IMMIGRATION AND ILLEGAL ALIENS

BURDEN OR BLESSING?

ISSN 1536-5263

IMMIGRATION AND ILLEGAL ALIENS
BURDEN OR BLESSING?

Cynthia S. Becker

INFORMATION PLUS® REFERENCE SERIES
Formerly Published by Information Plus, Wylie, Texas

THOMSON
✳
GALE

Detroit • New York • San Francisco • San Diego • New Haven, Conn. • Waterville, Maine • London • Munich

THOMSON

GALE

Immigration and Illegal Aliens: Burden or Blessing?
Cynthia S. Becker
Paula Kepos, Series Editor

Project Editor
John McCoy

Permissions
Margaret Abendroth, Edna Hedblad,
Emma Hull

Composition and Electronic Prepress
Evi Seoud

Manufacturing
Drew Kalasky

ISBN 0-7876-5103-6 (set)
ISBN 1-4144-0420-4
ISSN 1536-5263

This title is also available as an e-book.
ISBN 1-4144-0477-8 (set)
Contact your Thomson Gale sales representative for ordering information.

Printed in the United States of America
10 9 8 7 6 5 4 3 2 1

TABLE OF CONTENTS

PREFACE

Immigration and Illegal Aliens: Burden or Blessing? is part of the *Information Plus Reference Series*. The purpose of each volume of the series is to present the latest facts on a topic of pressing concern in modern American life. These topics include today's most controversial and most studied social issues: abortion, capital punishment, care for the elderly, crime, the environment, health care, immigration, minorities, national security, social welfare, women, youth, and many more. Although written especially for the high school and undergraduate student, this series is an excellent resource for anyone in need of factual information on current affairs.

By presenting the facts, it is Thomson Gale's intention to provide its readers with everything they need to reach an informed opinion on current issues. To that end, there is a particular emphasis in this series on the presentation of scientific studies, surveys, and statistics. These data are generally presented in the form of tables, charts, and other graphics placed within the text of each book. Every graphic is directly referred to and carefully explained in the text. The source of each graphic is presented within the graphic itself. The data used in these graphics are drawn from the most reputable and reliable sources, in particular from the various branches of the U.S. government and from major independent polling organizations. Every effort has been made to secure the most recent information available. The reader should bear in mind that many major studies take years to conduct, and that additional years often pass before the data from these studies are made available to the public. Therefore, in many cases the most recent information available in 2005 dated from 2002 or 2003. Older statistics are sometimes presented as well if they are of particular interest and no more recent information exists.

Although statistics are a major focus of the *Information Plus Reference Series*, they are by no means its only content. Each book also presents the widely held positions and important ideas that shape how the book's subject is discussed in the United States. These positions are explained in detail and, where possible, in the words of their proponents. Some of the other material to be found in these books includes: historical background; descriptions of major events related to the subject; relevant laws and court cases; and examples of how these issues play out in American life. Some books also feature primary documents or have pro and con debate sections giving the words and opinions of prominent Americans on both sides of a controversial topic. All material is presented in an even-handed and unbiased manner; the reader will never be encouraged to accept one view of an issue over another.

HOW TO USE THIS BOOK

America is known as a melting pot, a place where people of different nationalities, cultures, ethnicities, and races have come together to form one nation. This process has been shaped by the influx of both legal immigrants and illegal aliens, and American attitudes toward both groups have varied over time. Legal immigrants have faced discrimination based on prevailing social and political trends; illegal aliens have been seen by some as undesirable, particularly after it became apparent that some or all of the terrorists behind the September 11, 2001, attack had entered the United States legally but had overstayed their allotted time. This book discusses these and other legal, social, and political aspects of immigration and illegal aliens.

Immigration and Illegal Aliens: Burden or Blessing? consists of nine chapters and five appendices.

Each of the chapters is devoted to a particular aspect of immigration in the United States. For a summary of the information covered in each chapter, please see the synopses provided in the Table of Contents at the front of the book. Chapters generally begin with an overview of the basic facts and background information on the chapter's topic, then proceed to examine subtopics of particular interest. For example, Chapter 5, Illegal Aliens, begins with a discussion of what an illegal alien is and estimates how many are in the United States. It then presents statistics on the countries of origin for illegal aliens and examines some of the methods through which illegal aliens manage to enter and remain in the United States. This is followed by sections describing the law enforcement agencies responsible for keeping illegal aliens out and the number and types of illegal aliens apprehended in recent years. Next is an examination of the criminal enterprise of smuggling people into the United States. The chapter concludes with a discussion of the long and complicated history of U.S.-Mexican relations and immigration. Throughout the chapter, changes to immigration law and enforcement systems since September 11, 2001, are highlighted. Readers can find their way through a chapter by looking for the section and subsection headings, which are clearly set off from the text. They can also refer to the book's extensive index if they already know what they are looking for.

Statistical Information

The tables and figures featured throughout *Immigration and Illegal Aliens: Burden or Blessing?* will be of particular use to the reader in learning about this issue. These tables and figures represent an extensive collection of the most recent and important statistics on immigration and illegal aliens and related issues—for example, graphics in the book cover projections of the population by race/ethnicity; trends in the number of aliens admitted, the number of naturalized citizens, and the foreign-born population as a percentage of the U.S. population; and the number of illegal aliens apprehended each year by border patrol agents. Thomson Gale believes that making this information available to the reader is the most important way in which we fulfill the goal of this book: to help readers to understand the issues and controversies surrounding immigration and illegal aliens in the United States and to reach their own conclusions.

Each table or figure has a unique identifier appearing above it for ease of identification and reference. Titles for the tables and figures explain their purpose. At the end of each table or figure, the original source of the data is provided.

In order to help readers understand these often complicated statistics, all tables and figures are explained in the text. References in the text direct the reader to the relevant statistics. Furthermore, the contents of all tables and figures are fully indexed. Please see the opening section of the index at the back of this volume for a description of how to find tables and figures within it.

Appendices

In addition to the main body text and images, *Immigration and Illegal Aliens: Burden or Blessing?* has five appendices. The first is a reproduction of a pamphlet published by the U.S. Department of Justice entitled *Federal Protections against National Origin Discrimination—U.S. Department of Justice: Potential Discrimination against Immigrants Based on National Origin*. The second appendix features maps of the world to assist the reader in pinpointing the places of birth of America's immigrant population. The third is the Important Names and Addresses directory. Here the reader will find contact information for a number of government and private organizations that can provide further information on immigration and illegal aliens. The fourth appendix is the Resources section, which can also assist the reader in conducting his or her own research. In this section, the author and editors of *Immigration and Illegal Aliens: Burden or Blessing?* describe some of the sources that were most useful during the compilation of this book. The final appendix is the detailed Index, which facilitates reader access to specific topics in this book.

ADVISORY BOARD CONTRIBUTIONS

The staff of Information Plus would like to extend their heartfelt appreciation to the Information Plus Advisory Board. This dedicated group of media professionals provides feedback on the series on an ongoing basis. Their comments allow the editorial staff who work on the project to make the series better and more user-friendly. Our top priorities are to produce the highest-quality and most useful books possible, and the Advisory Board's contributions to this process are invaluable.

The members of the Information Plus Advisory Board are:
- Kathleen R. Bonn, Librarian, Newbury Park High School, Newbury Park, California

- Madelyn Garner, Librarian, San Jacinto College— North Campus, Houston, Texas

- Anne Oxenrider, Media Specialist, Dundee High School, Dundee, Michigan

- Charles R. Rodgers, Director of Libraries, Pasco-Hernando Community College, Dade City, Florida

- James N. Zitzelsberger, Library Media Department Chairman, Oshkosh West High School, Oshkosh, Wisconsin

COMMENTS AND SUGGESTIONS

The editors of the *Information Plus Reference Series* welcome your feedback on *Immigration and Illegal Aliens: Burden or Blessing?* Please direct all correspondence to:

Editors
Information Plus Reference Series
27500 Drake Rd.
Farmington Hills, MI 48331-3535

CHAPTER 1

IMMIGRATION—ALMOST FOUR HUNDRED YEARS OF AMERICAN HISTORY

There were probably as many reasons for coming to America as there were people who came. It was a highly individual decision. Yet it can be said that three large forces—religious persecution, political oppression and economic hardship—provided the chief motives for the mass migration to our shores. They were responding, in their own way, to the pledge of the Declaration of Independence: the promise of "life, liberty and the pursuit of happiness."

—John F. Kennedy, *A Nation of Immigrants*, 1964

This chapter covers the impact of immigration and related legislation from the founding of the first American colonies through the 1970s. Immigration from the 1980s to the present follows in Chapter 2. Information for these two chapters was drawn from a variety of resources, but in particular the U.S. Census Bureau; the U.S. Department of Homeland Security, Bureau of Citizenship and Immigration; the Department of State; the National Archives; and the Federation for American Immigration Reform.

COMING TO AMERICA

America, from its very beginning, has been a land of immigrants. People have come from all nations seeking free choice of worship, escape from cruel governments, and relief from war, famine, or poverty. All came with dreams of a better life for themselves and their families. America has accommodated these people of diverse backgrounds, customs, and beliefs, although not without considerable friction along the way.

On the eastern shore of the peninsula that is now Florida, Spanish conquistadors established a settlement in 1565. The city of St. Augustine survived to become the oldest continuously occupied settlement of European origin in North America. However, the series of northern colonies gained far more attention in history. In his book *Immigration: From the Founding of Virginia to the Closing of Ellis Island* (New York: Facts On File, Inc., 2002),

Dennis Wepman chronicles the immigrants who built America. Not long after English settlers established the first permanent colony on the James River in 1607, the French developed a settlement on the St. Lawrence River in what is now Canada. Dutch explorers soon built a fur-trading post along the Hudson River. Swedes settled on the Delaware River. German Quakers and Mennonites joined William Penn's experimental Pennsylvania colony. Jews from Brazil, Protestant Huguenots from France, Puritans and Catholics from England all came to escape persecution for their religious beliefs and practices.

During the colonial period, many immigrants came as indentured servants, required to work for four to seven years to earn back the cost of their passage. To the great aggravation of the colonists, some were convicts who accepted being shipped across the ocean as an alternative to imprisonment or death. In his book, Wepman estimated that as many as fifty thousand British felons were sent to the colonies. The first Africans arrived at Jamestown in 1619 as indentured servants but other Africans were soon brought in chains to be slaves.

The continual ebb and flow of immigrants provided settlers to develop communities along the Atlantic coast, pioneers to push the United States westward, builders for the Erie Canal and the transcontinental railways, pickers for cotton in the South and vegetables in the Southwest, laborers for American industrialization, and intellectuals in all fields. Together, these immigrants have built, in the opinion of many people, the most diverse and exciting nation in the world.

According to the 1790 census, the United States had a population of 3.2 million white persons and 757,206 slaves (Campbell Gibson and Kay Jung, *Historical Census Statistics on Population Totals by Race, 1790 to 1990, and by Hispanic Origin, 1790 to 1990, For the United States, Regions, Division, and States*, Washington,

DC: Population Bureau, U.S. Census Bureau, September 2002). All were immigrants or descendants of earlier seventeenth- and eighteenth-century arrivals. The population was predominantly English seasoned with people of German, Irish, Scottish, Dutch, French, and Spanish descent. Native Americans were not counted.

ATTITUDES TOWARD IMMIGRANTS

Immigration was the way of life in the country's first century. Nevertheless, negative attitudes began to appear among the already settled English population. In 1753 Benjamin Franklin warned about the Germans coming to Pennsylvania:

> Those who came hither are generally the most stupid of their own nation, and as ignorance is often attended with great credulity, when knavery [dishonest dealing] would mislead it, and with suspicion, when honesty would set it right; and, few of the English understand the German language, and so cannot address them either from the press or pulpit, it is almost impossible to remove any prejudices they may entertain. Not being used to liberty, they know not how to make modest use of it. (*The Complete Works in Philosophy, Politics, and Morals, of the Late Dr. Benjamin Franklin*, vol. II [London: J. Johnson, and Longman, Hurst, Rees, and Orme, 1806])

Officially, with the major exception of the 1798 Alien and Sedition Acts, the United States encouraged immigration. The Articles of Confederation (drafted in 1777) made citizens of each state citizens of every other state. The U.S. Constitution (written in 1787) made only one direct reference to immigration. Article I, Section 9, Clause I provided that the "immigration or importation of such persons as any of the states now existing shall think proper to admit shall not be prohibited by Congress prior to the Year (1808), but a tax or duty may be imposed on such importation, not exceeding ten dollars for each person." Article I also gave Congress power to establish "a uniform rule of naturalization [to grant U.S. citizenship]."

Alien and Sedition Acts of 1798

Early federal legislation established basic criteria for naturalization—five years residence in the United States, good moral character, and loyalty to the U.S. Constitution. These requirements were based on state naturalization laws. In 1798, in anticipation of war with France, the Federalist-controlled Congress proposed four laws intended to weaken the pro-immigrant Republican party.

Favoring caution in immigration policy, President John Adams asked, "Why should we take the bread out of the mouths of our own children and give it to strangers?" (*The Works of John Adams*, vol. IX, Boston: Little, Brown, 1856). Leading the opposition, Thomas Jefferson argued against restrictive immigration legisla-

tion. "Shall we refuse the unhappy fugitives from distress that hospitality which the savages of the wilderness extended to our fathers on arrival in this land? Shall oppressed humanity find no asylum on this globe?" (*The Writings of Thomas Jefferson*, Vol. 3, edited by Lipscomb and Bergh, Washington, DC, 1903–04).

Ultimately Congress passed the four laws, collectively called the Alien and Sedition Acts:

- The Naturalization Act lengthened the residence requirement for naturalization from five to fourteen years.

- The Alien Act authorized the president to arrest and/or expel allegedly dangerous aliens.

- The Alien Enemies Act allowed the imprisonment or deportation of aliens who were subjects of an enemy nation during wartime.

- The Sedition Act authorized fines and imprisonment for acts of treason including "any false, scandalous and malicious writing."

The Sedition Act was used to arrest and silence a number of mostly Republican newspaper editors. The strong public outcry against the Alien and Sedition Acts was partly responsible for the election of the Republican candidate, Thomas Jefferson, as the next president. Jefferson pardoned the individuals convicted under the Sedition Act. The Naturalization Act was repealed by Congress and the other three laws were allowed to lapse (*The Columbia Encyclopedia*, sixth edition, 2001).

THE FIRST CENTURY OF IMMIGRATION

In the early 1800s America's territory more than doubled in size with the addition of the 828,000 square miles of land, which came to be known as the Louisiana Purchase. Reports of rich farm land and virgin forests provided by explorers like Lewis and Clark drew struggling farmers and skilled craftsmen, merchants and miners, laborers, and wealthy investors to leave Europe for the land of opportunity. In 1820, the year when immigration records were first kept, only 8,385 immigrants entered the United States, according to the Office of Immigration Statistics. During the 1820s the number began to rise slowly, an increase that generally continued for more than a century, until the Great Depression in 1929.

A Wave of Irish and German Immigration

Europe suffered from a population explosion in the 1800s. As land in Europe became more and more scarce, tenant farmers were pushed off their farms into poverty. Some immigrated to America to start a new life. This situation was made worse in Ireland when a fungus that caused potato crops to rot struck in 1845. Many Irishmen were poor farmers who depended on potatoes for food.

They suffered greatly from famine when their crops rotted, and epidemics of cholera and typhoid spread from village to village. The Irish Potato Famine forced people to choose between starving to death or leaving their country. In the ten-year period from 1831 to 1840, a little over 207,000 Irish people arrived in America. Driven by the potato famine, between 1841 and 1850 the number of Irish immigrants rose more than 375% to 780,719. The flow of immigrants from Ireland peaked at more than 900,000 in the 1851–1860 decade. (See Table 1.1.)

TABLE 1.1

Immigration by region and selected country of last residence, 1820–2003

Region and country of last residence[a]	1820	1821–30	1831–40	1841–50	1851–60	1861–70	1871–80	1881–90
All countries	8,385	143,439	599,125	1,713,251	2,598,214	2,314,824	2,812,191	5,246,613
Europe	7,690	98,797	495,681	1,597,442	2,452,577	2,065,141	2,271,925	4,735,484
Austria-Hungary	b	b	b	b	b	7,800	72,969	353,719
Austria	b	b	b	b	b	7,124[c]	63,009	226,038
Hungary	b	b	b	b	b	484[c]	9,960	127,681
Belgium	1	27	22	5,074	4,738	6,734	7,221	20,177
Czechoslovakia	d	d	d	d	d	d	d	d
Denmark	20	169	1,063	539	3,749	17,094	31,771	88,132
France	371	8,497	45,575	77,262	76,358	35,986	72,206	50,464
Germany	968	6,761	152,454	434,626	951,667	787,468	718,182	1,452,970
Greece	—	20	49	16	31	72	210	2,308
Ireland[e]	3,614	50,724	207,381	780,719	914,119	435,778	436,871	655,482
Italy	30	409	2,253	1,870	9,231	11,725	55,759	307,309
Netherlands	49	1,078	1,412	8,251	10,789	9,102	16,541	53,701
Norway-Sweden	3	91	1,201	13,903	20,931	109,298	211,245	568,362
Norway	f	f	f	f	f	f	95,323	176,586
Sweden	f	f	f	f	f	f	115,922	391,776
Poland	5	16	369	105	1,164	2,027	12,970	51,806
Portugal	35	145	829	550	1,055	2,658	14,082	16,978
Romania	g	g	g	g	g	g	11[g]	6,348
Soviet Union	14	75	277	551	457	2,512	39,284	213,282
Spain	139	2,477	2,125	2,209	9,298	6,697	5,266	4,419
Switzerland	31	3,226	4,821	4,644	25,011	23,286	28,293	81,988
United Kingdom[e, h]	2,410	25,079	75,810	267,044	423,974	606,896	548,043	807,357
Yugoslavia	i	i	i	i	i	i	i	i
Other Europe	—	3	40	79	5	8	1,001	682
Asia	6	30	55	141	41,538	64,759	124,160	69,942
China[j]	1	2	8	35	41,397	64,301	123,201	61,711
Hong Kong	k	k	k	k	k	k	k	k
India	1	8	39	36	43	69	163	269
Iran	l	l	l	l	l	l	l	l
Israel	m	m	m	m	m	m	m	m
Japan	n	n	n	n	n	186	149	2,270
Korea	o	o	o	o	o	o	o	o
Philippines	16							
Turkey	1	20	7	59	83	131	404	3,782
Vietnam	11	k	k	k	k	k	k	k
Other Asia	3	—	1	11	15	72	243	1,910
America	387	11,564	33,424	62,469	74,720	166,607	404,044	426,967
Canada & Newfoundland[q, r]	209	2,277	13,624	41,723	59,309	153,878	383,640	393,304
Mexico[r]	1	4,817	6,599	3,271	3,078	2,191	5,162	1,913[s]
Caribbean	164	3,834	12,301	13,528	10,660	9,046	13,957	29,042
Cuba	i	i	i	i	i	i	i	i
Dominican Republic	t	t	t	t	t	t	t	t
Haiti	t	t	t	t	t	t	t	t
Jamaica	u	u	u	u	u	u	u	u
Other Caribbean	164	3,834	12,301	13,528	10,660	9,046	13,957	29,042
Central America	2	105	44	368	449	95	157	404
El Salvador	t	t	t	t	t	t	t	t
Other Central America	2	105	44	368	449	95	157	404
South America	11	531	856	3,579	1,224	1,397	1,128	2,304
Argentina	t	t	t	t	t	t	t	t
Colombia	t	t	t	t	t	t	t	t
Ecuador	t	t	t	t	t	t	t	t
Other South America	11	531	856	3,579	1,224	1,397	1,128	2,304
Other America	v	v	v	v	v	v	v	v
Africa	1	16	54	55	210	312	358	857
Oceania	1	2	9	29	158	214	10,914	12,574
Not specified[v]	300	33,030	69,902	53,115	29,011	17,791	790	789

Also affected by a potato famine and failed political revolutions, increasing numbers of German immigrants paralleled that of the Irish. From 1851 to 1860 the number of German immigrants (951,667) exceeded the Irish (914,119) by 37,548. The influx of Germans continued to rise to a peak of more than 1.4 million arrivals from 1881 to 1890. (See Table 1.1.)

Immigration, Politics, and the Civil War

This new wave of immigration led to intense anti-Irish, anti-German, and anti-Catholic sentiments among Americans, many of whom had been in America for only a few generations. It also triggered the creation of secret nativist societies (groups professing to protect the interests of the native-born against immigrants). Out of

TABLE 1.1

Immigration by region and selected country of last residence, 1820–2003 [CONTINUED]

Region and country of last residence[a]	1891–1900	1901–10	1911–20	1921–30	1931–40	1941–50	1951–60	1961–70
All countries	3,687,564	8,795,386	5,735,811	4,107,209	528,431	1,035,039	2,515,479	3,321,677
Europe	3,555,352	8,056,040	4,321,887	2,463,194	347,566	621,147	1,325,727	1,123,492
Austria-Hungary	592,707[w]	2,145,266[w]	896,342[w]	63,548	11,424	28,329	103,743	26,022
Austria	234,081[c]	668,209[c]	453,649	32,868	3,563[x]	24,860[x]	67,106	20,621
Hungary	181,288[c]	808,511[c]	442,693	30,680	7,861	3,469	36,637	5,401
Belgium	18,167	41,635	33,746	15,846	4,817	12,189	18,575	9,192
Czechoslovakia	[d]	[d]	3,426[d]	102,194	14,393	8,347	918	3,273
Denmark	50,231	65,285	41,983	32,430	2,559	5,393	10,984	9,201
France	30,770	73,379	61,897	49,610	12,623	38,808	51,121	45,237
Germany	505,152[w]	341,498[w]	143,945[w]	412,202	114,058[x]	226,578[x]	477,765	190,796
Greece	15,979	167,519	184,201	51,084	9,119	8,973	47,608	85,969
Ireland[e]	388,416	339,065	146,181	211,234	10,973	19,789	48,362	32,966
Italy	651,893	2,045,877	1,109,524	455,315	68,028	57,661	185,491	214,111
Netherlands	26,758	48,262	43,718	26,948	7,150	14,860	52,277	30,606
Norway-Sweden	321,281	440,039	161,469	165,780	8,700	20,765	44,632	32,600
Norway	95,015	190,505	66,395	68,531	4,740	10,100	22,935	15,484
Sweden	226,266	249,534	95,074	97,249	3,960	10,665	21,697	17,116
Poland	96,720[w]	[w]	4,813[w]	227,734	17,026	7,571	9,985	53,539
Portugal	27,508	69,149	89,732	29,994	3,329	7,423	19,588	76,065
Romania	12,750	53,008	13,311	67,646	3,871	1,076	1,039	2,531
Soviet Union	505,290[w]	1,597,306[w]	921,201[w]	61,742	1,370	571	671	2,465
Spain	8,731	27,935	68,611	28,958	3,258	2,898	7,894	44,659
Switzerland	31,179	34,922	23,091	29,676	5,512	10,547	17,675	18,453
United Kingdom[e, h]	271,538	525,950	341,408	339,570	31,572	139,306	202,824	213,822
Yugoslavia	[i]	[i]	1,888[i]	49,064	5,835	1,576	8,225	20,381
Other Europe	282	39,945	31,400	42,619	11,949	8,486	16,350	11,604
Asia	74,862	323,543	247,236	112,059	16,595	37,028	153,249	427,642
China[j]	14,799	20,605	21,278	29,907	4,928	16,709	9,657	34,764
Hong Kong	[k]	[k]	[k]	[k]	[k]	[k]	15,541[k]	75,007
India	68	4,713	2,082	1,886	496	1,761	1,973	27,189
Iran	[l]	[l]	[l]	241[l]	195	1,380	3,388	10,339
Israel	[m]	[m]	[m]	[m]	[m]	476[m]	25,476	29,602
Japan	25,942	129,797	83,837	33,462	1,948	1,555	46,250	39,988
Korea	[o]	[o]	[o]	[o]	[o]	107[o]	6,231	34,526
Philippines	[p]	[p]	[p]	[p]	528[p]	4,691	19,307	98,376
Turkey	30,425	157,369	134,066	33,824	1,065	798	3,519	10,142
Vietnam	[k]	[k]	[k]	[k]	[k]	[k]	335[k]	4,240
Other Asia	3,628	11,059	5,973	12,739	7,435	9,551	21,572	63,369
America	38,972	361,888	1,143,671	1,516,716	160,037	354,804	996,944	1,716,374
Canada & Newfoundland[q, r]	3,311	179,226	742,185	924,515	108,527	171,718	377,952	413,310
Mexico[r]	971[s]	49,642	219,004	459,287	22,319	60,589	299,811	453,937
Caribbean	33,066	107,548	123,424	74,899	15,502	49,725	123,091	470,213
Cuba	[t]	[t]	[t]	15,901[t]	9,571	26,313	78,948	208,536
Dominican Republic	[t]	[t]	[t]	[t]	1,150[t]	5,627	9,897	93,292
Haiti	[t]	[t]	[t]	[t]	191[t]	911	4,442	34,499
Jamaica	[u]	[u]	[u]	[u]	[u]	[u]	8,869[u]	74,906
Other Caribbean	33,066	107,548	123,424	58,998	4,590	16,874	20,935[u]	58,980
Central America	549	8,192	17,159	15,769	5,861	21,665	44,751	101,330
El Salvador	[t]	[t]	[t]	[t]	673[t]	5,132	5,895	14,992
Other Central America	549	8,192	17,159	15,769	5,188	16,533	38,856	86,338
South America	1,075	17,280	41,899	42,215	7,803	21,831	91,628	257,940
Argentina	[t]	[t]	[t]	[t]	1,349[t]	3,338	19,486	49,721
Colombia	[t]	[t]	[t]	[t]	1,223[t]	3,858	18,048	72,028
Ecuador	[t]	[t]	[t]	[t]	337[t]	2,417	9,841	36,780
Other South America	1,075	17,280	41,899	42,215	4,894	12,218	44,253	99,411
Other America	[v]	[v]	[v]	31[v]	25	29,276	59,711	19,644
Africa	350	7,368	8,443	6,286	1,750	7,367	14,092	28,954
Oceania	3,965	13,024	13,427	8,726	2,483	14,551	12,976	25,122
Not specified[v]	14,063	33,523[y]	1,147	228	—	412	12,491	93

these groups grew a new political party, the American Party (also called the "Know-Nothings"), who claimed to support the rights of Protestant, American-born, male voters. According to Dennis Wepman, the Know-Nothings managed to win seventy-five seats in Congress and six governorships in 1855 before the party dissolved (*Immigration: From the Founding of Virginia to the Closing of Ellis Island*, New York: Facts on File, Inc., 2002).

In contrast to the nativists, the 1864 Republican party platform, written in part by Abraham Lincoln, stated, "Resolved, That foreign immigration, which in the past has added so much to the wealth, development of resources, and increase of power to the nation, the asylum of the oppressed of all nations, shall be fostered and encouraged by a liberal and just policy" (Felix S. Cohen, in *Immigration and National*

TABLE 1.1

Immigration by region and selected country of last residence, 1820–2003 [CONTINUED]

Region and country of last residence [a]	1971–80	1981–90	1991–2000	2000	2001	2002	2003	Total 184 years, 1820–2003
All countries	4,493,314	7,338,062	9,095,417	849,807	1,064,318	1,063,732	705,827	68,923,308
Europe	800,368	761,550	1,359,737	133,362	177,833	177,652	102,843	38,919,125
Austria-Hungary	16,028	24,885	24,882	2,024	2,318	4,016	2,181	4,376,179[w, x]
Austria	9,478	18,340	15,500	997	1,004	2,657	1,163	1,849,270[b, c]
Hungary	6,550	6,545	9,382	1,027	1,314	1,359	1,018	1,680,833[b, c]
Belgium	5,329	7,066	7,090	827	1,002	842	518	220,008
Czechoslovakia	6,023	7,227	9,816	1,415	1,921	1,862	1,474	160,874[d]
Denmark	4,439	5,370	6,079	556	741	655	436	378,323
France	25,069	32,353	35,820	4,093	5,431	4,596	2,933	836,367
Germany	74,414	91,961	92,606	12,372	22,093	21,058	8,102	7,227,324[w, x]
Greece	92,369	38,377	26,759	5,138	1,966	1,516	914	735,059
Ireland[e]	11,490	31,969	56,950	1,279	1,550	1,419	1,010	4,786,062
Italy	129,368	67,254	62,722	2,695	3,377	2,837	1,904	5,443,948
Netherlands	10,492	12,238	13,308	1,466	1,895	2,305	1,329	393,069
Norway-Sweden	10,472	15,182	17,893	1,977	2,561	2,097	1,520	2,170,025
Norway	3,941	4,164	5,178	513	588	464	386	760,335[f]
Sweden	6,531	11,018	12,715	1,464	1,973	1,633	1,134	1,264,263[f]
Poland	37,234	83,252	163,747	9,773	12,355	13,304	11,016	806,758[w]
Portugal	101,710	40,431	22,916	1,402	1,654	1,320	821	527,972
Romania	12,393	30,857	51,203	6,521	6,224	4,525	3,311	270,104[g]
Soviet Union	38,961	57,677	462,874	43,807	55,099	55,464	33,563	4,050,706[w]
Spain	39,141	20,433	17,157	1,406	1,889	1,603	1,107	306,904
Switzerland	8,235	8,849	11,841	1,349	1,796	1,503	867	375,446
United Kingdom[e, h]	137,374	159,173	151,866	14,532	20,258	18,057	11,220	5,320,551
Yugoslavia	30,540	18,762	66,557	12,213	21,937	28,100	5,312	258,177
Other Europe	9,287	8,234	57,651	8,517	11,766	10,573	10,321	272,285
Asia	1,588,178	2,738,157	2,795,672	255,860	337,566	326,871	236,039	9,715,328
China[i]	124,326	346,747	419,114	41,861	50,821	55,974	37,395	1,477,680
Hong Kong	113,467	98,215	109,779	7,199	10,307	7,952	5,020	435,288[k]
India	164,134	250,786	363,060	39,072	65,916	66,864	47,157	998,713
Iran	45,136	116,172	68,556	6,505	8,063	7,730	4,709	265,909[l]
Israel	37,713	44,273	39,397	3,893	4,925	4,938	3,719	190,519[m]
Japan	49,775	47,085	67,942	7,730	10,464	9,150	6,724	556,524[n]
Korea	267,638	333,746	164,166	15,214	19,933	20,114	12,177	858,638[o]
Philippines	354,987	548,764	503,945	40,587	50,870	48,674	43,258	1,673,400[p]
Turkey	13,399	23,233	38,212	2,713	3,477	3,934	3,332	461,282
Vietnam	172,820	280,782	286,145	25,340	34,648	32,425	21,270	832,765[k]
Other Asia	244,783	648,354	735,356	65,746	78,142	69,116	51,278	1,964,610
America	1,982,735	3,615,225	4,486,806	397,201	473,351	478,777	306,793	18,813,275
Canada & Newfoundland[q, r]	169,939	156,938	191,987	21,475	30,203	27,299	16,555	4,561,296
Mexico[r]	640,294	1,655,843	2,249,421	171,748	204,844	217,318	114,984	6,675,296[s]
Caribbean	741,126	872,051	978,787	85,875	96,958	94,240	67,660	3,940,822
Cuba	264,863	144,578	169,322	19,322	26,073	27,520	8,722	980,347[t]
Dominican Republic	148,135	252,035	335,251	17,441	21,256	22,474	26,157	915,274[t]
Haiti	56,335	138,379	179,644	22,004	22,535	19,189	11,942	468,067[t]
Jamaica	137,577	208,148	169,227	15,654	15,099	14,567	13,082	641,475[u]
Other Caribbean	134,216	128,911	125,343	11,454	11,995	10,490	7,757	935,659
Central America	134,640	468,088	526,915	62,708	73,063	66,520	53,435	1,539,561
El Salvador	34,436	213,539	215,798	22,332	31,054	30,539	27,915	579,973[t]
Other Central America	100,204	254,549	311,117	40,376	42,009	35,981	25,520	959,588
South America	295,741	461,847	539,656	55,392	68,279	73,400	54,155	1,985,779
Argentina	29,897	27,327	26,644	2,485	3,459	3,811	3,217	168,249[t]
Colombia	77,347	122,849	128,499	14,191	16,333	18,488	14,455	473,128[t]
Ecuador	50,077	56,315	76,592	7,658	9,694	10,564	7,040	259,657[t]
Other South America	138,420	255,356	307,921	31,058	38,793	40,537	29,443	1,084,745
Other America	995	458	40	3	4	3	4	110,188

TABLE 1.1

Immigration by region and selected country of last residence, 1820–2003 [CONTINUED]

Region and country of last residence[a]	1971–80	1981–90	1991–2000	2000	2001	2002	2003	Total 184 years, 1820–2003
Africa	80,779	176,893	354,939	40,969	50,209	56,135	45,640	841,068
Oceania	41,242	45,205	55,845	5,962	7,253	6,536	5,102	279,358
Not specified[v]	12	1,032	42,418	16,453	18,106	17,761	9,410	355,154

[a]Data for years prior to 1906 relate to country whence alien came; data from 1906–79 and 1984–99 are for country of last permanent residence; and data for 1980–83 refer to country of birth. Because of changes in boundaries, changes in lists of countries, and lack of data for specified countries for various periods, data for certain countries, especially for the total period 1820–1999, are not comparable throughout. Data for specified countries are included with countries to which they belonged prior to World War I.
[b]Data for Austria and Hungary not reported until 1861.
[c]Data for Austria and Hungary not reported separately for all years during the period.
[d]No data available for Czechoslovakia until 1920.
[e]Prior to 1926, data for Northern Ireland included in Ireland.
[f]Data for Norway and Sweden not reported separately until 1871.
[g]No data available for Romania until 1880.
[h]Since 1925, data for United Kingdom refer to England, Scotland, Wales, and Northern Ireland.
[i]In 1920, a separate enumeration was made for the Kingdom of Serbs, Croats, and Slovenes. Since 1922, the Serb, Croat, and Slovene Kingdom recorded as Yugoslavia.
[j]Beginning in 1957, China includes Taiwan. As of January 1, 1979, the United States has recognized the People's Republic of China.
[k]Data not reported separately until 1952.
[l]Data not reported separately until 1925.
[m]Data not reported separately until 1949.
[n]No data available for Japan until 1861.
[o]Data not reported separately until 1948.
[p]Prior to 1934, Philippines recorded as insular travel.
[q]Prior to 1920, Canada and Newfoundland recorded as British North America. From 1820–98, figures include all British North America possessions.
[r]Land arrivals not completely enumerated until 1908.
[s]No data available for Mexico from 1886–94.
[t]Data not reported separately until 1932.
[u]Data for Jamaica not collected until 1953. In prior years, consolidated under British West Indies, which is included in "Other Caribbean."
[v]Included in countries "Not specified" until 1925.
[w]From 1899–1919, data for Poland included in Austria-Hungary, Germany, and the Soviet Union.
[x]From 1938–45, data for Austria included in Germany.
[y]Includes 32,897 persons returning in 1906 to their homes in the United States.
Note: From 1820–67, figures represent alien passengers arrived at seaports; from 1868–91 and 1895–97, immigrant aliens arrived; from 1892–94 and 1898–2003, immigrant aliens admitted for permanent residence. From 1892–1903, aliens entering by cabin class were not counted as immigrants. Land arrivals were not completely enumerated until 1908. For recent changes in geographic definitions for Hong Kong, and the former Czechoslovakia, Soviet Union, and Yugoslavia, see Notice of Special Geographic Definitions. Data for Czechoslovakia, Soviet Union, and Yugoslavia include independent republics.

SOURCE: "Table 2. Immigration by Region and Selected Country of Last Residence, Fiscal Years 1820–2003," in *2003 Yearbook of Immigration Statistics*, Office of Immigration Statistics, U.S. Department of Homeland Security, September 2004, http://uscis.gov/graphics/shared/aboutus/statistics/IMM03yrbk/2003IMM.pdf (accessed January 27, 2005)

Welfare, New York: League for Industrial Democracy, 1940).

In 1862 Lincoln signed the Homestead Law, which offered 160 acres of free land to any adult citizen or prospective citizen who agreed to occupy and improve the land for five years. Wepman noted that between 1862 and 1904 more than 147 million acres of western land were claimed by adventurous citizens and eager new immigrants. Efforts to complete a transcontinental railroad provided work for predominantly Irish and Chinese laborers.

The Civil War itself (1861–1865) seemed to have little impact on immigration. Although the number of immigrants dropped from 153,640 in 1860 to just under 92,000 in both 1861 and 1862, there were more than 176,000 new arrivals in 1863 and the numbers continued to grow.

Post-Civil War Growth in Immigration

Post-Civil War America was characterized by the rapid growth of the Industrial Revolution, which fueled the need for workers in the nation's flourishing factories. The number of arriving immigrants continued to grow in the 1870s, dominated by people from Germany, Great Britain, Ireland, Sweden, and Norway. (See Table 1.1.) Opposition to immigration continued among some factions of established citizens. Secret societies of white supremacists, such as the Ku Klux Klan, formed throughout the South to oppose not only African-American suffrage but also the influence of the Roman Catholic Church and rapid naturalization of foreign immigrants.

Immigration Swelled and the Source of Immigrants Shifted in the 1880s

The decade from 1881 to 1890 marked a new era in immigration. The volume of immigrants nearly doubled from 2,812,191 in the 1870s to 5,246,613 in the 1880s. German immigration peaked at nearly 1.5 million and immigration from Norway, Sweden, England, Scotland, and Wales also reached their highest levels. A new wave of immigrants began to arrive from Russia (including a significant number of Jews fleeing massacres called pogroms), Poland, Austria-Hungary, and Italy. (See

Table 1.1.) The mass exodus from eastern Europe foretold events that would result in World War I. These newcomers were different: they came from countries with limited public education and no sense of social equality; they were often unskilled and illiterate; and they tended to form tight ethnic communities within the large cities where they clung to their own language and customs, which further limited their ability to assimilate into American culture.

A Developing Federal Role in Immigration

The increasing numbers of immigrants prompted a belief that there should be some type of administrative order to the ever-growing influx. In 1864 Congress created a Commission of Immigration under the U.S. Department of State. A one-man office was set up in New York City to oversee immigration.

The 1870s witnessed a national debate over the importation of contract labor and limiting of such immigration. In 1875, after considerable debate, Congress passed the Page Law (18 Stat. 477). This first major piece of restrictive immigration legislation prohibited alien convicts and prostitutes from entering the country.

With the creation of the Commission of Immigration, the federal government began to play a central role in immigration, which had previously been handled by the individual states. Court decisions beginning in 1849 strengthened the federal government's role and limited the states' role in regulating immigration. In 1875 the Supreme Court ultimately ruled in *Henderson v. Mayor of the City of New York* (92 U.S. 259) that the immigration laws of New York, California, and Louisiana were unconstitutional. This ended the states' right to regulate immigration and exclude undesirable aliens. From then on Congress and the federal government had complete responsibility for immigration.

In 1882 Congress passed the first general immigration law. The Immigration Act of August 3, 1882 (22 Stat. 214) established a centralized immigration administration under the Secretary of the Treasury. The law also allowed the exclusion of "undesirables" including paupers, criminals, and the insane. A head tax was added at fifty cents per arriving immigrant to defray the expenses of immigration regulation and caring for the immigrants after their arrival in the United States.

The Influx of Immigrants from Asia

Before the discovery of gold in California in 1848, very few Asians (little more than two hundred, including Asian Indians) came to the United States (*2003 Yearbook of Immigration Statistics*, Washington, DC: Office of Immigration Statistics, U.S. Department of Homeland Security, September 2004). Between 1849 and 1852 large numbers of Asian immigrants began arriving in the United States. These early arrivals came mostly from southern China, spurred on by economic depression, famine, war, and flooding. Thousands of Chinese immigrants were recruited to build railroads and work in mines, construction, or manufacturing. Many became domestic servants. Former mining camp cooks who had saved a little money opened restaurants. Others invested small amounts in equipment to operate one-man laundries, performing a service few other people wanted to tackle. Between 1851 and 1880 about a quarter of a million immigrants arrived from China, while only a few thousand arrived from other Asian countries. (See Table 1.1.)

Some people became alarmed by this increase in Chinese immigration. Their fears were fueled by a combination of racism and fears among American-born workers that employers were bringing over foreign workers to replace them and keep unskilled wages low. The public began to call for restrictions on Chinese immigration.

The Chinese Exclusion Act

In 1882 Congress passed the Chinese Exclusion Act (22 Stat. 58), which prohibited further immigration of Chinese laborers to the United States for ten years. Exceptions included teachers, diplomats, students, merchants, and tourists. The Chinese Exclusion Act marked the first time the United States barred immigration of a national group. The law also prohibited Chinese immigrants in the United States from becoming naturalized American citizens. Fewer than fifteen thousand Chinese arrived during the last decade of the nineteenth century. (See Table 1.1.)

Four other laws that prohibited the immigration of Chinese laborers followed the Chinese Exclusion Act. The 1892 Geary Act (27 Stat. 25) extended the Chinese Exclusion Act for ten more years. In cases brought before the U.S. Supreme Court, the Court upheld the constitutionality of these two laws. The Immigration Act of 1904 (33 Stat. 428) made the Chinese exclusion laws permanent. Under the Immigration Act of 1917 (39 Stat. 874), the United States suspended the immigration of laborers from almost all Asian countries.

During World War II, the United States and China became allies against the Japanese in Asia. As a gesture of goodwill, on December 17, 1943, President Franklin D. Roosevelt signed the Act to Repeal the Chinese Exclusion Acts, to Establish Quotas, and for Other Purposes (57 Stat. 600-1). The new law lifted the ban on naturalization of Chinese nationals but established a quota or limit of 105 Chinese immigrants to be admitted per year.

The Beginning of Japanese Immigration

Until the passage of the Chinese Exclusion Act, Japanese immigration was hardly noticeable, with the total flow at 335 between 1861 and 1880. Because Japanese immigrants were not covered by the Chinese Exclusion Act, however, Japanese laborers were brought in to replace Chinese workers. Consequently Japanese immigration increased from 2,270 in the 1880s to almost 130,000 during the first decade of the twentieth century (1901–1910). (See Table 1.1.) Japanese workers labored in the rapidly expanding sugarcane plantations in Hawaii and the fruit and vegetable farms of California.

The same anti-Asian attitudes that had led to the Chinese Exclusion Act culminated in President Theodore Roosevelt's "Gentleman's Agreement" of 1907, an informal arrangement between the U.S. and Japanese governments that cut the flow of Japanese immigration to a trickle. This anti-Asian attitude resurfaced a generation later in the National Origins Act (Immigration Act of 1924; 43 Statutes-at-Large 153). The immigration quota for any nationality group had been based on the number of persons of that nationality resident in the United States in the 1910 census. The new law reduced quotas from 3% to 2% and shifted the base for quota calculations from 1910 back to 1890. Since few Asians lived in the United States in 1890, the reduction in Asian immigration was particularly dramatic. Asian immigration was not permitted to increase until after World War II.

Greater Government Control

In "Overview of INS History" (http://uscis.gov/graphics/aboutus/history/articles/OVIEW.htm), Marion L. Smith describes the development of the federal role in control of immigration. With the exception of Asian immigration, the federal government had done little to restrict immigration. In 1891 the federal government assumed total control over immigration issues. The Immigration Act of March 3, 1891 (26 Stat. 1084), authorized the establishment of the U.S. Office of Immigration under the Treasury Department. This first comprehensive immigration law added to the list of inadmissible persons those suffering from certain contagious diseases, polygamists (married persons who had more than one mate at the same time), and aliens convicted of minor crimes. The law also prohibited using advertisements to encourage immigration.

On January 2, 1892, a new federal immigration station began operating on Ellis Island in New York. According to the Statue of Liberty–Ellis Island Foundation, during its years of operation (1892–1954) more than twelve million immigrants were processed through Ellis Island (http://ellisisland.org/genealogy/ellis_island_history.asp). That figure represented about half of the 24,178,969 immigrants who entered the United States during that period.

In 1895 the Office of Immigration became the Bureau of Immigration under the Commissioner-General of Immigration.

In 1903 the Bureau of Immigration was transferred to the Department of Commerce and Labor. The Basic Naturalization Act of 1906 (34 Stat. 596) consolidated the immigration and naturalization functions of the federal government under the new title Bureau of Immigration and Naturalization. When the Department of Labor and Commerce was separated into two cabinet departments in 1913, two bureaus were formed—the Bureau of Immigration and the Bureau of Naturalization. In 1933 the two bureaus were reunited as the Immigration and Naturalization Service (INS).

Immigrants from Eastern Europe Continued to Come

By the 1890s the origins of those arriving in America had changed. Fewer immigrants came from northern Europe while immigrants from southern, central, and eastern European countries grew in numbers every year. Of the 8.1 million European immigrants who arrived between 1901 and 1910, 72% came from Italy, the Soviet Union, and Austria-Hungary. (See Table 1.1.) The 1923 report "The Immigration Problem in the United States" prepared by the National Industrial Conference Board noted that immigration from northern and western Europe was referred to as "old" immigration, whereas that from southern and eastern European countries was commonly called "new" immigration. The same report noted racial problems between "old" and "new" immigrants; the term "race" generally included nationalities or ethnic groups. The National Industrial Conference Board report displayed graphs of immigrant groups by race, including among others Hebrew, German, English, Irish, Scotch, Scandinavian, Slovak, and Armenian.

The exodus of Jews (called Hebrews in the National Industrial Conference Board report) from eastern Europe was particularly significant. The 1923 report stated that an average of greater than 57,000 Hebrew[s] per year arrived between 1908 and 1922. This was double the average arrivals of any other group. The American Immigration Law Foundation noted that many of these Jewish immigrants were merchants, shopkeepers, craftsmen, and professionals, contrary to the stereotype of poor, uneducated immigrants coming out of eastern Europe.

IMMIGRATION AT THE TURN OF THE TWENTIETH CENTURY

A Million Immigrants a Year

Immigration and Naturalization Service annual records reported that the nation's already high immigration rate at the turn of the century doubled between 1902 and 1907. Immigration reached a million per year in

TABLE 1.2

Aliens excluded, by administrative reason for exclusion, 1892–1990

Year	Total	Subversive or anarchist	Criminal or narcotics violations	Immoral	Mental or physical defect	Likely to become public charge	Stowaway	Attemped entry without inspection or without proper documents	Contract laborer	Unable to read (over 16 years of age)	Other
1892–1990	650,252	1,369	17,465	8,209	82,590	219,399	16,240	204,943	41,941	13,679	44,417
1892–1900	22,515	—	65	89	1,309	15,070	—	—	5,792	—	190
1901–10	108,211	10	1,681	1,277	24,425	63,311	—	—	12,991	—	4,516
1911–20	178,109	27	4,353	4,824	42,129	90,045	1,904	—	15,417	5,083	14,327
1921–30	189,307	9	2,082	1,281	11,044	37,175	8,447	94,084	6,274	8,202	20,709
1931–40	68,217	5	1,261	253	1,530	12,519	2,126	47,858	1,235	258	1,172
1941–50	30,263	60	1,134	80	1,021	1,072	3,182	22,441	219	108	946
1951–60	20,585	1,098	2,017	361	956	149	376	14,657	13	26	932
1961–70	4,831	128	383	24	145	27	175	3,706	—	2	241
1971–80	8,455	32	814	20	31	31	30	7,237	—	—	260
1981–90	19,759	NA	3,675	NA	NA	NA	NA	14,960	—	—	1,124

Note: From 1941–53, statistics represent all exclusions at sea and air ports and exclusions of aliens seeking entry for 30 days or longer at land ports. After 1953, includes aliens excluded after formal hearings.
—Represents.
NA Not available.

SOURCE: Adapted from "Table 44. Aliens Excluded by Administrative Reason for Exclusion: Fiscal Years 1892–1990," in Enforcement Supplemental Tables for *2003 Yearbook of Immigration Statistics*, U.S. Department of Homeland Security, Office of Immigration Statistics, September 2004, http://uscis.gov/graphics/shared/aboutus/statistics/ENF03yrbk/ENFExcel/Table44.xls (accessed February 9, 2005)

1905, 1906, 1907, 1910, 1913, and 1914 but declined to less than 325,000 per year from 1915 through 1919 due to World War I. Many Americans worried about the growing influx of immigrants, whose customs were unfamiliar to the majority of the native population. Anti-Catholic, anti-political radicalism (usually expressed as anti-socialism), and racist movements became more prevalent along with a resurgence of nativism.

The Immigration Act of 1907 (34 Stat. 898) barred the immigration of feeble-minded persons, those with physical or mental defects that might prevent them from earning a living, and persons with tuberculosis. Increasing the head tax on each arriving immigrant to five dollars, the 1907 law also officially classified the arriving aliens as "immigrants" (persons planning to take up residence in the United States) and "nonimmigrants" (persons visiting for a short period of time to attend school, conduct business, or travel as tourists). All arrivals were required to declare their intentions for permanent or temporary stays in the United States. The law further authorized the president to refuse admission to persons he considered harmful to the labor conditions in the nation.

Reflecting national concerns about conflicts between old and new immigrant groups, Bureau of Immigration annual reports proposed that the immigrants should be more widely dispersed throughout the rest of the country, instead of being concentrated mostly in the northeastern urban areas. Not only would such a distribution of aliens help relieve the nation's urban problems, but the bureau thought it might promote greater racial and cultural assimilation.

The Immigration Act of 1917

The mounting negative feelings toward immigrants resulted in the Immigration Act of 1917 (39 Stat. 874), which was passed despite President Woodrow Wilson's veto. In addition to codifying (compiling into a complete system of written law) previous immigration legislation, the 1917 act required that immigrants be able to read and write in their native language and pass a literacy test, which proved to be a controversial clause. The new act also added the following groups to the inadmissible classes of immigrants: "illiterates, persons of constitutional psychopathic inferiority, men and women entering for immoral reasons, chronic alcoholics, stowaways, vagrants, persons who had suffered a previous attack of insanity," and those coming from the designated Asiatic "barred zone," comprising mostly Asia and the Pacific Islands. This provision was a continuation of the Chinese Exclusion Act and the "Gentleman's Agreement" of 1907, in which the Japanese government had agreed to stop the flow of workers to the United States. In 1918 passports were required by presidential proclamation for all entries into the United States.

Denied Entry

Despite the restrictive immigration legislation, only a small percentage of those attempting to migrate to the United States were turned away. Between 1892 and 1990, 650,252 persons were denied entry for a variety of reasons. (See Table 1.2.) Aside from those attempting to enter without proper papers, the largest group excluded was 219,399 persons considered "likely to become public charges." The thirty-year period from 1901 to 1930 was the peak era for exclusion of immigrants deemed likely to become public charges, mentally or physically defective, or immoral. The 1917 ban on illiterate immigrants excluded 13,679 aliens over the next 50 years.

RESTRICTIONS ON IMMIGRATION TIGHTEN

World War I temporarily stopped the influx of immigrants. In 1914, 1.2 million immigrants arrived; a year later the number dropped to barely 326,700. By 1918, the final year of the war, just over 110,000 immigrants ventured to America. However, the heavy flow started again after the war as people fled the war-ravaged European continent. More than 800,000 immigrants arrived in 1921.

The new wave of immigrants flocked to major cities where they hoped to find relatives or other immigrants from their native country as well as jobs. The 1920 census reported that for the first time in America's history the population living in cities exceeded that living in rural areas.

The First Quota Law

Concern over whether America could continue to absorb such huge numbers of immigrants led Congress to introduce a major change in American immigration policy. Other factors influencing Congress included racial fears about the "new" immigrants and apprehension over many of the immigrants' politically radical ideas.

The Quota Law of 1921 (42 Stat. 5) was the first quantitative immigration law. Congress limited the number of aliens of any nationality who could enter the United States to 3% of the number of foreign-born persons of that nationality who lived in the United States in 1910 (based on the U.S. Census Report). By 1910, however, many southern and eastern Europeans had already entered the country, a fact many legislators had overlooked. Consequently, in order to restructure the makeup of the immigrant population, Congress approved the Immigration Act of 1924 (43 Stat. 153). This act set the first permanent limitation on immigration, or the "national origins quota system." The law immediately limited the number of persons of each nationality to 2% of the population of that nationality who lived in the United States in 1890.

The 1924 law provided that after July 1, 1927, an overall cap would allow a total of 150,000 immigrants per year. Quotas for each "national origin" group were to be developed based on the 1920 census. Exempted from the quota limitation were spouses or dependents of U.S. citizens, returning alien residents, or natives of Western Hemisphere countries not subject to quotas (natives of Mexico, Canada, or other independent countries of Central or South America). The 1924 law further required that all arriving nonimmigrants present visas obtained from a U.S. consulate abroad. Visas were government authorizations permitting entry into a country. The 1917 and 1924 acts remained the American immigration law until 1952.

The Impact of Quotas

The new laws also barred all Asian immigration, which soon led to a shortage of farm and sugar-plantation workers. Filipinos filled the gap; since the Philippines was an American territory, they did not come under the immigration quota laws. In addition, large numbers of immigrants arrived from the Caribbean, peaking during the 1911–1920 period, when more than 123,000 Caribbean immigrants entered the United States. (See Table 1.1.)

Prior to World War I Caribbean workers had moved among the islands and to parts of South and Central America. Following the war many went north in search of work. Similarly, after World War II (1939–1945), when agricultural changes in the Caribbean forced many people off the farms and into the cities, many continued on to the United States or the United Kingdom in search of jobs.

With the new quota laws, the problem of illegal aliens arose for the first time. Previously, only a few of the small number of immigrants who had failed the immigration standards tried to sneak in, usually across the U.S.–Mexico border. With the new laws, the number of illegal aliens began to increase. Subsequently, Congress created the Border Patrol in 1924 (under 43 Stat. 240) to oversee the nation's borders and prevent illegal aliens from coming into the United States. This in turn resulted in a system of appeals and deportation actions.

DEPRESSION AND WAR

Changes at the Immigration and Naturalization Service

Immigration dropped well below 100,000 arrivals per year during the Great Depression of the 1930s, since America offered no escape from the unemployment that was rampant throughout most of the world. However, in the latter half of the 1930s Nazi persecution caused a new round of immigrants to flee Europe. In 1940 the INS was transferred from the Department of Labor to the Department of Justice. This move reflected the growing fear of war, making surveillance of aliens a question of national security rather than a question of how many to admit. The job of the INS shifted from the exclusion of aliens to combating alien criminal and subversive elements. This required closer cooperation with the U.S. attorney general's office and the Federal Bureau of Investigation (FBI).

Alien Registration

World War II began with the German invasion of Poland in September 1939. Growing concern about an increase in refugees that might result from the war in Europe led Congress to pass the Alien Registration Act of 1940 (54 Stat. 670), also known as the Smith Act. Among other provisions, this act required all aliens to register and those over fourteen years old to be fingerprinted. All registration and fingerprinting took place at local post offices between August 27 and December 26, 1940. During that four-month period, five million aliens registered, nearly 4% of the total U.S. population of 132 million people. Each alien was identified by an alien registration number, known as an A-number. For the first time the government had a means of identifying an individual immigrant. (The A-number system is still in use today.) Following registration each alien received by mail an Alien Registration Receipt Card, which they were required to carry with them to prove they were registered. Each alien was required to report any change of address within five days. Managing such a vast number of registrants and documents in a short time created a monumental challenge for the INS. The ranks of employees in the Alien Registration Division of the INS swelled from 55 in August 1940 to a peak of 985 in July 1941 ("This Month in Immigration History: June 1940," U.S. Citizenship and Immigration Services, http://uscis.gov/graphics/aboutus/history/6june40.htm).

The United States officially entered World War II on December 8, 1941, the day after the Japanese attack on Pearl Harbor. President Roosevelt immediately proclaimed all "nationals and subjects" of nations with which the country was at war to be enemy aliens. Various intelligence and military services quickly rounded up and detained some two thousand people. On January 14, 1942, the president issued a proclamation requiring further registration of aliens from enemy nations (primarily Germany, Italy, and Japan). All such aliens age fourteen and over were directed to apply for a Certification of Identification during the month of February 1942.

Alien registrations were used by a variety of government agencies and private industry to locate possible enemy subversives, such as aliens working for defense contractors, aliens with radio operator licenses, and aliens trained to pilot aircraft. According to the U.S. Citizenship and Immigration Services, one out of every twenty workers in American industry at that time was a noncitizen ("This Month in Immigration History: June 1940").

Japanese Internment

On the recommendation of military advisors, the president issued Executive Order 9066 on February 19, 1942, which authorized the forcible internment of people of Japanese ancestry. Lieutenant General J. L. DeWitt was placed in charge of removal of the Japanese to internment camps. In a June 5, 1943, letter to the Chief of Staff of the U.S. Army, which accompanied his *Final Report; Japanese Evacuation from the West Coast 1942*, DeWitt summed up the fears that drove the Japanese removal. "The continued presence of a large, unassimilated, tightly knit and racial group, bound to an enemy nation by strong ties of race, culture, custom and religion along a frontier vulnerable to attack constituted a menace which had to be dealt with. Their loyalties were unknown and time was of the essence." DeWitt's report revealed that over a period of less than ninety days, 110,442 persons of Japanese ancestry were evacuated from the West Coast. More than two-thirds were U.S. citizens. Relocation began in April 1942 and the last camp was vacated in March 1946.

Executive Order 9066 was never formally terminated after the war ended. Over the years many Japanese-Americans expressed concern that it could be implemented again. On February 19, 1976, President Gerald Ford issued a proclamation officially terminating the provisions of Executive Order 9066 retroactive to December 31, 1946. President Ford said, "We now know what we should have known then—not only was that evacuation wrong, but Japanese-Americans were and are loyal Americans. On the battlefield and at home, Japanese-Americans … have been and continue to be written in our history for the sacrifices and the contributions they have made to the well-being and security of this, our common Nation."

POST-WAR IMMIGRATION LAW

A growing fear of "communist infiltration" arose during the post-World War II period. One result was the passage of the Internal Security Act of 1950 (64 Stat. 987; PL 81-831), also known as the McCarran Act, which made membership in communist or totalitarian organizations cause for exclusion (denial of an alien's entry into the United States), deportation, or denial of naturalization. The law also required resident aliens to report their addresses annually and made reading, writing, and speaking English prerequisites for naturalization.

The Immigration and Nationality Act of 1952 (66 Stat. 163; PL 82-414), also known as the McCarran–Walter Act after its sponsors, added preferences for relatives and skilled aliens, gave immigrants and aliens certain legal protections, made all races eligible for immigration and naturalization, and absorbed most of the Internal Security Act of 1950. The act changed the national origin quotas to only one-sixth of 1% of the number of people in the United States in 1920 whose ancestry or national origin was attributable to a specific area of the world. It also excluded aliens on ideological grounds, homosexuality, health restrictions, criminal records, narcotics addiction, and involvement in terrorism.

Once again, Western Hemisphere countries were not included in the quota system. President Harry Truman vetoed the legislation, declaring:

> Today we are "protecting" ourselves as we were in 1924, against being flooded by immigrants from Eastern Europe. This is fantastic. The countries of Eastern Europe have fallen under the Communist yoke—they are silenced, fenced off by barbed wire and minefields—no one passes their borders but at the risk of his life. We do not need to be protected against immigrants from these countries—on the contrary, we want to stretch out a helping hand, to save those who have managed to flee into Western Europe, to succor those who are brave enough to escape from barbarism, to welcome and restore them against the day when their countries will, as we hope, be free again. These are only a few examples of the absurdity, the cruelty of carrying over into this year of 1952 the isolationist limitation of our 1924 law. (*Public Papers of the Presidents of the United States* [Washington, DC: U.S. Government Printing Office, 1961])

Congress overrode Truman's veto. Although there were major amendments, the Immigration and Nationality Act remained the basic statute governing who could gain entry into the United States until the passage of new laws following the September 11, 2001, terrorist attacks.

During the 1950s a half-dozen special laws allowed the entrance of additional refugees. Many of the laws resulted from World War II, but some stemmed from new developments. An example was the law affecting refugees fleeing the failed 1955 Hungarian revolution.

A TWO-HEMISPHERE SYSTEM

In 1963 President John F. Kennedy submitted a plan to change the quota system. Two years later Congress passed the Immigration and Nationality Act Amendments of 1965 (PL 89-236). Since 1924 sources of immigration had changed. In the 1950s immigration from Asia more than quadrupled from 37,028 (between 1941 and 1950) to 153,249 (between 1951 and 1960). In the same period immigration from North, Central, and South America increased dramatically. (See Table 1.1.)

The 1965 legislation cancelled the national origins quota system and made visas available on a first-come, first-serve basis. A seven-category preference system was implemented for families of U.S. citizens and permanent resident aliens for the purpose of family reunification. In addition, the law set visa allocations for persons with special occupational skills, abilities, or training needed in the United States. It also established an annual ceiling of 170,000 Eastern Hemisphere immigrants with a 20,000 per-country limit, and an annual limit of 120,000 for the Western Hemisphere without a per-country limit or preference system.

The Immigration and Nationality Act Amendments of 1976 (PL 94-571) extended the 20,000 per-country limit to Western Hemisphere countries. Some legislators were concerned that the 20,000-person limit for Mexico was inadequate, but their objections were overruled. The Immigration and Nationality Act Amendments of 1978 (PL 95-412) combined the separate ceilings for the Eastern and Western Hemispheres into a single worldwide ceiling of 290,000.

WAR CREATED REFUGEES

Official American refugee programs began in response to the devastation of World War II, which created millions of refugees and displaced persons (DPs). (A displaced person was a person living in a foreign country as a result of having been driven from his or her home country due to war or political unrest.) This was the first time the United States formulated policy to admit persons fleeing persecution. The Presidential Directive of December 22, 1945, gave priority in issuing visas to about 40,000 DPs. The directive was followed by the Displaced Persons Act of 1948 (PL 80-744), which authorized admission of 202,000 persons from Eastern Europe, and the Refugee Relief Act of 1953 (PL 83-203), which approved entry of another 209,000 defectors from Communist countries over a three-year period (*A History of U.S. Refugee Policy*, Washington, DC: USA for UNHCR, 1992). The Displaced Persons Act counted the refugees in the existing immigration quotas, while the Refugee Relief Act admitted them outside the quota system.

Parole Authority—A Temporary Admission Policy

In 1956 the U.S. attorney general used the parole authority (temporary admission) under Section 212(d) (15) of the Immigration and Nationality Act of 1952 for the first time on a large scale. This section authorized the attorney general to temporarily admit any alien to the United States. While parole was not admission for permanent residence, it could lead to permanent resident or immigrant status. Aliens already in the United States on a temporary basis could apply for asylum (to stay in the United States) on the grounds they were likely to suffer persecution if returned to their native lands. The attorney general was authorized to withhold deportation on the same grounds.

According to the U.S. Citizenship and Immigration Service, this parole authority was used to admit approximately 32,000 of the 38,000 Hungarians who fled the failed Hungarian Revolution in 1956 (*An Immigrant Nation: United States Regulation of Immigration, 1798–1991*, June 18, 1991). The other 6,000 entered under the Refugee Relief Act of 1953 and were automatically admitted as permanent residents. This parole provision was also used in 1962 to admit 15,000 refugees from Hong Kong to the United States.

Refugees as Conditional Entrants

In 1965, under the Immigration and Nationality Act Amendments, Congress added Section 203(a) (7) to the Immigration and Nationality Act of 1952, creating a group of "conditional entrant" refugees from communist or Middle Eastern countries, with status similar to the refugee parolees. Sections 203(a) (7) and 212(d) (15) were used to admit thousands of refugees, including Czechoslovakians escaping their failed revolution in 1968, Ugandans fleeing their dictatorship in the 1970s, and Lebanese avoiding the civil war in their country in the 1980s.

Not until the Refugee Act of 1980 did the United States have a general policy governing the admission of refugees. The Refugee Act of 1980 (PL 96-212) eliminated refugees as a category in the preference system and set a worldwide ceiling on immigration of 270,000, not counting refugees. It also removed the requirement that refugees had to originate from a Communist or Middle Eastern nation.

CHAPTER 2

IMMIGRATION LAWS AND POLICIES SINCE THE 1980s

Remember, remember always, that all of us ... are descended from immigrants and revolutionists.

—Franklin D. Roosevelt

In "Immigration: Shaping and Reshaping America" (*Population Bulletin* 58, no. 2, June 2003), Philip Martin and Elizabeth Midgley point out that before the 1980s, U.S. immigration laws might have changed once in a generation, but the quickening pace of global change since 1980 brought major new immigration legislation in 1986, 1990, and 1996. The September 11, 2001, terrorist attacks led to antiterrorism laws that had considerable impact on immigration policies and procedures, and that effected changes to immigration legislation. This chapter covers the most significant immigration laws from the 1980s to 2005.

THE IMMIGRATIOIN REFORM AND CONTROL ACT OF 1986 (IRCA)

On November 6, 1986, after thirty-four years with no new major immigration legislation and a six-year effort to send an acceptable bill through both houses of Congress, the Immigration Reform and Control Act of 1986 (IRCA; PL 99-603) was signed into law by President Ronald Reagan. IRCA tried to resolve the following problems:

- Jobs lost by citizens and taken by illegal aliens, with resulting lower wages paid to illegal aliens

- Costs of services and welfare for illegal aliens and their low tax payments

- Exploitation of illegal aliens

- Social fragmentation of local communities

- The need to reestablish the power of law and the principle of U.S. sovereignty

To control illegal immigration IRCA adopted three major strategies:

- Legalization of a portion of the undocumented population (aliens in the country without legal papers), thereby reducing the number of aliens illegally resident in the United States

- Sanctions against employers who knowingly hired illegal aliens

- Additional border enforcement to impede further unlawful entries

The "Pre-1982 Cohort"

Two groups of immigrants became eligible to apply for legalization under IRCA. The largest group consisted of those who could prove they had continuously resided in the United States without authorization since January 1, 1982. This large group of aliens had entered the United States in one of two ways: (1) they could have arrived as illegal aliens before January 1, 1982; or (2) they may have been temporary visitors before January 1, 1982, with their authorized stay expiring before that date or with the government's knowledge of their unlawful status before that date. The latter category would include those who arrived legally on a tourist visa and then stayed to work and live illegally in the United States.

To adjust to the legal status of permanent resident, aliens were required to prove eligibility for admission as immigrants (with no serious criminal record and a negative test for HIV, the virus that causes AIDS), and have at least a minimal understanding and knowledge of the English language and U.S. history and government. They could apply for citizenship five years from the date permanent resident status was granted. Illegal aliens who did not apply for residence could no longer remain in the United States and adjust to permanent resident status unless they were immediate relatives of U.S. citizens.

TABLE 2.1

Effects of Immigration Reform and Control Act legalization through 2001

Category of admission	Applicants for temporary residence	Applicants granted permanent residence	Percent of applicants granted permanent residence	Applicants who naturalized	Naturalized as a percentage of applicants granted permanent residence
	(1)	(2)	(3)=(1)/(2)	(4)	(5)=(2)/(4)
Total	3,040,475	2,688,730	88%	889,033	33%
Legalization applicants					
Total	1,763,434	1,595,766	90%	634,456	40%
Entered illegally prior to 1/1/1982	1,444,925	1,312,058	91%	480,871	37%
Overstayed nonimmigrant visa prior to 1/1/1982	311,071	277,337	89%	149,676	54%
Blanket enforced voluntary departure/unknown	7,438	6,371	86%	3,909	61%
SAW applicants					
Total	1,277,041	1,092,964	86%	254,577	23%
Group I seasonal agricultural workers 1984–86	67,308	59,975	89%	12,124	20%
Group II seasonal agricultural workers in 1986	1,209,733	1,032,989	85%	242,453	23%
Unknown	473	—	—	—	—

SOURCE: Nancy Rytina, "Exhibit 1-IRCA Legalization: Temporary Residence, Permanent Residence, and Naturalization through 2001," in *IRCA Legalization Effects: Lawful Permanent Residence and Naturalization through 2001*, U.S. Department of Homeland Security, Office of Citizenship and Immigration Services, October 25, 2002, http://uscis.gov/graphics/shared/aboutus/statistics/IRCA_REPORT/irca0114int.pdf (accessed February 14, 2005)

Special Agricultural Workers (SAWs)

The second group of immigrants to become eligible to apply for legalization under IRCA were referred to as Special Agricultural Workers (SAWs). This category was created because many fruit and vegetable farmers feared they would lose their workers, many of whom were illegal aliens, if the IRCA provisions regarding length of continuous residence were applied to seasonal laborers. Most of these workers were migrants who returned home to live in Mexico when there was no work available in the fields. The SAW program permitted aliens who had performed labor in perishable agricultural commodities for a minimum of ninety days between May 1985 and May 1986 to apply for legalization.

HOW MANY WERE LEGALIZED? The Immigration and Naturalization Service (INS) estimated that three to five million illegal aliens were living in the United States in 1986. As shown in Table 2.1, more than three million aliens applied for temporary residence status under IRCA. Nearly 2.7 million (88%) of these applicants were eventually approved for permanent residence. By 2001, one-third (889,033) of these applicants had become naturalized citizens.

PROFILE OF THE LEGALIZED POPULATION. A majority (75%) of applicants under IRCA provisions were born in Mexico according to the INS. Table 2.1 shows that by 2001 a higher percentage of pre-1982 entrants (40%) had been naturalized than had SAW applicants (23%). According to Nancy Rytina in "IRCA Legalization Effects: Lawful Permanent Residence and Naturalization through 2001" (paper presented at the conference The Effects of Immigrant Legalization Programs on the United States, Bethesda, Maryland, October 25, 2002), more of the

pre-1982 entrants came to America with the intention of naturalizing, were better educated, and had a better grasp of the English language than the SAWs.

IRCA barred newly legalized aliens from receiving most federally funded public assistance for five years. Exceptions included access to Medicaid for pregnant women, children, the elderly, the handicapped, and for emergency care. The State Legalization Impact Assistance Grant (SLIAG) program reimbursed state and local governments the costs for providing public assistance, education, and public health services to the legalized aliens. The Department of Health and Human Services, which administered SLIAG, reported that the program reimbursed states $3.5 billion, averaging $1,167 per eligible legalized alien, during its seven years of operation (David Simcox, *Measuring the Fallout: The Cost of IRCA Amnesty After 10 Years*, Washington, DC: Center for Immigration Studies, May 1997).

Employer Sanctions

The employer sanctions provision of IRCA was intended to correct a double standard that prohibited unauthorized aliens from working in the United States but permitted employers to hire them. IRCA prohibited employers from hiring, recruiting, or referring for a fee aliens known to be unauthorized to work in the United States. Employers who violated the law were subject to a series of civil fines or criminal penalties when a pattern or practice of violations was found.

The burden of proof was on employers to demonstrate that their employees had valid proof of identity and were authorized to work. IRCA required employers to complete the Employment Eligibility Verification form, known as Form I-9 (see Figure 2.1), for each employee

FIGURE 2.1

Employment Eligibility Verification Form I-9

U.S. Department of Justice
Immigration and Naturalization Service

OMB No. 1115-0136
Employment Eligibility Verification

Please read instructions carefully before completing this form. The instructions must be available during completion of this form. **ANTI-DISCRIMINATION NOTICE:** It is illegal to discriminate against work eligible individuals. Employers **CANNOT** specify which document(s) they will accept from an employee. The refusal to hire an individual because of a future expiration date may also constitute illegal discrimination.

Section 1. Employee Information and Verification. To be completed and signed by employee at the time employment begins.

Print Name: Last	First	Middle Initial	Maiden Name

Address *(Street Name and Number)*	Apt. #	Date of Birth *(month/day/year)*

City	State	Zip Code	Social Security #

I am aware that federal law provides for imprisonment and/or fines for false statements or use of false documents in connection with the completion of this form.	I attest, under penalty of perjury, that I am (check one of the following): ☐ A citizen or national of the United States ☐ A Lawful Permanent Resident (Alien # A _____ ☐ An alien authorized to work until ___/___/___ (Alien # or Admission #) _____

Employee's Signature	Date *(month/day/year)*

Preparer and/or Translator Certification.   *(To be completed and signed if Section 1 is prepared by a person other than the employee.)* I attest, *under penalty of perjury, that I have assisted in the completion of this form and that to the best of my knowledge the information is true and correct.*

Preparer's/Translator's Signature	Print Name

Address *(Street Name and Number, City, State, Zip Code)*	Date *(month/day/year)*

Section 2. Employer Review and Verification. To be completed and signed by employer. Examine one document from List A OR examine one document from List B and one from List C, as listed on the reverse of this form, and record the title, number and expiration date, if any, of the document(s)

List A	OR	List B	AND	List C
Document title: _____		_____		_____
Issuing authority: _____		_____		_____
Document #: _____		_____		_____
Expiration Date *(if any):* ___/___/___		___/___/___		___/___/___
Document #: _____				
Expiration Date *(if any):* ___/___/___				

CERTIFICATION - I attest, under penalty of perjury, that I have examined the document(s) presented by the above-named employee, that the above-listed document(s) appear to be genuine and to relate to the employee named, that the employee began employment on *(month/day/year)* ___/___/___ and that to the best of my knowledge the employee is eligible to work in the United States. (State employment agencies may omit the date the employee began employment.)

Signature of Employer or Authorized Representative	Print Name	Title

Business or Organization Name	Address *(Street Name and Number, City, State, Zip Code)*	Date *(month/day/year)*

Section 3. Updating and Reverification. To be completed and signed by employer.

A. New Name *(if applicable)*	B. Date of rehire *(month/day/year)* *(if applicable)*

C. If employee's previous grant of work authorization has expired, provide the information below for the document that establishes current employment eligibility.

Document Title: _____   Document #: _____   Expiration Date (if any): ___/___/___

I attest, under penalty of perjury, that to the best of my knowledge, this employee is eligible to work in the United States, and if the employee presented document(s), the document(s) I have examined appear to be genuine and to relate to the individual.

Signature of Employer or Authorized Representative	Date *(month/day/year)*

Form I-9 (Rev. 11-21-91)N Page 2

SOURCE: "Employment Eligibility Verification," U.S. Department of Homeland Security, U.S. Citizenship and Immigration Services, November 21, 1991, http://uscis.gov/graphics/formsfee/forms/files/i-9.pdf (accessed February 14, 2005).

TABLE 2.2

Documents that can be used to demonstrate employment eligibility, with October 2000 changes noted

List A Documents that establish both identity and employment eligibility	OR	List B Documents that establish identity	AND	List C Documents that establish employment eligibility
1. U.S. Passport (unexpired or expired) 2. Certificate of U.S. Citizenship (INS from N-560 or N-561) 3. Certificate of Naturalization (INS from N-550 or N-570) 4. Unexpired foreign passport, with *I-551 stamp* or attached *INS form I-94* indicating unexpired employment authorization 5. Permanent Resident Card or Alien Registration Receipt Card with photograph (INS form I-151 or I-551) 6. Unexpired Temporary Card (INS form I-688) 7. Unexpired Employment Authorization Card (INS form I-688A) 8. Unexpired Reentry Permit (INS form I-327) 9. Unexpired Refugee Travel Document (INS form I-571) 10. Unexpired Employment Authorization Document issued by the INS which contains a photograph (INS form I-688B)		1. Driver's license or ID card issued by a state or outlying possession of the United States provided it contains a photograph or information such as name, date of birth, gender, height, eye color and address 2. ID card issued by federal, state or local government agencies or entities, provided it contains a photograph or information such as name, date of birth, gender, height, eye color and address 3. School ID card with a photograph 4. Voter's registration card 5. U.S. Military card or draft record 6. Military dependent's ID card 7. U.S. Coast Guard Merchant Mariner Card 8. Native American tribal document 9. Driver's license issued by a Canadian government authority **For persons under age 18 who are unable to present a document listed above:** 10. School record or report card 11. Clinic, doctor or hospital record 12. Day-care or nursery school record		1. U.S. social security card issued by the Social Security Administration (other than a card stating it is not valid for employment) 2. Certification of Birth Abroad issued by the Department of State (Form FS-545 or form DS-1350) 3. Original or certified copy of a birth certificate issued by a state, county, municipal authority or outlying possession of the United States bearing an official seal 4. Native American tribal document 5. U.S. Citizen ID Card (INS form I-197) 6. ID Card for use of Resident Citizen in the United States (INS form I-179) 7. Unexpired employment authorization document issued by the INS (other than those listed under list A)

The form above was last updated on October 4, 2000. The following changes were made to the I-9 process since then (as of July 14, 2003).
- Form I-766 (Employment Authorization Document), although not listed on the 11/21/91 version of the Form I-9, is an acceptable list A document #10.
- Form I-151 is no longer an acceptable list A document #5. However, form I-551 remains an acceptable list A document #5.
- The following documents have been removed from the list of acceptable identity and work authorization documents: Certificate of U.S. Citizenship (list A #2), Certificate of Naturalization (list A #3), Unexpired Reentry Permit (list A #8), and Unexpired Refugee Travel Document (list A #9).

SOURCE: "List of Acceptable Documents," U.S. Department of Homeland Security, U.S. Citizenship and Immigration Services, October 4, 2000, http://uscis.gov/graphics/formsfee/forms/files/I-9.pdf (accessed February 14, 2005)

hired. In completing the form the employer certified that the employee had presented valid proof of identity and eligibility for employment, and that these documents appeared genuine. Table 2.2 lists documents acceptable for proof of identity and employment eligibility. (A number of the documents were later deleted from the list, as noted at the bottom of Table 2.2. The Bureau of Citizenship and Immigration Services announced a revised version of Form I-9 and the list of eligible documents, to be available sometime in 2005.) IRCA also required employers to retain the completed I-9 forms and produce them in response to an official government request.

IMMIGRATION MARRIAGE FRAUD AMENDMENTS OF 1986

Prior to 1986 the INS granted permanent residence fairly quickly to the foreign spouses of U.S. citizens or lawful permanent residents (LPRs). However, a number of marriages between American citizens or LPRs and foreigners occurred in order to attain U.S. permanent residence status for the foreigner. Some American citizens or LPRs agreed to marry aliens for money. After the alien gained permanent residence, the marriage was dissolved. Other cases involved aliens entering into marriages by deceiving U.S. citizens or LPRs with declarations of love, only to seek divorce after gaining permanent residence.

Concerns regarding alleged marriage fraud led to the passage of the Immigration Marriage Fraud Amendments of 1986 (PL 99-639). The law specified that aliens basing their immigrant status on a marriage of less than two years were considered conditional immigrants. To remove the conditional immigrant status, the alien had to apply for permanent residence within ninety days after the second-year anniversary of receiving conditional status. The alien and his or her spouse were required to show that the marriage was and continued to be a valid one; otherwise, conditional immigrant status was terminated, and the alien could be deported.

Battered Brides

Unfortunately, cases of spousal abuse were an unintentional result of the two-year conditional immigrant status. Particularly in cases of mail-order brides and brides from countries where women had few, if any, rights, some husbands took advantage of the power they had as the wife's sponsor. The new wives were dependent on their husbands to obtain permanent U.S. residence. Reports surfaced with the Department of Justice about wives who were virtual prisoners, afraid they would be deported if they defied their husbands or reported abuse. In addition, some of the women came from cultures in which divorced women were outcasts with no place in society.

Subsequently two laws were passed to address the plight of such abused women and their children: the Violence Against Women Act (VAWA) of 1994—part of the Violent Crime Control and Law Enforcement Act of 1994 (PL 103-322)—and the Victims of Trafficking and Violence Prevention Act (PL 106-386) of 2000. The 1994 law allowed the women and/or children to self-petition for immigrant status without the abuser's participation or consent. Abused males could also file a self-petition under this law. The 2000 law created a new nonimmigrant U-visa for victims of serious crimes. Recipients of the U-visa, including victims of crimes against women, could adjust to lawful permanent resident status based on humanitarian grounds as determined by the U.S. attorney general.

THE IMMIGRATION ACT OF 1990 (IMMACT)

It took six years of commitment and negotiation to pass the 1986 Immigration Reform and Control Act. Almost as soon as that law was passed, Senators Edward Kennedy (a Democrat from Massachusetts) and Alan Simpson (a Republican from Wyoming) began work to change the Immigration and Nationality Act Amendments of 1965 (PL 89-236), which determined legal immigration into the United States. Senators Kennedy and Simpson claimed that the "family-oriented" system allowed one legal immigrant to bring too many relatives into the country. Instead, they wanted immigration policy to cut back the number of dependents admitted and replace them with individuals who had the skills or money to immediately benefit the American economy.

The result was the Immigration Act of 1990 (IMMACT; PL 101-649). Enacted on November 29, 1990, IMMACT represented a major overhaul of immigration law. The law's focus was to increase the numerical limits on immigrants and change the preference system, giving a greater priority to employment-based immigration. The law also created a diversity program enabling immigrants from countries that had been ignored in the recent past to be admitted more easily to the United States.

The total number of immigrants was set at 700,000 annually from FY 1992 through FY 1994 and then revised to an annual level of 675,000 beginning in FY 1995. (FY stands for fiscal year. The government fiscal year begins on October 1 and ends on September 30 of the following calendar year.) The 675,000 level allowed 480,000 family-sponsored immigrants,

140,000 employment-based immigrants, and 55,000 immigrants who were eligible under the diversity program.

Employment-Based Immigration

IMMACT nearly tripled the allowed level of employment-based immigration—from 54,000 to 140,000. The goal was to attract professional people with skills that would promote economic development in the United States. This was in contrast to the unskilled workers who were legalized through IRCA. The allotment of 140,000, however, included both workers and their families so the actual number of workers was considerably lower. IMMACT allocations included:

- Preference 1—forty thousand visas for priority workers with extraordinary ability, outstanding professors and researchers, and certain multinational executives and managers

- Preference 2—forty thousand visas for members of the professions holding advanced degrees or aliens of exceptional ability, both requiring the Secretary of Labor to certify that U.S. workers were not available and would not be hurt by the aliens' admission

- Preference 3—forty thousand visas for skilled workers with at least two years of vocational training or experience, professionals with the equivalent of a college degree, or needed unskilled workers (limited to ten thousand), all requiring labor certification

- Preference 4—ten thousand visas for special immigrants, including ministers of religion, persons working for religious organizations, foreign medical graduates, alien employees of the U.S. government abroad, and alien retired employees of international organizations, of which not more than five thousand could be religious workers

- Preference 5—ten thousand visas for employment-creation investors who invested at least one million dollars (or $500,000 in rural areas or areas of high unemployment) to create at least ten new jobs

Diversity Visa Program

IMMACT made new provisions for the admission of immigrants from countries with low rates of immigration to the United States. The program was introduced as a temporary or transitional program from 1992 to 1994. In the first year of the diversity program (1992) the INS ran a lottery; the "winners" were chosen based on the chronological order of the receipt of the visa applications. Applicants were permitted to file multiple applications to improve their chances. In 1993 and 1994, selections were made randomly rather than by chronological receipt of applications. In addition, only one application per immigrant was permitted. The permanent Diversity Visa Program began in 1995.

Under the permanent program, initially no country was permitted more than 7% (3,850) of the total 55,000 visas, and Northern Ireland was treated as a separate state. To be eligible, aliens were required to have at least a high school education or its equivalent, or at least two years of work experience in an occupation that required a minimum of two years training or experience. The work experience had to be within the past five years. A person selected under the lottery program could apply for permanent residence and, if granted, the person was authorized to work in the United States. The individual's spouse and unmarried children under the age of 21 were also allowed to enter the United States.

Beginning with fiscal year 1999, the number of visas was reduced to fifty thousand so that five thousand visas could be allotted to participants in the 1997 Nicaraguan Adjustment and Central American Relief Act (NACARA; PL-105-100). This law provided various immigration benefits and relief from deportation to certain Nicaraguans, Cubans, Salvadorans, Guatemalans, nationals of former Soviet-bloc countries, and their dependents.

Results of the 2005 Diversity Lottery

The U.S. Department of State reported that 5.9 million qualified applications were received for the 2005 lottery during the sixty-day period November 1 to December 30, 2003 (*Diversity Visa Lottery 2005 Results*, Washington, DC: Bureau of Consular Affairs, U.S. Department of State, April 15, 2005). Assuming that some of the applicants would not pursue their visas, a total of 100,000 applications were drawn at random by a computer. Table 2.3 lists the FY 2005 lottery results by regions and countries.

According to the U.S. Department of State, between 2.5 and 3 million applications are rejected each year for failing to follow directions or because they were received outside of the submission period (U.S. House of Representatives Judiciary Committee, *Security and Fairness Enhancement for America Act of 2003*, 108th Congress, 2d session, October 6, 2004, H. Rept. 108-747). Of the 90,000 to 110,000 lottery "winners" each year, about 45% either fail to meet the minimum educational, work experience, or training requirements; fail to supply the required medical information; or fail to complete the additional required paperwork fully or on time. The remaining qualifying "winners" were issued diversity visas on a first-come, first-served basis until the requisite number of visas were issued or the fiscal year ended (September 30, 2005, for the 2005 lottery). Winners already living legally in the United States could apply to have their status adjusted.

For the fiscal year 2005 application period, natives of the following countries were ineligible to apply: Canada, China (mainland-born), Colombia, Dominican Republic, El Salvador, Haiti, India, Jamaica, Mexico, Pakistan, Philippines, Russia, South Korea, the United Kingdom (except Northern Ireland) and its dependent territories, and Vietnam. However, persons born in Hong Kong SAR (Special Administrative Region), Macau SAR, and Taiwan were eligible.

On February 10, 2005, the U.S. Department of State announced that more than 6.3 million entries were received for the 2006 Diversity Visa Lottery ("2006 Diversity Lottery Registrations," http://www.state.gov/r/pa/prs/ps/2005/42131.htm). The two-month electronic registration period ran from noon on November 5, 2004, through noon, January 7, 2005. New antifraud technology in use for the 2006 Diversity Visa Lottery detected 31,334 exact duplicates, which were eliminated from the eligible entry pool. An additional 5,221 fraudulent entries were eliminated through the utilization of facial recognition and knowledge discovery software.

Efforts to End the Diversity Visa Program

In 2003 a bill was introduced in the U.S. House of Representatives to eliminate the diversity program. In its October 6, 2004, report in favor of the bill (*Security and Fairness Enhancement for America Act of 2003,* H. Rept. 108-747), the Judiciary Committee noted that it was commonplace for aliens to file multiple applications for the lottery using different aliases. The report stated that a partial check on applications filed in the 2003 lottery identified 364,000 duplicates. The report further noted that fraudulent documents were common in many countries due to poor control of vital records and identity documents. In addition to entry fraud, the visa lottery program had spawned a cottage industry of websites that offered to help applicants win the lottery for a fee. The problem became so widespread that the government posted electronic notices warning applicants that paying someone a fee to complete their application would not improve their chances in a random lottery drawing.

According to the Judiciary Committee report, the Diversity Visa Program posed a threat to U.S. national security. It noted that in the fiscal year 2004 lottery "24 Libyans, 1,183 Sudanese, 1,431 Iranians, 4 North Koreans, 64 Syrians, and 674 Cubans were selected. Each country is a state-sponsor of terrorism." While the report noted that the Department of State had implemented an electronic facial recognition system for processing applicants and had increased the verification of background information, the Judiciary Committee suggested that these efforts were not sufficient protection. At an April 29, 2004, hearing on the Diversity Visa Program before the House of Representatives Subcommittee on Immigration, Border

Security, and Claims (House Judiciary Committee, *Diversity Visa Program and Its Susceptibility to Fraud and Abuse*, 108th Congress, 2d session, serial 82), Anne Patterson, Deputy Inspector General with the State Department, testified that the program "contains significant vulnerabilities to national security as hostile intelligence officers, criminals, and terrorists attempt to use it to enter the United States as permanent residents."

The Judiciary Committee report cited two specific examples of individuals, both admitted as family members of lottery "winners," who later were involved in

TABLE 2.3

Results of the diversity immigrant visa lottery, 2005

Africa

Algeria	1,489	Eritrea	556	Namibia	11
Angola	14	Ethiopia	6,060	Niger	53
Benin	233	Gabon	29	Nigeria	6,725
Botswana	7	Gambia, the	136	Rwanda	51
Burkina Faso	76	Ghana	3,974	Sao Tome and Principe	0
Burundi	34	Guinea	268	Senegal	409
Cameroon	1,540	Guinea-Bissau	3	Seychelles	4
Cape Verde	6	Kenya	3,618	Sierra Leone	594
Central African Rep.	4	Lesotho	0	Somalia	364
Chad	22	Liberia	714	South Africa	390
Comoros	3	Libya	35	Sudan	1,015
Congo	47	Madagascar	28	Swaziland	6
Congo, Democratic		Malawi	44	Tanzania	356
Republic of the	844	Mail	124	Togo	2,857
Côte d'Ivoire	321	Mauritania	25	Tunisia	134
Djibouti	12	Mauritius	23	Uganda	244
Egypt	6,070	Morocco	5,298	Zambia	118
Equatorial Guinea	2	Mozambique	12	Zimbabwe	141

Asia

Afghanistan	22	Iraq	48	Nepal	2,698
Bahrain	1	Israel	116	Oman	0
Bangladesh	7,404	Japan	373	Qatar	1
Bhutan	1	Jordan	44	Saudi Arabia	30
Brunei	1	North Korea	1	Singapore	35
Burma	531	Kuwait	16	Sri Lanka	386
Cambodia	164	Laos	4	Syria	26
Hong Kong Special		Lebanon	83	Thailand	102
Admin. Region	77	Malaysia	87	Taiwan	367
Indonesia	258	Maldives	0	United Arab Emirates	13
Iran	820	Mongolia	55	Yemen	40

Europe

Albania	3,380	Georgia	375	Northern Ireland	75
Andorra	1	Germany	1,275	Norway	25
Armenia	1,004	Greece	78	Poland	6,211
Austria	91	Hungary	181	Portugal	51
Azerbaijan	235	Iceland	5	Macau	12
Belarus	925	Ireland	205	Romania	2,521
Belgium	81	Italy	202	San Marino	0
Bosnia & Herzegovina	103	Kazakhstan	296	Serbia & Montenegro	425
Bulgaria	4,068	Kyrgyzstan	206	Slovakia	398
Croatia	69	Latvia	158	Slovenia	6
Cyprus	14	Liechtenstein	1	Spain	134
Czech Republic	169	Lithuania	1,114	Sweden	115
Denmark	42	Luxembourg	2	Switzerland	136
Estonia	64	Macedonia, Former		Tajikistan	83
Finland	59	Yugoslav Rep. of	306	Turkey	1,803
France	384	Malta	0	Turkmenistan	78
French Southern &		Moldova	383	Ukraine	5,361
Antarctic Lands	1	Monaco	0	Uzbekistan	1,551
Martinique	2	Netherlands	130	Vatican City	0
New Caledonia	1	Netherlands' Antilles	10		
Reunion	3	Aruba	2		

North America

Bahamas, The	14

Oceania

Australia	787	Nauru	0	Samoa	6
Cocos Islands	2	New Zealand	290	Solomon Islands	1
Fiji	530	Cook Islands	0	Tonga	96
Kiribati	0	Niue	1	Tuvalu	0
Marshall Island	0	Palau	2	Vanuatu	0
Micronesia, Federated		Papua New Guinea	5		
States of	0				

TABLE 2.3

Results of the diversity immigrant visa lottery, 2005 [CONTINUED]

South America, Central America, and the Caribbean

Antigua and Barbuda	4	Dominica	8	Peru	2,514
Argentina	221	Ecuador	308	Saint Kitts and Nevis	3
Barbados	12	Grenada	7	Saint Lucia	4
Belize	3	Guatemala	25	Saint Vincent and the Grenadines	14
Bolivia	108	Guyana	27	Suriname	3
Brazil	592	Honduras	35	Trinidad and Tobago	96
Chile	43	Nicaragua	14	Uruguay	18
Costa Rica	24	Panama	17	Venezuela	299
Cuba	674	Paraguay	14		

Note: Natives of the following countries were not eligible to participate in DV-2005: Canada, China (mainland-born, excluding Hong Kong S.A.R., and Taiwan), Colombia, Dominican Republic, El Salvador, Haiti, India, Jamaica, Mexico, Pakistan, the Philippines, Russia, South Korea, United Kingdom (except Northern Ireland) and its dependent territories, and Vietnam.

SOURCE: "Diversity Visa Lottery 2005 (DV-2005) Results," U.S. Department of State, Bureau of Consular Affairs, http://travel.state.gov/visa/immigrants_types_diversity2.html (accessed February 15, 2005)

terrorist activity. In one case a man who entered as a visitor applied for asylum, and was in deportation proceedings when his wife became a diversity lottery winner. As her spouse, the man was able to adjust his status. He was a lawful permanent resident when he killed two people and wounded several others in an incident at Los Angeles International Airport. In the second case, a man entered the United States with his parents who were lottery winners. In 2002 he pleaded guilty to conspiring to destroy buildings, affecting interstate commerce by means of fire or explosives.

Changing Grounds for Entry

IMMACT changed the political and ideological grounds for exclusion and deportation. The law repealed the ban against the admission of communists and representatives of other totalitarian regimes that had been in place since 1950. In addition, immigration applicants who had been excluded previously because of associations with communism were provided exceptions if the applicants had been involuntary members of the communist party, had terminated membership, or merely had close family relationships with people affiliated with communism.

Temporary Protected Status

IMMACT authorized the U.S. attorney general to grant temporary protected status (TPS) to undocumented alien nationals present in the United States when a natural disaster, ongoing armed conflict, or other extraordinary occurrence in their countries posed a danger to their personal safety. TPS lasted for six to eighteen months unless conditions in the alien national's country warranted an extension of stay.

TPS did not lead to permanent resident status, although such aliens could obtain work authorization. Foreign nationals who had been convicted in the United States of either a felony or two or more misdemeanors were not eligible for TPS. Once the TPS designation ended, the foreign nationals resumed the same immigrant status they had before TPS (unless that status had expired) or returned to any other status obtained while in TPS.

According to a January 7, 2005, posting on the Bureau of Citizenship and Immigration Services Web site (www.uscis.gov/graphics/services/tps_inter.htm), TPS reregistration periods ended December 6, 2004, for nationals of Burundi and Sudan and January 3, 2005, for Honduras and Nicaragua. TPS ended February 27, 2005, for Montserrat. TPS registration periods were established August 24, 2004, to February 21, 2005, for Liberia, and January 7 to March 8, 2005, for El Salvador.

THE WELFARE REFORM LAW OF 1996

Under Title IV of the Personal Responsibility and Work Opportunity Reconciliation Act of 1996 (PRWORA; PL 104-193)—also called the Welfare Reform Law—federal welfare benefits for legal immigrants were cut substantially and the responsibility for public assistance was shifted from the federal government to the states. (Illegal immigrants were already ineligible for most major welfare programs.) The law was designed to ensure that available welfare benefits did not serve as an incentive for immigration and that immigrants admitted to the United States would be self-reliant.

In the past, legal immigrants had generally been eligible for the same welfare benefits as citizens. Under the new rules, immigrants who had become naturalized citizens remained eligible for federal benefits, but most noncitizens were barred from participating in federal programs such as Temporary Assistance for Needy Families (TANF), food stamps, Supplemental Security Income (SSI), and Medicaid. The states were given the option of using federal funds for TANF and Medicaid for immigrants who arrived before the act took effect. Immigrants who arrived legally after the law took effect were ineligible for any federal funds until five years had elapsed; the states then had the option of granting their applications for TANF and/or Medicaid. As of December 2004, TANF was extended to March 31, 2005, pending reauthorization. (Medicaid is a joint federal-state health insurance program for certain low-income and needy people, while TANF is the federal block grant program for needy families with dependent children that replaced the Aid to Families with Dependent Children, Emergency Assistance, and Job Opportunities and Basic Skills programs.)

Restoration of Government Benefits

With support from both Democrats and Republicans, and intense lobbying by immigration advocates, on August 15, 1997, the Balanced Budget Act (PL 105-34) restored SSI and Medicaid benefits to legal immigrants who were receiving these benefits when the welfare reform law was passed.

On October 28, 1998, the Noncitizen Benefit Clarification and Other Technical Amendments Act of 1998 (PL 105-306) amended the welfare reform law, requiring that nonqualified aliens who were receiving SSI and Medicaid benefits on August 22, 1996, could retain these benefits.

FOOD STAMPS. In 1997, when the food stamp restrictions went into effect, an estimated 940,000 of the 1.4 million legal immigrants receiving food stamps lost their eligibility. Nearly one-fifth were immigrant children. In *Welfare Reform: Many States Continue Some Federal or State Benefits for Immigrants* (Washington, DC, July 1998), the U.S. General Accounting Office (GAO) reported to the Senate Subcommittee on Children and Families that in 1997 and 1998, fourteen states had created food stamp programs that served about one-quarter of this immigrant group nationwide. Most recipients were children, the elderly, and the disabled. Some states continued to provide food assistance to ineligible legal immigrants.

In June 1998 the Agricultural Research, Extension, and Education Reform Act (PL 105-185) restored food stamp benefits to approximately 250,000 legal immigrants who would otherwise have been ineligible. According to a July 2002 estimate from the Food Research and Action Center, the Farm Security and Rural Investment Act of 2002 (PL 107-171), also known as the Food Stamp Reauthorization Act, restored access to food stamps to 400,000 legal immigrants (*Food Stamp Participation Increases in July 2002*, Washington, DC, October 2, 2002). As of December 2004, eight states provided food assistance to certain immigrants who were ineligible for federal food stamp benefits as a result of welfare reform. (See Table 2.4.)

TABLE 2.4

State-funded food programs for legal immigrants, January–March 2005

States	Starting date	Targeted population	Persons served (monthly estimate)*	Issuance (monthly estimate)*
California	9-1-97	Legal immigrants otherwise eligible.	21,048	$1,835,743
Nebraska	8-1-97	Legal immigrants otherwise eligible.	160	$14,013
New York	9-1-97	Immigrants legally residing in the US on 8/22/96 who are victims of domestic violence or 60–65 years of age.	0	0
Wisconsin	8-1-98	Legal immigrants otherwise eligible.	420	$30,796
Total			21,628	$1,880,552

States	Starting date	Targeted population	Served (monthly estimate)*	(Monthly estimate)*
Connecticut	4-1-98 STATE EBT	Legal immigrants otherwise eligible.	Unknown	Unknown
Maine	9-1-98 STATE EBT	Legal immigrants otherwise eligible.	Unknown	Unknown
Minnesota	9-1-97 STATE EBT	Legal immigrants otherwise eligible.	Unknown	Unknown
Washington	11-1-99 STATE EBT	Legal immigrants otherwise eligible.	Unknown	Unknown

*Estimates are based on information reported by states to USDA (United States Department of Agriculture) and are an average of the prior 3 months.

SOURCE: "State-Funded Food Programs for Legal Immigrants," *Food Stamp Program*, U.S. Department of Agriculture, Food & Nutrition Service, December 2004, http://www.fns.usda.gov/fsp/rules/Memo/PRWORA/StatePrograms.htm (accessed April 6, 2005)

Welfare Reform Does Not Diminish Immigrant Dependence

A March 2003 report from the Center for Immigration Studies asserted that PRWORA had failed to cut immigrants' use of welfare (Steven A. Camarota, "Back Where We Started: An Examination of Trends in Immigrant Welfare Use Since Welfare Reform," *Backgrounder*, Washington, DC, March 2003). The report contended that "[i]n 1996, 22% of immigrant-headed households used at least one major welfare program, compared to 15% of native households. After declining in the late 1990s, welfare use returned to 1996 levels by 2001, with 23% of immigrant households using welfare compared to 15% of native households."

ILLEGAL IMMIGRATION REFORM AND IMMIGRANT RESPONSIBILITY ACT (IIRIRA) OF 1996

On September 30, 1996, the Illegal Immigration Reform and Immigrant Responsibility Act (IIRIRA; PL 104-208) became law. In an effort to reduce illegal immigration, IIRIRA included the following among its many provisions:

- Required doubling the number of U.S. Border Patrol agents to 10,000 by the year 2001 and increasing equipment and technology at air and land ports of entry

- Authorized improvements of southwest border barriers

- Toughened penalties for immigrant smuggling (up to ten years in prison, fifteen years for third and subsequent offenses) and document fraud (up to fifteen years in prison)

- Increased the number of INS investigators for work site enforcement, tracking aliens who overstayed visas, and investigating alien smuggling

- Increased detention space for criminals and other deportable aliens

- Instituted a new "expedited removal" proceeding (denial of an alien's entry into the United States without a hearing) to speed deportation of aliens with no documents or with fraudulent documents

- Authorized three voluntary pilot programs to enable employers to verify the immigrant status of job applicants and to reduce the number and types of documents needed for identification and employment eligibility

- Required a legally binding affidavit of support from immigrant sponsors, who must have an income of at least 125% of the poverty level (in 2005 the poverty guidelines issued by the Department of Health and Human Services were set at $19,350 for a family of four and $25,870 for a family of six living in the forty-eight contiguous states and District of Columbia)

- Instituted a bar on admissibility for aliens seeking to reenter the United States after having been unlawfully present in the country—a bar of three years for aliens unlawfully present from six months to a year and a bar of ten years for those unlawfully present for more than a year

By 2001 the INS reported approximately 8,400 agents guarding America's borders—400 assigned to the 4,000-mile northern border and 8,000 assigned to the 2,000-mile southern border.

Employment Verification Process

Although the 1986 Immigration Reform and Control Act (IRCA) established a process by which employers could verify an applicant's eligibility to work in the United States, fraudulent documentation and employers who overlooked documentation in favor

of "cheap labor" continued to be problems. In May 2003 the Bureau of Citizenship and Immigration Services began accepting electronic filing of two of the most commonly submitted immigration forms, the Application for Employment Authorization (Form I-765) and the application used to renew or replace a "green card" (Form I-90). These two forms represented about 30% of the seven million applications filed annually with immigration authorities. IIRIRA authorized reduction of the number and types of documents used for identification and employment eligibility. As shown in the notes in Table 2.2, the INS took some steps to implement this policy by reducing the number of acceptable documents.

Many Aliens Detained in U.S. Jails

To allow for the construction of more detention facilities, Congress delayed the mandatory detention provisions of the 1996 laws until October 9, 1998. However, the INS continued to rely on county jails, federal prisons, and private lockups to accommodate the increasing number of detained noncitizens. Some aliens without criminal convictions, such as asylum seekers, were held with the nation's toughest criminals. A June 2003 report from Amnesty International charged that 5,385 unaccompanied immigrant children were detained by the INS in 2001 in facilities that also held juvenile offenders (*United States of America: Unaccompanied Children in Immigration Detention*, New York).

The average daily population of criminal aliens in detention between FY 1994 and FY 2001 grew from approximately 3,300 to 13,210 according to a December 19, 2001, statement made before the House Subcommittee on Immigration and Claims by Joseph Greene, Acting Deputy Executive Associate Commissioner for Field Operations, and Edward McElroy, New York District Director, both of the U.S. Immigration and Naturalization Service. The INS detainees were housed in a variety of facilities, including five that were owned and operated by the INS and others owned by state or local governments that contracted space to the INS. The median length of stay was reported by Greene and McElroy to be fourteen days, but cases of detainment lasting more than three years have been documented.

THE "GREEN CARD"

In January 2005 the U.S. Citizenship and Immigration Web site stated, "A 'green card' gives you official immigration status (Lawful Permanent Residency) in the United States." A lawful permanent resident (LPR) carries that document as proof of legal status in the country. Yet, the card is not green. What we know as a "green card" came in a variety of different colors at different times in history. The card, formally known as the Alien Registration Receipt Card, Form I-151 or I-551, entitles an alien to certain benefits, and those benefits originated at a time when the card was actually green.

The first receipt cards, Form AR-3, resulted from the Alien Registration Act of 1940, a World War II-era national defense measure. The act required all non–U.S. citizens (legal or illegal) to register at post offices. From there, the registration forms were forwarded to the INS. The receipt card was mailed to each alien as proof of their compliance with the law. These receipts were printed on white paper.

When the war ended, alien registration became part of the regular immigration procedure. Aliens registered at ports of entry and the INS issued different types of Alien Registration Receipt Cards based on each alien's admission status. Temporary foreign laborers, for example, received an I-100a card while visitors received an I-94c. Permanent residents received the I-151. Cards were different colors to make it easy to identify the immigration status of each alien. The permanent resident card was green and was necessary to get a job.

The Internal Security Act of 1950 made the I-151 even more valuable. Effective April 17, 1951, any alien holding an AR-3 card (the type issued to all aliens during the war) had to apply to have it replaced with the green I-151 card. Anyone who could not prove their legal admission to the United States (people not listed in INS legal admission records) did not qualify for a green card and could be subject to prosecution for violation of immigration laws.

By 1951 the green card represented security for an alien. It indicated the right to permanently live and work in the United States and instantly communicated that right to law enforcement officials. The Alien Registration Receipt Card, Form I-151, became commonly known to aliens, immigration attorneys, enforcement officers, and employers by its color. The term "green card" designated not only the document but also the official status so desired by many legal nonimmigrants (students, tourists, and temporary workers) and by illegal aliens.

The "green card" was so desirable that counterfeiting became a problem. To combat this fraud the INS issued nineteen different designs of the card between 1940 and 1977. The 1964 version was pale blue and in 1965 the card became dark blue. During the mid-1970s the INS studied methods to produce a counterfeit-proof card. In January 1977 the INS introduced the new style, machine-readable Alien Registration Receipt Card, Form I-551, which has since been issued in a variety of colors including pink and a pink and blue combination. Form I-151 and its successor, Form I-551, have such vital meaning to immigrants that despite changes in form number, design, and color it will probably always be known as a "green card."

BIRTHRIGHT CITIZENSHIP

On October 30, 2000, Congress passed the Child Citizenship Act of 2000 (PL 106-395), granting automatic U.S. citizenship to foreign-born biological and adopted children of American citizens. In a November 19, 2004, press release the U.S. Citizenship and Immigration Services announced that since January 2004 more than 13,000 Certificates of Citizenship had been issued to children from eighty-two countries who had been adopted by U.S. citizens.

USA PATRIOT ACT OF 2001

Following the terrorist attacks of September 11, 2001, it became apparent that some, if not all, of the perpetrators had entered the United States legally and many had overstayed their allotted time with no notice taken by the INS or any other enforcement agency. Since then several laws have been passed or proposed and policy changes have been implemented to address immigration concerns. The first law was the Uniting and Strengthening America by Providing Appropriate Tools Required to Intercept and Obstruct Terrorism, more commonly known as the USA PATRIOT Act (PL 107-56), signed into law in October 2001. With reference to immigration, the act included the following legislation:

- It mandated that the number of personnel at the northern border be tripled, appropriated funds for technology improvements, and gave the INS access to the FBI's criminal databases. The INS was to begin the task of locating hundreds of thousands of foreigners who had been ordered deported and entering their names into the FBI database.

- The Immigration and Nationality Act (INA) was amended in order to clarify that an alien who solicits funds or membership or provides material support to a certified terrorist organization could be detained or removed from the country.

- The attorney general was directed to implement an entry/exit system, with particular focus on biometric information gathered during the visa application process and the development of tamper-resistant documents. The system required that certain nonimmigrants register with the INS and submit fingerprints and photographs upon arrival in the United States; report to the INS in person within thirty days of arrival and annually thereafter; and notify an INS agent of their departure. Those who failed to comply could face criminal prosecution.

- Funds totaling $36.8 million were appropriated in order to implement a foreign-student monitoring system in which all institutions of higher education that enrolled foreign students or exchange visitors were required to participate. The act expanded the list of participating institutions to include air flight schools, language training schools, and vocational schools.

- Provisions were established to ensure that the immigration status of victims of the September 11 terrorist attacks and their families was not adversely affected as a result of the attacks. The family members of some victims were facing deportation.

HOMELAND SECURITY ACT OF 2002

On November 25, 2002, President George W. Bush signed into law the Homeland Security Act of 2002 (PL 107-296), a document totaling nearly five hundred pages that represented the largest restructuring of the government in several decades. The Homeland Security Act created the cabinet-level Department of Homeland Security (DHS). "The department will gather and focus all our efforts to face the challenge of cyberterrorism, and the even worse danger of nuclear, chemical and biological terrorism," President Bush said in announcing the signing of the document ("Remarks by the President at the Signing of H.R. 5005 The Homeland Security Act of 2002," The White House, November 25, 2002). The DHS consolidated the functions of more than twenty federal agencies into one department employing over 170,000 people. One of the affected agencies was the INS.

INS Reorganization

Title IV, Section 402 of the Homeland Security Act transferred the responsibilities of the INS from the Department of Justice to the DHS. With the goal of separating immigration services from immigration law enforcement, on March 1, 2003, the INS became the U.S. Citizenship & Immigration Services (USCIS), responsible for processing visas and petitions for naturalization, asylum, and refugee status. Immigration enforcement became the responsibility of Immigration and Customs Enforcement (called the Bureau of Border Security in the act).

Border Security

Section 402 of the Homeland Security Act outlined the responsibilities of the Under Secretary for Border and Transportation Security. These included:

- Preventing the entry of terrorists and the instruments of terrorism into the United States

- Securing the borders, territorial waters, ports, terminals, waterways, and air, land, and sea transportation systems of the United States

- Administering the immigration and naturalization laws of the United States, including the establishment of rules governing the granting of visas and other forms of permission to enter the United States to individuals who are not citizens or lawful permanent residents

- Administering the customs laws of the United States

- Ensuring the speedy, orderly, and efficient flow of lawful traffic and commerce in carrying out these responsibilities

OTHER POST-9/11 CHANGES

Since September 11, 2001, hundreds of policy changes have been inaugurated by the Department of Justice, the INS, and its successor the USCIS.

In November 2001 the U.S. Department of State issued directives mandating background checks on all male visa applicants between the ages of sixteen and forty-five from twenty-six mostly Muslim countries. The Enhanced Border Security and Visa Entry Reform Act of 2002 (PL 107-173) prohibited the issuing of a nonimmigrant visa to nationals of seven countries (Cuba, Iran, Iraq, Libya, North Korea, Sudan, and Syria) unless it was determined after a lengthy background check that the individuals were not security threats. The list of prohibited countries could change as directed by the attorney general.

Foreign Students Face Increased Visa Restrictions

The IIRIRA had mandated the creation of a database that stored information about international students, but the system had not yet been launched when the September 11 attacks occurred. In March 2002 the INS acknowledged that student visas had been issued to two of the perpetrators of the September 11 attacks, six months after the men died carrying them out. In May 2002 the INS launched the Student and Exchange Visitor Information System (SEVIS) to track foreigners who enter the country on student visas. New rules required that foreign students present a confirmation of acceptance from an American school before they would be allowed to enter the country, and that colleges report enrollment information and date of students' arrival or their failure to arrive.

Reporting Change of Address

The INS took steps to enforce the longstanding but essentially ignored requirement that all noncitizens in the country for more than thirty days must report any change of address within ten days of moving. Failure to report could be grounds for fines, penalties, or deportation.

Police Enforcement of Immigration Laws

The Justice Department ruled that effective August 2002 local police could detain individuals for immigration violations, a right formerly reserved for federal agents. The measure was part of IIRIRA but had not previously been finalized. Florida became the test state, initiating a Memorandum of Understanding with the Justice Department, which authorized specially training local police officers to assist federal agents in locating and detaining wanted aliens.

Indefinite Detention of Illegal Aliens

On April 17, 2003, Attorney General John Ashcroft issued a decision that illegal aliens could be detained indefinitely, whether they were known to have ties to terrorist groups or not (23 I&N Dec. 572 [AG 2003] Interim Decision #3488). The ruling involved the case of a Haitian immigrant who had won the right to be released on bail while he awaited a decision on his plea for asylum.

INTELLIGENCE REFORM AND TERRORISM PREVENTION ACT OF 2004

On December 17, 2004, President George W. Bush signed into law the Intelligence Reform and Terrorism Prevention Act of 2004 (PL 108-408). This new law set national standards for driver's licenses, Social Security cards, and birth certificates.

The law required the Secretary of Transportation to issue within eighteen months regulations governing any driver's license or identity cards to be accepted for any official purpose by a federal agency. The documents were required to include: full legal name, date of birth, gender, license or ID card number, digital photograph, address, and signature of the individual. In addition, cards were required to contain physical security features designed to prevent tampering, counterfeiting, or duplicating for fraudulent purposes. They also had to conform to specified requirements for a common machine-readable technology. States would be required to confiscate a driver's license or ID card if any of the security features were compromised. The regulations would include standards for documentation required by the applicant for a license or ID card and procedures for verifying the documents. States retained the right to determine what categories of individuals (for example, legal or illegal immigrants) were eligible for a license.

The law required that within one year the Commissioner of Social Security would restrict issuance of replacement Social Security cards for any individual to three in one year or ten in a lifetime; create minimum standards for verification of documents to be submitted to obtain initial or replacement Social Security cards; and add death and fraud indicators to verification systems used by employers, state agencies, and other entities. The commissioner was also required to improve controls for issuing Social Security numbers (SSNs) to newborns to prevent multiple numbers being issued to one child and to avoid fraud. The law also created an interagency task force to develop methods to prevent counterfeiting, tampering, theft, and alteration of Social Security cards. Finally, it amended the Social Security Act to prevent states from displaying SSNs on driver's licenses, motor vehicle registrations, or any other document issued to an individual for identification.

The law charged the Secretary of Health and Human Services with establishing minimum standards for birth certificates for use by federal agencies for any official purpose. This included requiring state or local issuing officials to certify the birth certificate. States would be required to use safety paper or other methods to prevent tampering, counterfeiting, or other birth certificate fraud. Also, procedures would be established for verifying proof of identity in issuing birth certificates, with additional security measures for issuing a birth certificate to someone other than the applicant (parents, adoptive parents, etc.).

LEGISLATION PENDING IN THE 109TH CONGRESS

In a January 11, 2005, interview with Joseph Curl of the *Washington Times*, President George W. Bush said he would spend political capital to push his proposal to grant temporary work visas to foreign workers as long as U.S. workers would not or did not want to fill the job ("Bush Vows Push on Immigration," January 12, 2005). Estimating the number of illegal aliens in the country at eight million, he said, "We've got people living in the shadows of our society, and we've got a border patrol that's overstressed because we've got people streaming across. The system has broken down. And I think that by legalizing workers, we take a lot of pressure off our borders."

The new Congress also appeared to place a priority on immigration reform. The first session of the 109th Congress convened on January 4, 2005. Seventy-six immigration-related bills were introduced within the first thirty days—forty-five in the House of Representatives and thirty-one in the Senate. The fastest-moving bill was the REAL ID Act of 2005 (H.R. 418). Introduced January 26, 2005, in the House of Representatives with 140 cosponsors, it passed by a 261-161 vote February 10, 2005, and was forwarded to the Senate February 14, 2005. In addition to focusing on security standards for state-issued driver's licenses, the bill included provisions for preventing terrorists from abusing U.S. asylum laws, unifying terrorism-related grounds for inadmissibility and removal, and ensuring expeditious construction of the San Diego border fence. Specific to the driver's license, the REAL ID Act required the expiration date of a license or ID card issued to a temporary foreign visitor to match the expiration date of the visa. If the visa had no expiration date, the license would expire in one year. It also strengthened requirements for proof of identification and lawful presence in the United States when applying for a driver's license.

REPERCUSSIONS OF POST-SEPTEMBER 11 POLICIES

The U.S. government was aggressive in its pursuit of terrorism suspects. The Justice Department reported that in the year following the September 11 attacks, approximately 1,200 aliens were apprehended (Allison Parker and Jamie Fellner, *Above the Law: Executive Power after September 11 in the United States*, Washington, DC: Human Rights Watch, January 2004). More than 700 were confined on immigration-related charges, and Attorney General John Ashcroft ordered officials to keep their names secret. In certain cases, their mail and communications with their attorneys were monitored.

Interested parties charged that the government's policies were unconstitutional or in violation of civil liberties or laws regarding public disclosure. Numerous lawsuits were filed seeking information about the September 11 detainees and protesting secret deportation hearings.

Many also inquired into the status of the nearly 600 people from Afghanistan, Pakistan, and other nations who were captured by U.S. soldiers in the October 2001 retaliatory attack on Afghanistan. Some of these individuals were taken to the U.S. naval base in Guantánamo Bay, Cuba. Reuters News Service ("Red Cross Head Discusses Guantanamo Inmates with Bush," February 15, 2005) reported that in a February 14, 2005, meeting with President Bush and Secretary of State Condoleezza Rice, the president of the International Committee of the Red Cross, Jakob Kellenberger, raised concerns about detainees at Guantánamo Bay and elsewhere.

In a January 2005 press release, Wendy Patten, U.S. Advocacy Director for Human Rights Watch, said, "Guantánamo has become the Bermuda Triangle of human rights. Basic rights vanish there. By flouting international law in its treatment of detainees, the Bush administration has drawn worldwide criticism and undermined support for U.S. counterterrorism efforts" ("Guantanamo: Three Years of Lawlessness," *Human Rights News*, Washington, DC: Human Rights Watch, January 11, 2005). The Human Rights Watch statement counted some 550 people being held as "enemy combatants" and noted that only four faced charges at that time. Also in a January 2005 statement ("Guantanamo Bay—A Human Rights Scandal," http://www.amnestyusa.org/waronterror/guantanamo/), Amnesty International described the condition of detainees from some thirty-five different nations who were "without access to any court, legal counsel or family visits. Denied their rights under international law and held in conditions which may amount to cruel, inhuman or degrading treatment, the detainees face severe psychological distress."

The Courts Rule

FREEDOM OF INFORMATION. On August 2, 2002, U.S. District Court Judge Gladys Kessler ordered the Justice Department to release the names of the aliens being detained on immigration charges and their attorneys. Her ruling stated: "Secret arrests are a concept odious to a democratic society and profoundly antithetical to the bedrock values that characterize a free and open one such as ours."

On June 17, 2003, the U.S. Court of Appeals for the District of Columbia Circuit issued its decision on appeal (*Center for National Security Studies, et al., v. U.S. Department of Justice* [No. 02-5254 & No. 02-300]). The court found that the Justice Department was justified in withholding information about the detainees, whose status as of June 2002 was described in the court's opinion:

- Of the more than 700 detainees held on immigration-related charges, 74 remained in custody. Many had been deported.

- Of the 134 individuals detained on federal criminal charges, 99 were found guilty either through pleas or trials.

- An undisclosed number of persons believed to have information relating to the events of September 11 were detained after a judge issued a material witness warrant to secure their testimony before a grand jury. The government is prohibited by court orders from releasing any information about the proceedings.

SECRET DEPORTATION HEARINGS. On September 21, 2001, Chief Immigration Judge Michael Creppy issued an order stating that typically open deportation hearings should be closed in any case deemed of "special interest" in the investigation of the terrorist attacks. A lawsuit was filed by the American Civil Liberties Union (ACLU) on behalf of Representative John Conyers (a Democrat from Michigan) and Michigan newspapers challenging Judge Creppy's order after the public and press were denied access to the deportation hearing of a Muslim religious leader who had overstayed a tourist visa.

On August 26, 2002, the U.S. Court of Appeals for the Sixth Circuit ruled in *Detroit News, Inc., et al., v. Ashcroft, et al.* that the Bush administration acted unlawfully in holding hundreds of deportation hearings in secret on the sole grounds that those involved were terrorism suspects. "Democracies die behind closed doors," Judge Damon Keith wrote. His ruling characterized the September 11 attacks as "egregious, deplorable, and despicable" events that led to vigorous prosecution of immigration laws, but he described governmental secrecy as "profoundly undemocratic" (2002 FED App. 0291P [6th Cir.] No. 02-1437).

In a separate suit, the ACLU represented the media seeking information on "special interest" detainees taken into custody in New Jersey. A lower court judge in Newark ordered the government to open all such hearings to the public unless it could offer case-by-case proof of the need for secrecy. The Third U.S. Circuit Court of Appeals reversed the lower court ruling (*North Jersey Media Group, Inc.; New Jersey Law Journal v. John Ashcroft, Attorney General of the United States; Michael Creppy, Hon.*, No. 02-2524). The case was appealed to the U.S. Supreme Court, which declined to review it.

The decisions of the courts in these two cases left the government in a position where its power to hold secret hearings was restricted in the four states belonging to the Sixth Circuit (Tennessee, Michigan, Ohio, and Kentucky) but not in the remaining forty-six states.

SUSPECTED TERRORISTS HELD IN CUBA. In March 2003 a federal appeals court ruled that 650 suspected members of the al-Qaeda terrorist network and the former Taliban regime in Afghanistan who were being held at a U.S. naval base in Guantánamo Bay had no legal rights in the United States and could not ask courts to review their detentions (*Al Odah v. United States*, No. 02-5251). The case, brought by relatives of some of the detainees, contested the legality and conditions of their confinement. Earlier, a *Washington Post* article, "U.S. Decries Abuse but Defends Interrogations" (Dana Priest and Barton Gellman, December 26, 2002), described alleged inhumane treatment of the individuals being held in Cuba.

Treatment of September 11 Detainees

A June 2, 2003, report from the Justice Department's inspector general, Glenn A. Fine, found "significant problems" in the treatment of some of the September 11 detainees, including physical and verbal abuse, long delays in charging detainees, a pattern of confining detainees in cells for twenty-three hours a day, the use of handcuffs and leg irons, and limitations on the ability of detainees to communicate with legal counsel (*The September 11 Detainees: A Review of the Treatment of Aliens Held on Immigration Charges in Connection with the Investigation of the September 11 Attacks*, Washington, DC: U.S. Department of Justice). During his June 25, 2003, testimony on the Justice Department's report before the Senate Judiciary Committee (http://www.usdoj.gov/oig/testimony/0306.htm), Fine acknowledged the tireless and dedicated work on the part of Justice Department employees under extraordinary circumstances and further stated that "the chaotic situation and uncertainties surrounding the detainees' role in the September 11 attacks, and the potential of additional attacks, explain many of the problems we found in our review, but they do not explain or justify all of them."

On the day the inspector general's report was released, Justice Department spokeswoman Barbara Comstock issued a statement asserting that "[t]he Justice Department believes that the Inspector General report is fully consistent with what courts have ruled over and over—that our actions are fully within the law and necessary to protect the American people. Our policy is to use all legal tools available to protect innocent Americans from terrorist attacks. We make no apologies for finding every legal way possible to protect the American public from further terrorist attacks" ("Statement of Barbara Comstock, Director of Public Affairs, Regarding the IG's Report on 9/11 Detainees," Washington, DC: U.S. Department of Justice, June 2, 2003).

Volunteers?

Between September 11 and November 9, 2001, the INS compiled a list of 7,602 names of aliens with characteristics similar to those of the hijackers and requested that the individuals on the list make themselves available for voluntary interviews. While many individuals expressed understanding regarding the need for such interviews, others expressed apprehension. The U.S. General Accounting Office (GAO) noted in *Homeland Security: Justice Department's Project to Interview Aliens after September 11, 2001* (GAO-03-459, Washington, DC, April 11, 2003) that "attorneys for interviewees and immigration advocates . . . expressed the view that interviewed aliens did not perceive the interviews to be truly voluntary . . . they worried about repercussions, such as future INS denials for visa extensions or permanent residence, if they refused to be interviewed."

Civil Rights Violations

The September 11, 2001, terrorist attacks caused Americans to take greater notice of foreign-born residents. People who appeared to be from the Middle East were suddenly suspect. Those who appeared "different" in dress or behavior became the subject of particular attention, suspicion, and sometimes even violence. Communities, and particularly law enforcement agencies, across the nation were faced with the challenges of fair treatment and even protection of foreign-born residents.

Even the Department of Justice, the enforcement agency for such civil rights violations, was not immune to complaints. Philip Shenon of the *New York Times* ("Report on U.S. Antiterrorism Law Alleges Violations of Civil Rights," July 21, 2003) noted that in a report presented to Congress in July 2003, the Justice Department's inspector general advised that in the six-month period that ended on June 15, 2003, the inspector general's office had received thirty-four credible complaints of violations of the civil rights and liberties of individuals held in connection with terrorism investigations. According to Shenon, Muslim and Arab immigrants held in detention had allegedly been beaten; the accused perpetrators were Justice Department employees.

The Chicago Police Department recognized the need to understand and more effectively communicate with the diverse ethnic and religious groups that populated the city. According to Stephen Kinzer of the *New York Times* ("Chicago Police Videos Offer Insights into Various Faiths," January 23, 2005), the department produced a series of short videotapes that focused on religious groups with a significant presence in Chicago—Sikhs, Muslims, Jews, Buddhists, and Hindus. Many members of these faiths might appear to be from the Middle East and/or might wear particular dress that made them look "different." The tapes provided a look into homes and houses of worship and interviews with religious and community leaders. A police officer narrator gave tips on things to do or to avoid when interacting with people of each faith. The intent was to help police officers respect people's cultural heritage while protecting the community and the city.

Viewing the tapes was required training for all Chicago police officers and it had a noticeable effect. Kinzer reported that one Sikh leader said the training helped the police understand that the display of swords in homes and as part of men's clothing was a religious tradition rather than intended for criminal activity. A leader of Chicago's Islamic community said the training "changed our community's relationship with the police ... people are beginning to see the Chicago Police Department as an ally rather than an opposing force."

For information on national origin discrimination, see Appendix I.

CHAPTER 3
CURRENT IMMIGRATION STATISTICS

Our borders and immigration system, including law enforcement, ought to send a message of welcome, tolerance, and justice to members of the immigrant communities in the United States and their countries of origin.

—*The 9/11 Commission Report: Final Report of the National Commission on Terrorist Attacks upon the United States*, New York: W. W. Norton & Co., 2004

To understand the scope of the immigration issue in the United States, it is important to know the number of immigrants in the country, where they came from, why they came, and why some did not get to stay. Because immigrant statistics have been the basis for legislation as well as the funding of projects, information about immigrants' ages, skills, ability to work, and location of settlement in the United States has been collected in a variety of forms.

U.S. immigration law defines an immigrant as a person legally admitted for permanent residence in the United States. Some arrive in the country with immigrant visas issued abroad at a consular office of the U.S. Department of State. (Visas are government authorizations permitting entry into a country.) Others who already reside in the United States adjust their status from temporary to permanent residence. These include illegal immigrants, foreign students, temporary workers, and refugees and asylees (those seeking asylum).

WHAT DOES IT COST TO GET A U.S. VISA?

Foreign visitors or immigrants who want to travel to the United States pay a variety of fees to obtain visas. Fees for visa services are collected by the U.S. Department of State, Bureau of Consular Affairs, and information on forms and fees can be found on the department's Web site (http://travel.state.gov). The following list of fees was effective March 8, 2005 (based on the Code of Federal Regulations, Title 22, Part 22, Sections 22.1 through 22.7). The U.S. Citizenship and Immigration Services (USCIS) had additional fees for some services.

Temporary Nonimmigrant Visa Services

Nonimmigrant visa application and border-crossing card processing fees (per person) are as follows:

- Nonimmigrant visa application processing fee (non-refundable; Form DS-156)—$100.00

- Border-crossing card (age 15 and over; non-refundable)—$100.00

- Border-crossing card (under age 15), for Mexican citizen if parent or guardian has or is applying for a border-crossing card (non-refundable) —$13.00

- L Visa, Fraud Prevention and Detection for visa applicant in the L blanket petition abroad only (principal applicant only)—$500.00

- Citizens of Visa Waiver Program participating countries, and meeting requirements, pay a small fee determined by USCIS

No fee services include the following:

- Applicants for A, G, C-3, NATO, and diplomatic visas (defined in 22 CFR 41.26)

- Applicants for J visas participating in official U.S. government sponsored educational and cultural exchanges

- Replacement of machine-readable visa when the original visa was not properly affixed or needs to be reissued through no fault of the applicant

- Applicants exempted by international agreement as determined by Visa Services, including members and staff of an observer mission to United Nations Headquarters recognized by the UN General Assembly, and their immediate families

- Applicants traveling to provide charitable services as determined by Visa Services

- U.S. government employees traveling on official business

FIGURE 3.1

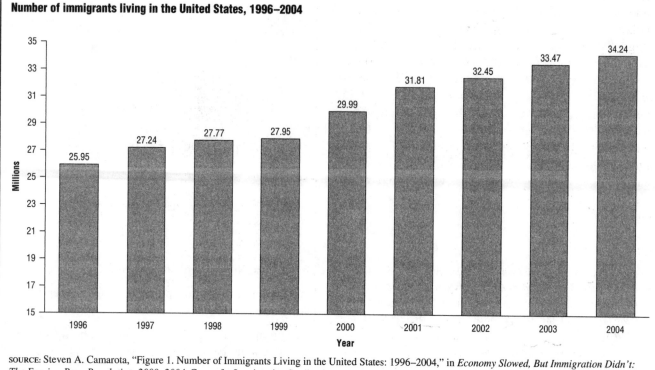

Number of immigrants living in the United States, 1996–2004

SOURCE: Steven A. Camarota, "Figure 1. Number of Immigrants Living in the United States: 1996–2004," in *Economy Slowed, But Immigration Didn't: The Foreign-Born Population, 2000–2004*, Center for Immigration Studies, November 2004, http://www.cis.org/articles/2004/back1204.pdf (accessed February 2, 2005)

- A parent, sibling, spouse, or child of a U.S. government employee killed in the line of duty who is traveling to attend the employee's funeral and/or burial; or a parent, sibling, spouse, or child of a U.S. government employee critically injured in the line of duty for visitation during emergency treatment and convalescence

Permanent Immigrant Services

Costs associated with obtaining permanent status include:

- Filing an immigrant visa petition to classify status of alien relative for issuance of immigrant visa (collected for USCIS and subject to change; USCIS Form I-130)—$185.00

- Petition to classify orphan as an immediate relative (collected for USCIS and subject to change; USCIS Form I-600)—$525.00

- Immigrant visa application processing fee (per person; Form DS-230)—$335.00

- Diversity Visa Lottery surcharge for immigrant visa application (per person applying as a result of the lottery program)—$375.00

- Immigrant visa security surcharge, for all immigrant visa and diversity visa applicants—$45.00

- Affidavit of Support review (only when AOS is reviewed domestically; Form I-864)—$70.00

Special Visa Services

Costs for special visa services include:

- Application for determining returning resident status (Form DSP-117)—$400.00

- Transportation letter for legal permanent residents of the United States—$165.00

- Application for waiver of two-year foreign residency requirement (J Waiver; Data Sheet, Form 3035)—$215.00

- Application for waiver of immigrant visa ineligibility (collected for USCIS and subject to change)—$250.00

- Refugee or significant public benefit parole case processing—No fee

- U.S. visa fingerprinting—$85.00

FOREIGN-BORN POPULATION

Figure 3.1 illustrates the annual increase in immigration from 1996 through 2004. In the United States the period from 1996 to 2000 was one of dramatic job growth and a rapidly expanding economy, while the economy slowed and the demand for labor was weak from 2000 to 2004. Despite these economic shifts, immigration increased. The Census Bureau's Current Population Studies (CPS) revealed that 6.1 million immigrants claimed they arrived between 2000 and early 2004, compared to 5.5 million who arrived between 1996 and 2000. In *Economy Slowed, But Immigration Didn't: The Foreign-Born Population, 2000–2004* (Washington, DC: Center for Immigration Studies, November 2004), Steven A. Camarota stated that, "[i]n contrast to past centuries, immigration levels are no longer tied to the business cycles." He noted that even when the U.S. economy was poor and unemployment was high, the high standard of living continued to attract immigrants.

Region of Birth

In 2003 the Census Bureau reported that the 33.5 million people who were born in foreign countries represented 11.7% of the U.S. population. More than half (53.3%) came from Latin America and one-quarter (25%) came from Asia. Reflecting the reversal from a century ago when the majority of immigrants were European, in 2003 just 13.7% of immigrants were from Europe. (See Figure 3.2.)

Table 3.1 provides greater detail on the place of origin of legal immigrants in the years 2001 through 2003. Total immigration numbers were fairly stable in 2001 and 2002 but dropped significantly from a little more than one million in 2002 to 705,827 in 2003. In its *2003 Yearbook of Immigration Statistics* (Washington, DC: U.S. Department of Homeland Security, September 2004), the U.S. Citizenship and Immigration Services reported that this 34% drop in persons granted lawful permanent residence was due primarily to increased security checks that slowed application processing.

Although the numbers of immigrants from various continents took a similar drop in 2003, a few groups increased in percentage share of total immigration. Immigrants from Africa grew from 5.7% of total immigrants to 6.9% between 2002 and 2003. In the same period immigrants from Asia increased from 32.2% to 34.7% of total immigrants. The share of immigrants from the Caribbean, Central America, and South America also increased from 2002 to 2003. The Dominican Republic was the only source of immigrants that showed an increase in actual numbers of immigrants (22,604 to 26,205) from 2002 to 2003. (See Table 3.1.)

Mexico continued to lead in total legal immigrants in 2003, although the number of immigrants dropped by almost half (47%) from 2002. At 115,864 legal immigrants in 2003, Mexico was still the source of twice as many immigrants as the next leading source—India, with 50,372 immigrants. (See Table 3.1.)

FIGURE 3.2

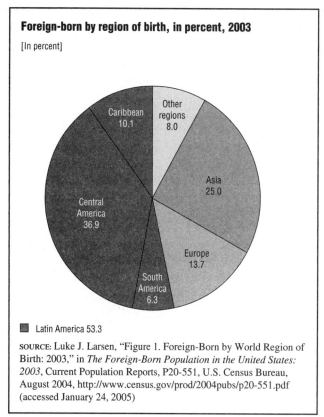

Foreign-born by region of birth, in percent, 2003

[In percent]

Caribbean 10.1
Other regions 8.0
Asia 25.0
Central America 36.9
Europe 13.7
South America 6.3

Latin America 53.3

SOURCE: Luke J. Larsen, "Figure 1. Foreign-Born by World Region of Birth: 2003," in *The Foreign-Born Population in the United States: 2003*, Current Population Reports, P20-551, U.S. Census Bureau, August 2004, http://www.census.gov/prod/2004pubs/p20-551.pdf (accessed January 24, 2005)

Where the Foreign-Born Population Chooses to Live

Two-thirds of the foreign-born population lived in the West (37.3%) or the South (29.2%) in 2003. (See Figure 3.3.) According to a U.S. Census Bureau report (Luke J. Larsen, *The Foreign-Born Population in the United States: 2003*, Current Population Reports, P20-551, Washington, DC, August 2004), the foreign-born from Asia and Latin America (comprising the Caribbean, Central America, and South America) were most likely to settle in the West, with the foreign-born from Central America concentrating in both the West and the South. Foreign-born residents were more likely to live in a central city of a major metropolitan area (44.4%) compared to the native population (26.9%). Just 5.3% of foreign-born residents lived in nonmetropolitan areas in 2003 while 20.2% of the native population lived away from large cities. (See Table 3.2.)

Immigrant Populations in the States

Table 3.3 shows the total number of immigrants living in each state in 2004, the number who said they arrived since 2000, and the percentage of the state's total population who were foreign-born in 2004. California's 9.5 million immigrants represented more than one-quarter (27%) of the state's total population. The 1.2 million new arrivals since 2000 accounted for 12.6% of the total

TABLE 3.1

Immigrants admitted by region and top 20 countries of birth, fiscal years 2001–03

Category of admission	2003 Number	2003 Percent	2002 Number	2002 Percent	2001 Number	2001 Percent
All countries	705,827	100.0	1,063,732	100.0	1,064,318	100.0
Africa	48,738	6.9	60,269	5.7	53,948	5.1
Asia	244,759	34.7	342,099	32.2	349,776	32.9
Europe	100,769	14.3	174,209	16.4	175,371	16.5
North America	*250,726*	*35.5*	*404,437*	*38.0*	*407,888*	*38.3*
Carribbean	68,815	9.7	96,489	9.1	103,546	9.7
Central America	54,565	7.7	68,979	6.5	75,914	7.1
Other North America	127,346	18.0	238,969	22.5	228,428	21.5
Oceania	4,377	.6	5,557	.5	6,113	.6
South America	55,247	7.8	74,506	7.0	68,888	6.5
Unknown	1,211	.2	2,655	.2	2,334	.2
Mexico	115,864	16.4	219,380	20.6	206,426	19.4
India	50,372	7.1	71,105	6.7	70,290	6.6
Philippines	45,397	6.4	51,308	4.8	53,154	5.0
China	40,659	5.8	61,282	5.8	56,426	5.3
El Salvador	28,296	4.0	31,168	2.9	31,272	2.9
Dominican Republic	26,205	3.7	22,604	2.1	21,313	2.0
Vietnam	22,133	3.1	33,627	3.2	35,531	3.3
Colombia	14,777	2.1	18,845	1.8	16,730	1.6
Guatemala	14,415	2.0	16,229	1.5	13,567	1.3
Russia	13,951	2.0	20,833	2.0	20,413	1.9
Jamaica	13,384	1.9	14,898	1.4	15,393	1.4
Korea	12,512	1.8	21,021	2.0	20,742	1.9
Haiti	12,314	1.7	20,268	1.9	27,120	2.5
Ukraine	11,666	1.7	21,217	2.0	20,975	2.0
Canada	11,446	1.6	19,519	1.8	21,933	2.1
Poland	10,526	1.5	12,746	1.2	11,818	1.1
United Kingdom	9,601	1.4	16,181	1.5	18,436	1.7
Pakistan	9,444	1.3	13,743	1.3	16,448	1.5
Peru	9,444	1.3	11,999	1.1	11,131	1.0
Cuba	9,304	1.3	28,272	2.7	27,703	2.6
Subtotal	**481,710**	**68.2**	**726,245**	**68.3**	**716,821**	**67.4**
Other	224,117	31.8	337,487	31.7	347,497	32.6

SOURCE: "Table B. Immigrants Admitted by Region and Top 20 Countries of Birth: Fiscal Years 2001–2003," in *2003 Yearbook of Immigration Statistics*, U.S. Department of Homeland Security, Office of Immigration Statistics, September 2004, http://uscis.gov/graphics/shared/aboutus/statistics/IMM03yrbk/2003IMM .pdf (accessed February 22, 2005)

foreign-born population in the state. New York was a distant second with 3.8 million immigrants representing one-fifth of the population (20.3%). While Hawaii was far down the list in total number of foreign-born residents, 17.6% of the population was foreign-born.

Table 3.4 compares educational attainment, poverty status, health insurance coverage, and receipt of welfare between natives and immigrants in selected states. Among the states selected in the report published by the Center for Immigration Studies (Steven A. Camarota, *Economy Slowed, But Immigration Didn't: The Foreign-Born Population, 2000–2004*, Washington, DC, November 2004), Texas, with the third largest immigrant population, had the greatest share of immigrants without a high school diploma (49.7%), immigrants and their children living in or near poverty (59.7%), and both immigrant and native families without health insurance (44.3% and 19.1%, respectively).

While nationwide 11.7% of the native population over age twenty-one lacked a high school diploma, almost three times as many immigrants (32.8%) had not completed high school. In every state a greater share of

immigrants than natives lacked high school diplomas. The educational gap between natives and immigrants was greatest in western states like California, Arizona, and Colorado. The widest gap was in Colorado, where 45.1% of immigrants had not completed high school compared to just 7.2% of natives. (See Table 3.4.) Camarota noted that this gap had "enormous implications for social and economic integration of immigrants because there is no single better predictor of one's economic and social status in America than education."

According to Camarota, "near" poverty level statistics were important because such families often did not pay income taxes and typically became eligible for means-tested programs including cash welfare, Medicaid, and the earned income tax credit. (Near poverty is defined as an income below 200% of poverty threshold. The 2004 poverty threshold for a family of four including two children was $19,157. At 200% of this figure, near-poverty level for that family was an annual income less than $38,314.) A greater share of immigrant households received some type of welfare benefits than did native households. (See Table 3.4.) Likewise the share of

FIGURE 3.3

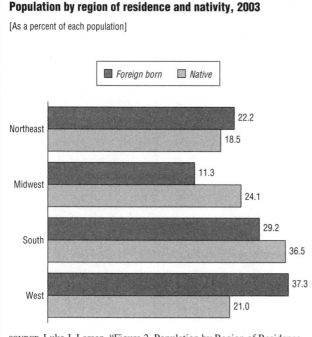

Population by region of residence and nativity, 2003

[As a percent of each population]

Legend: ■ Foreign born ▨ Native

- Northeast: Foreign born 22.2, Native 18.5
- Midwest: Foreign born 11.3, Native 24.1
- South: Foreign born 29.2, Native 36.5
- West: Foreign born 37.3, Native 21.0

SOURCE: Luke J. Larsen, "Figure 2. Population by Region of Residence and Nativity: 2003," in *The Foreign-Born Population in the United States: 2003*, Current Population Reports, P20-551, U.S. Census Bureau, August 2004, http://www.census.gov/prod/2004pubs/p20-551.pdf (accessed January 24, 2005)

TABLE 3.2

Native and foreign-born populations, by place of residence, 2003

[Percent]

	Population		
	Total	Native	Foreign-born
Metropolitan area			
Inside central city	29.0	26.9	44.4
Outside central city	52.6	52.9	50.3
Nonmetropolitan area	18.4	20.2	5.3
Total	**100.0**	**100.0**	**100.0**

SOURCE: "Table 9. Native and Foreign-Born Populations, by Place of Residence, 2003," in *A Description of the Immigrant Population*, Congressional Budget Office, November 2004, http://www.cbo.gov/ftpdocs/60xx/doc6019/11-23-Immigrant.pdf (accessed March 7, 2005)

immigrants without health insurance was more than double that of natives (30% compared to 12.9%). Camarota cited the impact of those lacking health insurance on the nation's health care system: people without insurance typically waited longer to seek care; when they finally did seek treatment, they often required greater care and the more expensive hospital emergency room care was often their only option for treatment.

Lack of health insurance was a persistent and pressing challenge for low-income adults. In 2003 low-income adults accounted for half of the uninsured population.

TABLE 3.3

Immigrant populations by state, 2004

[Numbers in thousands]

State	Total immigrant population	Post-2000 arrivals*	Immigrant share of state population
California	9,542	1,272	27.0%
New York	3,844	527	20.3%
Texas	3,328	643	15.2%
Florida	3,069	488	18.1%
New Jersey	1,544	247	18.0%
Illinois	1,382	207	10.9%
Arizona	922	200	16.5%
Massachusetts	845	206	13.3%
Maryland	728	184	13.3%
Virginia	703	172	9.5%
Washington	702	135	11.5%
Georgia	650	170	7.6%
North Carolina	641	200	7.8%
Michigan	548	101	5.5%
Pennsylvania	534	107	4.4%
Colorado	434	93	9.7%
Ohio	399	112	3.5%
Connecticut	376	53	11.0%
Oregon	363	49	10.2%
Nevada	355	57	15.8%
Minnesota	283	63	5.6%
Wisconsin	253	82	4.7%
Tennessee	238	96	4.0%
Indiana	224	55	3.6%
Hawaii	220	32	17.6%
Missouri	211	59	3.8%
Utah	176	24	7.5%
Kansas	158	41	5.9%
Oklahoma	140	19	4.1%
New Mexico	138	32	7.4%
Rhode Island	132	22	12.5%
South Carolina	128	39	3.1%
Iowa	113	34	3.9%
Kentucky	104	41	2.5%
Louisiana	96	13	2.2%
Nebraska	88	29	5.1%
Alabama	88	27	2.0%
New Hampshire	69	16	5.5%
Arkansas	69	13	2.6%
D.C.	68	18	12.3%
Mississippi	59	15	2.1%
Idaho	59	17	4.3%
Delaware	53	10	6.5%
Alaska	50	7	7.7%
Maine	41	9	3.2%
Vermont	22	2	3.6%
North Dakota	15	5	2.4%
West Virginia	14	9	0.8%
South Dakota	11	2	1.5%
Montana	10	1	1.1%
Wyoming	10	2	2.0%
Total	**34,244**	**6,057**	**11.9%**

*Based on year of arrival question.

SOURCE: Steven A. Camarota, "Table 1. State Immigrant Populations (Thousands)," in *Economy Slowed, But Immigration Didn't: The Foreign-Born Population, 2000–2004*, Center for Immigration Studies, November 2004, http://www.cis.org/articles/2004/back1204.pdf (accessed February 2, 2005)

While Medicaid and State Children's Health Insurance Programs (SCHIP) were major sources of coverage for low-income children, most of the adults did not work in jobs where employer-sponsored insurance was offered, or they could not afford coverage. A study by the Henry J. Kaiser Family Foundation (*Health Coverage for*

TABLE 3.4

Characteristics of immigrants and natives for selected states, 2004

	Educational attainment Percent without a high school degree[a]		In or near poverty[b] Immigrants and their children[c]		Natives and their children		Without health insurance Immigrants and their children[c]		Natives and their children		Households receiving welfare[d] Immigrant-headed households		Native-headed households	
	Immigrants	Natives	Percent	Number (thousands)	Percent	Number (thousands)	Percent	Number (thousands)	Percent	Number (thousands)	Percent	Number (thousands)	Percent	Number (thousands)
New York	26.8%	10.3%	40.8%	1,977	28.38%	3,995	26.1%	1,267	11.3%	1,599	32.1%	534	19.0%	1,084
New Jersey	21.4%	9.7%	33.3%	657	20.08%	1,326	26.0%	512	10.4%	689	16.9%	109	10.6%	273
Massachusetts	28.8%	10.1%	37.7%	394	22.78%	1,210	22.5%	235	8.4%	447	22.4%	84	13.7%	294
Illinois	30.3%	10.5%	38.4%	713	28.1%	3,020	29.0%	539	11.9%	1,279	15.4%	88	12.8%	547
Florida	27.7%	10.5%	44.4%	1,706	29.2%	3,806	30.7%	1,180	14.5%	1,892	24.3%	336	13.3%	744
Texas	49.7%	14.3%	59.7%	2,818	34.0%	5,814	44.3%	2,095	19.1%	3,279	29.8%	402	16.4%	1,100
Georgia	25.2%	13.8%	38.2%	335	27.3%	2,095	30.1%	264	14.9%	1,145	15.0%	38	15.8%	481
Maryland	26.8%	10.3%	37.5%	357	21.4%	972	31.3%	300	10.2%	461	16.6%	51	10.5%	190
Virginia	21.3%	10.6%	29.4%	267	22.1%	1,428	28.0%	255	10.9%	707	8.1%	23	12.3%	319
North Carolina	41.7%	17.0%	59.0%	477	34.8%	2,581	43.8%	355	14.4%	1,068	19.7%	46	19.0%	583
California	37.4%	8.3%	46.9%	6,133	24.7%	5,485	28.2%	3,692	12.6%	2,807	31.4%	1,217	13.8%	1,215
Arizona	43.0%	9.1%	59.3%	784	29.9%	1,269	34.2%	454	11.7%	497	31.2%	119	14.3%	248
Colorado	45.1%	7.2%	44.5%	272	23.4%	903	39.1%	239	13.8%	534	25.0%	41	13.2%	209
Nation	**32.8%**	**11.7%**	**45.0%**	**20,448**	**28.4%**	**68,915**	**30.0%**	**13,646**	**12.9%**	**31,315**	**25.7%**	**3,638**	**15.9%**	**15,524**

[a]Persons 21 years of age and older.

[b]In or near poverty defined as under 200 percent of the official poverty threshold.

[c]Includes U.S.-born children of immigrant mother under age 18.

[d]At least one person in household uses AFDC/TANF (Aid to Families with Dependent Children/Temporary Assistance for Needy Families), general assistance, food stamps, SSI (Supplemental Security Income), public/subsidized housing, or Medicaid.

SOURCE: Steven A. Camarota, "Table 3. Characteristics of Immigrants and Natives for Selected States," in *Economy Slowed, But Immigration Didn't: The Foreign-Born Population, 2000–2004*, Center for Immigration Studies, November 2004, http://www.cis.org/articles/2004/back1204.pdf (accessed February 2, 2005)

FIGURE 3.4

Native and foreign-born populations, by age and sex, 2003

[In percent]*

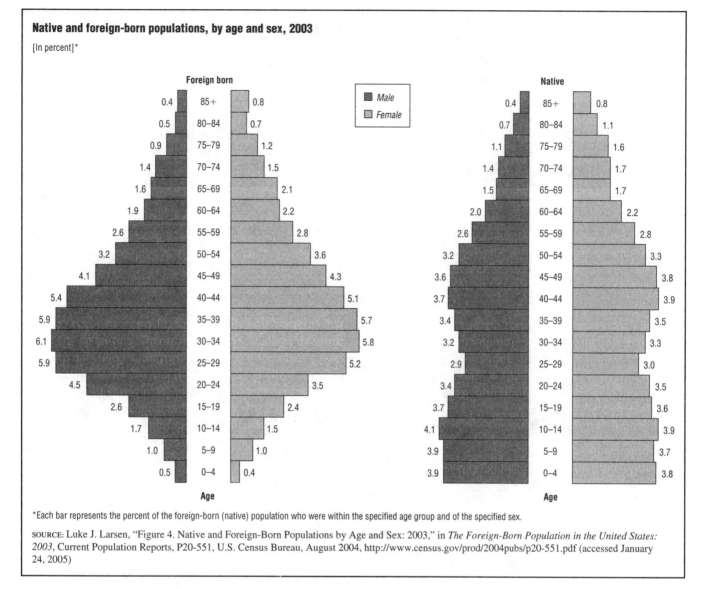

*Each bar represents the percent of the foreign-born (native) population who were within the specified age group and of the specified sex.

SOURCE: Luke J. Larsen, "Figure 4. Native and Foreign-Born Populations by Age and Sex: 2003," in *The Foreign-Born Population in the United States: 2003*, Current Population Reports, P20-551, U.S. Census Bureau, August 2004, http://www.census.gov/prod/2004pubs/p20-551.pdf (accessed January 24, 2005)

Low-Income Adults: Eligibility and Enrollment in Medicaid and State Coverage, Washington, DC: The Kaiser Commission on Medicaid and the Uninsured, 2002) revealed that of the 5.3 million low-income persons eligible for these programs, 75% were citizens and 25% were noncitizens. The breakdown of citizens and noncitizens was almost the same for the 12.8 million persons ineligible for Medicaid and state coverage. This result suggested that noncitizens accounted for about one-quarter of the low-income adult population and they were equally balanced with citizens in the eligible and ineligible groups.

Foreign-Born and Natives Compared by Age

Figure 3.4 illustrates the difference in age groups among the foreign-born and natives. In 2003 the majority of the foreign-born (55.9% of males and 50.9% of females) were between the prime working ages of 20 and 44. Among the native population, just 34.2% of males and 33.9% of females were in this age range. Over

age 65 there was little difference between foreign-born (11.5%) and native (12.1%). The other obvious difference was among the children. Just 8.9% of the foreign-born were age 18 and under compared to 27.8% of the native born. The Census Bureau noted that the small proportion of foreign-born children could be explained by the fact that most young children of immigrant parents were born in the United States and were counted as natives.

Individual and Family Incomes

In 2002, 30.5% of foreign-born, full-time, year-round workers and 16.5% of such native workers had annual incomes of less than $20,000. The share of Central American workers in this earning category was 45.3%. On the opposite end of the spectrum, 37.3% of Asian workers and 35.1% of European workers earned in excess of $50,000 compared to 30.2% of native workers. (See Figure 3.5.) When the Census Bureau compared household

FIGURE 3.5

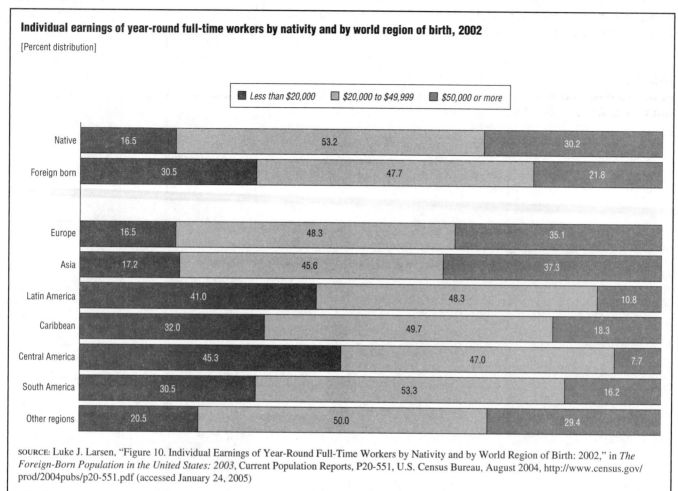

Individual earnings of year-round full-time workers by nativity and by world region of birth, 2002

[Percent distribution]

Legend: ■ Less than $20,000 ■ $20,000 to $49,999 ■ $50,000 or more

Group	Less than $20,000	$20,000 to $49,999	$50,000 or more
Native	16.5	53.2	30.2
Foreign born	30.5	47.7	21.8
Europe	16.5	48.3	35.1
Asia	17.2	45.6	37.3
Latin America	41.0	48.3	10.8
Caribbean	32.0	49.7	18.3
Central America	45.3	47.0	7.7
South America	30.5	53.3	16.2
Other regions	20.5	50.0	29.4

SOURCE: Luke J. Larsen, "Figure 10. Individual Earnings of Year-Round Full-Time Workers by Nativity and by World Region of Birth: 2002," in *The Foreign-Born Population in the United States: 2003*, Current Population Reports, P20-551, U.S. Census Bureau, August 2004, http://www.census.gov/prod/2004pubs/p20-551.pdf (accessed January 24, 2005)

incomes, more than half (53.8%) of Asian families had annual incomes in excess of $50,000 compared to 44% of native families.

IMMIGRATION AND POPULATION PROJECTIONS

The Census Bureau has projected that the U.S. population will reach 571 million by the year 2100, nearly double the estimated population of 290 million as of July 1, 2006. The overall foreign-born population could grow from 10.8% of the total population in 2006 to 13.3% in 2050 and then drop to 10.9% in 2100. (See Table 3.5.)

The foreign-born, Hispanic population could decline from 34.8% of the total Hispanic population in 2006 to 20% in 2050 and 9.3% in 2100. In comparison, the foreign-born, non-Hispanic white population—3.6% of the non-Hispanic whites in 2006—was projected to remain stable at 5.2% of this racial group in 2050 and 5.3% in 2100. (See Table 3.5.)

The foreign-born, non-Hispanic black population, representing 6.7% of the estimated total non-Hispanic black population in 2006, was projected to grow to 11.3%

of this racial group in 2050 and remain steady at 11.8% in 2100. In 2006 foreign-born, non-Hispanic Asians and Pacific Islanders (APIs) were projected to represent 60.6% of the overall API population in the United States. This proportion was projected to decline to 47.5% by 2050, and to 32.7% by 2100. On the other hand, the foreign-born, non-Hispanic Native American population, at 2.5% of the total Native American population in 2006, was projected to rise to 3.7% in 2050 and 3.8% in 2100. (See Table 3.5.)

Projected Total Population by Race and Hispanic Origin

It should be noted that foreign-born persons who became naturalized U.S. citizens were eventually added to the race and Hispanic-origin count of the Census Bureau. According to the bureau's projections, the Hispanic share of the U.S. population would nearly double from 13.5% in 2006 to 24.3% in 2050, and reach 33.3% (one-third of the total U.S. population) in 2100. The other population projected for growth was the API. Representing 4.4% of the estimated 2006 population, they could more than double to 8.9% of the population by 2050, and grow threefold to 12.6% by 2100. (See Table 3.5.)

In contrast to the growth groups, the non-Hispanic white population, an estimated 68.9% of the population in 2006, was projected to decline to 52.8% of the population in 2050 and 40.3% in 2100. The non-Hispanic black and non-Hispanic Native American populations were projected to remain relatively stable as a percentage

TABLE 3.5

Population projections, 2006–2100

[Numbers in thousands]

	July 1, 2006	July 1, 2025	July 1, 2050	July 1, 2075	July 1, 2100
Total					
Population	290,152	337,814	403,686	480,504	570,954
Percent of total	100.0	100.0	100.0	100.0	100.0
Native population	258,917	296,999	349,890	420,957	508,694
Percent of total	89.2	87.9	86.7	87.6	89.1
Foreign-born population	31,235	40,814	53,796	59,546	62,259
Percent of total	10.8	12.1	13.3	12.4	10.9
White					
Population	235,751	265,305	302,453	348,027	403,696
Percent of total	81.3	78.5	74.9	72.4	70.7
Native population	216,089	241,421	273,794	318,944	375,745
Percent of group	91.7	91.0	90.5	91.6	93.1
Foreign-born population	19,661	23,884	28,659	29,083	27,950
Percent of group	8.3	9.0	9.5	8.4	6.9
Black					
Population	38,084	47,089	59,239	71,705	85,579
Percent of total	13.1	13.9	14.7	14.9	15.0
Native population	34,816	42,205	51,887	62.805	75,614
Percent of group	91.4	89.6	87.6	87.6	88.4
Foreign-born population	3,267	4,883	7,352	8,900	9,965
Percent of group	8.6	10.4	12.4	12.4	11.6
American Indian					
Population	2,664	3,399	4,405	5,413	6,442
Percent of total	0.9	1.0	1.1	1.1	1.1
Native population	2,464	3,116	4,024	4,995	6,018
Percent of group	92.5	91.7	91.4	92.3	93.4
Foreign-born population	199	283	380	417	424
Percent of group	7.5	8.3	8.6	7.7	6.6
Asian and Pacific Islander					
Population	13,653	22,020	37,589	55,357	75,235
Percent of total	4.7	6.5	9.3	11.5	13.2
Native population	5,546	10,257	20,184	34,212	51,316
Percent of group	40.6	46.6	53.7	61.8	68.2
Foreign-born population	8,107	11,763	17,404	21,144	23,919
Percent of group	59.4	53.4	46.3	38.2	31.8
Hispanic					
Population	39,307	61,433	98,228	141,719	190,330
Percent of total	13.5	18.2	24.3	29.5	33.3
Native population	25,612	44,394	78,598	122,676	172,584
Percent of group	65.2	72.3	80.0	86.6	90.7
Foreign-born population	13,694	17,038	19,629	19,042	17,746
Percent of group	34.8	27.7	20.0	13.4	9.3
White, non-Hispanic					
Population	199,923	209,339	212,990	218,923	230,236
Percent of total	68.9	62.0	52.8	45.6	40.3
Native population	192,643	200,833	201,988	206,904	218,143
Percent of group	96.4	95.9	94.8	94.5	94.7
Foreign-born population	7,280	8,505	11,002	12,018	12,092
Percent of group	3.6	4.1	5.2	5.5	5.3
Black, non-Hispanic					
Population	35,845	43,527	53,466	63,348	74,360
Percent of total	12.4	12.9	13.2	13.2	13.0
Native population	33,446	39,732	47,399	55,716	65,585
Percent of group	93.3	91.3	88.7	88.0	88.2
Foreign-born population	2,398	3,794	6,066	7,631	8,775
Percent of group	6.7	8.7	11.3	12.0	11.8

TABLE 3.5

Population projections, 2006–2100 [CONTINUED]

[Numbers in thousands]

	July 1, 2006	July 1, 2025	July 1, 2050	July 1, 2075	July 1, 2100
American Indian, non-Hispanic					
Population	2,196	2,668	3,241	3,753	4,237
Percent of total	0.8	0.8	0.8	0.8	0.7
Native population	2,140	2,585	3,120	3,607	4,077
Percent of group	97.5	96.9	96.3	96.1	96.2
Foreign-born population	55	82	120	145	160
Percent of group	2.5	3.1	3.7	3.9	3.8
Asian and Pacific Islander, non-Hispanic					
Population	12,879	20,846	35,759	52,759	71,789
Percent of total	4.4	6.2	8.9	11.0	12.6
Native population	5,074	9,452	18,783	32,052	48,303
Percent of group	39.4	45.3	52.5	60.8	67.3
Foreign-born population	7,805	11,393	16,976	20,707	23,485
Percent of group	60.6	54.7	47.5	39.2	32.7

SOURCE: Adapted from "Projections of the Resident Population by Race, Hispanic Origin, and Nativity: Middle Series, 1999 to 2100 (NP-T5-C; NP-T5-F; NP-T5-G; NP-T5-H)," U.S. Census Bureau, Washington, DC, http://www.census.gov/population/www/projections/natsum-T5.html (accessed April 21, 2005)

of the total population from 2006 through 2100. (See Table 3.5.)

COUNTING IMMIGRANTS

There are various ways to qualify for immigration to the United States, but the U.S. Citizenship and Immigration Services (USCIS) generally classified admissions into four major groups:

- Family-sponsored preference
- Employment-based preference
- Diversity Program
- Other—including Amerasians (typically children of Asian mothers and American military or civilian personnel), parolees, refugees and asylees, individuals whose order for removal was cancelled, and other legal provisions.

With the passage of the Immigration Act (IMMACT) in 1990, the number of immigrants (persons granted permanent resident status) was limited to a total of 675,000 per year. The annual limit is flexible; it could exceed 675,000 if the maximum number of visas were not issued in the preceding year. Yet Table 3.6 counted total immigrants in both 2001 and 2002 in excess of one million and a total of 705,827 immigrants admitted in 2003. How did this happen?

The USCIS reports in the *2003 Yearbook of Immigration Statistics* (Washington, DC: Department of Homeland Security, September 2004) that some major categories of immigrants are exempt from the annual limits. These include:

- immediate relatives of U.S. citizens,
- refugee and asylee adjustments,
- certain parolees from the Soviet Union and Indochina,
- certain special agricultural workers (SAWs)
- cancelled removals, and
- aliens who applied for adjustment of status after having unlawfully resided in the United States since January 1, 1982.

The USCIS notes that immediate relatives of U.S. citizens, who are not subject to any numerical limitation, have for many years been the largest single category of immigrants. They represented 41.7% of total immigrants in 2001, 45.8% in 2002, and 47.2% in 2003. In each of those years, subtracting the immediate relatives category dropped the remaining total immigrants below the 675,000 annual limit. (See Table 3.6.)

New Arrivals

The United States offers two general methods for foreign-born persons to attain immigrant status. In the first method, aliens living abroad can apply for an immigrant visa and then become legal residents when approved for admission at a U.S. port of entry. In 2003, 358,411 such persons entered the United States; identified in statistics as "new arrivals," they accounted for 50.8% of all immigrants admitted in 2003. (See Table 3.6.)

Adjustment of Status

The second method of gaining immigrant status is by "adjustment of status." This procedure allows certain aliens already in the United States to apply for immigrant status. This includes certain undocumented residents, temporary workers, foreign students, and refugees who

TABLE 3.6

Immigrants admitted by major category of admission, fiscal years 2001–03

Category of admission	2003 Number	2003 Percent	2002 Number	2002 Percent	2001 Number	2001 Percent
Total	**705,827**	**100.0**	**1,063,732**	**100.0**	**1,064,318**	**100.0**
New arrivals	358,411	50.8	384,427	36.1	411,059	38.6
Adjustments of status	347,416	49.2	679,305	63.9	653,259	61.4
Family-sponsored immigrants	**492,297**	**69.7**	**673,817**	**63.3**	**676,107**	**63.5**
Family-sponsored preferences	158,894	22.5	187,069	17.6	232,143	21.8
Unmarried sons/daughters of U.S. citizens	21,503	3.0	23,567	2.2	27,098	2.5
Spouses and children of alien residents	53,229	7.5	84,860	8.0	112,260	10.5
Married sons/daughters of U.S. citizens	27,303	3.9	21,072	2.0	24,878	2.3
Siblings of U.S. citizens	56,859	8.1	57,570	5.4	67,907	6.4
Immediate relatives of U.S. citizens	333,403	47.2	486,748	45.8	443,964	41.7
Spouses	184,741	26.2	294,798	27.7	270,545	25.4
Parents	69,892	9.9	94,063	8.8	80,964	7.6
Children	78,024	11.1	97,099	9.1	91,526	8.6
Children born abroad to alien residents	746	.1	788	.1	929	.1
Legalization dependents	21	d	57	d	37	d
Employment-based preferences	**82,137**	**11.6**	**174,968**	**16.4**	**179,195**	**16.8**
Priority workers	14,544	2.1	34,452	3.2	41,801	3.9
Professionals with advanced degree or of exceptional ability	15,459	2.2	44,468	4.2	42,620	4.0
Skilled workers, professionals, unskilled workers	46,613	6.6	88,555	8.3	86,058	8.1
Special immigrants	5,456	.8	7,344	.7	8,523	.8
Investors	65	d	149	d	193	d
Diversity program	**46,347**	**6.6**	**42,829**	**4.0**	**42,015**	**3.9**
Permanent	46,347	6.6	42,829	4.0	42,015	3.9
Transition	c	d	c	d	c	d
Other categories	**85,025**	**12.0**	**172,061**	**16.2**	**166,964**	**15.7**
Amerasians	120	d	348	d	376	d
Parolees, Soviet and Indochinese	4,199	.6	6,012	.6	5,468	.5
Refugees and asylees	*44,927*	*6.4*	*126,084*	*11.9*	*108,506*	*10.2*
Refugee adjustments	34,496	4.9	115,832	10.9	97,305	9.1
Asylee adjustments	10,431	1.5	10,252	1.0	11,201	1.1
Subject to annual limit	10,026	1.4	9,713	.9	10,111	.9
Not subject to limit	405	.1	539	.1	1,090	.1
NACARA Sec. 202[a]	2,577	.4	9,495	.9	18,926	1.8
Cancellation of removal	29,109	4.1	23,827	2.2	22,506	2.1
Subject to annual limit	2,009	.3	2,224	.2	3,157	.3
Not subject to limit (NACARA, Sec. 203)	27,100	3.8	21,603	2.0	19,349	1.8
IRCA legalization	39	d	55	d	263	d
HRIFA[b]	1,414	.2	5,383	.5	10,111	.9
Other	2,640	.4	857	.1	808	.1

[a]Nicaraguan Adjustment and Central American Relief Act of November, 1997.
[b]Haitian Refugee Immigration Fairness Act of 1998.
[c]Not applicable.
[d]Rounds to less than .05 percent.

SOURCE: "Table A. Immigrants Admitted by Major Category of Admission: Fiscal Years 2001–2003," in *2003 Yearbook of Immigration Statistics*, U.S. Department of Homeland Security, Office of Immigration Statistics, September 2004, http://uscis.gov/graphics/shared/aboutus/statistics/IMM03yrbk/2003IMM.pdf (accessed February 22, 2005)

could apply to have their status adjusted. In 2001 and 2002, individuals who had their status adjusted accounted for about two-thirds of all immigrants (61.4% in 2001 and 63.9% in 2002). However, in 2003, adjustment of status cases dropped to just half (49.2%) of all immigrants admitted. (See Table 3.6.)

The sudden decrease in adjustment-of-status immigrants in 2003 resulted from the Legal Immigration Family Equity (LIFE) Act of 2002, which resolved three class action lawsuits. Eligible persons had one year (until June 4, 2003) to apply for this particular adjustment of status. Key to eligibility was proof that by October 1, 2000, the applicant had filed a written claim for class membership in one of three lawsuits commonly referred to as CSS, LULAC, and Zambrano. Applicants also had to prove they entered the United States before January 1, 1982, resided in continuous unlawful status through May 4, 1988, and that they were continuously physically present in the United States from November 6, 1986, through May 4, 1988. Eligible applicants, and certain spouses and children, were protected from removal or deportation while their adjustment applications were pending. Also, they could be eligible for employment authorization while waiting.

LIFE Act applications poured in. In the *2003 Yearbook of Immigration Statistics*, the USCIS noted a

TABLE 3.7

Immigrant orphans adopted by U.S. citizens, by gender, age, region, and most frequent country of birth, fiscal year 2003

Region and country of birth	Total	Gender			Age			
		Male	Female	Unknown	Under 1 year	1–4 years	5–9 years	Over 9 years
All countries	21,320	7,435	13,884	1	9,728	8,853	1,680	1,059
Europe	7,652	3,694	3,958	—	2,067	3,934	1,028	623
Russia	5,134	2,513	2,621	—	1,559	2,559	608	408
Asia	10,018	1,990	8,028	—	5,519	4,000	328	171
China, People's Republic	6,638	313	6,325	—	3,262	3,206	140	30
Africa	417	190	227	—	59	146	108	104
Ethiopia	166	75	91	—	18	50	60	38
Oceania	52	21	31	—	22	17	12	ᵉ
North America	2,773	1,348	1,424	1	1,830	672	162	109
Guatemala	2,327	1,163	1,163	1	1,766	480	65	16
South America	406	192	214	—	231	82	42	51
Colombia	275	134	141	—	206	29	23	17

SOURCE: Adapted from "Table 10. Immigrant-Orphans Adopted by U.S. Citizens by Gender, Age, and Region and Country of Birth, Fiscal Year 2003," in *2003 Yearbook of Immigration Statistics*, Office of Immigration Statistics, U.S. Department of Homeland Security, September 2004, http://uscis.gov/graphics/shared/aboutus/statistics/IMM03yrbk/2003IMM.pdf (accessed January 27, 2005)

backlog of 1.2 million adjustment-of-status cases pending decisions at the end of the 2003 fiscal year (September 30, 2003). The volume of applications clogged the system, resulting in fewer approved adjustments in 2003. (See Table 3.6.)

New Arrivals by Adoption

Included in the category of immediate relatives are orphans adopted by American citizens. In 2003, 21,320 foreign adopted children were admitted to the United States. (See Table 3.7.) Almost half of the children (10,018) came from Asia. The People's Republic of China was the largest single source with 6,638 children adopted. Ninety-five percent of the Chinese children were females, primarily under the age of four years. According to the Web site for Holt International Children's Services, a nonprofit adoption service, nearly all children available for adoption from China were abandoned, usually left in public places with no identifying information ("FAQs about the China Adoption Process: How Do Children Come into Care?" http://www.holtintl.org/china/chinafaq.shtml).

In a January 6, 2005, story for Radio Free Europe/ Radio Liberty ("China: Population May Peak Under 'One-Child' Policy"), Daisy Sindelar explained China's efforts at birth control. Fear of widespread famine if the population continued to grow at the 1950s birth rate of six children per woman drove the Chinese government to implement a 1979 one-child-per-family policy. While some rural families were allowed a second child if the first was a girl, in most areas enforcement was strict. Punishment for exceeding the limit included forced abortions, beating of men whose wives gave birth to too many children, and sometimes jail terms or sterilization. The restrictions brought the fertility rate down to 1.8 by 2005 but not without negative side effects. The strong cultural preference for a son resulted in the abortion of female fetuses and the killing or abandonment of infant girls.

The vast majority of foreign adopted children were four years of age or younger. Of the 2,739 children aged five to nine years and over nine years, more than one-third (37%) came from Russia, the country that was second to China as a source of children adopted by American families. (See Table 3.7.)

Employment-Based Admissions

According to the Immigration and Naturalization Service (INS), in the decade before 1991 employment-based preferred immigrants accounted for a very small percentage of total immigration. One of the major goals of the Immigration Act of 1990 (IMMACT) was to increase the number of highly skilled workers entering the United States. However, spouses and children continued to claim a significant portion of this class of admission.

Of the 82,137 employment-based admissions in 2003, 32,534 were identified as having "no occupation/ not working outside the home," the majority of which were categorized as homemakers, students, and children. The 36,502 employment-based admissions who were actually seeking jobs represented just 5.2% of total immigrants admitted for the fiscal year. The majority (23,744 or 65%) of the actual job seekers in this category were prepared by training and experience to fill professional and technical positions. (See Table 3.8.)

NATURALIZATION—BECOMING A CITIZEN

Naturalization refers to the conferring of U.S. citizenship, by any means, upon a person after birth. A naturalization court grants citizenship if the naturalization

TABLE 3.8

Immigrants admitted, by major class of admission and selected demographic characteristics, 2003

Characteristic	Total	Family-sponsored preferences	Employment-based preferences	Immediate relatives of U.S. citizens	Diversity programs	Refugee and asylee adjustments	Other
Total	705,827	158,894	82,137	332,657	46,347	44,927	40,865
Gender							
Male	316,225	76,109	41,761	129,394	24,938	22,932	21,091
Female	389,507	82,783	40,362	203,255	21,404	21,950	19,753
Unknown	95	b	14	8	b	45	21
Age							
Under 16 years	129,497	39,212	15,127	53,921	9,554	8,827	2,856
16–20 years	68,390	25,103	6,333	25,819	3,498	4,785	2,852
21 years and over	507,904	94,568	60,676	252,904	33,289	31,314	35,153
Under 1 year	11,994	611	234	10,022	495	a	632
1–4 years	24,658	5,592	2,190	12,896	2,519	1,002	459
5–9 years	36,282	11,754	5,737	11,905	3,096	3,227	563
10–14 years	45,536	17,012	5,707	15,455	2,912	3,638	812
15–19 years	61,632	22,891	6,144	22,572	2,933	4,755	2,337
20–24 years	65,121	13,502	3,385	35,551	5,630	4,691	2,362
25–29 years	91,709	11,820	11,182	53,226	8,271	4,338	2,872
30–34 years	96,190	15,224	17,869	42,685	7,297	5,161	7,954
35–39 years	70,235	13,721	12,112	25,563	4,948	4,890	9,001
40–44 years	51,572	13,373	8,194	16,533	3,540	4,009	5,923
45–49 years	39,621	13,245	5,082	12,517	2,178	2,891	3,708
50–54 years	30,074	10,067	2,481	12,086	1,370	1,914	2,156
55–59 years	23,427	5,623	1,086	13,820	660	1,256	982
60–64 years	20,564	2,755	481	15,448	301	1,055	524
65–74 years	28,207	1,584	226	24,318	159	1,461	459
75 years and over	8,969	109	26	8,047	32	638	117
Unknown	36	11	b	13	6	b	b
Marital status							
Single	275,047	98,446	30,768	84,126	21,721	21,646	18,340
Married	401,134	57,088	50,012	229,757	23,787	19,860	20,630
Widowed	17,436	1,029	157	14,475	173	1,163	439
Divorced/separated	10,882	2,298	1,027	4,180	645	1,439	1,293
Unknown	1,328	33	173	119	21	819	163
Occupation							
Executive and managerial	22,295	4,292	6,394	5,104	5,870	413	222
Professional and technical	46,495	6,046	23,744	9,223	6,323	902	257
Sales	12,594	4,752	776	4,240	1,436	1,168	222
Administrative support	9,870	3,449	759	3,320	1,740	419	183
Farming, forestry, and fisheries	8,685	4,588	165	3,392	306	88	146
Operators, fabricators, and laborers	24,595	7,760	975	8,798	1,324	3,949	1,789
Precision production, craft, and repair	7,698	1,961	1,025	2,109	912	1,045	646
Service	29,117	9,091	2,661	8,416	4,795	2,895	1,259
Military	56	12	3	28	4	5	4
No occupation/not working outside home	310,197	87,987	32,534	150,862	17,460	16,602	4,752
Homemakers	79,667	17,879	10,118	47,800	1,412	1,686	772
Students or children	188,082	62,325	20,748	73,137	14,896	13,346	3,630
Retirees	2,603	259	41	1,766	20	475	42
Unemployed	39,845	7,524	1,627	28,159	1,132	1,095	308
Unknown	234,225	28,956	13,101	137,165	6,177	17,441	31,385

ªRepresents zero.
ᵇDisclosure standards not met.

SOURCE: "Table 7. Immigrants Admitted by Major Class of Admission and Selected Demographic Characteristics, Fiscal Year 2003," in *2003 Yearbook of Immigration Statistics*, Office of Immigration Statistics, U.S. Department of Homeland Security, September 2004, http://uscis.gov/graphics/shared/aboutus/statistics/IMM03yrbk/2003IMM.pdf (accessed January 27, 2005)

occurs within the United States, while a representative of the U.S. Citizenship and Immigration Services confers naturalization if it is performed outside the United States. Beginning in 1992 IMMACT also permitted persons to naturalize through administrative hearings with the INS (now USCIS). When individuals become U.S. citizens, they pledge allegiance to the United States and renounce allegiance to their former country of nationality.

General Requirements

In order to naturalize, most immigrants have to meet certain general requirements. They have to be at least eighteen years old, have been legally admitted to the United States for permanent residence, and have lived in this country continuously for at least five years. They also have to be able to speak, read, and write English; know how the U.S. government works; have a basic knowledge of U.S. history; and be of good moral character. According to the *2003 Yearbook of Immigration Statistics*, 91% of the immigrants who became naturalized in fiscal year 2003 did so by meeting these general provisions.

Special Provisions

The remaining 9% of persons naturalized in 2003 did so under special provisions of the naturalization laws that exempted them from one or more of the general requirements. Spouses and children of U.S. citizens and military personnel made up most of those attaining citizenship through special provisions. Spouses of U.S. citizens can become naturalized in three years instead of the normal five. Children who immigrated with their parents generally receive their U.S. citizenship through the naturalization of their parents. Aliens with lawful permanent resident status who served honorably in the U.S. military are also entitled to certain exemptions from the naturalization requirements.

Naturalization Rates

The longer immigrants lived in the United States, the more likely they were to become naturalized citizens. Figure 3.6 shows that 80.9% of those who entered the United States before 1970 were naturalized, compared to 14.7% of those who arrived in 1990 or later. The Census Bureau reported that of the foreign-born residents in 2003, 13.6% had arrived since 2000, 36.6% came in the 1990s, 24% came in the 1980s, 13.7% came in the 1970s, and 12.2% arrived before 1970 (Luke J. Larsen, *The Foreign-Born Population in the United States: 2003*, P20-551, Current Population Reports, Washington, DC, August 2004).

National Origins of Naturalized Citizens

For much of the twentieth century, quotas established by immigration legislation favored persons from Europe, resulting in higher numbers of naturalizations from European countries. Once the quotas ended with the Immigration and Nationality Act Amendments in 1965, the regional origin of persons immigrating and naturalizing shifted to Asian countries. Asian immigrants historically had higher naturalization rates than other immigrants. With increased legal immigration from such Western Hemisphere countries and regions as Canada, Mexico, and the Caribbean beginning in the mid-1980s, the share of naturalizations from those areas peaked at 49% in 1996 (*2003 Yearbook of Immigration Statistics*, Washington DC: U.S. Citizenship and Immigration Services, Department of Homeland Security, September 2004). Since 2001, Asia has been the leading region for naturalizations. In 2003, 42% of persons naturalizing were born in Asian countries compared to 28% for North American countries. Figure 3.7 illustrates the shift from European to Asian immigration during the last four decades of the twentieth century. The decade-by-decade growth in naturalization of immigrants from North America is also shown. From just 20.9% of

FIGURE 3.6

U.S. citizenship of the foreign-born, by year of entry, 2003

[In percent]

Before 1970	80.9
1970–1979	69.6
1980–1989	48.3
1990 or later	14.7

SOURCE: Luke J. Larsen, "Figure 5. U.S. Citizenship of the Foreign-Born by Year of Entry: 2003," in *The Foreign-Born Population in the United States: 2003*, Current Population Reports, P20-551, U.S. Census Bureau, August 2004, http://www.census.gov/prod/2004pubs/p20-551.pdf (accessed January 24, 2005)

naturalizations in the 1961–70 period, naturalizations from North America rose to 40% by the 1991–2000 period.

The USCIS *2003 Yearbook of Immigration Statistics* identified Mexico as the leading country of birth of persons naturalized in 2003, accounting for 56,093 new citizens. Other countries contributing large numbers to 2003 naturalizations were India (29,790), the Philippines (29,081), Vietnam (25,995), the People's Republic of China (24,014), South Korea (15,968), the Dominican Republic (12,627), Jamaica (11,232), Iran (10,807), and Poland (9,140). These ten countries represented almost half (49%) of the 463,204 new naturalized citizens in 2003.

Trends in Naturalization

In 2003 the Urban Institute, a nonpartisan economic and social policy research organization, published an analysis of the recently naturalized, the pool of eight million immigrants eligible to be naturalized, and the estimated 2.7 million legal immigrants soon-to-be eligible (Michael E. Fix, Jeffrey S. Passel, and Kenneth Sucher, *Trends in Naturalization*, Washington, DC: The Urban Institute, September 17, 2003). Noting the shift in sources of immigrants from Europe to Asia and Latin America, the study considered naturalization rates for immigrants from those three regions. Immigrants from Mexico were considered separately because Mexico had become the largest source country for immigrants. In 2001, 67% of eligible immigrants from Asia were naturalized, a greater rate of naturalization than for immigrants from Europe and Canada (65%). Eligible immigrants from Latin America lagged behind with 58% naturalized; Mexico was farther behind with 34% of eligible immigrants naturalized. (See Figure 3.8.)

Figure 3.9 illustrates three areas of concern about future naturalization candidates—limited English skills, little formal education, and low incomes. The study

FIGURE 3.7

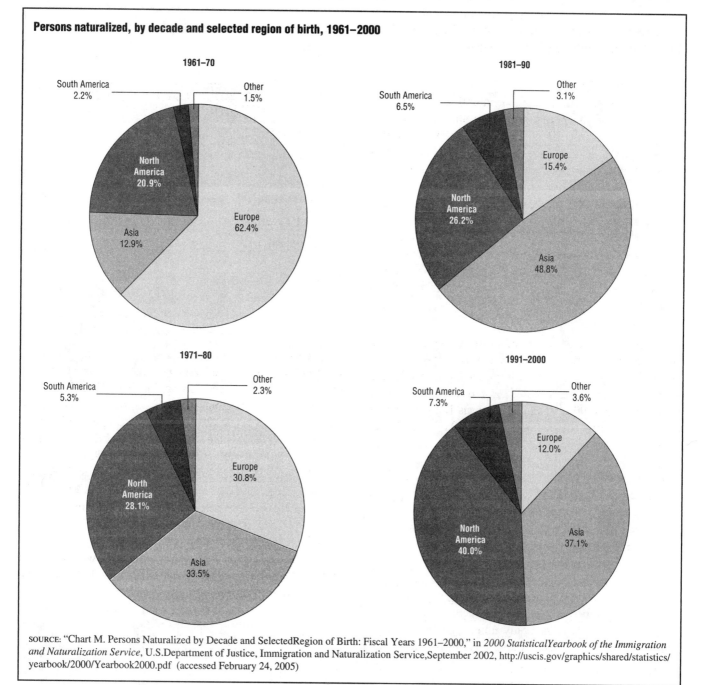

Persons naturalized, by decade and selected region of birth, 1961–2000

1961–70

South America 2.2%
Other 1.5%
North America 20.9%
Asia 12.9%
Europe 62.4%

1981–90

South America 6.5%
Other 3.1%
Europe 15.4%
North America 26.2%
Asia 48.8%

1971–80

South America 5.3%
Other 2.3%
North America 28.1%
Europe 30.8%
Asia 33.5%

1991–2000

South America 7.3%
Other 3.6%
Europe 12.0%
North America 40.0%
Asia 37.1%

SOURCE: "Chart M. Persons Naturalized by Decade and SelectedRegion of Birth: Fiscal Years 1961–2000," in *2000 StatisticalYearbook of the Immigration and Naturalization Service*, U.S.Department of Justice, Immigration and Naturalization Service,September 2002, http://uscis.gov/graphics/shared/statistics/yearbook/2000/Yearbook2000.pdf (accessed February 24, 2005)

found that 52% of the recently naturalized had only limited English proficiency. By contrast, 60% (about 3.5 million adults) of the legal immigrant population currently eligible to naturalize and 67% (about 1.5 million adults) of the soon-to-be eligible had only limited English skills. The study suggested that publicly supported English classes and civics courses might be needed to help this population achieve the language skills and knowledge of American history and government required for citizenship.

In education, the study described two significant clusters of immigrants—those with less than a high school education and those with college degrees. Compared to 9% of the recently naturalized with less than a ninth-grade education, 25% of current and 21% of soon-to-be eligible candidates for naturalization had less than a ninth-grade education. This suggested that literacy was a significant issue, in addition to English language skills, in preparing this group of immigrants to qualify for citizenship. The study also found that, while 35% of the recently naturalized had bachelor's degrees or higher, just 23% of currently eligible and 30% of the soon-to-be eligible held such degrees. (See Figure 3.9.)

FIGURE 3.8

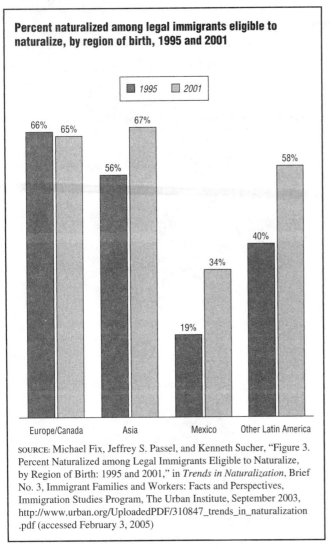

Percent naturalized among legal immigrants eligible to naturalize, by region of birth, 1995 and 2001

SOURCE: Michael Fix, Jeffrey S. Passel, and Kenneth Sucher, "Figure 3. Percent Naturalized among Legal Immigrants Eligible to Naturalize, by Region of Birth: 1995 and 2001," in *Trends in Naturalization*, Brief No. 3, Immigrant Families and Workers: Facts and Perspectives, Immigration Studies Program, The Urban Institute, September 2003, http://www.urban.org/UploadedPDF/310847_trends_in_naturalization.pdf (accessed February 3, 2005)

FIGURE 3.9

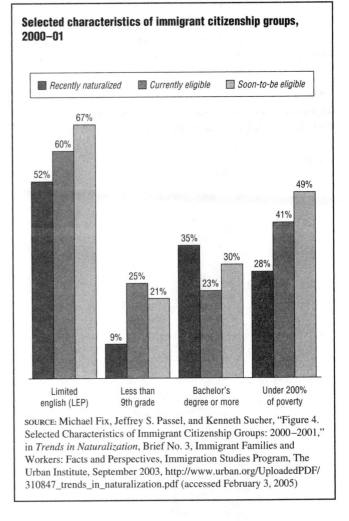

Selected characteristics of immigrant citizenship groups, 2000–01

SOURCE: Michael Fix, Jeffrey S. Passel, and Kenneth Sucher, "Figure 4. Selected Characteristics of Immigrant Citizenship Groups: 2000–2001," in *Trends in Naturalization*, Brief No. 3, Immigrant Families and Workers: Facts and Perspectives, Immigration Studies Program, The Urban Institute, September 2003, http://www.urban.org/UploadedPDF/310847_trends_in_naturalization.pdf (accessed February 3, 2005)

In addition, the study found a far greater share of the future naturalization candidates had incomes under 200% of the poverty level. The study noted that the combination of limited English skills, low level of education, and low income presented greater barriers to naturalization. (See Figure 3.9.)

NONIMMIGRANTS

Tourists, Business People, Foreign Government Officials, and Foreign Students

Table 3.9 lists nonimmigrant visa classifications and numbers of nonimmigrant visas issued by the U.S. Department of State for fiscal years 1998 through 2002. The impact of increased security following the 2001 terrorist attacks can be seen in the almost 24% drop from 7,588,778 total visas issued in 2001 to a total of 5,769,437 in 2002. The largest category of nonimmigrant visas was visitors for business or pleasure (B-1, B-2, and B-1/B-2). The majority of persons with business in the United States also included plans for tourist or pleasure activities (B-1/B-2).

A combined total of 2,859,232 B class visas were issued in 2002—nearly half (49.6%) of all visas issued for the fiscal year. Students and their family members totaled 256,534 in 2002, or 4.4% of all visas issued.

There were no restrictions on the number of nonimmigrants allowed to enter the United States. In fact, the United States, like most other countries, encourages tourism and tries to attract as many visitors as possible. However, while it is easy to get in, strict rules do apply to the conditions of the visit. For example, students can stay only long enough to complete their studies, and business people can stay only six months (although a six-month extension is available). Most nonimmigrants are not allowed to hold jobs while in the United States, although exceptions are made for students and the families of diplomats. However, a certain undetermined number, amounting to many tens of thousands, chose to overstay their nonimmigrant visas and continue to live in the United States illegally.

Temporary Foreign Workers

A temporary worker is an alien coming to the United States to work for a temporary period. The major nonimmigrant visa category for legal temporary workers is the H visa, which includes the H-2/H-2A, H-1B/H-1B1, and H-1C visas.

THE H-2/H-2A PROGRAM. The H-2 Temporary Agricultural Worker Program, authorized by the Immigration and Nationality Act of 1952, was a flexible response to seasonal agricultural labor demands. Since 1964 it has been the only legal temporary foreign agricultural worker program in the United States. (The year 1964 marked the end of the Mexican Bracero program, a temporary foreign agricultural

TABLE 3.9

Nonimmigrant visas issued by classification, FY 1998–2002

Visa symbol/class		1998	1999	2000	2001	2002
A1	Ambassador, public minister, career diplomat, consul, and immediate family	10,437	10,757	10,698	9,662	10,452
A2	Other foreign government official or employee, and immediate family	66,998	66,335	69,079	66,398	71,728
A3	Attendant, servant, or personal employee of A1 and A2, and immediate family	2,148	2,279	2,486	2,228	1,971
B1	Temporary visitor for business	192,837	93,019	75,919	84,201	75,642
B2	Temporary visitor for pleasure	854,738	642,676	509,031	381,431	255,487
B1/B 2	Temporary visitor for business and pleasure	3,226,799	3,447,822	3,567,580	3,527,118	2,528,103
B1/B2/BCC	Combination B1/B2 and Border Crossing Card[a]	289,883	676,386	1,510,133	1,990,402	1,399,819
C1	Person in transit	31,457	26,494	26,407	27,231	24,207
C1/D	Combination transit/crew member (indiv. iss.)[b]	172,955	161,723	165,556	167,435	175,446
C2	Person in transit to United Nations Headquarters	34	25	37	24	8
C3	Foreign government official, immediate family, attendant, servant, or personal employee in transit	8,388	7,805	6,606	5,697	6,024
D Indiv. Iss.	Crew Member (sea or air) (individual issuance)	20,174	19,175	21,195	21,615	13,671
D Crewlist	Crewlist Visas	11,260	10,768	9,817	8,480	8,399
E1	Treaty trader, spouse and children	9,457	9,973	9,539	9,309	7,811
E2	Treaty investor, spouse and children	20,775	22,975	26,981	27,577	25,633
F1	Student (academic or language training program)	251,565	262,542	284,053	293,357	234,322
F2	Spouse or child of student	21,845	22,893	24,981	26,160	22,212
G1	Principal resident representative of recognized foreign member government to international organization, staff, and immediate family	4,957	5,090	5,166	5,274	4,905
G2	Other representative of recognized foreign member government to international organization, and immediate family	8,847	8,466	11,225	8,825	9,144
G3	Representative of nonrecognized or nonmember foreign government to international organization, and immediate family	150	165	258	134	99
G4	International organization officer or employee, and immediate family	15,245	17,142	16,960	16,999	17,374
G5	Attendant, servant, or personal employee of G1 through G4, and immediate family	1,614	1,737	1,737	1,645	1,482
H1A	Temporary worker performing services as a registered nurse[c]	18	5	2		
H1B	Temporary worker of distinguished merit and ability performing services other than as a registered nurse	91,360	116,513	133,290	161,643	118,352
H1C	Nurse in health professional shortage area[c]			—	34	212
H2A	Temporary worker performing agricultural services	22,676	28,568	30,201	31,523	31,538
H2B	Temporary worker performing other services	20,192	30,642	45,037	58,215	62,591
H3	Trainee	1,830	1,892	1,514	1,613	1,387
H4	Spouse or child of H1A/B/C, H2A/B, or H3	54,595	69,194	79,518	95,967	79,725
I	Representative of foreign information media, spouse and children	11,627	12,694	13,928	13,799	18,187
J1	Exchange visitor	192,451	211,349	236,837	261,769	253,841
J2	Spouse or child of exchange visitor	33,177	34,394	37,122	38,189	32,539
K1	Fiance(e) of U.S. citizen	12,968	17,025	21,471	24,973	28,338
K2	Child of fiance(e) of U.S. citizen	1,499	2,431	3,275	3,735	4,298
K3	Spouse of U.S. citizen awaiting availability of immigrant visa[d]				3	5,078
K4	Child of K3[d]				1	1,294
L1	Intracompany transferee (executive, managerial, and specialized personnel continuing employment with international firm or corporation)	38,307	41,739	54,963	59,384	57,721
L2	Spouse or child of intracompany transferee	44,176	46,289	57,069	61,154	54,903
M1	Vocational and other nonacademic student	6,515	6,240	6,107	5,373	4,116
M2	Spouse or child of vocational student	457	337	358	285	161
NATO1	Principal permanent representative of member state to NATO (including any of its subsidiary bodies) resident in the U.S., and resident members of official staff; principal NATO officers; and immediate family	4	22	17	4	24
NATO2	Other representatives of member states to NATO (including any of its subsidiary bodies), and immediate family; dependents of member of a force entering in accordance with provisions of NATO agreements; members of such force if issued visas	4,339	4,865	5,031	4,282	5,195
NATO3	Official clerical staff accompanying a representative of member state to NATO, and immediate family	—	—	—	—	—
NATO4	Officials of NATO (other than those classifiable as NATO1), and immediate family	80	211	97	95	89
NATO5	Experts, other than NATO4 officials, employed in missions on behalf of NATO, and their dependents	18	28	33	121	179

TABLE 3.9

Nonimmigrant visas issued by classification, FY 1998–2002 [CONTINUED]

Visa symbol/class		1998	1999	2000	2001	2002
NATO6	Members of a civilian component accompanying a force entering in accordance with the provisions of NATO agreements, and their dependents	150	256	209	220	192
NATO7	Attendant, servant, or personal employee of NATO1 through NATO6, and immediate family	2	6	3	1	8
N8	Parent of SK3 special immigrant	15	10	12	8	8
N9	Child of N8 or of SK1, SK2 or SK4 special immigrant	11	9	8	6	4
O1	Person with extraordinary ability in the sciences, arts, education, business, or athletics	4,257	5,009	6,466	6,666	6,026
O2	Person accompanying and assisting in the artistic or athletic performance by O1	1,778	2,185	1,894	1,918	1,972
O3	Spouse or child of O1 or O2	1,056	1,480	2,101	2,287	1,760
P1	Internationally recognized athlete or member of an internationally recognized entertainment group	20,598	22,306	23,786	24,378	24,287
P2	Artist or entertainer in a reciprocal exchange program	175	198	238	125	119
P3	Artist or entertainer in a culturally unique program	9,291	8,068	10,501	8,495	8,131
P4	Spouse or child of P1, P2, or P3	628	742	868	1,020	938
Q1	Participant in an international cultural exchange program	1,312	1,836	2,024	1,432	1,469
Q2	Irish Peace Process trainee[e]			358	186	329
Q3	Spouse or child of Q2[e]			3	—	1
R1	Person in a religious occupation	5,450	6,497	7,418	8,503	8,646
R2	Spouse or child of R1	1,395	2,003	2,489	3,009	3,175
S5	Informant possessing critical reliable information concerning criminal organization or enterprise[f]	—	—	—	—	—
S6	Informant possessing critical reliable information concerning terrorist organization, enterprise, or operation[f]	—	—	—	—	—
S7	Spouse, married or unmarried son or daughter, or parent of S5 or S6[f]	—	—	—	—	—
TN	NAFTA professional	295	484	906	787	699
TD	Spouse or child of TN	530	704	1,128	1,041	856
T1	Victim of a severe form of trafficking in persons[g]				—	—
T2	Spouse of T1[g]				—	—
T3	Child of T1[g]				—	—
T4	Parent of T1 under 21 years of age[g]				—	—
U1	Victim of criminal activity[h]				—	—
U2	Spouse of U1[h]				—	—
U3	Child of U1[h]				—	—
U4	Parent of U1 under 21 years of age[h]				—	—
V1	Spouse of lawful permanent resident awaiting availability of immigrant visa[i]				9,127	18,020
V2	Child of lawful permanent resident awaiting availability of immigrant visa[i]				14,805	19,523
V3	Derivative child of V1 or V2[i]				1,400	19,567
Other nonimmigrant classes						
BCC	Border Crossing Cards [a]	8,358				
Grand total		**5,814,153**	**6,192,478**	**7,141,636**	**7,588,778**	**5,769,437**

[a]Border Crossing Cards (BCC) were issued at posts in Canada and Mexico; issuance ceased in Fiscal Year 1998. Combination B1/B2 and Border Crossing Card (B/B2/BCC) issuances began in Fiscal Year 1984 at posts in Mexico and in Fiscal Year 1992 at posts in Canada; issuance ceased in Fiscal Year 1998 at posts in Canada.
[b]Combination C1/D visas (issued in lieu of separate concurrent C1 and D visas) are counted as one visa, not two.
[c]The H1C category was established by Section 2(a) of the Nursing Relief for Disadvantaged Areas Act of 1999 (Pub. L. 106 95) enacted November 12, 1999; it is effective from June 11, 2001 (the date the Immigration and Naturalization Service published implementing regulations) through June 11, 2005 only. Section 2(c) of Pub. L. 106 95 repealed the former H1A category relating to registered nurses.
[d]Nonimmigrant status for spouses of U.S. citizens (and their children) awaiting the availability of an immigrant visa was provided by Section 1103 of the Legal Immigration Family Equity (LIFE) Act of 2000 (Title XI of Pub. L. 106 553) enacted December 21, 2000.
[e]Category established by the Irish Peace Process Cultural and Training Program Act of 1998 (Pub. L. 105 319), and effective October 30, 1998 through September 30, 2005 only.
[f]Category established by the Violent Crime Control and Law Enforcement Act of 1994 (Pub. L. 103 322), and effective September 13, 1994 through September 12, 1999. Section 2 of Pub. L. 106 104 extended this category through September 12, 2001. The category was made permanent by Pub. L. 107 45 enacted October 1, 2001.
[g]Category established by Section 107(e)(1), division A (Trafficking Victims Protection Act of 2000) of the Victims of Trafficking and Violence Protection Act of 2000 (Pub. L. 106 386) enacted October 28, 2000.
[h]Category established by Section 1513(b), title V (Battered Immigrant Women Protection Act of 2000), division B (Violence Against Women Act of 2000) of the Victims of Trafficking and Violence Protection Act of 2000 (Pub. L. 106 386) enacted October 28, 2000.
[i]Nonimmigrant status for spouses and children of lawful permanent residents (and their children) awaiting the availability of an immigrant visa was provided by Section 1102 of the Legal Immigration Family Equity (LIFE) Act of 2000 (Title XI of Pub. L. 106 553) enacted December 21, 2000.

SOURCE: "Table XVI (B). Nonimmigrant Visas Issued by Classification (Including Crewlist Visas and Border Crossing Cards): Fiscal Years 1998–2002," in *Report of the Visa Office 2002*, U.S. Department of State, Bureau of Consular Affairs, December 2004, http://travel.state.gov/pdf/visa_office_report_2002.pdf (accessed February 25, 2005)

worker program negotiated between the United States and Mexico.) In 1986 the H-2 program was amended as the H-2A program. No numerical limit on the number of workers allowed per year has been set for this program.

Under the H-2A temporary agricultural program, employers who anticipate a shortage of domestic workers can bring nonimmigrant foreign workers to the United States to perform agricultural labor or services of a temporary or seasonal nature. The employer files an application with the Labor Department stating that there are not enough workers able, willing, qualified, and available, and that the employment of aliens will not adversely affect the wages and working conditions of similarly employed U.S. workers. The employer must also certify that the jobs are not vacant due to a labor dispute. The employer pays a fee of $100, plus $10 for each job opportunity certified, up to a maximum fee of $1,000 for each certification granted.

Hiring foreign workers under the H-2A program places a number of requirements on the employer, including advertising for and hiring qualified domestic workers, providing workers compensation insurance or equivalent insurance for all workers, and following specific pay and recordkeeping procedures. In some situations the employer could be required to pay for transportation and provide housing and meals for workers.

The employer is required to pay all workers the higher of (1) the Adverse Effect Wage Rate (AEWR) determined by the Labor Department for each state, (2) the applicable prevailing wage for the state, or (3) the statutory minimum wage. The federal minimum wage in 2004 was $5.15 per hour. Table 3.10 lists the 2004 AEWR for all states. State hourly AEWRs ranged from a low of $7.38 in Arkansas, Louisiana, and Mississippi to $9.28 in Iowa and Missouri. Hawaii was highest at $9.60.

The numbers of certified H-2A jobs have varied over the years. In a study for the Pew Hispanic Center (*Guest Workers: New Solution, New Problem?*, Washington, DC, March 21, 2002), Philip Martin noted that in 1990 the number of jobs certified was 25,412, dropping to 17,000 in 1993, to 15,117 in 1995, then tripling to 44,017 in 2000. Compared to the total number of U.S. farm workers, the number of H-2A workers has been small. In 2001 the U.S. Department of Labor reported in their *National Agricultural Workers Surveys* that during the 1990s an estimated 2.5 million people were employed on U.S. farms in a typical year, including about 1.8 million on crop farms. The Labor Department also reported that more than half of the farm workforce consisted of unauthorized foreigners.

According to the Department of State, 6,564 employers applied for H-2A certification of 45,716 workers in fiscal year (FY) 2003. A total of 6,360 employers were approved to hire 44,033 workers (*United States Department of Labor H-2A Regional Summary, Fiscal Year 2003*, Washington, DC, 2004). Almost half of the approved jobs (21,221) were in the Atlanta Region (Alabama, Florida, Georgia, Kentucky, Mississippi, North Carolina, South Carolina, and Tennessee). Table 3.11 identifies the number of certified employers and foreign workers by agricultural category for the Atlanta Region. By far the largest agricultural need was for tobacco workers (11,123)

TABLE 3.10

Adverse effect wage rates, 2004

State	2004
Alabama	$7.88
Arizona	$7.54
Arkansas	$7.38
California	$8.50
Colorado	$8.36
Connecticut	$9.01
Delaware	$8.52
Florida	$8.18
Georgia	$7.88
Hawaii	$9.60
Idaho	$7.69
Illinois	$9.00
Indiana	$9.00
Iowa	$9.28
Kansas	$8.83
Kentucky	$7.63
Louisiana	$7.38
Maine	$9.01
Maryland	$8.52
Massachusetts	$9.01
Michigan	$9.11
Minnesota	$9.11
Mississippi	$7.38
Missouri	$9.28
Montana	$7.69
Nebraska	$8.83
Nevada	$8.36
New Hampshire	$9.01
New Jersey	$8.52
New Mexico	$7.54
New York	$9.01
North Carolina	$8.06
North Dakota	$8.83
Ohio	$9.00
Oklahoma	$7.73
Oregon	$8.73
Pennsylvania	$8.52
Rhode Island	$9.01
South Carolina	$7.88
South Dakota	$8.83
Tennessee	$7.63
Texas	$7.73
Utah	$8.36
Vermont	$9.01
Virginia	$8.06
Washington	$8.73
West Virginia	$7.63
Wisconsin	$9.11
Wyoming	$7.69

Note: Adverse effect wage rates are the minimum wage rates which the Department of Labor has determined must be offered and paid to U.S. and foreign workers by employers of nonimmigrant foreign agricultural workers (H2-A visa holders).

SOURCE: "Adverse Effect Wage Rates: Year 2005," U.S. Department of Labor, Employment & Training Administration, http://www.ows.doleta.gov/foreign/adverse.asp (accessed March 4, 2005)

who represented 52% of the H-2A certified workers in the eight-state Atlanta Region. Christmas tree harvesters were needed only in North Carolina, cotton and corn pickers in Mississippi, grape and pecan pickers in Georgia, and sugarcane cutters in Florida.

THE H-1B PROGRAM. The H-1B program allows an employer to temporarily employ a foreign worker in the United States on a nonimmigrant basis in a specialty occupation or as a model of distinguished merit and ability. A specialty occupation requires the theoretical

TABLE 3.11

TABLE 3.12

H-2A activity, Atlanta region, FY 2003

Agricultural category	Employers certified	Workers certified
Bee keeper	5	20
Catfish	1	3
Christmas trees	57	699
Cook	1	1
Corn	1	20
Cotton	3	23
Dairy	1	1
Fish	6	151
Fruit	45	1,563
Grain	25	69
Grape	1	90
Hay	3	9
Horses	1	3
Horticulture	108	1,419
Livestock	2	8
Onion	5	622
Peach	23	1,815
Pecans	2	40
Rice	2	9
Sheep herding	2	10
Sod	6	55
Sugar cane	2	4
Tobacco	2,137	11,124
Vegetables	106	3,455
Wheat	1	8
Total	**2,546**	**21,221**

SOURCE: Adapted from "United States Department of Labor H-2A Crop Activity Summary, Fiscal Year 2003," in *United States Department of Labor H-2A Regional Summary, Fiscal Year 2003*, U.S. Department of Labor, Employment & Training Administration, http://www.ows.doleta.gov/foreign/h-2a_region.asp (accessed March 4, 2005)

H-1B visas issued by fiscal year, 1992–2005

Fiscal year	H-1Bs counted against cap
1992	48,600
1993	61,600
1994	60,300
1995	54,200
1996	55,100
1997	65,000
1998	65,000
1999	115,000
2000	115,000
2001	163,600
2002	79,100
2003	78,000
2004	65,000
2005	65,000*

Note: In FY 1997, 5,000 petitions were carried over and applied to the FY 1998 cap. In FY 1998, 14,000 petitions were carried over and applied to the FY 1999 cap. In FY 1999, an audit showed the cap was exceeded by 22,000 and thousands of other petitions were carried forward to FY 2001. In FY 2000, the cap was reached July 21, 2000 and under legislation thousands of approved petitions were not included in the cap count. In FY 2001, the new cap of 195,000 was not reached; legislation exempted from the cap count initial beneficiaries employed by non-profit organizations.
*CIS has reported receiving sufficient applications to reach the ceiling of 65,000 for FY 2005.

SOURCE: "H-1Bs Issued by Fiscal Year, 1992–2005," National Foundation for American Policy, 2004, http://www.nfap.net/researchactivities/immigrationresearch/H-1BVisasByYear.pdf (accessed March 18, 2005)

and practical application of a body of specialized knowledge and a bachelor's degree or the equivalent in the specific specialty (e.g., sciences, medicine and health care, education, biotechnology, business specialties, etc.). Effective January 1, 2004, the H-1B1 program became available, allowing employers to request such specialty foreign workers from Chile and Singapore. To hire a foreign worker on an H-1B or H-1B1 visa, the job had to be a professional position that normally requires a bachelor's degree as a minimum for entry into the occupation.

A foreign worker can be in H-1B status for a maximum continuous period of six years. After the H-1B expires, the worker has to remain outside the United States for one year before another H-1B petition can be approved. Certain foreign workers with labor certification applications or immigrant visa petitions in process for extended periods may stay in H-1B status beyond the normal six-year limitation, in one-year increments. Extensions and renewals were allowed under the H-1B1 program, however, adjustment-of-status to another non-immigrant category or to legal permanent residency is not permitted.

The Immigration Act of 1990 set the ceiling on H-1B admissions for initial employment at 65,000 beginning in FY 1992, but demand for H-1B workers grew. The

American Competitiveness and Workforce Improvement Act of 1998 (PL 105-277) temporarily raised the maximum number of petitions for initial H-1B employment to 115,000 for fiscal years 1999 and 2000.

The American Competitiveness in the Twenty-First Century Act of 2000 (PL 106-311) increased the H-1B annual limit for initial employment to 195,000 for fiscal years 2001, 2002, and 2003. The cap would revert back to 65,000 for FY 2004. When the H-1B1 visa was introduced in 2004, the 6,800 allowable H-1B1 visas were deducted from the total H-1B program. This left 58,200 H-1B visas available per year. On October 1, 2004, the first day of FY 2005, USCIS announced that it had already received enough H-1B petitions to meet the annual cap for FY 2005. Table 3.12 shows the number of H-1B visas issued annually from 1992 through 2005.

The American Competitiveness and Workforce Improvement Act of 1998 required employers to offer H-1B workers benefits and wages comparable to those offered to U.S. workers. It also imposed on employers a $500 fee per alien hired. The fees were to fund the education and training of U.S. workers. Both the INS and the Labor Department would administer the H-1B program.

The American Competitiveness in the Twenty-First Century Act increased fees for employers hiring foreign workers under the H-1B program to $1,000 per alien

FIGURE 3.10

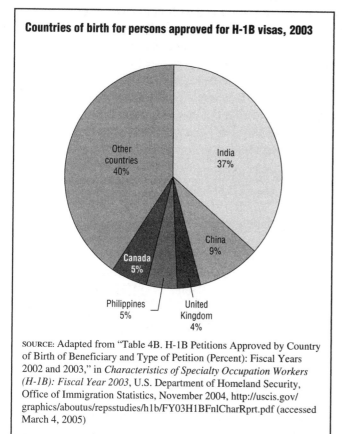

Countries of birth for persons approved for H-1B visas, 2003

SOURCE: Adapted from "Table 4B. H-1B Petitions Approved by Country of Birth of Beneficiary and Type of Petition (Percent): Fiscal Years 2002 and 2003," in *Characteristics of Specialty Occupation Workers (H-1B): Fiscal Year 2003*, U.S. Department of Homeland Security, Office of Immigration Statistics, November 2004, http://uscis.gov/graphics/aboutus/repsstudies/h1b/FY03H1BFnlCharRprt.pdf (accessed March 4, 2005)

hired plus a $110 filing fee. The $1,000 fees would be used to prepare U.S. workers to fill the jobs for which foreign workers were being recruited by funding job training, scholarships, and grants for mathematics, science, and engineering courses.

The typical 2003 H-1B recipient was thirty-two years old, was born in India (37%), had a bachelor's degree (50%) or higher, worked in a computer-related field (39%), and earned an annual salary of $60,000 (*Characteristics of Specialty Occupation Workers (H-1B): Fiscal Year 2003*, Washington, DC: Office of Immigration Statistics, U. S. Department of Homeland Security, November 2004). Figure 3.10 shows major source countries for H-1B workers in 2003. As in previous years, India supplied by far the most workers (37%). China was a distant second (9%).

H-1C PROGRAM ASSISTED HOSPITALS. The Nursing Relief for Disadvantaged Areas Act of 1999 (NRDAA) allowed qualifying hospitals to employ temporary foreign workers as registered nurses (RNs) for up to three years under H-1C visas. Only 500 H-1C visas could be issued each year during the four-year period of the H-1C program (2000–2004). The sponsoring employer paid a filing fee of $250 for each application filed with the Labor Department. H-1C nurses were admitted for a period of three years and the law did not provide for an

extension of that time frame. The H-1C program expired September 20, 2004.

ALIENS TURNED AWAY FROM THE UNITED STATES

Customs and Border Protection inspectors determine the admissibility of aliens who arrive at any of the approximately 300 U.S. ports of entry. Aliens who arrive without required documents, present improper or fraudulent documents, or who are on criminal wanted lists are deemed inadmissible. New rules that became effective in 1997 under the Illegal Immigration Reform and Immigrant Responsibility Act (IIRIRA) provide two options to the inadmissible alien—voluntary departure or removal proceedings. Most removal proceedings involve a hearing before an immigration judge, which could result in removal or adjustment to a legal status such as granting asylum. Removal proceedings can also involve fines or imprisonment. IIRIRA empowers immigration officers to order an alien removed without a hearing or review through a process called expedited removal. This process applies to cases in which the officers determine that the alien is inadmissible because the alien engaged in fraud or misrepresentation or lacked proper documents.

The *2003 Yearbook of Immigration Statistics* (Washington, DC: U.S. Citizenship and Immigration Services, Department of Homeland Security, September 2004) reported that in FY 2003 inspectors determined that about 497,000 arriving aliens were inadmissible. Of these, about 181,000 were subject to expedited removal. However, 128,000 of these aliens were allowed to withdraw their applications for admission and leave the country. The remaining 53,000 were placed in expedited removal. Approximately 6,000 of these aliens reported a fear of returning to their country of origin and were referred to an asylum officer. About 90% of those were found to have credible fears of persecution and were scheduled for hearings with an immigration judge. The remaining 43,248 aliens were removed under the expedited removal process. Expedited removals accounted for 23% of the total 186,151 alien removals in FY 2003. (See Table 3.13.)

While aliens with formal removals came from 178 countries, the *2003 Yearbook of Immigration Statistics* reported that just nine countries accounted for almost 92% of all formal removals. With 137,819 aliens removed, Mexico alone accounted for the majority (74%) of the 186,151 alien removals in FY 2003. (See Table 3.14.) Beginning in 2002 Brazil displaced Canada from the top nine countries with the most aliens removed.

The removal of criminal aliens increased dramatically after the 1986 passage of the Immigration Reform and Control Act (IRCA). In 1986 the INS reported 1,978 aliens removed for criminal violations; in 2003 there

TABLE 3.13

Formal removals, 1994–2003

Fiscal year	Total removals	Expedited removals
2003	186,151	43,248
2002	150,084	34,500
2001	177,739	69,827
2000	185,987	85,921
1999	180,902	89,160
1998	173,146	76,078
1997	114,432	23,242
1996	69,680	X
1995	50,924	X
1994	45,674	X

X Not applicable.

SOURCE: "Formal Removal (Tables 40–46)," in *2003 Yearbook of Immigration Statistics*, U.S. Department of Homeland Security, Office of Immigration Statistics, September 2004, http://uscis.gov/graphics/shared/aboutus/statistics/ENF03yrbk/2003ENFtext.pdf (accessed January 27, 2005)

TABLE 3.14

Removals, by country and types of crimes resulting in criminals removed, FY 2003

Country	Number removed	Number of criminals
Mexico	137,819	62,518
Honduras	7,700	1,862
Guatemala	6,674	1,483
El Salvador	4,933	1,982
Brazil	3,797	210
Dominican Republic	3,284	2,139
Colombia	2,081	1,319
Jamaica	1,999	1,480
Haiti	1,032	516

Crime	Number removed	Percent of total crimes
Dangerous drugs	31,352	39
Immigration	11,413	14
Assault	8,336	11
Burglary	3,206	4
Robbery	2,806	4
Larceny	2,494	3
Sexual assault	2,191	3
Family offenses	2,238	3
Sex offenses	1,609	2
Stolen vehicles	1,525	2

SOURCE: "Country of Nationality (Table 43) and Criminal Activity (Table 43)," in *2003 Yearbook of Immigration Statistics*, U.S. Department of HomelandSecurity, O ffice of Immigration Statistics,September 2004, http://uscis.gov/graphics/shared/aboutus/statistics/ENF03yrbk/2003ENFtext.pdf (accessed January 27,2005)

were 79,395 criminals removed. Table 3.14 identifies the ten most common categories of crime resulting in removals in FY 2003. Transporting or dealing in dangerous drugs accounted for more than a third (39%) of crimes for which aliens were removed.

Aliens with Communicable Diseases

Aliens with "communicable diseases of public health significance" are not permitted to enter the United States.

In 1990 the U.S. Department of Health and Human Services, as part of the Immigration Act of 1990, declared that tuberculosis and AIDS were a public health threat. In 1993 Congress added HIV (human immunodeficiency virus), the virus that causes AIDS, to the list of grounds for exclusion (denial of an alien's entry into the United States). It was not, however, a legal ground for deportation of immigrants who were already in the country. Illegal aliens bypassed any screening or treatment for communicable diseases.

TUBERCULOSIS. The Centers for Disease Control (CDC) reported 2004 data on U.S. tuberculosis (TB) cases in a March 17, 2005, press release ("Tuberculosis in the United States, 2004," Atlanta, GA: Office of Communication, The Centers for Disease Control, U.S. Department of Health and Human Services). National surveillance showed a significant decline in the case rate of TB. In 2004 a total of 14,511 TB cases were reported in the country, marking the lowest overall TB case rate (4.9 per 100,000 persons) recorded since reporting began in 1953. However, the decline in the case rate from 2003 to 2004 was one of the smallest in more than a decade (3.3% compared with an average of 6.8% per year).

The TB rate among foreign-born individuals (22.5/100,000) was nearly nine times the rate among persons born in the United States (2.6/100,000). Individuals born outside the United States accounted for more than half (7,701 cases, or 53.7%) of all new TB cases in 2004. Of Asians in the United States reported to have TB in 2004, 95% were foreign-born. Among Hispanics in the United States, foreign-born individuals also accounted for the majority (74%) of TB cases.

During the ten-year period from 1993 to 2003, the number of TB cases among those born in the United States dropped from about 17,500 in 1993 to about 7,500 in 2003. The number of TB cases among foreign-born persons showed no decrease during that period. In fact by 2002 there were more cases of TB among the foreign-born than among U.S.-born persons. (See Figure 3.11.) During the same period the incidence of TB cases among the foreign-born spread across the country. In 1993 only the states along the Pacific coast and Hawaii had greater than a 50% incidence rate of TB cases among foreign-born residents. Ten years later nearly half of the states (22) reported 50% or more of TB cases among foreign-born residents. (See Figure 3.12.)

According to the CDC press release, seven states bore more than half the total burden of TB disease by 2004: California, Florida, Georgia, Illinois, New Jersey, New York, and Texas accounted for 59.9% of the national case total. The toll continued to be greatest among minority and foreign-born individuals, who consistently had higher rates of TB. The CDC reported its

FIGURE 3.11

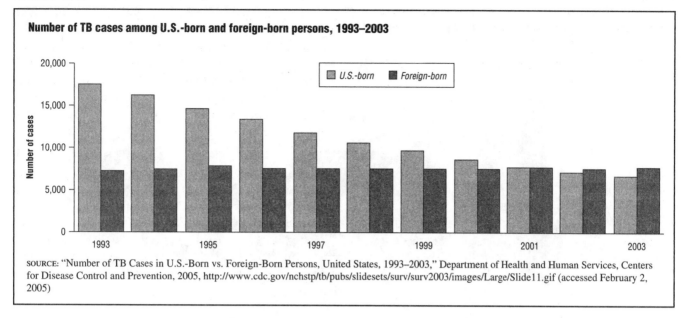

Number of TB cases among U.S.-born and foreign-born persons, 1993–2003

SOURCE: "Number of TB Cases in U.S.-Born vs. Foreign-Born Persons, United States, 1993–2003," Department of Health and Human Services, Centers for Disease Control and Prevention, 2005, http://www.cdc.gov/nchstp/tb/pubs/slidesets/surv/surv2003/images/Large/Slide11.gif (accessed February 2, 2005)

efforts to strengthen global partnerships to combat TB. These efforts included improving overseas screening for immigrants and refugees, and testing recent arrivals from countries with a high-incidence rate of TB infection. CDC was also improving the system that alerted local health departments about the arrival of immigrants who were known or believed to have TB, and collaborating with public health teams in Mexico to improve TB control among those who frequently crossed the U.S.–Mexico border.

HIV. In late 1991, a large number of Haitians fled their country following the military takeover of President Jean-Bertrand Aristide's democratic government. The U.S. Navy and Coast Guard intercepted more than 8,000 Haitian refugees at sea. In 1992 and 1993 another 34,000 refugees were intercepted. Many were returned to Haiti. Some were detained at the U.S. naval base at Guantánamo Bay, Cuba. In 1993 HIV-infected Haitian refugees being detained at Guantánamo Bay held a hunger strike to protest being denied entry to the United States after they were approved for asylum proceedings. On June 8, 1993, a federal judge in New York ordered the U.S. government to release 158 HIV-positive Haitians who had been detained for up to twenty months and permit them to enter the United States.

VISITING THE UNITED STATES
The Visa Waiver Program

Under the Visa Waiver Program (VWP), citizens of certain countries can travel to the United States for tourism or business for ninety days or less without obtaining a visa. Travelers from countries participating in the program can apply for entry to the United States on a passport issued by their country of citizenship. Representatives of the foreign press, radio, film, journalists, or other information media cannot enter the United States on a visa waiver when traveling for professional pursuits. In *Fact Sheet: The Visa Waiver Program and Biometric and Machine-Readable Passport Requirements* (Washington, DC: Department of Homeland Security, 2004), the State Department's Bureau of Consular Affairs estimated that thirteen million visitors each year had entered the United States under the VWP.

The following twenty-seven countries participated in the VWP as of October 2004: Andorra, Australia, Austria, Belgium, Brunei, Denmark, Finland, France, Germany, Iceland, Ireland, Italy, Japan, Liechtenstein, Luxembourg, Monaco, Netherlands, New Zealand, Norway, Portugal, San Marino, Singapore, Slovenia, Spain, Sweden, Switzerland, and the United Kingdom (for citizens with the unrestricted right of permanent abode in England, Scotland, Wales, Northern Ireland, the Channel Islands, and the Isle of Man).

US-VISIT

Congress mandated in the Enhanced Border Security and Visa Entry Reform Act of 2002 (PL 107-173), as amended, that by October 26, 2005, machine-readable, biometric passports (MRP) were required for all visa waiver travelers and children were no longer able to travel on their parents' passports. This deadline required that VWP countries certify that they have programs in place to issue their citizens machine-readable passports that incorporate biometric identifiers and comply with standards established by the International Civil Aviation Organization (ICAO). These new requirements became

FIGURE 3.12

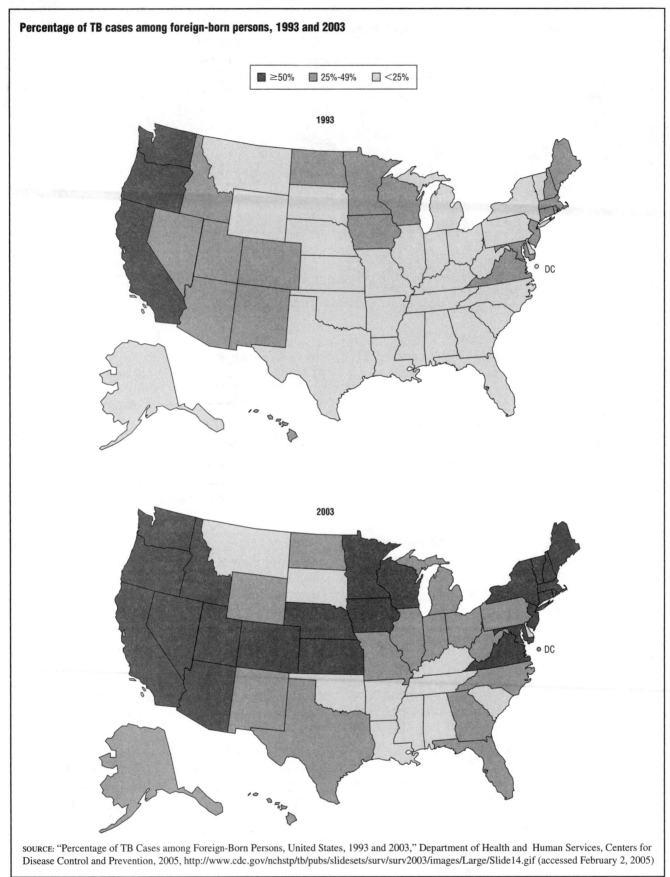

Percentage of TB cases among foreign-born persons, 1993 and 2003

≥50%   25%-49%   <25%

1993

2003

SOURCE: "Percentage of TB Cases among Foreign-Born Persons, United States, 1993 and 2003," Department of Health and Human Services, Centers for Disease Control and Prevention, 2005, http://www.cdc.gov/nchstp/tb/pubs/slidesets/surv/surv2003/images/Large/Slide14.gif (accessed February 2, 2005) part of a program called US-VISIT introduced by the Department of Homeland Security (DHS) to improve border security. The new passport features were developed to allow officials at the ports of entry to more accurately verify the identity of each traveler, to cross-check identities with national and international security watch lists, and to screen for fraudulent documents.

Biometric data, according to the DHS Web site, is a measurable physical characteristic or personal behavioral trait used to recognize the identity or verify the claimed identity of an enrollee. Among the features that can be measured are face, fingerscans, hand geometry, handwriting, iris, retina, vein, and voice. Initially only fingerprint and photo were used.

A machine-readable passport carries encoded biographical data. The size of the passport and photograph, and arrangement of data fields, especially the two lines of data that must be read by an Optical Character Reader, style B (OCR-B), have to meet the standards of the International Civil Aviation Division (Doc 9303, Part 1: Machine-Readable Passports). Biometric technology includes digital, inkless fingerprint scans and digital photographs. According to the DHS, all domestically produced U.S. passports would be biometric passports by the end of 2005. On January 5, 2004, the DHS announced that US-VISIT entry procedures were operational at 115 airports and 14 seaports. Pilot testing of biometric exit procedures (for departing visitors) have begun at one airport and one seaport.

US-VISIT applies to all visitors (with limited exemptions) holding nonimmigrant visas, regardless of country of origin. US-VISIT does not apply to U.S. citizens. Foreign visitors traveling to the United States have their two index fingers scanned and a digital photograph taken to match and authenticate their travel documents at the port of entry. Visas are required for most students, business travelers (depending on their length of stay), and millions of other visitors, regardless of where they lived.

CHAPTER 4
THE REFUGEE INFLUX

Refugees are people, not statistics and global trends. Their protection is a humanitarian necessity, not a political choice.

—Ruud Lubbers, United Nations High Commissioner for Refugees, in a speech before the 55th annual session of the UNHCR Executive Committee, Geneva, Switzerland, October 7, 2004

Every year millions of people around the world are displaced by war, famine, civil unrest, and political unrest. Others are forced to flee their countries in order escape the risk of death and torture at the hands of persecutors. Generally, refugees are people who have been persecuted in their homeland, or have a well-founded fear of persecution there, on account of race, religion, nationality, membership in a particular social group, or political opinion.

The United States has worked with other governmental, international, and private organizations to provide food, health care, and shelter to millions of refugees throughout the world. Resettlement in another country, including the United States, is considered for refugees in urgent need of protection, refugees for whom other long-term solutions were not feasible, and refugees able to join close family members. The United States gives priority to the safe, voluntary return of refugees to their homelands. This policy, recognized in the Refugee Act of 1980, is also the preference of the United Nations High Commissioner for Refugees (UNHCR). If repatriation is not feasible, refugees can be resettled in countries within their geographic region or in more distant countries, such as the United States.

In 2003 the UNHCR referred refugees to twenty-four countries for resettlement. Table 4.1 lists several of those countries and the number of refugees they accepted. The UNHCR noted that the European Union had recently endorsed a plan in support of refugee resettlement that could generate additional interest in participation by European countries.

In March 2005 the UNHCR announced that the number of asylum seekers (includes refugees and asylees in U.S. terms) arriving in industrialized countries fell sharply for the third year in a row, to the lowest level in sixteen years. (See Figure 4.1.) According to the UNHCR (*UNHCR: Asylum Claims Fall to Lowest Level since 1988*, Geneva, Switzerland, March 1, 2004), France became the top receiving country with an estimated 61,600 asylum seekers in 2004, followed by the United States (52,400), the United Kingdom (40,200), Germany (35,600), and Canada (25,500). Leading countries of origin for asylum seekers were the Russian Federation, Serbia and Montenegro, and China. (See Figure 4.2.) The UNHCR noted that asylum seekers from Afghanistan had dropped 82% since 2001, and Iraqi asylum seekers had declined 80% since 2002. (See Figure 4.3.)

WHO IS A REFUGEE?

Before World War II, the U.S. government had no arrangements for admitting people seeking refuge. The only way oppressed people were able to enter the United States was through regular immigration procedures.

After World War II, refugees were admitted through special legislation passed by Congress. The Immigration and Nationality Act of 1952 (INA; PL 82-414) did not specifically mention refugees, but it did allow entry to large groups of people, such as Hungarians after their unsuccessful uprising in 1956, Cubans who left after Fidel Castro's takeover in 1959, and Southeast Asians after the defeat of South Vietnam in 1975.

Refugees were legally recognized for the first time in the Immigration and Nationality Act Amendments of 1965 (PL 89-236) with a preference category reserved for refugees from the Middle East or from countries ruled by a communist government.

TABLE 4.1

Countries participating in UN refugee resettlements, 2003

Resettlement countries	Total	Percent of total admissions
United States	15,588	53.98%
Canada	4,991	17.28%
Australia	4,354	15.08%
Norway	1,391	4.82%
Sweden	805	2.79%
Denmark	518	1.79%
Finland	451	1.56%
New Zealand	443	1.53%
Netherlands	137	.47%
Great Britain	119	.41%
Germany	82	.28%
Other*	219	.76%
Total	**29,098**	**100%**

*Principally to Ireland, Italy, Belgium, Chile, Iceland, Brazil, and Austria.

SOURCE: "Table VIII. UNHCR Resettlement Statistics by Resettlement Country FY 2003," in *Proposed Refugee Admissions for FY 2005: Report to Congress*, Submitted on behalf of The President of the United States to the Committees on the Judiciary, United States Senate and United States House of Representatives in fulfillment of the requirements of Section 207(e) (1)-(7) of the Immigration and Nationality Act, September 2004, http://www.state.gov/documents/organization/36228.pdf (accessed March 1, 2005)

The Refugee Act of 1980

The Refugee Act of 1980 (PL 96-212) changed the definition of the term "refugee," which previously applied only to those fleeing a communist or Middle Eastern nation. The Refugee Act of 1980 adopted the definition of "refugee" contained in the 1951 United Nations Convention Relating to the Status of Refugees and its 1967 Protocol.

The definition of "refugee" found in Section 101(a)(42) of the Immigration and Nationality Act, as amended by the Refugee Act of 1980, is as follows:

The term "refugee" means (A) any person who is outside any country of such person's nationality or, in the case of a person having no nationality, is outside any country in which such person last habitually resided, and who is unable or unwilling to return to, and is unable or unwilling to avail himself or herself of the protection of, that country because of persecution or a well-founded fear of persecution on account of race, religion, nationality, membership in a particular social group, or political opinion, or (B) in such circumstances as the President after appropriate consultation [as defined in Section 207(e) of this Act] may specify, any person who is within the country of such person's nationality or, in the case of a person having no nationality, within the country in which such a person is habitually residing, and who is persecuted or who has a well-founded fear of persecution on account of race, religion, nationality, membership in a particular social group, or political opinion.

The term "refugee" does not include any person who ordered, incited, assisted, or otherwise participated in the persecution of any person on account of race, religion, nationality, membership in a particular social group, or political opinion.

[A] person who has been forced to abort a pregnancy or to undergo involuntary sterilization, or who has been persecuted for failure or refusal to undergo such a procedure or for other resistance to a coercive population control program, shall be deemed to have been persecuted on account of political opinion, and a person who has a well-founded fear that he or she will be

FIGURE 4.1

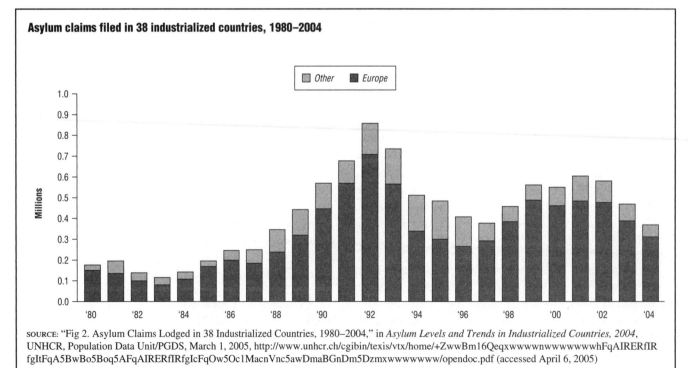

Asylum claims filed in 38 industrialized countries, 1980–2004

SOURCE: "Fig 2. Asylum Claims Lodged in 38 Industrialized Countries, 1980–2004," in *Asylum Levels and Trends in Industrialized Countries, 2004*, UNHCR, Population Data Unit/PGDS, March 1, 2005, http://www.unhcr.ch/cgibin/texis/vtx/home/+ZwwBm16QeqxwwwwnwwwwwwwhFqAIRERfIR fgItFqA5BwBo5Boq5AFqAIRERfIRfgIcFqOw5Oc1MacnVnc5awDmaBGnDm5Dzmxwwwwwww/opendoc.pdf (accessed April 6, 2005)

FIGURE 4.2

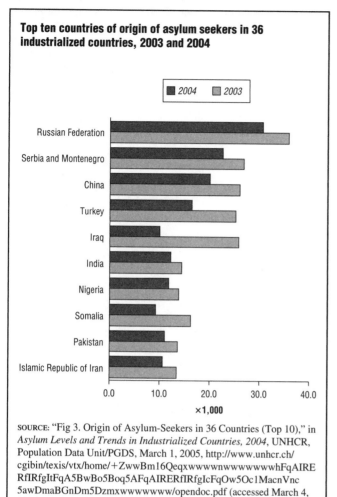

Top ten countries of origin of asylum seekers in 36 industrialized countries, 2003 and 2004

SOURCE: "Fig 3. Origin of Asylum-Seekers in 36 Countries (Top 10)," in *Asylum Levels and Trends in Industrialized Countries, 2004*, UNHCR, Population Data Unit/PGDS, March 1, 2005, http://www.unhcr.ch/cgibin/texis/vtx/home/+ZwwBm16QeqxwwwwnwwwwwwhFqAIRERfIRfgItFqA5BwBo5Boq5AFqAIRERfIRfgIcFqOw5Oc1MacnVnc5awDmaBGnDm5Dzmxwwwwwww/opendoc.pdf (accessed March 4, 2005)

FIGURE 4.3

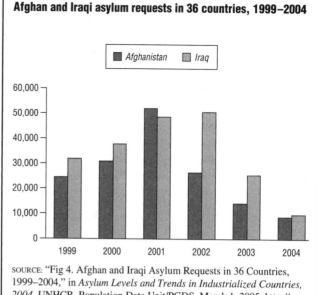

Afghan and Iraqi asylum requests in 36 countries, 1999–2004

SOURCE: "Fig 4. Afghan and Iraqi Asylum Requests in 36 Countries, 1999–2004," in *Asylum Levels and Trends in Industrialized Countries, 2004*, UNHCR, Population Data Unit/PGDS, March 1, 2005, http://www.unhcr.ch/cgi-bin/texis/vtx/home/+ZwwBm16QeqxwwwwnwwwwwwwhFqAIRERfIRfgItFqA5BwBo5Boq5AFqAIRERfIRfgIcFqOw5Oc1MacnVnc5awDmaBGnDm5Dzmxwwwwwww/opendoc.pdf (accessed March 4, 2005)

forced to undergo such a procedure or be subject to persecution for such failure, refusal or resistance shall be deemed to have a well-founded fear of persecution on account of political opinion.

The Refugee Act of 1980 requires the president of the United States, at the beginning of each fiscal year (FY), to determine the number of refugees to be admitted. (The federal fiscal year begins on October 1 and ends on September 30 of the following calendar year. It is identified by the calendar year in which it ends.) Refugee numbers are determined without consideration of any overall immigrant quota. The law also regulates U.S. asylum policy. A refugee is someone who applies for protection while outside the United States; an asylee is someone who is already in the United States when they apply for protection.

The Lautenberg Amendment

Normal procedures require refugees to establish a well-founded fear of persecution on an individual, case-by-case basis. A provision of the Foreign Operations, Export Financing, and Related Programs Appropriations Act of 1990 (PL 101-167), called the Lautenberg Amendment, addresses persecution based on group identity. Applicants are only required to prove that they are members of a protected category (or group) with a credible, but not necessarily individual, fear of persecution (U.S. Department of State, Bureau of Population, Refugees, and Migration, "Refugee Admissions Program for the New Independent States and the Baltics," http://www.state.gov/g/prm/rls/fs/15373.htm, November 19, 2002). In the former Soviet Union, for example, Jews, evangelical Christians, and certain members of the Ukrainian Catholic or Ukrainian Orthodox churches are identified as groups subject to persecution.

Since 1990 the Lautenberg Amendment has been reauthorized each year as a provision of various laws. In FY 2002 it was extended under the Labor, Health and Human Services, and Education Appropriation Act (PL 107-116). As of FY 2004 nearly 470,000 individuals had entered the United States as Lautenberg refugees, representing over 35% of all refugees admitted since 1989 (U.S. Department of State, Bureau of Population, Refugees, and Migration, "Refugee Admissions Program for Europe and Central Asia," http://www.state.gov/g/prm/rls/fs/2004/28215.htm, January 16, 2004).

HOW MANY ARE ADMITTED?

The United States has resettled refugees for more than fifty years. Table 4.2 shows the trends in refugee and asylee admissions from 1946 to 2003. The table

TABLE 4.2

Refugee and asylee admissions, fiscal years 1946–2003, and legislation affecting the flow of refugees and asylees, 1949–2003

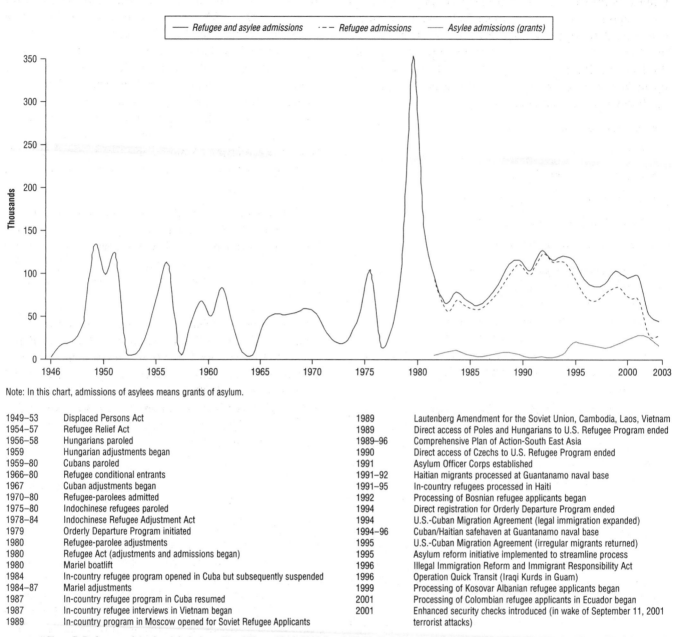

Note: In this chart, admissions of asylees means grants of asylum.

1949–53	Displaced Persons Act
1954–57	Refugee Relief Act
1956–58	Hungarians paroled
1959	Hungarian adjustments began
1959–80	Cubans paroled
1966–80	Refugee conditional entrants
1967	Cuban adjustments began
1970–80	Refugee-parolees admitted
1975–80	Indochinese refugees paroled
1978–84	Indochinese Refugee Adjustment Act
1979	Orderly Departure Program initiated
1980	Refugee-parolee adjustments
1980	Refugee Act (adjustments and admissions began)
1980	Mariel boatlift
1984	In-country refugee program opened in Cuba but subsequently suspended
1984–87	Mariel adjustments
1987	In-country refugee program in Cuba resumed
1987	In-country refugee interviews in Vietnam began
1989	In-country program in Moscow opened for Soviet Refugee Applicants

1989	Lautenberg Amendment for the Soviet Union, Cambodia, Laos, Vietnam
1989	Direct access of Poles and Hungarians to U.S. Refugee Program ended
1989–96	Comprehensive Plan of Action-South East Asia
1990	Direct access of Czechs to U.S. Refugee Program ended
1991	Asylum Officer Corps established
1991–92	Haitian migrants processed at Guantanamo naval base
1991–95	In-country refugees processed in Haiti
1992	Processing of Bosnian refugee applicants began
1994	Direct registration for Orderly Departure Program ended
1994	U.S.-Cuban Migration Agreement (legal immigration expanded)
1994–96	Cuban/Haitian safehaven at Guantanamo naval base
1995	U.S.-Cuban Migration Agreement (irregular migrants returned)
1995	Asylum reform initiative implemented to streamline process
1996	Illegal Immigration Reform and Immigrant Responsibility Act
1996	Operation Quick Transit (Iraqi Kurds in Guam)
1999	Processing of Kosovar Albanian refugee applicants began
2001	Processing of Colombian refugee applicants in Ecuador began
2001	Enhanced security checks introduced (in wake of September 11, 2001 terrorist attacks)

SOURCE: "Chart C. Refugee and Asylee Admissions: Fiscal Years 1946–2003," and "Table D. Major Legislation and Events Affecting the Flow of Refugees and Asylees," in *2003 Yearbook of Immigration Statistics*, U.S. Department of Homeland Security, Office of Immigration Statistics, September 2004, http://uscis .gov/graphics/shared/aboutus/statistics/ RA2003yrbk/2003RA.pdf (accessed March 2, 2005)

below the graph lists major legislation and events that affected the flow of refugees and asylees. Early refugees were admitted under existing immigrant programs or via specially targeted legislation. For example, the Displaced Persons Act of 1948 (PL 80-774) brought 400,000 Eastern Europeans who fled or lost their homes during World War II (*2003 Yearbook of Immigration Statistics*, Washington, DC: Department of Homeland Security, Office of Immigration Statistics, September 2004). Between 1953 and 1956 more than 200,000 arrivals came

from what were called "Iron Curtain" countries under the Refugee Relief Act. With the Soviet invasion of Hungary in 1956, the attorney general's parole authority was used to admit refugees. The largest group admitted under this parole authority was several hundred thousand Indochinese at the fall of South Vietnam in 1975. The Refugee Act of 1980 coupled with that year's exodus of refugees from the Cuban port of Mariel (known as the Mariel Boatlift) created an unprecedented spike in refugee levels in 1981.

Annual Refugee Admissions Limits

Before the start of a new fiscal year, the president, after consultation with Congress, must set the number of refugee admissions for that fiscal year. In a September 2004 report to the congressional Judiciary Committees ("Proposed Refugee Admissions for FY 2005—Report to Congress," http://www.state.gov/g/prm/asst/rl/rpts/36116.htm), President George W. Bush proposed that up to 70,000 refugees be admitted during FY 2005 by the following regional allocations:

- Africa—20,000

- East Asia—13,000

- Europe and Central Asia—9,500

- Latin America and the Caribbean—5,000

- Near East and South Asia—2,500

- Unallocated reserve—20,000

The president specified that the allocation for East Asia was to include Amerasian immigrants and their families. He further specified that refugees of the former Soviet Union (part of the Europe and Central Asia allocation) would include nationals of the former Soviet Union as well as persons having no nationality who were habitual residents of the former Soviet Union prior to September 2, 1991.

An additional 10,000 refugee admissions were to be made available for adjustment to permanent resident status of aliens who had been granted asylum under special provisions. The president's report noted that the 10,000-person statutory limitation on the number of asylees who could adjust their status had resulted in a backlog of adjustment-of-status applications some seventeen years long. According to the *2003 Yearbook of Immigration Statistics*, nearly 22,500 individuals were granted asylum during FY 2003. It was estimated that these asylees from 2003 would not be eligible to apply for U.S. citizenship until at least 2025 if the cap remained at 10,000 adjustments per year.

The 20,000 "unallocated reserve" was to be used, at the discretion of the secretary of state (with notice to the congressional Judiciary Committees), where additional refugee needs arose. The president further authorized persons from the following countries, if otherwise qualified, could be considered refugees for the purpose of admission to the United States: persons in Vietnam; persons in Cuba; persons in the former Soviet Union; and, in exceptional circumstances, persons identified by a U.S. embassy in any location.

Declining Refugee Admissions

In the press release announcing the FY 2005 refugee authorizations (White House, Office of the Press Secretary, "Presidential Determination on FY 2005 Refugee Admissions Numbers," http://www.state.gov/g/prm/refadm/rls/39348.htm, October 1, 2004), the White House noted that security concerns and immigration policy reviews stemming from the September 2001 terrorist attacks had slowed refugee admissions. Admissions for both FY 2002 and FY 2003 were less than 30,000, while refugee admissions for FY 2004 were anticipated to be slightly more than 50,000. Security was not the only issue affecting the predictability of projected admissions. For example, in Africa, relationship fraud had resulted in the disqualification of many previously approved family reunification cases. In the countries of the former Soviet Union, the number of new religious minority group applicants ("Lautenberg Amendment" refugees) and the percentage of those appearing for interviews continued to decline.

Table 4.3 details refugee admissions for FY 2004 by region and country. With a total refugee ceiling of 70,000 admissions available, 52,868 refugees were actually admitted. More than half of the refugees (29,125) came from the African continent with the largest group from Somalia (13,331).

The February 2005 issue of *U.S. Refugee News*, a publication of the State Department's Bureau of Population, Refugees, and Migration, reported that through January 2005 the United States had processed 14,073 admissions for FY 2005. This represented 20% of the 70,000 total admissions authorized for that year. The largest share, 5,655 (40%), came from Africa and 3,919 (27.8%) came from Asia.

GAINING ENTRY INTO THE UNITED STATES

Processing Priority System

The United States has established three priority categories for admitting refugees. These categories were restated and updated by President Bush in his "Proposed Refugee Admissions for FY 2005—Report to Congress." Table 4.4 shows the breakdown of FY 2005 refugee admissions by the three priority groups for each region. Of the total 70,000 admissions, 25,000 were "approved pipeline from FY 2004" or carryover persons already in process.

PRIORITY 1: INDIVIDUAL REFERRALS. This category is reserved for compelling individual protection cases or refugees for whom no other durable solution existed, and who were identified and referred to the program by the United Nations High Commissioner for Refugees (UNHCR), a U.S. embassy, or a nongovernmental organization (NGO). This processing priority is available to persons of any nationality. Historically the United States has resettled approximately 50% of all the UNHCR's resettlement referrals worldwide.

TABLE 4.3

Refugee admissions for fiscal year 2004 (October 1, 2003–September 30, 2004)

Country of chargeability	Refugee admissions ceiling	FY total admitted into U.S. as of report
Africa	30,000	
Angola		20
Burundi		276
Cameroon		1
Central Africa		24
Chad		4
Congo		73
Congo, Democratic Republic of		569
Djibouti		6
Eritrea		128
Ethiopia		2,710
Gambia		3
Ghana		1
Liberia		7,140
Nigeria		34
Rwanda		176
Sierra Leone		1,084
Somalia		13,331
Sudan		3,500
Togo		35
Uganda		8
Zambia		2
Total Africa	**30,000**	**29,125**
East Asia	8,500	
Burma		1,056
Cambodia		3
China		3
Indonesia		5
Laos		6,005
Vietnam		1,007
Total East Asia	**8,500**	**8,079**
Europe & Central Asia	13,000	
Albania		2
Bosnia		244
Croatia		92
Serbia		143
Yugoslavia		8
Subtotal Europe		**489**
Armenia		88
Azerbaijan		407
Belarus		659
Estonia		27
Georgia		33
Kazakhstan		312
Kyrgyzstan		100
Latvia		52
Lithuania		13
Moldova		1,711
Russia		1,446
Tajikistan		2
Turkmenistan		7
Ukraine		3,482
Uzbekistan		426
Subtotal NIS		**8,765**
Total Europe & Central Asia	**13,000**	**9,254**

TABLE 4.3

Refugee admissions for fiscal year 2004 (October 1, 2003–September 30, 2004) [CONTINUED]

Country of chargeability	Refugee admissions ceiling	FY total admitted into U.S. as of report
Latin America & Caribbean	3,600	
Colombia		577
Costa Rica		1
Cuba		2,959
Ecuador		2
Haiti		17
Total Latin America & Caribbean	**3,600**	**3,556**
Near East & South Asia	3,000	
Afghanistan		959
Algeria		1
Egypt		3
India		1
Iran		1,787
Iraq		66
Kuwait		14
Lebanon		2
Nepal		1
Pakistan		11
Sri Lanka		1
Yemen		8
Total Near East & South Asia	**3,000**	**2,854**
Unallocated reserve	11,900	
Grand total	**70,000**	**52,868**

SOURCE: Adapted from "Summary of Refugee Admissions for Fiscal Year 2004," U.S. Department of State, Bureau of Population, Refugees, and Migration, October 1, 2004, http://www.state.gov/documents/organization/37128.pdf (accessed February 3, 2005).

PRIORITY 2: GROUP REFERRALS. This category is used for groups of special humanitarian concern to the United States who are designated for resettlement processing. It includes specific groups (within certain nationalities, clans, or ethnic groups) identified by the Department of State in consultation with U.S. Citizenship and Immigration Services (USCIS), NGOs, the UNHCR, and other experts. Some Priority 2 groups are processed in their countries of origin, including:

- Former Soviet Union—Jews, evangelical Christians, and Ukrainian Catholic and Orthodox religious activists identified in the Lautenberg Amendment who had close family in the United States.

- Cuba—members of persecuted religious minorities, human rights activists, former political prisoners, forced-labor conscripts (1965–68), persons deprived of their professional credentials or subjected to other disproportionately harsh or discriminatory treatment resulting from their perceived or actual political or religious beliefs or activities, and persons who experienced or feared harm because of their family or social relationship to someone who falls under one of the preceding categories.

- Vietnam—persons eligible under the former Orderly Departure Program (ODP), and Resettlement Opportunity for Vietnamese Returnees (ROVR) programs; also included are Amerasian immigrants, whose numbers are counted in the refugee ceiling.

- For FY 2005 the following new Priority 2 groups were added—Meskhetian Turks in Russia; Hmong Lao at Wat Tham Krabok in Thailand; Iranian religious minorities, primarily in Austria; Vietnamese in

TABLE 4.4

Proposed refugee regional ceilings by priority, FY 2005

Africa

Approved pipeline from FY 2004	9,000
Priority 1 individual referrals	2,500
Priority 2 groups	5,000
Priority 3 family reunification refugees	3,500
Total proposed:	**20,000**

East Asia

Approved pipeline from FY 2004	8,000
Priority 1 individual referrals	4,000
Priority 2 groups	1,000
Total proposed:	**13,000**

Europe/Central Asia

Approved pipeline from FY 2004	4,000
Priority 1 individual referrals	100
Priority 2 groups	5,400
Total proposed:	**9,500**

Latin America/Caribbean

Approved pipeline from FY 2004	3,000
Priority 1 individual referrals	700
Priority 2 groups	1,200
Priority 3 family reunification refugees	100
Total proposed:	**5,000**

Near East/South Asia

Approved pipeline from FY 2004	1,000
Priority 1 individual referrals	400
Priority 2 groups	1,000
Priority 3 family reunification refugees	100
Total proposed:	**2,500**
Unallocated reserve	20,000
Total proposed ceiling:	**70,000**

SOURCE: "Table II. Proposed FY 2005 Regional Ceilings by Priority," in *Proposed Refugee Admissions for FY 2005: Report to Congress*, Submitted on behalf of The President of the United States to the Committees on the Judiciary, United States Senate and United States House of Representatives in fulfillment of the requirements of Section 207(e) (1)-(7) of the Immigration and Nationality Act, Department of State, U.S. Department of Homeland Security, Department of Health and Human Services, September 2004, http://www.state.gov/documents/organization/36228.pdf (accessed March 1, 2005).

the Philippines; Somali Benadir in Kenya; Burundians in Tanzania; Somali group in Uganda; and Liberian groups in Ghana and Guinea.

- Additional populations under active consideration for group designation in FY 2005 included Bhutanese in Nepal; Kunama in Ethiopia; Ethiopians in Yemen; and Burmese in camps along the Thai border.

PRIORITY 3: FAMILY REUNIFICATION CASES. In FY 2005, eligibility for a refugee interview was extended to nationals of fourteen countries (Burma, Burundi, Congo [Brazzaville], Colombia, Cuba, Democratic Republic of Congo [DRC], Eritrea, Ethiopia, Haiti, Iran, Liberia, Rwanda, Somalia, and Sudan) who were the spouses, unmarried children under twenty-one, or parents of persons granted asylum, admitted to the United States as refugees, or persons who were lawful permanent residents or U.S. citizens and were initially admitted to the United States as refugees or granted asylum.

TABLE 4.5

Refugee-status applications filed and approved by top 20 nationalities, fiscal year 2003

Nationality	Refugee applications filed	Refugee applications approved
All nationalities	**42,705**	**25,329**
Ukraine	7,654	4,612
Cuba	4,963	1,599
Somalia	3,739	1,331
Ethiopia	2,937	1,311
Russia	2,895	1,894
Moldova	2,606	1,575
Sierra Leone	2,237	1,430
Vietnam	2,032	1,772
Bosnia-Herzegovina	1,819	1,145
Iran	1,784	1,755
Sudan	1,739	1,609
Afghanistan	1,318	1,031
Belarus	1,228	737
Azerbaijan	1,131	907
Liberia	1,124	981
Iraq	759	147
Uzbekistan	419	280
Kazakhstan	417	255
Congo, Democratic Republic	353	90
Burma	242	227
Other	1,309	641

SOURCE: "Table E. Refugee-Status Applications Filed and Approved by Top 20 Nationalities, Fiscal Year 2003," in *2003 Yearbook of Immigration Statistics*, U.S. Department of Homeland Security, Office of Immigration Statistics, September 2004, http://uscis.gov/graphics/shared/aboutus/statistics/RA2003yrbk/2003RA.pdf (accessed March 2, 2005)

Refugees in the United States

According to the *2003 Yearbook of Immigration Statistics*, a publication of the Department of Homeland Security's Office of Immigration Statistics, 42,705 individuals applied for refugee status in the United States in FY 2003. Of these, 59% (25,329) were approved. Table 4.5 shows the top twenty countries of origin for refugee applications in FY 2003. The Ukraine accounted for 18% of all applications filed and applications approved. Cuba, on the other hand, with the second-highest number of applications, represented 11.6% of all applications filed but just 6.3% of all those approved. Of the 28,134 refugees who actually arrived in the United States in FY 2003, 31% were from countries such as the Ukraine, Russia, Belarus, Azerbaijan, Uzbekistan, and Kazakhstan, all part of the former Soviet Union. (See Table 4.6.)

The greatest share of refugees (14.9%) settled in California. As might be expected, New York and Texas were popular choices with 8.0% and 5.5% of refugees. Washington was the second most popular choice, however, receiving 9.8% of refugees. Minnesota attracted 6.2%. (See Table 4.7.)

Those Granted Lawful Permanent Residence

For a refugee or an asylee to adjust to permanent resident status, he or she must have lived in the United States for at least one year. From 1946 through 2003

TABLE 4.6

Refugee arrivals by top ten countries of origin, 2003

Country	Number of refugees	Percent of total refugees
Former Soviet Union	8,728	31.0%
Liberia	2,915	10.4%
Former Yugoslavia	2,500	8.9%
Iran	2,428	8.6%
Sudan	2,090	7.4%
Somalia	1,708	6.1%
Ethiopia	1,669	5.9%
Vietnam*	1,461	5.2%
Afghanistan	1,446	5.1%
Sierra Leone	1,350	4.8%
All Other	1,839	6.6%
Total	**28,134**	

*Includes 67 Amerasians

SOURCE: Adapted from "Table VI. Refugee Arrivals by Country of Origin, FY 2003," in *Proposed Refugee Admissions for FY 2005: Report to Congress*, Submitted on behalf of The President of the United States to the Committees on the Judiciary, United States Senate and United States House of Representatives in fulfillment of the requirements of Section 207(e) (1)-(7) of the Immigration and Nationality Act, Department of State, U.S. Department of Homeland Security, Department of Health and Human Services, September 2004, http://www.state.gov/g/prm/asst/rl/rpts/36116 .htm#table5 (accessed March 1, 2005)

TABLE 4.7

Refugee arrivals by state of initial resettlement, FY 2003

State	Refugee arrivals	Amerasian arrivals	Total arrivals to state	Percentage of total arrivals
Alabama	46	0	46	0.16%
Alaska	28	0	28	0.10%
Arizona	967	0	967	3.44%
Arkansas	4	0	4	0.01%
California	4,166	12	4,178	14.85%
Colorado	472	0	472	1.68%
Connecticut	204	1	205	0.73%
Delaware	36	0	36	1.13%
District of Columbia	107	0	107	0.38%
Florida	911	7	918	3.26%
Georgia	1,080	4	1,084	3.85%
Hawaii	15	0	15	0.05%
Idaho	257	0	257	0.91%
Illinois	936	0	936	3.33%
Indiana	262	0	262	0.93%
Iowa	220	7	227	0.81%
Kansas	99	0	99	0.35%
Kentucky	314	0	314	1.12%
Louisiana	77	0	77	0.27%
Maine	105	0	105	0.37%
Maryland	786	0	786	2.79%
Massachusetts	807	0	807	2.87%
Michigan	443	5	448	1.59%
Minnesota	1,749	0	1,749	6.22%
Mississippi	3	0	3	0.01%
Missouri	437	4	441	1.57%
Montana	34	0	34	0.12%
Nebraska	211	0	211	0.75%
Nevada	185	0	185	0.66%
New Hampshire	240	0	240	0.85%
New Jersey	562	0	562	2.00%
New Mexico	27	0	27	0.10%
New York	2,239	5	2,244	7.98%
North Carolina	576	4	580	2.06%
North Dakota	105	0	105	0.37%
Ohio	655	0	655	2.33%
Oklahoma	54	6	60	0.21%
Oregon	789	0	789	2.80%
Pennsylvania	1,227	0	1,227	4.36%
Rhode Island	129	0	129	0.46%
South Carolina	110	0	110	0.39%
South Dakota	159	0	159	0.57%
Tennessee	451	0	451	1.60%
Texas	1,520	12	1,532	5.45%
Utah	400	0	400	1.42%
Vermont	78	0	78	0.28%
Virginia	796	0	796	2.83%
Washington	2,750	0	2,750	9.77%
West Virginia	2	0	2	0.01%
Wisconsin	236	0	236	0.84%
Wyoming	1	0	1	0.00%
Total	**28,067**	**67**	**28,134**	**100.0%**

Note: Arrival figures do not reflect secondary migration.

SOURCE: "Table V. Refugee Arrivals by State of Initial Resettlement, FY 2003," in *Proposed Refugee Admissions for Fiscal Year 2005: Report to Congress*, Submitted on behalf of The President of the United States to the Committees on the Judiciary, United States Senate and United States House of Representatives in fulfillment of the requirements of Section 207(e) (1)-(7) of the Immigration and Nationality Act, Department of State, U.S. Department of Homeland Security, Department of Health and Human Services, September 2004, http://www.state.gov/documents/organization/ 36228.pdf (accessed March 1, 2005)

more than 3.7 million refugees and asylees were granted lawful permanent resident status. (See Table 4.8.)

EAST ASIAN REFUGEES

President Bush's September 2004 *Proposed Refugee Admissions for FY 2005—Report to Congress* included information on recent refuge programs in Southeast Asia. In FY 2004 Thailand continued to host the largest population of refugees in East Asia. More than 140,000 Burmese, mostly ethnic minorities, were recognized by the UNHCR and lived in nine Thai-administered refugee camps along the Thai–Burma border. In FY 2004, at the request of the Thai government, some 15,500 Lao Hmong at Wat Tham Krabok and several thousand urban Burmese were expeditiously processed for resettlement in the United States.

As of June 2004 nearly one hundred Vietnamese Montagnards had sought UNHCR protection—more than eighty in Cambodia and others in Thailand. Most were referred to the United States for resettlement. Over 19,000 Burmese Muslim Rohingyas remained in two UNHCR camps in southern Bangladesh. From 1995 to 2005 more than 200,000 of this group had repatriated to Burma.

In April 2004 the U.S. and Philippine governments announced plans for the majority of a group of some 1,885 Vietnamese longstayers in the Philippines to be considered for possible resettlement in the United States. The Philippine government agreed to make efforts to regularize the status of those not approved for the U.S. program.

In 2003 Malaysia became the largest UNHCR refugee status determination operation in the world. From January 2003 to April 2004 the UNHCR registered 18,092 persons of concern. They included asylum seekers

TABLE 4.8

Refugees and asylees granted lawful permanent resident status by region, fiscal years 1946–2003

Region and country of birth	Total	1946–50	1951–60	1961–70	1971–80	1981–90	1991–2000	2002	2003
All countries	**3,772,411**	**213,347**	**492,371**	**212,843**	**539,447**	**1,013,620**	**1,021,266**	**126,084**	**44,927**
Europe	1,513,325	211,983	456,146	55,235	71,858	155,512	426,565	62,911	17,290
Asia	1,379,836	1,106	33,422	19,895	210,683	712,092	351,347	21,414	9,885
Africa	112,146	20	1,768	5,486	2,991	22,149	51,649	13,454	7,723
Oceania	523	7	75	21	37	22	291	33	18
North America	752,825	163	831	132,068	252,633	121,840	185,333	26,807	8,454
Caribbean	708,540	3	6	131,557	251,825	114,213	154,235	25,706	7,547
Central America	40,795	*	*	4	289	6,973	30,582	974	806
South America	12,992	32	74	123	1,244	1,986	5,857	1,222	1,518
Unknown or not reported	764	36	55	15	*	19	224	243	39

*Disclosure standards not met.

SOURCE: Adapted from "Table 21. Refugees and Asylees Granted Lawful Permanent Resident Status by Region and Selected Country of Birth, Fiscal Years 1946–2003," in *2003 Yearbook of Immigration Statistics*, U.S. Department of Homeland Security, Office of Immigration Statistics, September 2004, http://uscis.gov/graphics/shared/aboutus/statistics/RA2003yrbk/2003RA.pdf (accessed March 2, 2005)

from Burma—mainly Chin, Rohingyas, and other Burmese Muslims—and Acehnese from Indonesia. The UNHCR estimated that more than 2,000 persons would be in need of resettlement from Malaysia in 2005 and was preparing referrals of some 1,000 Burmese Chin to the U.S. program. Indonesia continued to host a number of asylum seekers from East Asia and elsewhere.

AFRICAN REFUGEES

According to the president's *Proposed Refugee Admissions for FY 2005—Report to Congress*, there was cause for optimism on several fronts across Africa. Thanks to progress made toward resolution of several long-term conflicts on the continent, repatriations organized by the United Nations (UN) were underway in Angola, Eritrea, Rwanda, Sierra Leone, and parts of Somalia. Similar operations were under discussion for Burundi, Liberia, Sudan, and parts of Democratic Republic of Congo (DRC). In all, nearly 300,000 African refugees returned to their countries of origin in 2004. At the same time, fresh violence occurred in eastern DRC, the Darfur region of Sudan, western Ethiopia, and Ivory Coast, creating new refugee flows or threatening refugees in their countries of first asylum. There were approximately 3.2 million refugees across the African continent, more than 30% of the worldwide population of refugees and asylum seekers.

REFUGEES FROM THE NEAR EAST AND SOUTH ASIA

Although the Near East (an area often considered to consist of countries in southeastern Europe, northwestern Africa, and southwestern Asia) and South Asia regions have the largest number of the world's refugees, countries within these regions have historically taken in refugees from neighboring countries. The majority of refugees have been Iraqi, Iranian, and Afghan nationals. According to the

U.S. Department of State, between 1980 and 2002 more than 133,000 refugees from Near East and South Asian countries resettled in the United States (U.S. Department of State, Bureau of Population, Refugees, and Migration, "Refugee Admissions Program for Near East and South Asia," http://www.state.gov/g/prm/rls/fs/15496.htm, November 25, 2002). Most came from Iraq (36,000), Iran (about 58,000), and Afghanistan (33,000).

By 2004 the Near East and South Asia regions remained host to the majority of the world's refugee population—some 6.5 million people, primarily Afghans, Palestinians, and Iraqis. The UNHCR, the International Committee for the Red Cross (ICRC), the United Nations Relief and Works Agency (UNRWA), and other humanitarian organizations worked with refugees in the region. Despite the voluntary return of some three million Afghan refugees from countries of asylum since November 2001, the government of Pakistan may need to indefinitely host some of the remaining Afghan population, who have been resident there for many years. Other countries in the region have provided long-term asylum for Tibetan, Bhutanese, Sri Lankan, and Iraqi refugees. Refugees identified by the UNHCR for resettlement in the region included Afghans in Pakistan, Iran, and India; Afghans and Iranians in Turkey; and some particularly vulnerable Iraqis throughout the region.

REFUGEES FROM THE FORMER SOVIET UNION AND EASTERN EUROPE

On December 21, 1991, the Union of Soviet Socialist Republics (USSR, or the Soviet Union) was dissolved. The fifteen USSR republics became independent countries. These countries were also referred to as the Newly Independent States (Armenia, Azerbaijan, Belarus, Georgia, Kazakhstan, Kyrgyzstan, Moldova, Russia, Tajikistan, Turkmenistan, Ukraine, and Uzbekistan) and the Baltics (Estonia, Latvia, and Lithuania).

Unfortunately, the chaos and turmoil in the new republics led to ethnic conflict, increased anti-Semitism, and persecution of certain Christian groups. On July 1, 2002, about 2,300 Baku Armenians in Russia received Priority 2 status for admission to the United States (*2002 Yearbook of Immigration Statistics*, Washington, DC: Department of Homeland Security, Office of Immigration Statistics, 2003). This group of displaced ethnic Armenians evacuated from Azerbaijan between 1988 and 1992 but was never permanently resettled. The president proposed that 14,000 people from the former Soviet Union be admitted to the United States in FY 2003, of which 11,500 were "Lautenberg-eligible cases."

Kosovo

From the beginning of January to late May of 1999, Serbian forces and the Yugoslav military expelled more than 780,000 ethnic Albanians from the Serbian province of Kosovo in a campaign of ethnic cleansing. In the largest European refugee exodus since the Bosnian war (1992–95), the homeless Kosovars fled to Albania (about 442,000), Macedonia (250,000), Montenegro (70,000), and Bosnia-Herzegovina (21,700). The ethnic Albanians had accounted for 90% of the Kosovar population.

In April 1999 the U.S. government offered to relocate as many as 20,000 Kosovar refugees to the United States. The priority lists consisted of those with families in America as well as persons in vulnerable circumstances. About 14,000 Kosovar refugees resettled in the United States.

In June 1999 the Yugoslav government accepted a peace agreement following seventy-eight days of NATO (North Atlantic Treaty Organization) bombing of military installations and other facilities throughout Serbia. To encourage refugees to return to Kosovo once the crisis was resolved, the U.S. Department of State funded the trip for those who left the United States before May 1, 2000. About 2,600 returned to their home country.

LATIN AMERICAN AND CARIBBEAN REFUGEES

The majority of refugee admissions from Latin America and the Caribbean have been from Cuba. Admission of Cubans as refugees is governed by the U.S.–Cuba Bilateral Migration Agreement, in effect since September 9, 1994. The United States agreed that a minimum of 20,000 Cubans could lawfully migrate to the United States each year. Cuba, on the other hand, took measures to prevent its citizens from embarking on unsafe journeys to reach the United States.

According to the president's *Proposed Refugee Admissions for FY 2005—Report to Congress*, the UNHCR estimated that as of January 1, 2004, the total number of refugees, asylum-seekers, and other people of concern in Latin America and the Caribbean was close to

1.5 million. Of those, about 48,000 were Colombians who had fled the continuing conflict in their country. As many as 2.1 million more were displaced within Colombia. Among the other nationals seeking refuge in 2003 were 30,000 Cubans and close to 26,000 Haitians. The UNHCR was helping to establish procedures for granting asylum in a number of countries in the region with large refugee populations, including Venezuela, Panama, the Dominican Republic, and Peru.

SEEKING ASYLUM

Like a refugee, an asylee (a person seeking asylum) is someone who wants refuge in another country, for example, the United States. The only difference is the location of the alien when he or she applies for refuge: a refugee is outside the United States when applying for refuge, while an asylee is already in the United States, perhaps on an expired tourist visa or at a port of entry. Just like a refugee applying for entrance into the country, an asylee seeks the protection of the United States because of persecution or a well-founded fear of persecution.

Asylees in the United States include sailors who jumped ship while their boat was docked in a U.S. port, athletes who ask for asylum while participating in a sports event, or women who base their claim on a fear of being compelled to undergo a coercive population-control measure. Any alien physically present in the United States or at a port of entry can request asylum in the United States. It is irrelevant whether the person is a legal or illegal alien. Like refugees, asylum applicants do not count against the worldwide annual U.S. limitation of immigrants.

Asylum Applications Exceeded Annual Limits

Thousands of people apply for asylum in the United States every year, but under the Immigration Act of 1990, only 10,000 asylees per year can be granted lawful permanent resident status. Moreover, they must be in the country for one year after being granted asylee status. Critics charge that many people seek asylum in the United States to avoid dismal economic conditions at home rather than the legitimate reasons to seek asylum under U.S. law: to escape political or religious persecution, or due to a well-founded fear of death. In addition, some illegal aliens try to obtain the legal right to work by filing for asylum. Unlike illegal aliens, asylees are legally permitted to work under certain circumstances.

How Many Asylees?

In FY 2003 the USCIS received 42,112 applications for asylum. More than one-fifth (9,175) were filed in the Miami office. During FY 2003, 15,470 individuals were granted asylum and 2,582 individuals were denied. Most

TABLE 4.9

Asylum cases filed with USCIS asylum officers, by asylum office, FY 2003

Asylum office and state of residence	Cases filed during year[a]	Cases reopened during year[b]	Cases granted during year	Percent approved	Individuals granted asylum during year	Cases denied during year
Total	42,114	4,158	11,434	29	15,470	1,539
Asylum office:						
Arlington	5,859	370	2,182	52	2,718	110
Chicago	3,480	276	700	21	990	220
Houston	1,948	111	255	12	397	210
Los Angeles	8,027	685	2,033	22	2,544	360
Miami	9,175	525	2,639	34	4,203	247
New York	3,807	677	697	18	841	56
Newark	4,475	800	824	20	1,101	145
San Francisco	5,343	714	2,104	43	2,676	191

Asylum office and state of residence	Individuals denied asylum during year	Cases referred to immigration judge, past filing deadline[c]	Cases otherwise closed during year[d]	Cases referred to immigration judge, not interviewed	Cases referred to immigration judge, interviewed
Total	2,582	11,221	45,005	3,055	15,262
Asylum office:					
Arlington	155	703	5,708	88	1,229
Chicago	329	987	1,423	631	1,420
Houston	313	565	2,421	238	1,035
Los Angeles	561	3,975	16,910	922	2,740
Miami	603	1,673	6,365	429	3,290
New York	101	1,077	4,633	133	2,059
Newark	206	1,328	2,657	41	1,825
San Francisco	314	913	4,888	573	1,664

[a]Cases filed and reopened in the same year are included only with cases filed.
[b]Cases reopened that were filed in a prior fiscal year.
[c]These cases referred because they were filed after the applicants had been in the United States for a year.
[d]Include ABC interview no show cases.
Note: USCIS represents U.S. Citizenship and Immigration Services

SOURCE: Adapted from "Table 19. Asylum Cases Filed with USCIS Asylum Officers by Asylum Office and State of Residence, FY 2003," in *2003 Yearbook of Immigration Statistics*, U.S. Department of Homeland Security, Office of Immigration Statistics, September 2004, http://uscis.gov/graphics/shared/aboutus/ statistics/RA2003yrbk/2003RA.pdf (accessed March 2, 2005)

other cases were referred to an immigration judge, or were closed for various reasons. (See Table 4.9.)

Filing Claims

A claim for asylum can be filed through an affirmative process or through a defensive process. In general, the affirmative asylum seeker is a person who mailed an application to U.S. Citizenship and Immigration Services within one year from the date of last arrival in the United States.

Defensive asylum seekers are those who requested asylum as a defense against being removed from the country. In general, aliens can be placed into defensive asylum processing in one of two ways:

• they are referred to an immigration judge by asylum officers who did not grant them asylum, or

• they are placed in expedited removal proceedings because they were (1) undocumented or in violation of their status when apprehended in the United States, or (2) caught trying to enter the country without proper documentation (usually at a port of entry) and were found to have a credible fear of persecution or torture.

Expedited Removal

Under the expedited removal provisions of the 1996 Illegal Immigration Reform and Immigrant Responsibility Act (IIRIRA), any alien subject to expedited removal due to fraud, misrepresentation, or a lack of valid documents has to be questioned by an immigration officer regarding the fear of persecution at home. If the alien expresses such a fear, they are detained until an asylum officer can determine the credibility of the fear. Aliens found to have a credible fear are referred to an immigration judge for a final determination and are generally released until their case is heard. In some cases the alien is detained while his or her case is pending before an immigration judge. If the fear is deemed not credible, the alien is refused admission and removed.

Critics charge that the expedited removal process denies aliens a fair chance to fully present their asylum claims, places unprecedented authority in the hands of asylum officers, is conducted so quickly that mistakes are inevitable, limits an alien's right to review of a deportation order, and results in the wrongful expulsion of individuals with legitimate fears of persecution.

An alien who is deported under the expedited removal process is barred from returning to the United States for five years.

ASYLUM REFORM

In *The Coming Conflict over Asylum: Does America Need a New Asylum Policy?* (Washington, DC: Center for Immigration Studies, March 2002), Don Barnett described the U.S. asylum system in the early 1990s as being overwhelmed by frivolous applications. Most were turned down, but most of the rejected applicants remained in the country, either disappearing completely or filing appeals that proceeded slowly through the system while the individual sought some other way to gain permanent residence status. "It was an open secret around the globe that claiming asylum was a means of immigrating to America," Barnett wrote.

In 1995 and 1996 laws were passed in an effort to reform the system. The new expedited removal process and the detention of asylum seekers for long periods generated considerable controversy and calls for reform. In August 2001 the Refugee Protection Act (S 1311) was introduced in the Senate. It is described as "a bill to amend the Immigration and Nationality Act to reaffirm the [nation's] historic commitment to protecting refugees who are fleeing persecution or torture." Since September 11, 2001, however, protection of refugees has not been a national priority, and as of June 2005 the Refugee Protection Act had failed to advance.

Post 9/11 Asylum Policies

In August 2002 U.S. Attorney General John Ashcroft ordered changes within the Board of Immigration Appeals (BIA). At that time, the BIA had a backlog of 56,000 cases pending processing. While most Immigration and Naturalization Services (INS) functions shifted to the Department of Homeland Security (DHS) on March 1, 2003, the BIA remained under the jurisdiction of the Department of Justice.

CRITERIA FOR GRANTING ASYLUM

Under the Immigration and Nationality Act, as amended, a person can be granted asylum only if he or she established a well-founded fear of persecution on account of one of five protected grounds: race, religion, nationality, membership in a particular social group, or political opinion. Some people charged that the United States constantly changed its definition of what constituted "membership in a particular social group" to accommodate the growing number of asylum-seekers. The Refugee Act of 1980 defined a social group as comprised of persons "all of whom share a common characteristic that is either immutable [not susceptible

to change], or should not be required to change because it is fundamental to their individual identities and consciences."

For example, Somali clan membership has been defined as social group membership, although the INS noted that "mere membership in a clan will not be sufficient to establish refugee status unless the applicant can establish special circumstances that would justify the conclusion that all members of the clan are threatened with persecution."

Those who believed the term should be interpreted broadly argued that the intent of the law was to provide a catch-all to include all the types of persecution that can occur. Those with a narrow view saw the law as a means of identifying and protecting individuals from known forms of harm, not in anticipation of future types of abuse.

Persecution Based on Gender and Sexual Orientation

As the United States and the world became more aware of persecution based on gender and sexual orientation, victims came to be considered members of a "social group." The UNHCR issued a formal statement that declared states "are free to adopt the interpretation that women asylum-seekers who face harsh or inhumane treatment due to their having transgressed the social mores of the society in which they live may be considered as a 'particular social group'" (*Guidelines on International Protection: Gender-Related Persecution within the Context of Article 1A(2) of the 1951 Convention and/or its 1967 Protocol Relating to the Status of Refugees*, Washington, DC: United Nations High Commissioner for Refugees, May 7, 2002). For example, the Presidential Advisory Council on HIV/AIDS (PACHA) recommended that the INS should "grant stays of deportation . . . and asylum based on the social group of HIV-positive individuals" (PACHA Recommendation II.D.4, http://www.pacha.gov/actions/recommendations/Discrimination/IID4/iid4.html, December 8, 1995).

On August 24, 2000, the U.S. Court of Appeals for the Ninth Circuit, in *Hernandez-Montiel v. INS* (No. 98-70582), ruled that "gay men with female sexual identities" constituted a "particular social group" eligible for asylum and withholding of deportation.

In 1994, nineteen-year-old Fauziya Kasinga fled her native Togo to escape genital mutilation. When she arrived in the United States, she asked for asylum and was held in a detention center for sixteen months waiting for her case to be heard by the Board of Immigration Appeals. In June 1996 (*In re Fauziya Kasinga*, A 73 479 695), she became the first individual granted asylum on the basis of gender persecution.

VICTIMS OF TRAFFICKING AND VIOLENCE

The Trafficking Victims Protection Act of 2000 (TVPA; PL 106-386) makes victims of severe forms of trafficking eligible for benefits and services to the same extent as refugees. In addition, the law attempts to identify and prosecute traffickers. Traffickers force their victims into the international sex trade, prostitution, slavery, and forced labor through coercion, threats of physical violence, psychological abuse, torture, and imprisonment. The United Nations estimates that trafficking generated $7-10 billion annually for traffickers (Sara L. Gottovi, "Sex Trafficking of Minors: International Crisis, Federal Response," *Child Protection, Exploitation, and Obscenity,* vol. 52, no. 2, March 2004).

Trafficking victims who meet requirements can be authorized to remain temporarily in the United States as potential witnesses. Victims can also apply for a T visa, which will allow them to remain for three years and then apply for lawful permanent residence. Victims who are age eighteen and over have to be certified by the U.S. Department of Health and Human Services (HHS). To receive a certification, adult victims have to make a bona fide application for a T visa or be an individual whose continued presence is necessary to assist the Attorney General in prosecuting traffickers. Child victims under age eighteen do not require certification.

The Trafficking Victims Protection Reauthorization Act of 2003 (TVPRA; PL 108-179) mandates informational awareness campaigns and created a new civil action provision that allowed victims to sue their traffickers in federal district court. It also requires an annual report to Congress on the results of U.S. government activities to combat trafficking.

Visa Applications and Prosecutions Related to Trafficking

According to the *Assessment of U.S. Government Activities to Combat Trafficking in Persons 2004* (Washington, DC: U.S. Department of Justice, June 2004), in FY 2003 there were 601 applications for T visas filed: 297 approved, 30 denied, and the rest were pending. In fiscal years 2001 through 2003 the Department of Justice and U.S. Attorney's Office initiated prosecution of 110 traffickers and secured 78 convictions and/or guilty pleas.

The June 2004 *Trafficking in Persons Report* issued by the Department of State estimates that 800,000 to 900,000 persons, primarily women and children, were trafficked across international borders annually. Approximately 18,000 to 20,000 of those victims were trafficked into the United States along with an unknown number of men.

Monitoring Foreign Governments

The Trafficking Victims Protection Act of 2000 (TVPA) and the Trafficking Victims Protection Reauthorization Act of 2003 (TVPRA) require the U.S.

TABLE 4.10

Tier placements, trafficking in persons, 2004

Tier 1

Australia	France	Macedonia	Spain
Austria	Germany	Morocco	Sweden
Belgium	Ghana	The Netherlands	Taiwan
Canada	Hong Kong	New Zealand	United Kingdom
Colombia	Italy	Norway	
Czech Republic	Republic of Korea	Poland	
Denmark	Lithuania	Portugal	

Tier 2

Afghanistan	Cameroon	Kyrgyz Republic	Saudi Arabia
Albania	Chile	Latvia	Singapore
Angola	China	Lebanon	Slovak Republic
Argentina	Costa Rica	Malaysia	Slovenia
Armenia	Egypt	Mali	South Africa
Bahrain	El Salvador	Mauritius	Sri Lanka
Belarus	Finland	Moldova	Switzerland
Benin	The Gambia	Mozambique	Togo
Bosnia/Herz	Guinea	Nepal	United Arab Emirates
Brazil	Hungary	Nicaragua	Uganda
Bulgaria	Indonesia	Niger	Ukraine
Burkina Faso	Iran	Panama	Uzbekistan
Burundi	Israel	Romania	
Cambodia	Kuwait	Rwanda	

Tier 2 watch list

Azerbaijan	Georgia	Malawi	Serbia-Montenegro
Belize	Greece	Mauritania	Suriname
Bolivia	Guatemala	Mexico	Tajikstan
Democratic Republic of Congo	Honduras	Nigeria	Tanzania
Côte d'Ivoire	India	Pakistan	Thailand
Croatia	Jamaica	Paraguay	Turkey
Cyprus	Japan	Peru	Vietnam
Dominican Republic	Kazakhstan	Philippines	Zambia
Estonia	Kenya	Qatar	Zimbabwe
Ethiopia	Laos	Russia	
Gabon	Madagascar	Senegal	

Tier 3

Bangladesh	Ecuador	North Korea	Venezuela
Burma	Equatorial Guinea	Sierra Leone	
Cuba	Guyana	Sudan	

Note: Bangladesh, Ecuador, Guyana, and Sierra Leone were updated to tier 2 watch list per President George W. Bush, Presidential Determination No. 2004-46, September 10, 2004

SOURCE: "Tier Placements," in *Trafficking in Persons Report*, U.S. Department of State, June 14, 2004, http://www.state.gov/g/tip/rls/tiprpt/2004/33187.htm (accessed March 3, 2005)

Department of State to monitor the efforts of foreign governments to eliminate trafficking. The *Trafficking in Persons Report 2004*, published by the U.S. Department of State, identified governments in full compliance with TVPA (Tier I), governments in compliance with minimum standards of TVPA (Tier II), governments that have shown positive efforts toward minimum compliance (Tier II Watch List), and those countries that have not taken serious action to stop trafficking (Tier III). (See Table 4.10.) In September 2004 President Bush announced sanctions against those countries on the Tier III list.

VICTIMS OF TORTURE

The Torture Victims Relief Act of 1998 (TVRA; PL 105-320) provides federal funds to help support treatment centers for refugees and asylees who are victims of torture in their home country. The Trafficking Victims Protection Reauthorization Act of 2003 increased funding as follows:

- For domestic torture treatment centers, to be administered by the Department of Health and Human Services—$20 million in 2004 and $25 million in 2005

- For foreign torture treatment centers, to be administered by the U.S. Agency for International Development—$11 million in 2004 and $12 million in 2005

- In contributions to the United Nations Voluntary Fund for Victims of Torture—$6 million in 2004 and $7 million in 2005

REFUGEE ADJUSTMENT TO LIFE IN THE UNITED STATES

The Office of Refugee Resettlement (ORR) under the Department of Health and Human Services administers programs to assist refugees and asylees in adjusting to life in the United States. The U.S. resettlement program is designed to function as a public-private partnership, with nongovernmental organizations (NGOs) playing a key role. Through the Reception and Placement program, refugees are welcomed on arrival and provided essential services (housing, clothing, food, referrals to medical and social services) during the first thirty days in the United States. During this initial period the resettlement agencies also link refugees to longer-term resettlement and integration programs funded by the ORR.

Some of the NGOs recruit church groups and volunteers from local communities to provide a variety of services, and to contribute clothing and household furnishings to meet the needs of arriving refugees. In addition, they often become mentors and friends of refugees, providing orientation to community services, offering supportive services such as tutoring children after school, and teaching families how to shop and handle other essential functions of living in the community.

Mutual Assistance Associations (MAAs), many of which have national networks, provide opportunities for refugees to meet their countrymen who are already settled in the United States. MAAs also help refugees connect with their ethnic culture through holiday and religious celebrations.

The Bush Administration requested a $473.2 million budget appropriation for ORR in FY 2005. This included $399.2 million for refugee assistance, $54.2 million for unaccompanied alien minors, and $10 million each for victims of torture and trafficking (the same amount approved for victims of torture and trafficking in FY 2003). The Refugee Council USA, a coalition of U.S. nongovernmental organizations focused on refugee protection, initiated a campaign to lobby Congress for an

ORR FY 2005 budget appropriation of $650 million. On February 7, 2005, President Bush unveiled his FY 2006 proposal, which included an ORR budget of $489 million, an increase of $59 million over the FY 2005 request but still far from the funding level advocated by groups involved in the work of assisting refugees.

Benefits to Assist Transition

Ongoing benefits for the newly arrived refugees include transitional cash assistance, health benefits, and a wide variety of social services, provided through ORR grants. English language training is a basic service offered to all refugees. The primary focus is preparation for employment through skills training, job development, orientation to the workplace, and job counseling. Early employment leads not only to early economic self-sufficiency for the family, but helps establish the family in their new country and community. Special attention is paid to ensure that women have equal access to training and services leading to job placement. Other services include family strengthening, youth and elderly services, adjustment counseling, and mental health services.

Transitional cash assistance benefits are provided to refugees on the basis of family composition. Single adults and childless couples are eligible for Refugee Cash Assistance for up to eight months after arrival. They are expected to be employed by that time. However, families with children under eighteen years of age are eligible for the mainstream welfare program that assisted unemployed families for a period of two years. The amount of monthly cash assistance depends on family composition, and is established by the individual states in which refugees settled.

Health benefits follow similar rules. Single people and childless couples are eligible for Refugee Medical Assistance for their first eight months in the United States. Families with minor children are eligible for the Medicaid program, which is the mainstream health benefits program for unemployed and low-income families in the United States. While there are certain federal requirements that state welfare programs have to follow, states have flexibility and options in designing their programs. Therefore the cash and medical benefits available in each state can vary in terms of time limits and benefits.

Social services provided through a refugee services system are available for the first five years after arrival in the United States. Continuing services beyond five years on a limited basis are available for refugees identified as difficult to employ. They are assisted in overcoming barriers and learning new skills that would improve their chances for employment.

ASYLEES GRANTED REFUGEE ASSISTANCE BENEFITS. In June 2000 the ORR announced that asylees could participate in refugee assistance benefits starting on the date they were granted asylum, rather than the date of their arrival in the country. Unlike refugees, asylees were not granted asylum at the time they physically entered the United States; they officially "entered" the country on the date asylum was granted. Under the previous ORR policy, asylees often lost out on some benefits because they were granted asylum some time after the date they arrived. Because of the new policy, asylees could obtain refugee assistance benefits, including Refugee Cash Assistance (RCA) and Refugee Medical Assistance (RMA) for eight months, and Refugee Social Services (RSS) for about five years.

Support for Elderly and Disabled Refugees

Refugees who are elderly or disabled received benefits from the Social Security Administration, the same as U.S. citizens. However, changes by Congress in the late 1990s limited the eligibility of noncitizens to their first seven years in the United States. Time limits for noncitizens do not apply once they became U.S. citizens. The refugee program offers citizenship classes to assist refugees who wished to study for the citizenship test.

UNACCOMPANIED MINOR CHILDREN AS REFUGEES

Each year thousands of children enter the United States illegally and unaccompanied by a parent or guardian; some of them were sent away by parents who feared for their safety in war-torn regions of the world. Beginning in 1984 the INS refused to release these children to anyone other than a parent or legal guardian. As a result, children whose parents were not in the United States were detained for months or years while immigration authorities decided what to do with them. In 1985 the National Center for Youth Law filed a class action lawsuit in which it challenged INS policies governing the release of children and the conditions of confinement of those who were not released.

Following the 1997 U.S. Supreme Court ruling in *Flores v. Reno* (507 U.S. 292), the INS pledged to improve conditions for children in its custody. A June 2003 report from Amnesty International (*Why Am I Here? Children in Immigration Detention*, New York: Amnesty International) charged, however, that more than 5,000 children who entered the country illegally and alone were being locked up each year, and some of them were "shackled, strip-searched, or subject to physical or verbal abuse." As of March 1, 2003, the Homeland Security Act transferred responsibility for the care and custody of these children to the Office of Refugee Resettlement (ORR) in the Department of Health and Human Services.

Support for Unaccompanied Children Seeking Asylum

On January 24, 2005, Senator Diane Feinstein (a Democrat from California) introduced the Unaccompanied Alien Child Protection Act of 2005 (S.1129). Similar legislation was introduced in both 2001 and 2003 without success. Among other things, the 2005 bill would prohibit placing such children in adult detention facilities or facilities housing delinquent children; prohibit the unreasonable use of restraints, solitary confinement, and strip searches; provide for appointing qualified and trained guardians for such children; and require guidelines be developed to ensure the children received appropriate legal counsel.

Actress Angelina Jolie, UNHCR Goodwill Ambassador and advocate for protection of unaccompanied alien children, launched the National Center for Refugee and Immigrant Children on March 8, 2005, in Washington, D.C. The center would provide better access to free legal counsel for children who arrived alone in the United States and were fleeing persecution. The center recruited major law firms willing to provide pro bono (free) assistance to unaccompanied alien children who requested asylum.

CHAPTER 5
ILLEGAL ALIENS

When you're undocumented in any country, it's like you're in a shadow. No one sees you. No one notices. They can see your work, that you're contributing to the economy and consuming goods, but you don't really exist.

—Norberto Terrazas, member of the Mexican consulate in New York City (Lisa Adams, "Kin Struggle for Proof of Foreign 9/11 Victims," *The Denver Post*, September 24, 2004)

WHAT IS AN ILLEGAL ALIEN?

Illegal aliens are also known as illegal immigrants, illegal migrants, unauthorized migrants, undocumented immigrants, undocumented residents, and undocumented aliens. People often assume that the term illegal aliens refers specifically to Mexicans who have crossed the U.S.–Mexico border to work illegally in the United States. Although Mexicans may account for a number of the unauthorized entrants to the United States, illegal aliens can come from anywhere in the world.

An illegal alien is defined as a person who is not a U.S. citizen and who is in the United States in violation of U.S. immigration laws. An illegal alien could be one of the following:

- An undocumented alien, also known as an EWI (Entry Without Inspection), who entered the United States without a visa (such as a stowaway), often between land ports of entry

- A person who entered the United States using fraudulent documentation

- A person who entered the United States legally with a temporary visa and then stayed beyond the time allowed; this person was referred to as a nonimmigrant overstay or a visa overstay

- A legal permanent resident who committed a crime after entry, became subject to an order of deportation, but failed to depart

HOW MANY ILLEGAL ALIENS ARE THERE?

Because illegal aliens do not readily identify themselves for fear of deportation, it is almost impossible to determine how many illegal aliens are in the United States. Various sources have estimated between two and twelve million, but most estimates are little more than educated guesses and are often politically influenced. (The wide variance among the estimates is an indication of their unreliability.) The figures also vary somewhat between winter months and summer months based on availability of agricultural work.

Illegal Alien Estimates

Figure 5.1 provides an estimate of the number of illegal aliens living in the United States from 1986 to 2002. It also indicates some of the differences in estimates between Census Bureau and Immigration and Naturalization Service (INS) demographers. (Karen Woodrow and Jeffrey Passel worked for the Census Bureau and Passel later joined the Urban Institute. Robert Warren worked for the INS.) These estimates indicate that the total number of illegal aliens rose from 3.2 million in 1986 to 9.3 million in 2002. In *Undocumented Immigrants: Facts and Figures* (Jeffrey Passell, Randy Capps, and Michael Fix, Washington, DC: The Urban Institute, January 12, 2004), the demographers estimated that nearly two-thirds of all illegal aliens lived in just six states: California (27%), Texas (13%), New York (8%), Florida (7%), Illinois (6%), and New Jersey (4%).

Figure 5.2 shows that in 2002, 57% of all illegal aliens in the United States were from Mexico, compared to an estimated 69% in 1986. While the percentage share of illegal aliens from Mexico decreased between 1986 and 2002, their total numbers still increased dramatically. Sixty-nine percent of 3.2 million total illegal aliens in 1986 equaled 2.2 million from Mexico. By 2002 the number of illegal aliens from Mexico rose to 5.3 million (57% of 9.3 million).

FIGURE 5.1

FIGURE 5.2

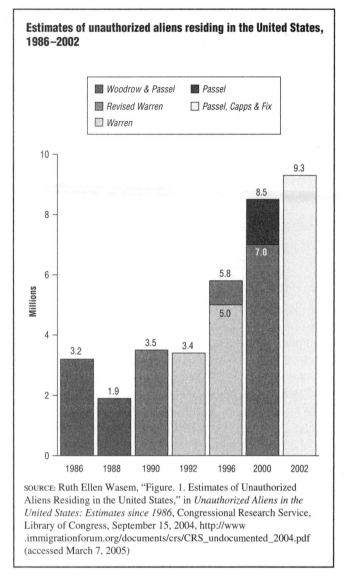

Estimates of unauthorized aliens residing in the United States, 1986–2002

SOURCE: Ruth Ellen Wasem, "Figure. 1. Estimates of Unauthorized Aliens Residing in the United States," in *Unauthorized Aliens in the United States: Estimates since 1986*, Congressional Research Service, Library of Congress, September 15, 2004, http://www.immigrationforum.org/documents/crs/CRS_undocumented_2004.pdf (accessed March 7, 2005)

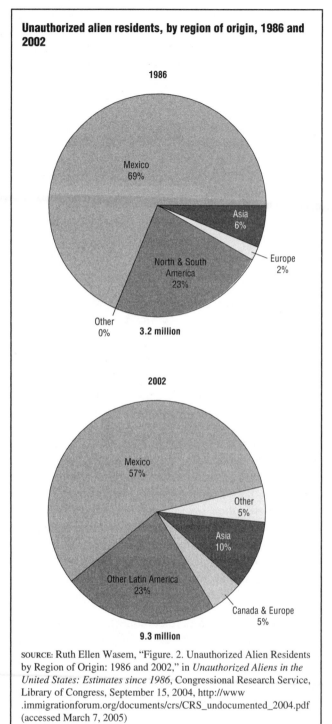

Unauthorized alien residents, by region of origin, 1986 and 2002

SOURCE: Ruth Ellen Wasem, "Figure. 2. Unauthorized Alien Residents by Region of Origin: 1986 and 2002," in *Unauthorized Aliens in the United States: Estimates since 1986*, Congressional Research Service, Library of Congress, September 15, 2004, http://www.immigrationforum.org/documents/crs/CRS_undocumented_2004.pdf (accessed March 7, 2005)

A November 2004 report by the Center for Immigration Studies (CIS) also estimated the number of illegal aliens in the country at about ten million (Steven A. Camarota, *Economy Slowed, But Immigration Didn't: The Foreign-Born Population, 2000–2004*, Washington, DC). However, in *The Underground Labor Force Is Rising to the Surface* (New York: Bear Stearns Asset Management, January 3, 2005), Robert Justich and Betty Ng disputed the estimates of the illegal alien population based on Census Bureau counts. Justich and Ng suggested that the Census Bureau accounted for only half of the illegal alien population. By the authors' projections, the 2004 illegal alien population was as high as twenty million. They based their projections on sources such as increases in school enrollments, foreign remittances (money sent by foreign workers to their families back home), border crossings, and housing permits. They suggested that more small businesses had taken advantage of illegal workers, moving four to six million jobs into the underground market. They

also noted that many employers of illegal aliens resorted to unrecorded revenue receipts (paying "under the table" or "off the books" by cash). Justich and Ng estimated five million illegal workers were being paid on such an untaxed cash basis. They argued that this "stealth workforce" distorted economic statistics and government budget projections by understating job growth, inflating U.S. productivity, and shortchanging tax revenues by some $35 billion per year.

Counting Who Comes and Goes

Section 110 of the Illegal Immigration Reform and Immigrant Responsibility Act of 1996 (IIRIRA; PL 104-208) mandated that the INS develop an automated system to track the entry and exit of all noncitizens—nonimmigrants and immigrant residents entering or leaving all ports of entry, including land borders and sea ports. The INS, the Canadian government, and the airline industry, among others, opposed Section 110. According to the INS, it lacked the resources to put in place such an integrated system. The Canadian government claimed that filling out the entry form (Form I-94) and having it checked by INS inspectors would cause large backups at the border. Airlines considered Section 110 an additional reporting burden.

On June 15, 2000, Congress passed the Immigration and Naturalization Service Data Management Improvement Act (PL 106-215) to amend Section 110 of the IIRIRA. It required the INS to develop an electronic system that "provides access to, and integrates, alien arrival and departure data," using available data to identify lawfully admitted nonimmigrants who might have overstayed their visits. A deadline of December 31, 2003, was set for all airports and seaports to have the system in place. Fifty land border ports, determined by the U.S. attorney general to have the highest number of arrivals and departures, were given until December 31, 2004, to have the system operating. All remaining land ports of entry were to have the system operating by December 31, 2005.

NATIONAL SECURITY ENTRY-EXIT REGISTRATION SYSTEM

Exactly one year after the terrorist attacks it was intended to prevent, the National Security Entry-Exit Registration System (NSEERS) was launched. It consisted of three components: point-of-entry registration, special registration, and exit/departure controls. Special registration established a national registry for temporary foreign visitors (nonimmigrant aliens) coming from twenty-five designated countries and others who met a combination of intelligence-based criteria that identified them as potential security risks.

One by one, immigration-related security deficiencies were being addressed by NSEERS. For example, as of January 2003 all commercial carriers were required to submit detailed passenger lists electronically before an aircraft or vessel arrived in or departed from the United States.

In December 2003 certain provisions in NSEERS were suspended, including the need to reregister each year, a process commonly known as "domestic registration." Certain provisions of NSEERS remained in place, however, including the requirement for foreign nationals

from Iran, Iraq, Libya, Syria, and the Sudan to go through special registration at ports of entry and to report to immigration officials before leaving the country. Foreign nationals from all other countries were registered if Customs and Border Protection Officers deemed it necessary based on initial questioning upon arrival. By January 2005, individuals from more than 160 countries had been registered in the NSEERS program. The registry provides detailed information about the background and purpose of an individual's visit to the United States as well as departure confirmation.

NONIMMIGRANT OVERSTAYS

An April 2002 report from the U.S. Department of Justice (*Follow-Up Report on INS Efforts to Improve the Control of Nonimmigrant Overstays*, Report no. I-2002-006, Washington, DC, April 2002) stated:

> Data from the 2000 Census suggests the number [of overstays] may be at least 8 million. Scholars at Boston's Northeastern University estimated the number as close to 13 million in a February 2001 study, *An Analysis of the Preliminary 2000 Census Estimates of the Resident Population of the U.S. and Their Implications for Demographic, Immigration, and Labor Market Analysis and Policymaking*. The common perception that the vast majority of illegal aliens entered the United States by surreptitiously crossing the southwest or northern border is inaccurate. INS officials have testified before Congress that 40% to 50% of the illegal alien population entered the United States legally as temporary visitors but failed to depart when required. The INS commonly refers to these illegal aliens as nonimmigrant overstays, and according to the INS this population is growing by at least 125,000 a year.

Under the Department of Homeland Security (DHS), the U.S. Immigration and Customs Enforcement (ICE) is responsible for collecting documents from incoming travelers, but airlines and shipping lines are responsible for collecting departure forms and for sending those forms to ICE. However, departure forms may have gone unrecorded because they were not collected, they were collected by the airline but not sent to ICE, or the forms were returned to ICE but incorrectly recorded. Therefore, the number of visa overstays is difficult to estimate.

In a May 2004 report to Congress (*Overstay Tracking: A Key Component of Homeland Security and a Layered Defense*, report to the chairman of the House Judiciary Committee, GAO-04-82, http://www.gao.gov/htext/d0482.html), the U.S. Government Accountability Office (GAO) reported the DHS had estimated the number of overstays in the United States to be 2.3 million in 2000. However, the GAO noted this figure did not account for an unknown number of short- and long-term overstays from Mexico and Canada. (See Figure 5.3.)

FIGURE 5.3

Key groups covered and not covered by DHS's overstay estimate

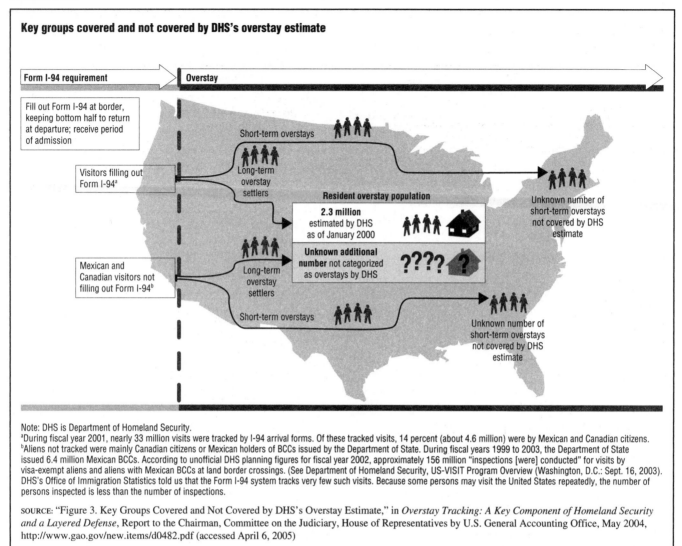

Note: DHS is Department of Homeland Security.
[a]During fiscal year 2001, nearly 33 million visits were tracked by I-94 arrival forms. Of these tracked visits, 14 percent (about 4.6 million) were by Mexican and Canadian citizens.
[b]Aliens not tracked were mainly Canadian citizens or Mexican holders of BCCs issued by the Department of State. During fiscal years 1999 to 2003, the Department of State issued 6.4 million Mexican BCCs. According to unofficial DHS planning figures for fiscal year 2002, approximately 156 million "inspections [were] conducted" for visits by visa-exempt aliens and aliens with Mexican BCCs at land border crossings. (See Department of Homeland Security, US-VISIT Program Overview (Washington, D.C.: Sept. 16, 2003). DHS's Office of Immigration Statistics told us that the Form I-94 system tracks very few such visits. Because some persons may visit the United States repeatedly, the number of persons inspected is less than the number of inspections.

SOURCE: "Figure 3. Key Groups Covered and Not Covered by DHS's Overstay Estimate," in *Overstay Tracking: A Key Component of Homeland Security and a Layered Defense*, Report to the Chairman, Committee on the Judiciary, House of Representatives by U.S. General Accounting Office, May 2004, http://www.gao.gov/new.items/d0482.pdf (accessed April 6, 2005)

Citizens of Canada admitted for up to six months and Mexican citizens with border crossing cards entering at a border in the southwest for a stay of less than seventy-two hours are exempt from the visa admissions procedure. The GAO report also noted weaknesses in the tracking system that identified who entered the country on visas but which did not accurately track when, or if, those individuals left.

In fiscal year (FY) 2001 the INS reported 32,799,000 arrivals at U.S. ports of entry, not including Mexican and Canadian business or pleasure visitors. Of these arrivals, 79% departed before their authorized stay expired and another 1% departed after their initial authorized stay expired. While there were no departure records for 15% of those persons who arrived by air or sea, departure records were missing for nearly three-fourths (71%) of all persons who arrived by land. The document that formed the basis of the tracking system was the Form I-94 completed on arrival. (See Figure 5.4.)

OPERATION TARMAC

Post–September 11 investigations identified "thousands of overstays and other illegal immigrant workers who (despite background checks) had obtained critical infrastructure jobs and security badges with access to, for example, airport tarmacs and U.S. military bases" (*Overstay Tracking: A Key Component of Homeland Security and A Layered Defense*, U.S. Government Accountability Office report to the chairman of the House Judiciary Committee, GAO-04-82, May 2004). The GAO report also claimed that of the six hijackers who actually flew the planes on September 11 or were apparent leaders, two were overstays and one had violated a student visa by not attending school. The DHS initiated an ongoing multiagency effort, known as Operation Tarmac, to identify unauthorized foreign nationals working in places vulnerable to terrorism, such as security areas of airports.

The GAO further reported in *Overstay Tracking* that as of April 2004, 195 airports had been investigated and

FIGURE 5.4

Form I-94

Front	Back

Front

U.S. Department of Justice
Immigration and Naturalization Service

OMB 1115-0077

Admission Number

601408904 00

Welcome to the United States

I-94 Arrival/Departure Record - Instructions

This form must be completed by all persons except U.S. Citizens, returning resident aliens, aliens with immigrant visas, and Canadian Citizens visiting or in transit.

Type of print legibly with pen in ALL CAPITAL LETTERS. Use English. Do not write on the back of this form.

This form is in two parts. Please complete both the Arrival Record (Items 1 through 13) and the Departure Record (Items 14 through 17).

When all items are completed, present this form to the U.S. Immigration and Naturalization Service Inspector.

Item 7 - If you are entering the United States by land, enter LAND in this space. If you are entering the United States by ship, enter SEA in this space.

Form I-94 (04-15-86)Y

Admission Number

601408904 00

Immigration and Naturalization Service

I-94
Arrival Record

1. Family Name
2. First (Given) Name
3. Birth Date (Day/Mo/Yr)
4. Country of Citizenship
5. Sex (Male or Female)
6. Passport Number
7. Airline and Flight Number
8. Country Where You Live
9. City Where You Boarded
10. City Where Visa Was Issued
11. Date Issued (Day/Mo/Yr)
12. Address While in the United States (Number and Street)
13. City and State

Departure Number

601408904 00

Immigration and Naturalization Service

I-94
Departure Record

14. Family Name
15. First (Given) Name
16. Birth Date (Day/Mo/Yr)
17. Country of Citizenship

See Other Side

STAPLE HERE

Back

This Side For Government Use Only
Primary Inspection

Applicant's Name
Date Referred _____ Time _____ Insp. # _____

Reason Referred

☐ 212A   ☐ PP   ☐ Visa   ☐ Parole   ☐ SLB   ☐ TWOV

☐ Other _____

Secondary Inspection

End Secondary Time _____ Insp. # _____

Disposition

18. Occupation

19. Waivers

20. INS File

A -

21. INS FCO

22. Petition Number

23. Program Number

24. ☐ Bond

25. ☐ Prospective Student

26. Itinerary/Comments

27. TWOV Ticket Number

Warning - A nonimmigrant who accepts unauthorized employment is subject to deportation.

Important - Retain this permit in your possession; you must surrender it when you leave the U.S. Failure to do so may delay your entry into the U.S. in the future. You are authorized to stay in the U.S. only until the date written on this form. To remain past this date, without permmission from immigration authorities, is a violation of the law.

Surrender this permit when you leave the U.S.:
   - By sea or air, to the transportation line;
   - Across the Canadian border, to a Canadian Official;
   - Across the Mexican border, to a U.S. Official.

Students planning to reenter the U.S. within 30 days to return to the same school, see "Arrival-Departure" on page 2 of Form I-20 prior to surrendering this permit.
Record of Changes

Port: _____ Departure Record

Date:

Carrier:

Flight #/Ship Name:

For sale by the Superintendent of Documents, U.S. Government Printing Office
Washington, D.C. 20402

SOURCE: "Appendix I: Copy of Form I-94," in *Overstay Tracking: A Key Component of Homeland Security and a Layered Defense*, Report to the Chairman, Committee on the Judiciary, House of Representatives by U.S. General Accounting Office, May 2004, http://www.gao.gov/new.items/d0482.pdf (accessed April 6, 2005)

TABLE 5.1

Operation Tarmac: overstays arrested

Airport	Overstays	Not overstays (EWIs and others)*	Total unauthorized workers arrested
Atlanta Hartsfield (ATL)	14	4	18
Austin (AUS)	1	22	23
Baltimore (BWI)	3	0	3
Boston Logan (BOS)	6	14	20
Burbank, California (BUR)	5	5	10
Chicago O'Hare (ORD) and Midway (MDW)	10	28	38
Dallas (DFW)	26	41	67
Denver (DIA)	6	36	42
Detroit (DTW)	2	4	6
Houston Bush (IAH)	3	100	103
Jacksonville (JAX)	2	1	3
Los Angeles (LAX)	5	18	23
Manchester, New Hampshire (MHT)	3	1	4
Newark, New Jersey (EWR)	8	5	13
New York JFK and La Guardia (LGA)	11	15	26
Omaha (OMA)	0	9	9
Orlando (MCO)	12	1	13
Phoenix Sky Harbor (PHX)	7	21	28
Salt Lake City, Utah (SLC)	23	25	48
San Francisco (SFO)	4	13	17
Sarasota (SRQ)	1	6	7
Tampa (TPA)	10	1	11
Washington Dulles (IAD)	7	40	47
Washington Reagan National (DCA)	13	15	28
Total number	**182**	**425**	**607**
Percent	30.0%	70.0%	100.0%

Note: Data are for operations conducted from October 2001 through April 2004.
*Entered without inspection (surreptitious border crosser).

SOURCE: "Table 2. Operation Tarmac Data for Selected Airports: Number of Overstays Arrested by Airport," in *Overstay Tracking: A Key Component of Homeland Security and a Layered Defense*, Report to the Chairman, Committee on the Judiciary, House of Representatives by U.S. General Accounting Office, May 2004, http://www.gao.gov/new.items/d0482.pdf (accessed April 6, 2005)

5,877 businesses had been audited. Checking I-9 employment eligibility forms and badging office records of some 385,000 workers located 4,918 unauthorized workers. Table 5.1 provides a profile of Operation Tarmac results in 25 airports. Of 607 unauthorized workers arrested, 30% were overstays. The greatest number of unauthorized workers arrested (103) were identified at Houston's Bush Intercontinental Airport. A total of ten unauthorized workers arrested were from countries identified as "of special interest" under the NSEERS program and five of these were overstays. According to the GAO report, the unauthorized workers with access to secured areas were employed by airports, airlines, and support service companies in jobs such as aircraft maintenance technicians, airline cabin service attendants, airplane fuelers, baggage handlers, and predeparture screeners. One unauthorized worker was employed in the airport badging office. In most cases these individuals had misused Social Security numbers and identity documents to obtain airport jobs and security badges.

Operation Tarmac also investigates employees working at critical infrastructure sites (such as nuclear power plants, sensitive national landmarks, military installations, or the Alaska pipeline) and special events (such as the 2002 Olympics in Salt Lake City and the annual Super Bowl game). Seventy-nine unauthorized workers were arrested at the 2003 Super Bowl in San Diego, according to the GAO report. Eight were overstayers and twelve others were from countries that became part of the NSEERS "special registration" requirements.

WHERE DO ILLEGAL ALIENS COME FROM?

The 2000 census data was used by the INS to estimate that a total of seven million unauthorized residents were in the United States, double the 3.5 million estimated for 1990. That analysis identified Mexico as the leading country of origin of illegal aliens to the United States, accounting for 68.7% (4.8 million) of the estimated undocumented population in 2000. Fourteen countries were each estimated to be the source of 50,000 or more illegal aliens. Of the top fifteen countries of origin, only China, the Philippines, India, and Korea are not within the Western Hemisphere. (See Table 5.2.)

TABLE 5.2

Estimated unauthorized resident population, top 15 countries of origin, 1990 and 2000

[Numbers in thousands; parts might not add to totals because of rounding]

Country of origin	Estimated population 2000 (1)	Estimated population 1990 (2)	Growth 1990–2000 (3)=(1)−(2)	Percent of total population 2000 (4)	Percent of total population 1990 (5)
All countries	**7,000**	**3,500**	**3,500**	**100.0%**	**100.0%**
Mexico	4,808	2,040	2,768	68.7%	58.3%
El Salvador	189	298	−109	2.7%	8.5%
Guatemala	144	118	26	2.1%	3.4%
Colombia	141	51	91	2.0%	1.4%
Honduras*	138	42	96	2.0%	1.2%
China	115	70	45	1.6%	2.0%
Ecuador	108	37	71	1.5%	1.0%
Dominican Republic	91	46	45	1.3%	1.3%
Philippines	85	70	14	1.2%	2.0%
Brazil	77	20	58	1.1%	0.6%
Haiti	76	67	8	1.1%	1.9%
India	70	28	41	1.0%	0.8%
Peru	61	27	34	0.9%	0.8%
Korea	55	24	31	0.8%	0.7%
Canada	47	25	22	0.7%	0.7%
All other countries	795	537	259	11.4%	15.3%

*Includes 105,000 Hondurans granted temporary protected status in December 1998.

SOURCE: "Table B. Estimated Unauthorized Resident Population, Top 15 Countries, 1990 and 2000," in *Estimates of the Unauthorized Immigrant Population Residing in the United States: 1990 to 2000*, Office of Policy and Planning, U.S. Immigration and Naturalization Service, January 2003, http://uscis.gov/graphics/shared/aboutus/statistics/Ill_Report_1211.pdf (accessed March 9, 2005)

FIGURE 5.5

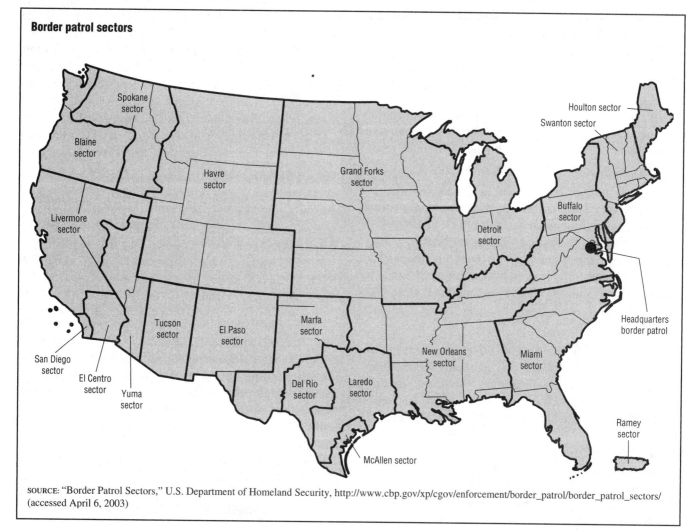

Border patrol sectors

SOURCE: "Border Patrol Sectors," U.S. Department of Homeland Security, http://www.cbp.gov/xp/cgov/enforcement/border_patrol/border_patrol_sectors/ (accessed April 6, 2003)

WHO ENFORCES IMMIGRATION LAWS?

Following the terrorist attacks of September 11, 2001, it became apparent that some or all of the perpetrators had entered the United States legally and many had overstayed their allotted time with no notice taken by the INS or any other enforcement agency. On March 1, 2003, INS functions and those of the U.S. Customs Service were folded into the newly created Department of Homeland Security (DHS). Within the DHS, the new U.S. Customs and Border Protection (CBP) oversees the movement of goods and people into the United States, while Immigration and Customs Enforcement (ICE) is responsible for enforcing immigration laws within the United States and along its land and water boundaries. On March 17, 2004, Under Secretary for Border and Transportation Security Asa Hutchinson reported before the Subcommittee on Infrastructure and Border Security of the House Select Committee on Homeland Security (http://www.globalsecurity.org/security/library/congress/2004_h/040317-hutchinson.doc) that ports of entry into the United States stretched across 7,500 miles of land border with Mexico and Canada, and 95,000 miles of

shoreline and navigable rivers. Conditions and venues varied considerably, from air and sea ports of entry in metropolitan New York City with dozens of employees, to a two-person land entry point in North Dakota.

The U.S. Border Patrol

The U.S. Border Patrol, the mobile uniformed law enforcement arm of the CBP, is responsible for the detection and apprehension of illegal aliens and smugglers of aliens at or near U.S. land borders—a difficult, sometimes dangerous, and often frustrating job. The United States is divided into twenty-one Border Patrol Sectors. Nine of the Border Patrol sectors are along the southwest border. (See Figure 5.5.)

THE SOUTHWEST BORDER. The biggest illegal entry problems occur along the 1,956-mile border between the United States and Mexico. The four states bordering Mexico—Texas, New Mexico, Arizona, and California—have 39 ports of entry. About five million Mexican nationals reside in the Mexican municipalities (municipios) along the southwest border.

RECRUITING BORDER PATROL AGENTS. The Illegal Immigration Reform and Immigrant Responsibility Act of 1996 (IIRIRA) mandated that the Immigration and Naturalization Service (INS) add 1,000 Border Patrol agents each year starting fiscal year (FY) 1997 through 2001. In 1997 and 1998 the INS fulfilled the law's mandate but fell short in 1999, when just 363 agents were added. In March 1999 the Clinton administration announced it would not request more funding for Border Patrol positions, citing the problems that could result from having too many inexperienced agents.

In 2000 the INS strengthened its recruiting efforts by training Border Patrol agents as recruiters and offering entrance exams throughout the country. It advertised in movie theaters, on television, and on the Internet. About 80% of those interested applied over the Internet. In addition, the INS offered a $2,000 recruitment bonus to each recruit. As a result, the INS reported that more than 1,700 new agents were hired, bringing the total number of agents to 9,212.

The aggressive recruitment effort continued, and in 2001 legislation was passed that increased the base pay for new agents to about $41,000. After the terrorist attacks of September 11, the need for Border Patrol agents became acute. In his testimony on October 17, 2001, before the House Committee on Government Reform, INS Commissioner James W. Ziglar pointed out that even before September 11, Border Patrol agents were routinely recruited away by other federal law enforcement agencies that offered better pay. In fact, as Jonathan Peterson of the *Los Angeles Times* reported, about 2,000 Border Patrol agents and immigration inspectors left the INS between October 2001 and August 2002 ("'Mass Exodus' of Agents Leaves INS Scrambling," August 5, 2002). Many took better-paid airline security jobs with the newly created Transportation Security Administration. According to Peterson, in FY 2002, 1,499 new Border Patrol agents were hired—but 1,459 veterans left. Border Patrol agents complained of low job satisfaction, low pay, and the poor image of the INS as well as uncertainty over its continued existence.

After INS responsibilities were turned over to the DHS, a recruiting campaign was launched on college campuses in an effort to meet President George W. Bush's goal of hiring 570 new Border Patrol agents in FY 2003. The nation's post–September 11 southwest border strategy called for 14,000 Border Patrol agents to be in place by 2010 (Jerry Seper, "14,000 Agents Needed to Patrol Mexico Border," *Washington Times*, September 23, 2002).

THE NORTHERN BORDER. The September 11 terrorist attacks also highlighted the vulnerability of the nation's northern border, where fewer than 300 Border Patrol agents guarded the nearly 4,000-mile border with Canada, and several ports of entry were not staffed around-the-clock. In FY 2002, 245 Border Patrol agents were allocated to the northern border. On July 2, 2003, CBP Commissioner Robert Bonner announced that 375 additional Border Patrol agents would be deployed to the northern border, bringing the total number of agents there to 1,000 (http://www.customs.gov/xp/cgov/newsroom/press_releases/archives/cbp_press_releases/072003/07022003.xml).

APPREHENSION OF ILLEGAL ALIENS

In FY 2003 the Border Patrol located 931,557 deportable aliens, down from 955,310 in 2002, and from more than one million in each of the previous five years. The majority (882,012, or 94.7%) of the deportable aliens were from Mexico. Most of the Mexican aliens located (810,671) were identified as "seeking employment." (See Table 5.3.)

More than one million aliens were expelled from CBP field offices in 2003. (See Table 5.4.) The majority (887,115) were voluntary removals compared to 186,151 formal removals, including deportations and exclusions. Given the high volume of migrant traffic along the Southwest border, it was no surprise that the San Diego, California, and Phoenix, Arizona, offices had the greatest number of removals. The Phoenix field office processed 44% (395,757) of all voluntary departures and 17.5% (32,609) of all formal removals.

Customs and Border Patrol FY 2004 Activities

In a January 11, 2005, press release ("Border Agency Reports First-Year Successes," http://www.cbp.gov/xp/cgov/newsroom/press_releases/0012005/01112005.xml), the CBP reported that 428 million passengers and pedestrians were processed and cleared through U.S. air, land, and sea ports of entry during FY 2004. A total of 121 million privately owned vehicles entered the United States—91 million at the U.S.–Mexico border and 30 million at the U.S.–Canada border. CBP officers processed more than 262 million aliens at U.S. ports of entry. Of that number, 643,091 were deemed inadmissible under U.S. laws, including 19,740 criminal aliens. Since new fingerprint matching systems were installed on the Mexican and Canadian borders, arrests of criminals and criminal suspects attempting to enter the country jumped from 2,612 in FY 2002 to 29,501 in FY 2004. In tallying its successes, the CBP noted that officers at ports of entry arrested 6,709 persons on drug-related charges and 7,516 on outstanding state or federal warrants, a 41% increase over FY 2003. They also intercepted 566 stowaways. Nationwide, Border Patrol agents arrested 1,158,800 illegal aliens, including 643 special interest aliens, and intercepted 78,255 fraudulent documents.

TABLE 5.3

Border patrol activities, 1997–2003

Activities and accomplishments	1997	1998	1999	2000	2001	2002	2003
Persons processed by the border patrol[a]	1,422,829	1,566,984	1,591,969	1,689,195	1,277,576	967,044	946,684
Deportable aliens located by the border patrol	1,412,953	1,555,776	1,579,010	1,676,438	1,266,213	955,310	931,557
Mexican aliens	1,387,650	1,522,918	1,534,515	1,636,883	1,224,046	917,994	882,012
Working in agriculture	3,521	3,270	1,599	1,330	1,248	1,821	1,908
Working in trades, crafts, industry, and service	10,146	6,616	2,383	2,167	2,678	2,897	3,856
Seeking employment	1,279,923	1,398,892	1,422,970	1,525,422	1,107,550	822,161	810,671
Canadian aliens	2,935	2,329	2,724	2,211	2,539	1,836	1,611
All others	22,368	30,529	41,771	37,344	39,628	35,480	47,934
Smugglers of aliens located	12,523	13,908	15,755	14,406	8,720	8,701	11,128
Aliens located who were smuggled into the United States	124,605	174,514	221,522	236,782	112,927	68,192	110,605
Seizures (conveyances)	11,792	14,401	16,803	17,269	5,892	7,250	9,355
Value of seizures (millions of dollars)	1,095	1,405	2,004	1,945	1,581	1,564	1,168
Narcotics	1,046	1,340	1,919	1,848	1,519	1,499	1,608
Other	49	64	86	97	62	65	72

*Includes deportable aliens located and non-deportable (e.g., U.S. citizens).
Note: Data for aliens previously expelled, aliens located with previous criminal records, and conveyances examined are not available starting in fiscal year 1990. Data for narcotics for fiscal year 1995 and for other for 1992–94 and 1996–97 have been revised.

SOURCE: "Table 38. Principal Activities and Accomplishments of the Border Patrol, Fiscal Years 1997–2003," in *2003 Yearbook of Immigration Statistics*, U.S. Department of Homeland Security, Office of Immigration Statistics, September 2004, http://uscis.gov/graphics/shared/aboutus/statistics/ENF03yrbk/2003ENFtables.pdf (accessed February 9, 2005)

TABLE 5.4

Aliens expelled by field office, fiscal year 2003

Field office	Formal removals[a]	Voluntary departures[b]
All field offices	**186,151**	**887,115**
Atlanta, GA	3,647	1,918
Baltimore, MD	4,546	416
Boston, MA	1,979	2,379
Buffalo, NY	1,366	375
Chicago, IL	5,279	1,404
Dallas, TX	5,378	2,966
Denver, CO	4,027	2,914
Detroit, MI	1,500	1,695
El Paso, TX	11,431	93,811
Houston, TX	11,144	1,759
Los Angeles, CA	13,116	6,435
Miami, FL	7,695	6,074
New Orleans, LA	4,339	552
New York, NY	2,877	162
Newark, NJ	3,162	271
Phoenix, AZ	32,609	395,757
San Antonio, TX	15,372	165,005
San Diego, CA	40,325	195,678
San Francisco, CA	7,355	3,625
Seattle, WA	4,321	2,249
St. Paul, MN	3,342	1,408
Washington, DC	1,341	262

[a]Formal removals include deportations, exclusions, and removals.
[b]Voluntary departures include aliens under docket control required to depart and voluntary departures not under docket control.

SOURCE: "Table 41. Aliens Expelled by Field Office, Fiscal Year 2003," in *2003 Yearbook of Immigration Statistics*, U.S. Department of Homeland Security, Office of Immigration Statistics, September 2004, http://uscis.gov/graphics/shared/aboutus/statistics/ENF03yrbk/2003ENFtables.pdf (accessed February 9, 2005)

Source Countries of Apprehended Aliens

According to the *2002 Yearbook of Immigration Statistics* (Washington, DC: U.S. Department of Homeland Security, Office of Immigration Statistics, October 2003), in FY 2002 nationals of 186 countries were apprehended by the INS. Almost all of those arrested were from Mexico (94%). The next largest source countries were Honduras, El Salvador, Guatemala, Brazil, Canada, the Dominican Republic, Cuba, the People's Republic of China, Jamaica, Colombia, Pakistan, Haiti, and Ecuador. However, the INS counted apprehensions, not individuals. Many of those apprehended and returned to Mexico would return to the border to attempt to cross again. According to U.S. Border Patrol statistics reported in a *USA Today* article ("Despite New Technology Border Patrol Overwhelmed," http://www.usatoday.com/news/nation/2005-02-22-border-patrol_x.htm, March 22, 2005), 1,073,468 persons from Mexico were caught illegally crossing the southwestern border in 2004, compared to 865,850 the previous year. The number of persons from countries other than Mexico who were caught trying to cross the southwestern border totaled 65,814 in 2004, up from 39,215 in 2003.

Removal of Illegal Aliens

Noncriminal aliens apprehended while attempting illegal entry into the United States are offered voluntary departure. If they accept, they waive their right to a hearing and are supposed to leave the country under supervision. Aliens who are apprehended after entering the United States could also be allowed to depart voluntarily. In both cases, an immigration judge or a DHS Field Office Director grants permission to depart. The Office of Immigration Statistics reported that most voluntary departures (99%) involve aliens apprehended and quickly removed by the Border Patrol (*2003 Yearbook of Immigration Statistics*, Washington, DC: U.S. Department of Homeland Security, Office of Immigration Statistics, September 2004).

TABLE 5.5

Aliens removed, by administrative reason for removal, fiscal years 1991–2003

Year	Total	Attempted entry without proper documents or through fraud or misrepresentation	Criminal	Failed to maintain status	Previously removed ineligible for reentry	Present without authorization*	Security	Smuggling or aiding illegal entry	Other	Unknown
1991	33,189	3,058	14,475	1,135	735	13,347	7	28	191	213
1992	43,671	3,630	20,098	1,076	1,008	17,403	31	177	57	191
1993	42,542	2,968	22,470	783	913	15,018	54	208	95	33
1994	45,674	3,482	24,581	716	1,052	15,500	57	218	51	17
1995	50,924	5,822	25,684	611	1,432	17,069	34	196	63	13
1996	69,680	15,412	27,655	708	2,005	23,522	36	275	49	18
1997	114,432	35,737	34,113	1,031	3,302	39,297	30	385	522	15
1998	173,146	79,290	35,946	986	7,103	48,477	15	497	816	16
1999	180,902	91,858	41,995	789	9,287	34,898	10	404	1,651	10
2000	185,987	89,893	41,076	729	11,653	40,254	13	490	1,874	5
2001	177,739	76,212	40,112	714	10,668	47,889	12	507	1,619	6
2002	150,084	41,295	37,723	1,226	12,809	55,322	11	572	1,101	25
2003	186,151	52,014	39,600	1,240	17,630	73,609	12	597	1,442	7

*Includes those aliens charged under the statutes previous to April 1, 1997 as "entered without inspection."
Note: The administrative reason for formal removal is the legal basis for removal. Some aliens who are criminals may be removed under a different administrative reason (or charge) for the convenience of the government. Removals include those actions known as deportation and exclusion prior to the revision of law that was effective April 1, 1997.

SOURCE: Adapted from "Table 42. Aliens Removed by Administrative Reason for Removal: Fiscal Years 1991–2003," in Enforcement Supplemental Tables for *2003 Yearbook of Immigration Statistics*, U.S. Department of Homeland Security, Office of Immigration Statistics, September 2004, http://uscis.gov/graphics/shared/aboutus/statistics/ENF03yrbk/ENFExcel/Table42.xls (accessed February 9, 2005)

Prior to the passage of Illegal Immigration Reform and Immigrant Responsibility in 1996, the INS used the term "exclusion" to mean denial of an alien's entry into the United States. "Deportation" referred to the formal removal of an alien from the United States after being found in violation of immigration laws. IIRIRA consolidated the two procedures into one category called "removals."

Table 5.5 compares removals by reason for fiscal years 1991 through 2003. The increasing number of removals—33,189 total in 1991 compared to 186,151 in 2003—reflects not only growth in the number of immigrants but changes in immigration laws and enforcement activities. According to data in the *2003 Yearbook of Immigration Statistics*, 497,000 arriving aliens initially were determined to be inadmissible in FY 2003. Although approximately 181,000 of these were inadmissible for reasons that made them subject to expedited removal, 128,000 chose to withdraw their applications for admission. Of the remaining 53,000 who were scheduled for expedited removal, about 6,000 expressed a fear of being returned to their countries of origin and were referred to an asylum officer. Expedited removals totaled 23% of removals in 2003.

The INS contended that as many as 314,000 "absconders" who had been ordered deported by an immigration judge remained at large as of early 2002 ("Guidance for Absconder Apprehension Initiative," Washington, DC: Office of Deputy Attorney General, January 25, 2002). In January 2002 the Department of Justice launched the Absconder Apprehension Initiative, which was to begin with the deportation of about 1,000 immigrants from Middle Eastern countries who had been convicted of felonies in the United States but remained at large. After the campaign was announced, the INS predicted that it would take a minimum of a year just to enter the names of the absconders in the FBI database and that the agency was unlikely to be able to locate more than 10% of the absconders.

In 2003 U.S. Immigration and Customs Enforcement (ICE) took over responsibility for locating absconders. In a November 16, 2004, press release ("ICE Detention and Removal Sets Record for Fiscal Year 2004," http://www.ice.gov/graphics/news/newsreleases/articles/droFY04.htm), ICE announced that the removal of criminal and other illegal aliens from the United States reached record levels in FY 2004. A total of 157,281 aliens were removed. In addition, ICE recorded a sizable increase in apprehensions under a new program specifically targeting fugitive aliens.

"Removing criminal aliens and other illegal aliens from the United States is critical to the integrity of our immigration system and important to the safety of our communities," Michael J. Garcia, DHS Assistant Secretary for ICE, was quoted as saying in the 2004 press release. "The 9/11 Commission Report details how our immigration system was exploited by terrorists, and we know that other dangerous criminals have sought illegal entry by similar means. We are bringing to bear the full force of our authorities to locate and remove those in the country illegally."

On May 14, 2003, ICE initiated a Most Wanted list on its website (http://www.ice.gov/graphics/investigations/mostwanted.htm). The list included "Most Wanted Criminal Aliens" who had been convicted of mostly violent crimes and had evaded final removal orders. On

February 18, 2005, for example, the list included ten individuals convicted of crimes against children, assault and weapons offenses, and manslaughter. There were also five individuals wanted for human smuggling, most of which involved deaths. A separate "Most Wanted Fugitives" list included eleven individuals wanted for customs violations such as drug smuggling, firearms smuggling, stolen vehicles, child pornography, and money laundering. The website lists included a photo of each individual and personal information. The website provided a telephone number that any member of the public could call with information about individuals on the lists.

Field Fugitive Operations Teams Seek Absconders

On February 25, 2003, the National Fugitive Operations Program was established with a mission to identify, locate, apprehend, and remove fugitive aliens. The Absconder Initiative under this program established eighteen Field Fugitive Operations Teams around the country to perform the work.

In "Outnumbered in a Hunt for Aliens" for the *Washington Times* (July 20, 2004), Jerry Seper reported on the activities of one field team operating in the Los Angeles area. In a pre-dawn raid the team arrested "three Mexican nationals and a Guatemalan, all convicted criminals, and an Israeli national sought by the U.S. government as a potential terrorist threat." Seper noted that in the city of Los Angeles more than 90% of outstanding homicide warrants and 65% of fugitive felony warrants were for illegal aliens.

Seper's article reported that the eighteen squads nationwide were seeking to arrest 80,000 criminal aliens—including killers, rapists, drug dealers, and child molesters—and at least 320,000 absconders. Barely 200 agents were searching for nearly a half-million criminal aliens and absconders hiding in communities from Seattle and Los Angeles to Miami and New York City.

Operation Predator

Operation Predator, an initiative targeting criminals who sexually exploit children, began in July 2003. As of March 2005 Operation Predator had resulted in more than 5,000 arrests nationwide ("Operation Predator," http://www.ice.gov/graphics/news/factsheets/operation predator.htm, March 9, 2005). Approximately 85% of those arrested were foreign-national sexual predators whose crimes made them deportable. Between July 2003 and March 2005 more than 2,100 child predators were deported.

JOINING FORCES TO LOCATE CRIMINAL ALIENS

Charlie LeDuff reported for the *New York Times* ("100 Members of Immigrant Gang Held," March 15, 2005) that federal immigration authorities had arrested more than one hundred members of a violent Central American street gang in a nationwide crackdown. The gang, known as "Mara Salvatrucha" or MS-13, originated in Los Angeles and spread across the continent. Gang members were involved in narcotics, gun trafficking, murder, and prostitution. Many of the gang members were illegal aliens, including some who had been deported and returned, and some deportees who never left. The article quoted the opinion of Officer Frank Flores, a gang expert with the Los Angeles Police Department, that members of MS-13 "pose as much a threat to the well-being of ordinary citizens as any foreign terrorist group."

A longstanding problem faced by immigration officials is lack of support from local law enforcement. The Los Angeles Police Department, for example, has a policy that prohibits its officers from informing federal immigration officials about illegal aliens they discover in the normal course of their duties. By letting the immigrant community see that local law officers will not report them, police departments hope to gain the trust of illegal aliens so they will seek assistance when needed and report crimes. Such written or unwritten "sanctuary laws" have been in place in a number of major cities. Several cities prohibit their employees from even asking about a person's immigration status. The arrests of MS-13 gang members appeared to mark a new cooperation between federal, state, and local enforcement agencies.

Supporting the concept of "sanctuary laws," the National Council of La Raza (a nonprofit, nonpartisan organization focused on reducing poverty and discrimination and improving opportunities for Hispanic Americans) charges that allowing local police agencies to enforce federal immigration laws results in racial profiling, police misconduct, and civil rights violations. The council also thinks local police involvement with immigration enforcement undercuts effective law enforcement and hampers antiterrorism efforts.

ALIEN SMUGGLING AND TRAFFICKING

Aliens often pay smugglers to help them enter the United States illegally. In cases of trafficking the smugglers then use the aliens for forced labor or commercial sexual exploitation. ICE makes a distinction between alien smuggling and human trafficking. Alien smuggling produces short-term profits, while trafficking garners profits over both the long and short term.

A Growing Problem

According to an ICE press release, Agent Thomas Homan asserted in a statement before the House Judiciary Committee's Immigration, Border Security, and Claims Subcommittee on June 24, 2003, that the international trade in men, women, and children is a growing and lucrative business, generating an estimated

FIGURE 5.6

Estimated number of people trafficked annually into the U.S., by region[a]

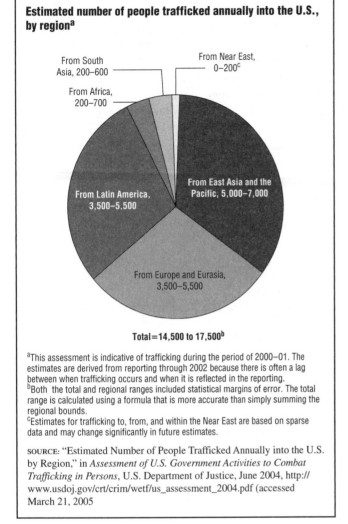

Total=14,500 to 17,500[b]

[a]This assessment is indicative of trafficking during the period of 2000–01. The estimates are derived from reporting through 2002 because there is often a lag between when trafficking occurs and when it is reflected in the reporting.
[b]Both the total and regional ranges included statistical margins of error. The total range is calculated using a formula that is more accurate than simply summing the regional bounds.
[c]Estimates for trafficking to, from, and within the Near East are based on sparse data and may change significantly in future estimates.

SOURCE: "Estimated Number of People Trafficked Annually into the U.S. by Region," in *Assessment of U.S. Government Activities to Combat Trafficking in Persons*, U.S. Department of Justice, June 2004, http://www.usdoj.gov/crt/crim/wetf/us_assessment_2004.pdf (accessed March 21, 2005

TABLE 5.6

Trafficking prosecutions, FY 2001–03

TVPA prosecutions	FY01	FY02	FY03
Cases filed			
Total	5	7	9
Sex (subset of total)	2	5	7
Defendants charged			
Total	11	21	24
Sex (subset of total)	6	13	20
Convictions			
Total	5	6	17
Sex (subset of total)	3	6	14

SOURCE: "Trafficking Prosecutions, FY 2001–2003," in *Assessment of U.S. Government Activities to Combat Trafficking in Persons*, U.S. Department of Justice, June 2004, http://www.usdoj.gov/crt/crim/wetf/us_assessment_2004.pdf (accessed March 21, 2005)

On February 21, 2003, the Justice Department announced that a federal jury delivered a guilty verdict in the human trafficking case against Kil Soo Lee ("Garment Factory Owner Convicted in Largest Ever Human Trafficking Case Prosecuted by the Department of Justice," http://www.usdoj.gov/opa/pr/2003/February/03_crt_108.htm). According to the announcement, from March 1999 through November 2000 Lee and his underlings used threats, starvation, confinement, and beatings to hold over two hundred Vietnamese and Chinese garment workers in servitude in Lee's factory in American Samoa. The women had paid $5,000 to $8,000 (the equivalent of five to ten years' salary in their home countries), what they believed was a legitimate fee for a new job that would lead to a better way of life.

A Dangerous Journey

In order to avoid detection, persons who smuggle illegal aliens into the United States often use transporting methods that are not safe. Aliens who cross the U.S.–Mexico or U.S.–Canada borders might travel in enclosed, packed trucks with little ventilation. Others, who travel by sea for thousands of miles from such countries as the People's Republic of China and India, might be stowed on cargo ships and subjected to extreme conditions, including lack of comfort facilities and stifling heat.

In the deadliest illegal border-crossing in more than fifteen years, nineteen men, women, and children died of suffocation, heat exposure, and thirst while locked inside an unventilated trailer in May 2003. The victims were among at least seventy-four illegal aliens from Mexico and Central America abandoned at a truck stop about one hundred miles southwest of Houston. The driver of the truck that brought the aliens across the U.S.–Mexico border was Tyrone M. Williams, a Jamaican citizen and

$9.5 billion each year (http://www.ice.gov/graphics/news/newsreleases/articles/humanTraf062403.htm, June 24, 2003). The international smuggling trade is highly organized, consisting of a sophisticated network of persons who set up smuggling transactions, forge documents, transport aliens, and handle aliens at the destination.

The State Department estimated that 600,000 to 800,000 persons are victims of global trafficking each year ("Office to Monitor and Combat Trafficking in Persons," http://www.state.gov/g/tip/). Likewise, according to 2004 U.S. Department of Justice estimates, 14,500 to 17,500 people are trafficked into the United States annually. About 40% (5,000–7,000) come from East Asia and the Pacific and 31% (3,500–5,500) come from Latin America. (See Figure 5.6.) Table 5.6 summarizes the Justice Department's trafficking cases for fiscal years 2001 through 2003. During that time a total of 56 defendants were charged and 28 were convicted of trafficking. Twenty-three (82%) of the convictions were for sex-related trafficking charges.

resident of New York state. Williams had received $7,500 to smuggle the group across the border and deliver them to Houston. Indicted on 58 counts of conspiracy, and harboring and transporting illegal immigrants, Williams became the first person to face possible execution for human smuggling deaths under the Trafficking Victims Protection Act of 2000. While fourteen people were indicted, including ring-leaders of the Brownsville, Texas, smuggling ring, prosecutors said Williams was the only one facing the death penalty because he alone had the power to release the immigrants from the airless tractor-trailer.

After a series of appeals based on Williams's charges of discrimination, the trial began March 8, 2005, in federal district court in Houston. Williams testified that he turned off the air conditioning in the truck so that he could say that he was hauling an empty trailer when he went through a Border Patrol checkpoint. He also contended that he did not hear the passengers pounding on the sides of the trailer and screaming for help. A passenger in the cab, Fatima Holloway, testified that Mr. Williams ignored the sounds of the desperate passengers. On March 23, 2005, the jury returned a verdict of guilty on thirty-eight counts of transporting illegal aliens. However, they were deadlocked on twenty potential death penalty charges of conspiracy and harboring, resulting in a mistrial on those counts (trial coverage from the *New York Times, Houston Chronicle, Christian Science Monitor*, and *National Public Radio*, March 2005).

Some illegal aliens have drowned while trying to swim across the Rio Grande, which forms the border between Texas and Mexico. Others have fallen prey to border bandits who stole from them and injured or killed them. Some illegal aliens who brought in drugs as payment for their entry into the United States put themselves in harm's way because of the dangerous nature of their undertakings.

Between October 2002 and July 2003, 123 illegal aliens died in Arizona from the heat, accidents, and other causes (Anabelle Garay, "Immigrant Death Toll in Ariz. Near Record," *Newsday*, July 24, 2003). William Aceves, a professor of international and human rights law at the California Western School of Law, estimated that between 1994 and 2003 more than 2,200 migrants died while trying to cross the southwestern border through remote passages (*Summary of Migrant Civil Rights Issues Along the Southwest Border*, Washington, DC: U.S. Commission on Civil Rights, April 2003).

Tucson's *Arizona Daily Star* newspaper established a searchable database (http://regulus.azstarnet.com/border-deaths/search.php) of deaths occurring on the U.S.–Mexico border. The database not only counts the death toll but can be used by relatives searching for missing family members

who left to cross the border and were never heard from again. The Coalición de Derechos Humanos/Alianza Indigena sin Fronteras, a Tucson human rights organization, also maintains a list of migrant border deaths including name (if known), sex, age, date discovered, location where discovered, and cause of death. Between October 1, 2003, and September 30, 2004, the Coalición added 233 people to its list. Approximately 47% (110 bodies) were unknown—found with no identification papers. Many were only bones. Attesting to the risks of dealing with some of the guides who led illegal aliens across the border for a fee, nineteen of the dead suffered blunt trauma injuries and one had a gunshot wound.

MEXICO'S UNIQUE RELATIONSHIP WITH THE UNITED STATES

In no other place in the world does a nation as wealthy as the United States share a border with a nation as poor as Mexico. Huge disparities exist between the rich and poor people of Mexico, so it is understandable that Mexico's poor are attracted to the United States.

An Open Border

Before the twentieth century, Mexicans moved easily back and forth across completely open borders to work in the mines, on the ranches, and on the railroad. While fewer than 1,000 Mexicans immigrated between 1891 and 1900, almost 50,000 came during the period 1901 to 1910. The flow from Mexico soared to almost 220,000 between 1911 and 1921 and reached nearly 460,000 between 1921 and 1930. (See Table 1.1 in Chapter 1.)

This increase in Mexican immigration occurred even as overall immigration declined because of the growing tension in Europe that led to World War I (1914–18). It was fueled by the growing need for labor as America prepared to supply its allies and sent many thousands of its young men off to Europe to fight. While legal immigration rose after the war, a large amount of illegal immigration also occurred. Some historians estimated that during the 1920s there might have been more illegal Mexican aliens than legal immigrants. The need for Mexican labor was so great that in 1918 the commissioner-general of immigration exempted Mexicans from meeting most immigration conditions, such as head taxes (small amounts paid to come into the country) and literacy requirements.

The First Illegal Alien "Problem"

The increase in the number of illegal aliens from Mexico led to the creation of the U.S. Border Patrol in 1924. The United States had maintained a small force of mounted guards to deter alien smuggling, but this force was inadequate to stop large numbers of illegal aliens. The efforts of the Border Patrol contributed to a sharp increase in the number of aliens deported during the 1920s and 1930s.

In 1929 administrative control along the Mexican border was significantly tightened as the Great Depression led many Americans to blame the nation's unemployment on the illegal aliens. Consequently, thousands of Mexicans—both legal immigrants and illegal aliens—were repatriated (sent back to Mexico). According to the 1940 U.S. Census Report, the Mexican-born population in the United States declined from 639,000 in 1930 to 377,000 in 1940.

The Bracero Program (1942 to 1964)

World War II (1941–45) brought the country out of the Great Depression. Industry expanded and drew rural laborers into the cities. Other workers were drafted and went off to war. Once more, the United States needed laborers, especially farm workers, and the nation again turned to Mexico. The Bracero Program was a negotiated treaty between Mexico and the United States, permitting the entry of Mexican farm workers on a temporary basis under contract to U.S. employers. (The term *bracero* literally meant a pair of arms, or *brazos*; in this case, it signified a laborer.) The entire program lasted 22 years and involved approximately 4.8 million Mexican workers (Handbook of Texas Online, http://www.tsha.utexas.edu/handbook/online/articles/view/BB/omb1.html).

The Bracero Program, however, did not end illegal immigration but further contributed to its increase. Many Mexicans became accustomed to working in the United States and earning higher wages than they could get in Mexico. They told friends and relatives that while conditions were not always satisfactory, the pay was better than in Mexico.

MISSING MONEY. Between 1942 and 1949 American employers deducted 10% from the braceros weekly wages for a savings plan. The U.S. government transferred the money to banks in Mexico. It was estimated that, with interest, the aggregate savings accounts should have yielded $500 million or more. However, when the braceros went back to their country, no money could be found. In April 2001 a group of former braceros filed a class-action lawsuit seeking reparations for the money deducted from their salaries (*Senorino Ramirez Cruz, et al., v. United States of America* [C-01-0892]). In August 2002, Federal District Judge Charles R. Brever dismissed the lawsuit on the grounds that the government-owned Mexican banks could not be sued and the statute of limitations permitting claims against the U.S. government had expired. His ruling stated that he did "not doubt that many braceros never received Savings Fund withholdings to which they were entitled."

North American Free Trade Agreement (NAFTA)

In December 1993 the North American Free Trade Agreement (NAFTA; PL 103-182) was passed to eliminate trade and investment barriers among the United States, Canada, and Mexico over a fifteen-year period. NAFTA was intended to promote economic growth in each country so that, in the long run, the number of illegal immigrants seeking to enter the United States for work would diminish. One of NAFTA's provisions facilitated temporary entry on a reciprocal basis among the three countries. It established procedures for Canadian and Mexican citizens who were professional businesspeople to temporarily enter the United States to render services for pay. President Clinton claimed that more jobs on both sides of the southwest border meant more income for Mexican nationals, which would help reduce the number of undocumented aliens entering the United States.

K. Larry Storrs reported in *Mexico–U.S. Relations: Issues for the 107th Congress* (Washington, DC: The Library of Congress, Congressional Research Service, May 4, 2001) that total U.S. trade with Mexico grew from $100 billion to $248 billion between 1994 and 2000. However, due partly to the devaluation of the peso (the unit of Mexican currency) in 1994, the U.S. trade balance with Mexico had gone from a surplus of $1.3 billion in 1994 to a deficit of $24.2 billion in 2000. According to the American Farm Bureau Federation, however, by 2001 the United States had an agricultural trade surplus with Mexico of $2.1 billion.

A Guide for the Illegal Migrant

In the January 9, 2005, article, "A Guide for the Illegal Migrant," in the *New York Times*, James C. McKinley Jr. reported that the Mexican government had published and distributed a thirty-one page guide to assist illegal migrants in entering the United States. Members of the U.S. Congress protested what they saw as "blatantly encourage[ing] people to break United States law." Mexican officials compared the pamphlet to providing information about AIDS to illegal drug users. They argued that the document was intended to save lives by warning Mexican people of the dangers of illegal border crossing. The *New York Times* reproduced translated excerpts from the guide. While outlining the legal methods of gaining entry into the United States and noting the hazards of illegal entry, the guide listed the migrant's rights once inside the United States and offered tips on how to avoid being discovered after successful illegal entry. In a January 5, 2005, story entitled "Mexico Issues Illustrated Migrant Guide," the Associated Press reported that 1.5 million copies of the guide had been distributed in December 2004. Despite U.S. protests, Mexico's Secretariat of Foreign Relations announced on January 22, 2005, that Mexico would reprint the guide

TABLE 5.7

Uses of *matrícula consular*

	7/25/04 Los Angeles	9/24/04 New York	10/29/04 Dallas	11/19/04 Chicago	12/3/04 Fresno	12/10/04 Raleigh	1/28/05 Atlanta	Total	Matrícula ID	No U.S. ID
As an ID card in the U.S.	63	73	72	70	48	68	77	68	100	83
To cash checks in the U.S.	33	26	37	29	21	28	29	31	41	38
To mail money to Mexico from the U.S.	25	28	32	25	16	18	25	25	34	30
To open a bank account in the U.S.	41	46	43	39	21	32	40	39	48	47
To get a driver's license in the U.S.	18	22	22	15	11	31	24	19	24	22
To travel to Mexico from the U.S.	47	28	39	44	63	44	36	43	34	29

SOURCE: Roberto Suro, "Table 16. Uses of the *Matrícula Consular*," in *Survey of Mexican Migrants: Attitudes about Immigration and Major Demographic Characteristics*, Pew Hispanic Center, March 2, 2005, http://pewhispanic.org/files/reports/41.pdf (accessed March 7, 2005) © 2005, Pew Hispanic Center, a Pew Research Center project.

and continue distribution (Natalia Gomez, "Mexican Government to Reprint Migrant Guide," *El Universal*, January 22, 2005).

ATTITUDES OF MEXICAN MIGRANTS SURVEYED

For its *Survey of Mexican Migrants: Attitudes about Immigration and Major Demographic Characteristics* (Washington, DC, 2005), the Pew Hispanic Center interviewed nearly 5,000 Mexican migrants who were applying for a matrícula consular, an identity document issued by Mexican consulates in the United States. The surveys were conducted at the consulates in Los Angeles and Fresno, California; New York City; Chicago, Illinois; Atlanta, Georgia; Dallas, Texas; and Raleigh, North Carolina. The majority of individuals surveyed had no U.S. government-issued identification (80% of those who had lived in the United States two years or less; 75% of those who had lived in the country five years or less).

The matrícula consular was a laminated photo ID card bearing the person's name and home address in the United States, which was issued by Mexican officials without inquiring about the individual's immigration status in the United States. The cards included a number of antiforgery techniques used in ID cards issued by the U.S. government. The Mexican government began issuing these cards March 6, 2003, and as of February 2005 some 2.8 million matrícula consulars had been disbursed.

Obtaining a U.S. Driver's License

While it is not accepted as proof of legal status in the United States, the matrícula consular is accepted as identification by many law enforcement officials and local governments. The U.S. Treasury Department ruled in 2003 that the card could be used to open bank accounts, an option previously unavailable to aliens without proof of legal status. Of the migrants surveyed, 39% had used the card to open a U.S. bank account. The Pew study

noted that, according to the National Immigration Law Center, as of January 2005 ten states accepted the matrícula consular as ID for persons seeking driver's licenses. Nineteen percent of all individuals surveyed reported they had used the card to obtain a U.S. driver's license, despite the fact that, of the cities in which the survey was conducted, only Dallas was in a state that issued driver's licenses based on a matrícula consular. From 11% to 31% of respondents in the other cities said they had used it to get a driver's license. (See Table 5.7.)

The Pew survey noted that applying for a matrícula consular did not mean that an individual was an unauthorized migrant (illegal alien). However, both permanent and temporary legal immigrants would have other forms of ID, such as a valid Mexican passport; permanent legal immigrants also would have a green card and be eligible for a Social Security card and driver's license in all states.

Where Do Mexican Immigrants Settle in the United States?

Mexican migrants, both legal and illegal, were once found primarily in the South and border states where agricultural employment was most available. Since 1990 more Mexican migrants have moved into other areas of the country in search of job opportunities. Figure 5.7 provides a visual image of where Mexican-born migrants lived in greatest numbers according to the 2000 census. Some researchers have suggested that illegal aliens did not respond to the census and therefore they were not counted in the census figures. However, many census enumerators, who went in person to addresses that had not responded to the census by mail, told a different story. They related that in face-to-face interviews, illegal aliens frequently identified themselves. Some said they thought it was an honor to be counted in the U.S. census. Often they stated that they wanted to be sure their children were listed in the census, regardless of whether they were born in the United States.

FIGURE 5.7

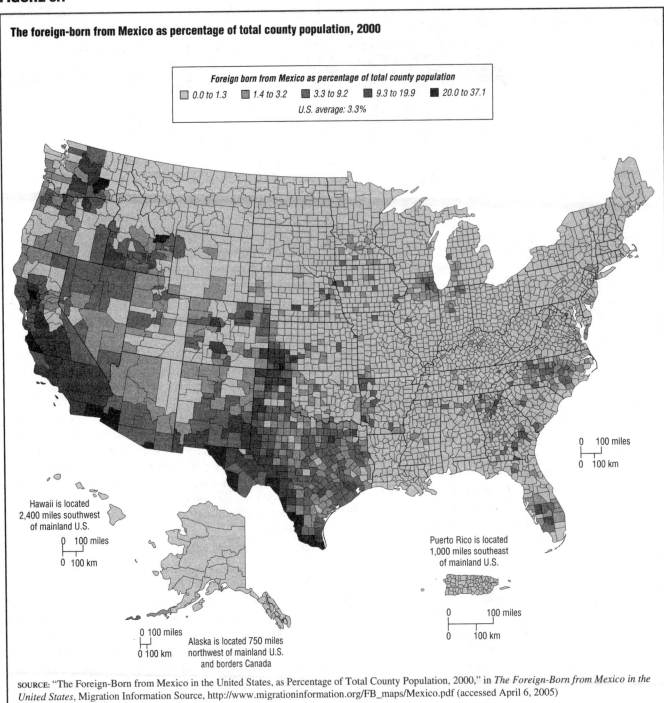

The foreign-born from Mexico as percentage of total county population, 2000

Foreign born from Mexico as percentage of total county population

☐ *0.0 to 1.3* ☐ *1.4 to 3.2* ■ *3.3 to 9.2* ■ *9.3 to 19.9* ■ *20.0 to 37.1*

U.S. average: 3.3%

Hawaii is located
2,400 miles southwest
of mainland U.S.

0   100 miles
0   100 km

Puerto Rico is located
1,000 miles southeast
of mainland U.S.

0   100 miles
0   100 km

0   100 miles
0   100 km

Alaska is located 750 miles
northwest of mainland U.S.
and borders Canada

0   100 miles
0   100 km

SOURCE: "The Foreign-Born from Mexico in the United States, as Percentage of Total County Population, 2000," in *The Foreign-Born from Mexico in the United States*, Migration Information Source, http://www.migrationinformation.org/FB_maps/Mexico.pdf (accessed April 6, 2005)

Profile of Mexican Migrants

According to the Pew survey's findings, 48% of Mexican migrants interviewed were between the ages of nineteen and twenty-nine and 42% had been in the United States five years or less. Most (59%) wanted to remain in the United States as long as they could or for the rest of their lives. The Pew survey noted an increase of women (40%) in what had been a male-dominated flow of immigrants in the past. In addition, the group was better educated than the average population of Mexico (where only 7% of the adult population had completed high

school) and more came from cities than agricultural areas. Thirty-six percent of those surveyed had completed lower secondary school (equivalent to U.S. grades 7–9) or vocational school, and 22% had completed high school. The largest share (27%) said they earned between $200 and $299 per week in the United States. Of all individuals surveyed, 54% said they spoke little or no English.

Furthermore, 68% of respondents said they had children, while 35% reported they had children enrolled in U.S. schools. Eighty-two percent said they had relatives

TABLE 5.8

Major industries of employment for Mexican migrants surveyed in selected cities, July 2004–January 2005

[¿EN QUÉ INDUSTRIA TRABAJA PRINCIPALMENTE USTED AHORA AQUÍ EN LOS EE.UU.? (WHAT IS THE MAIN TYPE OF INDUSTRY YOU NOW WORK AT IN THE U.S.?)]

	Los Angeles	New York	Dallas	Chicago	Fresno	Raleigh	Atlanta	Total	Matrícula ID	No U.S. ID
Agriculture	3	5	5	4	52	10	5	8	7	6
Hospitality	13	26	16	17	6	10	16	15	17	18
Construction	9	15	26	12	5	37	26	16	17	17
Manufacturing	19	11	13	23	5	17	19	16	17	16
Janitorial and landscaping	9	9	11	9	4	10	8	9	9	10
Domestic service	6	8	2	2	3	2	2	4	4	4
Commerce/sales	10	8	4	7	5	2	4	7	7	7
Installation, maintenance and repair	3	2	3	3	1	4	1	3	2	2
Transportation and warehousing	3	2	1	3	3	*	1	2	1	1

SOURCE: Roberto Suro, "Table 15. Major Industries of Employment," in *Survey of Mexican Migrants: Part One, Attitudes about Immigration and Major Demographic Characteristics*, Pew Hispanic Center, March 2, 2005, http://pewhispanic.org/files/reports/41.pdf (accessed March 7, 2005) © 2005, Pew Hispanic Center, a Pew Research Center project.

other than children or spouse living in the United States. Of those who had been in the United States six to ten years, more than half (52%) had no photo ID issued by a U.S. government agency, and 26% of those who had lived in the United States fifteen years or more did not have such an ID.

While 47% of the total group surveyed worked in hospitality, construction, or manufacturing industries, the share varied greatly by the city in which the survey was conducted. The percentage employed in the hospitality industry (hotels, restaurants, and bars) was highest in New York City (26%). Manufacturing claimed the greatest share in Chicago (23%). In Dallas (26%), Raleigh (37%), and Atlanta (26%) the greatest share worked in construction. (See Table 5.8.) Construction workers tended to be male, younger than the average for the survey group, and earned more money. Agricultural workers tended to be older, less educated, and a disproportionate share had lived in the United States more than fifteen years. Only 10% of respondents said they did not work, and these were predominantly females.

Public Agenda, a nonpartisan opinion research organization, also interviewed immigrants for a study released in 2005 (*Now That I'm Here: What America's Immigrants Have to Say about Life in the U.S. Today*, New York). One section of the study compared Mexican immigrants to immigrants from other countries. Mexican immigrants were almost three times more likely to lack English language skills when they came to the United States (71% compared to 26%); almost four times as likely to lack a high school diploma (35% compared to 9%); more than twice as likely to lack health insurance (40% compared to 17%); and more likely to have an annual household income of $25,000 or less (44% compared to 27%). (See Figure 5.8.)

When Public Agenda asked immigrants what things were better in the United States and what things were better in their home country, Mexican immigrants found

the United States better in all categories to a greater degree than immigrants from other countries. Mexican immigrants differed most from all other immigrants on issues of health care and a place to raise children. Just 6% of Mexican immigrants thought their home country was better than the United States at making good health care available, while 22% of other immigrants preferred health care in their home countries. Similarly, 9% of Mexican immigrants thought their home country was a better place to raise children compared to 26% of immigrants from other countries. All immigrants agreed by a strong majority that the United States had a more honest government, a trustworthy legal system, and honored women's rights. (See Figure 5.9.)

DISASTERS CHALLENGED ILLEGAL ALIENS

An estimated five hundred people from ninety-one foreign countries were among the approximately three thousand people who died in the terrorist attacks of September 11, 2001. In New York City, some of these were undocumented workers employed in the World Trade Center. From the more than 7,000 claims filed with the September 11th Victim Compensation Fund, which was administered by the Department of Justice, about 250 foreigners qualified for compensation, according to reporter Lisa J. Adams ("Kin Struggle for Proof of Foreign 9/11 Victims," *Denver Post*, September 24, 2004). Administrators estimated that about fifty of the 250 were undocumented. No doubt there were more illegal aliens lost in the disaster for whom no claims were filed. Although fund administrators took great pains to ensure that undocumented immigrants who came forward would not be reported to the INS, many families of illegal aliens decided it was not worth the risk. The stakes were high. The average settlement was about $1.3 million per claim (Kenneth R. Feinberg, *Final Report of the Special Master for the September 11th Victim Compensation Fund of 2001*, Volume 1, Washington, DC: U.S. Department of Justice).

FIGURE 5.8

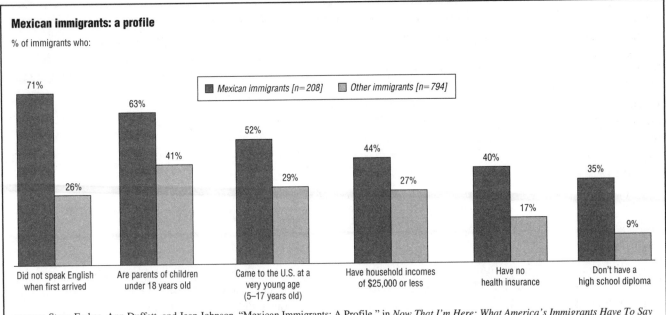

Mexican immigrants: a profile

% of immigrants who:

■ *Mexican immigrants [n=208]* □ *Other immigrants [n=794]*

Did not speak English when first arrived	Are parents of children under 18 years old	Came to the U.S. at a very young age (5–17 years old)	Have household incomes of $25,000 or less	Have no health insurance	Don't have a high school diploma
71% / 26%	63% / 41%	52% / 29%	44% / 27%	40% / 17%	35% / 9%

SOURCE: Steve Farkas, Ann Duffett, and Jean Johnson, "Mexican Immigrants: A Profile," in *Now That I'm Here: What America's Immigrants Have To Say about Life In the U.S. Today*, Public Agenda, 2003, http://www.publicagenda.org/research/pdfs/now_that_im_here.pdf (accessed February 21, 2005)

FIGURE 5.9

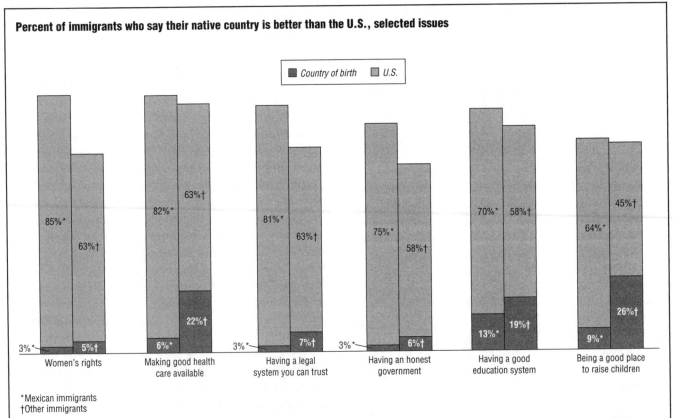

Percent of immigrants who say their native country is better than the U.S., selected issues

■ *Country of birth* □ *U.S.*

Women's rights	Making good health care available	Having a legal system you can trust	Having an honest government	Having a good education system	Being a good place to raise children
85%* / 63%†	82%* / 63%†	81%* / 63%†	75%* / 58%†	70%* / 58%†	64%* / 45%†
3%* / 5%†	6%* / 22%†	3%* / 7%†	3%* / 6%†	13%* / 19%†	9%* / 26%†

*Mexican immigrants
†Other immigrants

SOURCE: Steve Farkas, Ann Duffett, and Jean Johnson, "An Even Better Comparison," in *Now That I'm Here: What America's Immigrants Have To Say about Life In the U.S. Today*, Public Agenda, 2003, http://www.publicagenda.org/research/pdfs/now_that_im_here.pdf (accessed February 21, 2005)

For families of illegal aliens who did wish to make a claim, seeking compensation or just a death certificate ranges from difficult to impossible. Illegal aliens often use fake names and shared housing so they have no rent receipts or utility bills in their names. Many work in jobs where they are paid in cash. Without a paycheck stub, Social Security number, tax records, money transfer receipts, or an employer who would verify the deceased as an employee, grieving families were unable to prove that their relatives were at the World Trade Center at the time of the terrorist attacks.

U.S. authorities required little more than a photo of the victim in his/her former New York workplace to issue a death certificate for missing immigrants. Yet, of approximately sixteen undocumented Mexican victims, only five families were able to prove the person died in the 9/11 attacks and qualify for compensation.

When hurricanes Charley, Frances, Ivan, and Jeanne pounded the state of Florida in August and September 2004, thousands of people were left with damaged or destroyed homes. Power was out for weeks in some areas. Businesses, too, were damaged or destroyed, leaving employees with no paychecks. Among the victims were many foreign-born families, both legal and illegal, who formed the backbone of Florida's agriculture, construction, and service industries. Rob Williams of Florida Legal Services' Migrant Farmworker Justice Program estimated there were some 300,000 migrant agriculture workers in the state who lost $40 million in wages due to destroyed crops. The Federal Emergency Management Agency (FEMA) provided a variety of financial aid to individuals and communities impacted by the disaster. Sandra Hernandez, reporting for the *Ft. Lauderdale Sun-Sentinel* ("Change in Law Hurting the Needy," October 8, 2004), noted that 1996 welfare reforms prohibited FEMA from providing cash assistance, including loans to rebuild homes and money to recoup lost wages, to "nonqualified" immigrants. This included undocumented workers and some legal immigrants such as asylum applicants or people with temporary protected status. Undocumented residents with children born in the United States could apply for FEMA benefits in the child's name. However, many were afraid to identify themselves to a government agency. The "nonqualified" immigrants were then left to voluntary agencies that provided assistance such as water, food, and temporary shelter, but little financial aid in the midst of life-altering disaster.

CHAPTER 6

THE COST OF IMMIGRATION

WEIGHING THE COSTS AND BENEFITS OF IMMIGRATION

Immigration is a hotly contested issue. Immigration supporters contend that immigrants contribute considerable sums of money to the public coffers and that, in an aging society, immigration is the only hope for a secure economic future. Immigration opponents argue that immigrants cost taxpayers far more than they contribute. George J. Borjas, an immigrant who left Cuba at age twelve and became a professor of public policy at the John F. Kennedy School of Government at Harvard University, concluded in *Heaven's Door: Immigration Policy and the American Economy* (Princeton, NJ: Princeton University Press, 1999) that immigration returned a relatively small net economic benefit of less than $10 billion a year (in a then–$8 trillion economy). He believed that current immigration policy, which favored family ties over work skills, might harm American interests. Moreover, he argued that since immigration accounted for the continuing growth in U.S. population, immigrants played an increasing role in determining America's demographic and economic trends. Borjas claimed that the lower educational levels of the more recent immigrants would keep them at an economic disadvantage, which in the long run would result in greater use of welfare.

In testimony given before the House Subcommittee on Immigration and Claims at a hearing on "The U.S. Population and Immigration" ("U.S. Immigration at the Beginning of the 21st Century," Washington, DC: The Urban Institute, August 2, 2001), Census Bureau immigration analysts Michael E. Fix and Jeffrey S. Passel pointed out that it was difficult to measure the fiscal impact of immigration because "there is no general agreement and no clear rationale for deciding which costs and impacts to include, nor on how to measure them." Much public concern about immigrants (legal and illegal) focuses on their use of public benefits and their overall cost to the nation's taxpayers. Some people believe that too many immigrants come to the United States to take advantage of taxpayer-funded education, health care, and other social services without ever contributing to the system. Indeed, the fear that immigrants are too heavily reliant on welfare was one factor that influenced the passage of the Personal Responsibility and Work Opportunity Reconciliation Act (PRWORA) of 1996 (also called the welfare reform law; PL 104-193). Under Title IV of the act, federal welfare benefits for legal immigrants were cut substantially. Those who oppose this provision believe that the revenues produced by immigrants far outweighed the initial cost of their immigration.

A Study of Illegal Immigrants

A report released in August 2004 by the Center for Immigration Studies (CIS) concluded that American households headed by illegal immigrants used $26.3 billion in government services during 2002, but paid only $16 billion in taxes. According to the report this resulted in an annual cost of $10 billion to taxpaying U.S. citizens. CIS described itself as "an independent, nonpartisan, nonprofit research organization ... animated by a pro-immigrant, low-immigration vision which seeks fewer immigrants but a warmer welcome for those admitted." The CIS study, *Illegals Cost Feds $10 Billion a Year; Amnesty Would Nearly Triple Cost* (Washington, DC), was described as one of the first to estimate the impact of illegal immigration on the federal budget.

Table 6.1 compares social characteristics of legal immigrants, illegal aliens, and natives. Illegal aliens had the highest share of uninsured persons, those receiving welfare, and those living in poverty or near poverty. These figures referred only to federal programs; the study noted that costs at the state and local level were also likely to be significant.

TABLE 6.1

Selected social characteristics, 2004

	Rate	Number [thousands]
Poverty all persons	12.5%	35,874
All immigrants[a]	17.2%	5,900
Immigrants and their U.S.-born children (under 18)[b]	18.5%	8,148
Illegal aliens only (estimate)	22.6%	2,058
Natives	11.8%	29,974
Natives and their children[c]	11.3%	27,456
In or near poverty all persons[d]	31.1%	89,361
All immigrants[a]	43.0%	14,719
Immigrants and their U.S.-born children (under 18)[b]	45.0%	20,447
Illegal aliens only (estimate)	58.7%	5,349
Natives	29.4%	74,642
Natives and their children[c]	28.4%	68,914
Uninsured all persons	15.6%	44,961
All immigrants[a]	34.5%	11,815
Immigrants and their U.S.-born children (under 18)[b]	30.0%	13,647
Illegal aliens only (estimate)	64.5%	5,892
Natives	13.0%	33,146
Natives and their children[c]	12.9%	31,314
Welfare use[e] all households	17.1%	19,162
All immigrant households	25.7%	3,638
Illegal alien households (estimate)	30.0%	932
Native households	15.9%	15,524
Self employment[f] all persons	11.0%	13,929
Foreign born	9.7%	1,790
Natives	11.2%	12,139

[a]Includes all foreign-born individuals, including illegals aliens.
[b]Includes all immigrants and all children (under 18) of immigrant mothers, including those born in the United States.
[c]Excludes the U.S.-born children of immigrant mothers.
[d]In or near poverty defined as under 200 percent of the offical poverty threshold.
[e]Based on nativity of household head, at least one person in household uses TANF (Temporary Assistance for Needy Families), food stamps, SSI, public/subsidized housing or Medicaid.
[f]Self employment figures are for employed persons 18 years of age and older.

SOURCE: Steven A. Camarota, "Table 6. Selected Social Characteristics," in *Economy Slowed, But Immigration Didn't: The Foreign-Born Population, 2000–2004*, Center for Immigration Studies, November 2004, http://www.cis.org/articles/2004/back1204.pdf (accessed February 2, 2005).

The CIS study projected that, if illegal aliens were given amnesty, the fiscal deficit at the federal level would grow to nearly $29 billion. Some of the findings of the study included:

- Among the largest federal costs incurred were Medicaid ($2.5 billion); treatment for the uninsured ($2.2 billion); food assistance programs ($1.9 billion); the federal prison and court systems ($1.6 billion); and federal aid to schools ($1.4 billion).

- With nearly two-thirds of illegal aliens lacking a high school diploma, the primary reason they created a fiscal deficit was their low education levels and resulting low incomes and tax payments—not their legal status or any unwillingness to work.

- Amnesty would increase costs because illegal aliens would still be largely unskilled, and thus their tax payments would continue to be very modest—but once legalized they would be able to access many more government services.

- The fact that legal immigrants with little schooling were a fiscal drain on federal coffers did not mean that legal immigrants overall were a drain. Many legal immigrants were highly skilled.

- Because many of the costs were due to their U.S.-born children, who were awarded U.S. citizenship at birth, barring illegal aliens themselves from federal programs would not significantly reduce costs.

- Although they created a net drain on the federal government, the average illegal household paid more than $4,200 a year in federal taxes, for a total of nearly $16 billion.

- However, they imposed annual costs of more than $26.3 billion, or about $6,950 per illegal household.

- About 43%, or $7 billion, of the federal taxes illegal aliens paid went to Social Security and Medicare.

- Employers did not see the costs associated with less-educated immigrant workers because the costs were spread out among all taxpayers.

Educational Attainment

According to the U.S. Census Bureau's *The Foreign-Born Population in the United States: 2003* (Luke J. Larsen, Current Population Reports P20-551, Washington, DC, August 2004), in 2003 the share of both the native-born and foreign-born population who had completed a bachelor's degree or more was almost identical (about one-fourth of both groups). However, just 40% of the foreign-born had completed high school compared to 60.3% of the native-born. On the lower end of the educational scale, 21.5% of the foreign-born had less than a ninth-grade education compared to just 4.1% of the native-born population.

Countries of origin make a great difference in the education levels of immigrants. More than 80% of foreign-born residents from both Asia and Europe had at least a high school education compared to 37.7% from Central America. (See Figure 6.1.) According to the Census Bureau's report, fifty percent of the foreign-born from Asia had at least a bachelor's degree while just 11.6% of persons from Latin America had completed the same level of education.

The report's findings indicated that household income levels corresponded to education levels. Among foreign-born families from Asia, more than half (53.6%) had annual incomes of $50,000 or more in 2002, compared to just 29% of families from Latin America. Native-born

FIGURE 6.1

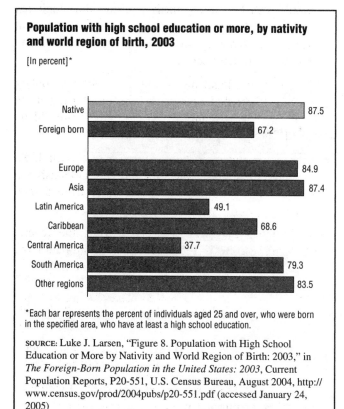

Population with high school education or more, by nativity and world region of birth, 2003

[In percent]*

Region	Percent
Native	87.5
Foreign born	67.2
Europe	84.9
Asia	87.4
Latin America	49.1
Caribbean	68.6
Central America	37.7
South America	79.3
Other regions	83.5

*Each bar represents the percent of individuals aged 25 and over, who were born in the specified area, who have at least a high school education.

SOURCE: Luke J. Larsen, "Figure 8. Population with High School Education or More by Nativity and World Region of Birth: 2003," in *The Foreign-Born Population in the United States: 2003*, Current Population Reports, P20-551, U.S. Census Bureau, August 2004, http://www.census.gov/prod/2004pubs/p20-551.pdf (accessed January 24, 2005)

families fell in between with 44% in the $50,000 or more household income range. (See Figure 6.2.)

Labor Force Characteristics of Immigrants

According to data in another U.S. Census Bureau report (Dianne Schmidley, *The Foreign-Born Population in the United States: March 2002*, Current Population Reports P20-539, Washington, DC, February 2003), as of March 2002 the foreign-born population (which comprised 12.4% of the civilian labor force of 140.5 million people) participated in the labor market at about the same rate as the native population (66.6% compared to 67.3%, respectively), thereby contributing income and payroll taxes. The labor force participation rate among males in their prime working years was higher for the foreign-born population (92.8%) than for native males (91.2%). For females, however, the labor force participation rate was lower at every age among the foreign-born population than among the native population.

Do Immigrants Cause Job Losses for Native Workers?

In *A Jobless Recovery? Immigrant Gains and Native Losses* (Washington, DC: Center for Immigration Studies, October 2004), Steven A. Camarota compared immigrant and native employment in 2000 and 2004. Table 6.2 shows that the number of working immigrants increased by 2.3 million in the four-year period while the number of working natives decreased by 482,000.

Camarota identified a number of factors that may have contributed to the reduced number of employed natives: early retirements, more mothers staying home to raise children, and an increased number of native students out of the job market while attending college. However, he concluded that economic conditions accounted for most of the loss of workforce participation by natives.

Camarota noted that the rapid increase in the number of immigrants made it possible for both the number of immigrants working and the number not working to increase at the same time. Camarota disputed the argument that "immigrants only take jobs Americans don't want," noting that half of the increase in jobs held by immigrants was in positions requiring more than a high school education. He also noted that while both immigrants and natives with less than a high school education experienced unemployment, the influx of immigrants may have made it more difficult for natives with limited education to find jobs.

Immigrant Occupations and Native Unemployment

Camarota also examined the impact of immigration by occupations. Farming, building maintenance, and construction had the highest percentage of immigrants for the total number of people in those occupations. They were also the occupations with the highest unemployment rates for natives. For example, 36% of all employees in farming were immigrants, and the native unemployment rate in farming was 11.9%. The greatest number of immigrants who arrived between 2000 and 2004 worked in construction (462,000) while that industry had the highest native unemployment rate at 12.7%. (See Table 6.3.) Camarota concluded that such data did not show immigrants to be the cause of native unemployment, but it also did not support the argument that there were no American workers available to fill lower-skilled jobs.

In Table 6.4 Camarota analyzed immigrant and native employment in the states that had experienced the greatest increase in immigrant workers. California, with the largest influx of immigrants, had a nearly even balance in employment growth between immigrants and natives. From 2000 to 2004, California saw a 3% growth in immigrant employment and a 2% growth in native employment. By contrast, during the same period, growth in the number of immigrants working in Texas was 25% while the number of natives working increased by just 1%. Camarota noted that in New York the number of both immigrant and native workers declined while in Massachusetts natives gained jobs and the number of immigrants working declined. Camarota concluded that "[i]mmigration is only one of many factors that can have an impact on labor market outcomes for natives."

Unemployment data for 2003 in the U.S. Census Bureau's *The Foreign-Born Population in the United*

FIGURE 6.2

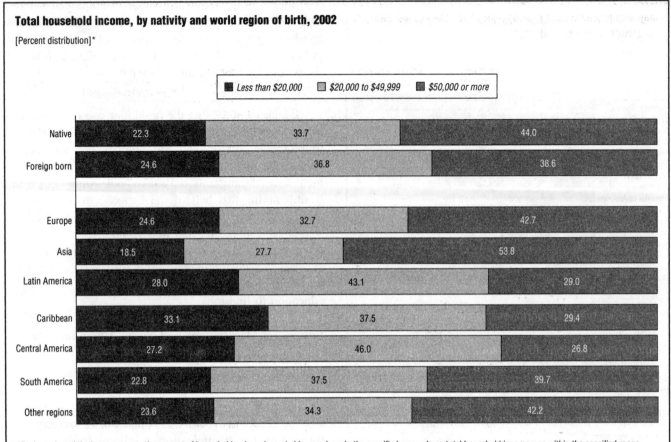

Total household income, by nativity and world region of birth, 2002

[Percent distribution]*

Legend: Less than $20,000 | $20,000 to $49,999 | $50,000 or more

Region	Less than $20,000	$20,000 to $49,999	$50,000 or more
Native	22.3	33.7	44.0
Foreign born	24.6	36.8	38.6
Europe	24.6	32.7	42.7
Asia	18.5	27.7	53.8
Latin America	28.0	43.1	29.0
Caribbean	33.1	37.5	29.4
Central America	27.2	46.0	26.8
South America	22.8	37.5	39.7
Other regions	23.6	34.3	42.2

*Each section of the bar represents the percent of households whose householder was born in the specified area, whose total household income was within the specified range.

SOURCE: Luke J. Larsen, "Figure 9. Total Household Income by Nativity and World Region of Birth: 2002," in *The Foreign-Born Population in the United States: 2003*, Current Population Reports, P20-551, U.S. Census Bureau, August 2004, http://www.census.gov/prod/2004pubs/p20-551.pdf (accessed January 24, 2005)

TABLE 6.2

Immigrant and native labor force status in thousands, 2000 and 2004

[In thousands]

	Immigrants	Natives
Number working 2000[a]	17,463	115,797
Number working 2004[a]	19,742	115,315
Change in number working 2000–2004[a]	2,279	−482
Number unemployed 2000[a]	904	4,812
Number unemployed 2004	1,292	7,085
Change in number unemployed 2000–2004[a]	388	2,273
Number not in labor force 2000[b]	5,883	30,846
Number not in labor force 2004[b]	6,923	34,813
Change in number not in labor force 2000–2004[b]	1,040	3,967

[a]Figures for those working or unemployed are for persons 18 years of age and older.
[b]Figures for those not in workforce are for persons 18 to 64 years of age. Persons not in the labor force are not working or looking for work.

SOURCE: Steven A. Camarota, "Table 1. Immigrant and Native Labor Force Status, 2000 and 2004 (in Thousands)," in *A Jobless Recovery? Immigrant Gains and Native Losses*, Center for Immigration Studies, October 2004, http://www.cis.org/articles/2004/back1104.pdf (accessed February 2, 2005)

States: 2003 (Larsen, Current Population Reports P20-551, August 2004), showed that 7.5% of the foreign-born in the civilian labor force were unemployed compared to 6.2% of the native-born. Among men, 7.2% of foreign-born and 6.9% of native-born were unemployed. The difference was much greater among women—7.9% of foreign-born women were unemployed compared to 5.5% of native-born women.

Income and Poverty Levels for Immigrants

In 2002 the median annual salary for all U.S. workers was $35,038. Native-born workers had a slightly higher median of $35,956. Foreign-born naturalized citizens were generally in line with the overall workforce at a median annual salary of $35,032. Noncitizens earned considerably less, with a median annual salary of $22,687, and female noncitizens had the lowest median annual earnings at $20,774. In a comparison by region of birth, foreign-born workers from Latin America earned the least at $21,943, while workers from Asia had the highest median annual income at $38,383. (See Table 6.5.)

In 2002, 16.6% of all foreign-born persons were living at or below the poverty level compared to 11.5% of natives.

TABLE 6.3

Immigrants and natives, by occupation, 2004 (ranked by immigrant share of occupation)

[In thousands]

	Share of all immigrants who work in occupation	Share of occupation comprised of immigrants	Number of employed natives	Number of unemployed natives*	Number of recently arrived immigrants (2000–2004) employed	Native unemployment rate
Farming, fishing, & forestry	2%	36%	540	73	63	11.9%
Building cleaning & maintenance	8%	35%	3,054	375	318	10.9%
Construction & extraction	10%	24%	5,999	874	462	12.7%
Food preparation	8%	23%	5,090	525	380	9.3%
Production manufacturing	11%	22%	7,249	566	272	7.2%
Computer mathematical	3%	19%	2,451	130	95	5.0%
Life, physical, & social science	1%	18%	1,059	48	39	4.3%
Healthcare support	2%	17%	2,342	166	59	6.6%
Personal care & service	3%	16%	3,549	218	87	5.8%
Transportation & moving	7%	16%	6,925	608	150	8.1%
Architecture & engineering	2%	15%	2,203	77	45	3.4%
Installation and repair	3%	13%	4,296	224	68	5.0%
Healthcare practitioner	4%	12%	5,932	88	66	1.5%
Sales	9%	12%	13,569	879	204	6.1%
Arts, entertainment & media	1%	11%	2,313	145	37	5.9%
Management	7%	10%	12,969	344	133	2.6%
Office & administrative support	9%	10%	17,278	994	162	5.4%
Business and financial	3%	10%	5,098	172	54	3.3%
Community & social service	1%	9%	1,944	55	23	2.8%
Protective service	1%	8%	2,538	134	29	5.0%
Education, training	3%	8%	7,464	101	102	1.3%
Legal occupations	1%	7%	1,454	40	10	2.7%
Totals	**100%**	**15%**	**115,316**	**6,836**	**2,857**	**5.6%**

Figures are for workers 18 years of age and older.
*Not all unemployed persons report an occupation.

SOURCE: Steven A. Camarota, "Table 5. Immigrants and Natives by Occupation in 2004, Ranked by Immigrant Share of Occupation (in Thousands)," in *A Jobless Recovery? Immigrant Gains and Native Losses*, Center for Immigration Studies, October 2004, http://www.cis.org/articles/2004/back1104.pdf (accessed February 2, 2005)

TABLE 6.4

States with the largest number of immigrant workers, in thousands, 2000 and 2004

[In thousands]

	2000		2004		Change in the number of immigrants working 2000–2004	Change in the number of natives working 2000–2004	Share of employment growth going to immigrants 2000–2004
	Number of immigrants working	Number of natives working	Number of immigrants working	Number of natives working			
Texas	1,534	8,049	1,921	8,114	387	65	86%
North Carolina	217	3,686	410	3,496	193	−190	100%
Maryland	302	2,303	490	2,236	188	−67	100%
Georgia	223	3,787	410	3,644	187	−143	100%
California	5,177	10,385	5,339	10,552	162	167	49%
Arizona	383	1,912	527	1,947	144	35	80%
New Jersey	782	3,326	924	3,199	142	−127	100%
Virginia	337	3,116	455	3,085	118	−31	100%
Florida	1,607	5,691	1,670	6,048	63	357	15%
Illinois	800	5,276	818	5,159	18	−117	No emp. increase
New York	2,162	6,489	2,121	6,329	−41	−160	No emp. increase
Massachusetts	524	2,617	478	2,652	−46	35	0%

Note: Figures are for workers 18 years of age and older.

SOURCE: Steven A. Camarota, "Table 6. States with the Largest Numbers of Immigrant Workers (in Thousands)," in *A Jobless Recovery? Immigrant Gains and Native Losses*, Center for Immigration Studies, October 2004, http://www.cis.org/articles/2004/back1104.pdf (accessed February 2, 2005)

Among the foreign-born population, noncitizens had double the share (20.7%) of persons living at or below the poverty level compared to naturalized citizens (10.0%). A lower percentage of naturalized citizens (10%) were living in poverty than native-born citizens (11.5%). (See Table 6.6.) Among the foreign-born population, those from Latin America had the highest poverty rate (21.6%) while those from Europe had the lowest rate (8.7%). (See Figure 6.3.)

TABLE 6.5

Median annual earnings of native and foreign-born workers, by region of origin, 2002

[In dollars]

	Total median earnings	Median earnings of men	Median earnings of women
All workers	35,038	39,429	30,203
Native workers	35,956	41,015	30,635
Foreign-born workers	27,047	28,994	25,195
Naturalized U.S. citizens	35,032	39,341	30,388
Not U.S. citizens	22,687	24,576	20,774
Region of origin of foreign-born workers			
Europe	36,738	45,474	31,399
Asia	38,383	43,296	31,833
Latin America	21,943	22,941	20,374
Other	32,348	35,802	30,484

Note: The data cover earnings by year-round, full-time workers.

SOURCE: "Table 15. Median Annual Earnings of Native and Foreign-Born Workers, by Region of Origin, 2002," in *A Description of the Immigrant Population*, Congressional Budget Office, November 2004, http://www.cbo.gov/ftpdocs/60xx/doc6019/11-23-Immigrant.pdf (accessed March 7, 2005)

TABLE 6.6

Percentage of native and foreign-born populations at or below poverty level, by age, 2002

	Total population	Native population	Foreign-born population	Foreign-born population Naturalized U.S. citizens	Not U.S. citizens
Total population					
All ages	12.1	11.5	16.6	10.0	20.7
Under 18	16.7	16.2	28.5	16.4	31.0
18 to 64	10.6	9.7	15.6	9.2	19.2
65 and older	10.4	9.9	14.7	11.9	21.0
Men					
All ages	10.9	10.2	15.4	9.3	18.8
Under 18	16.8	16.3	29.0	19.1	30.8
18 to 64	8.9	7.9	14.1	8.7	16.8
65 and older	7.7	7.1	13.4	9.6	21.8
Women					
All ages	13.3	12.7	17.9	10.6	22.9
Under 18	16.6	16.1	28.1	14.0	31.2
18 to 64	12.2	11.4	17.1	9.6	21.9
65 and older	12.4	12.0	15.8	13.6	20.4

SOURCE: "Table 18. Percentage of Native and Foreign-Born Populations at or Below the Poverty Level, by Age, 2002," in *A Description of the Immigrant Population*, Congressional Budget Office, November 2004, http://www.cbo.gov/ftpdocs/60xx/doc6019/11-23-Immigrant.pdf (accessed March 7, 2005)

Table 6.7 details the types of benefits received by U.S. households from different welfare programs in 2001. More than one-fifth (22.7%) of all immigrants received welfare benefits compared to 14.6% of natives. Refugees were the most likely to receive welfare benefits and received the greatest amount of benefits. Of all refugee households (based on the immigration status of the head of household), 28.5% received some type of welfare benefits at an average monthly payment of $3,402.00.

FIGURE 6.3

People living below the poverty level, by nativity and world region of birth, 2002

[In percent]*

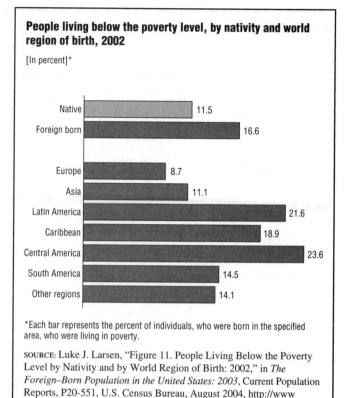

*Each bar represents the percent of individuals, who were born in the specified area, who were living in poverty.

SOURCE: Luke J. Larsen, "Figure 11. People Living Below the Poverty Level by Nativity and by World Region of Birth: 2002," in *The Foreign–Born Population in the United States: 2003*, Current Population Reports, P20-551, U.S. Census Bureau, August 2004, http://www.census.gov/prod/2004pubs/p20-551.pdf (accessed January 24, 2005)

Refugees were the greatest users of all types of welfare benefits—Temporary Assistance to Needy Families (TANF), Food Stamps, Supplemental Security Income (SSI), and Medicaid. While 24.3% of illegal immigrant households received welfare benefits, they received the lowest amount per month of any group, including natives. The primary welfare benefit received by illegal immigrants was Medicaid, which may have been available to U.S.-born children in the household.

THE FISCAL IMPACT OF IMMIGRANTS

Analyses of the Role of Immigrants in Social Security and Medicare

To illustrate the principal fiscal benefit of immigrants, Stephen Moore, an economist at the libertarian think tank called the Cato Institute, explained that through a "pay-as-you-go mechanism" current workers, through their taxes, funded the previous generation's Medicare and Social Security benefits (*A Fiscal Portrait of the Newest Americans*, Washington, DC: National Immigration Forum, 1998). Moore pointed out that while legal immigrants working in the United States paid into the Social Security and Medicare programs, their parents were not collecting benefits since they were, in most cases, not in the United States. According to Moore, "[t]hat creates a huge one-generation windfall to the Social Security system." In addition, he contended that

TABLE 6.7

Household welfare use by household head's immigration status, 2001

	2001	
	Percent using	Average payment
Using any program		
Natives	14.6%	$1,327
All immigrants	22.7%	$1,982
Legal immigrants	22.3%	$2,222
Legal non-refugees	21.3%	$2,029
Refugees	28.5%	$3,402
Illegal immigrants	24.3%	$1,040
TAN F/General assistance		
Natives	1.6%	$51
All immigrants	2.3%	$95
Legal immigrants	2.7%	$112
Legal non-refugees	2.5%	$96
Refugees	3.8%	$209
Illegal immigrants	0.7%	$27
Food stamps		
Natives	5.4%	$86
All immigrants	5.7%	$104
Legal immigrants	5.9%	$107
Legal non-refugees	5.2%	$94
Refugees	10.6%	$187
Illegal immigrants	4.8%	$35
SSI		
Natives	3.9%	$216
All immigrants	4.5%	$291
Legal immigrants	5.5%	$356
Legal non-refugees	4.7%	$293
Refugees	10.1%	$742
Illegal immigrants	0.6%	$35
Medicaid		
Natives	13.4%	$974
All immigrants	21.8%	$1,492
Legal immigrants	21.4%	$1,646
Legal non-refugees	20.5%	$1,545
Refugees	26.9%	$2,264
Illegal immigrants	23.0%	$888

Note: Welfare use rates reflect use of welfare by any member of household. Average payments are in constant 2001 dollars and reflect total value of payment or service received by households in each category divided by total number of households in each category.

SOURCE: Adapted from Steven A. Camarota, "Table 1. Household Welfare Use by Household Head's Immigration Status: 1996 to 2001," in *Back Where We Started: An Examination of Trends in Immigrant Welfare Use since Welfare Reform*, Center for Immigration Studies, March 2003, http://www.cis.org/articles/2003/back503.pdf (accessed April 6, 2005)

immigrants would help ease the financial hardship that is projected to begin in 2011, when the first baby boomers (persons born between 1946 and 1964; about forty million people) start collecting retirement benefits.

David Simcox of the Center for Immigration Studies (CIS) predicted, however, that Mexico would be the source of new immigrants through 2050, adding 300,000 to 400,000 unskilled workers to the economy each year. Simcox opined that "[t]hese cohorts are hardly a promising tax base for rescuing the Social Security fund" (*Another 50 Years of Mass Mexican Immigration: Mexican Government Report Projects Continued Flow Regardless of Economics or Birth Rates*, Washington, DC: Center for Immigration Studies, March 2002).

Taxes Paid by Legal Immigrants

Some analysts believe that immigrants pay more than their share of taxes. In testimony on April 4, 2001, before the Senate Judiciary Committee Subcommittee on Immigration, the Cato Institute's Stephen Moore estimated that immigrants paid $133 billion in direct taxes to federal, state, and local governments in 1998. Moore cited a study by the National Research Council of the National Academy of Sciences that estimated that the typical immigrant and his or her children will pay $80,000 more in taxes than they will receive in local, state, and federal benefits over their lifetimes. Using calculations by Social Security Administration actuaries, Moore said, "I find that the total net benefit (taxes paid over benefits received) to the Social Security system in 1998 dollars from continuing current levels of immigration is nearly $500 billion from 1998–2022 and nearly $2.0 trillion through 2072. Continuing immigration is an essential component to solving the long term financing problem of the Social Security system" (*Immigrants and the U.S. Economy*, Washington, DC: Cato Institute, April 4, 2001).

Taxes Paid by Illegal Immigrants

Before the Internal Revenue Service (IRS) made changes in 2003 to tighten the application process, illegal aliens could apply for an Individual Taxpayer Identification Number (ITIN), which can be used in place of a Social Security number, allowing those who were earning an income in the United States to file tax returns. FOXNews.com reported that tax filers with ITINs paid $300 million in taxes in 2001 ("IRS Keeps Tabs on Illegal Immigrant Filers," April 22, 2003). The *Washington Post* reported that between 1990 and 1998, more than $20 billion was paid into the Social Security fund by "mystery workers," many of whom the government believes to be illegal immigrants who gave their employers false Social Security numbers (Mary Beth Sheridan, "Illegals Paying Millions in Taxes; Most Don't Seek Refunds for Fear of INS Action," April 15, 2001).

Noncitizen Recipients of Supplemental Security Income (SSI)

Of 6.9 million persons receiving SSI benefits in 2003, 10.1% were noncitizens. This was a decrease from a peak of 12.1% in 1995. Those 696,772 noncitizen SSI beneficiaries represented 28.9% of all aged SSI recipients and 6% of all blind and disabled recipients in 2003. (See Table 6.8.)

A person's work history determines his or her eligibility for Social Security benefits, as well as SSI eligibility for some noncitizens. In 2004 one credit was added to a person's work record for each $900 of earnings, up to the maximum of four credits per year. Generally, noncitizens could be eligible for SSI if (1) they were lawfully living in the United States on August 22, 1996, and were blind or disabled on that date, or were receiving SSI on August 22, 1996; or (2) they

TABLE 6.8

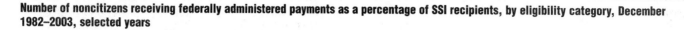

Number of noncitizens receiving federally administered payments as a percentage of SSI recipients, by eligibility category, December 1982–2003, selected years

Year	All noncitizens		Aged		Blind and disabled	
	Number	Percentage of total SSI	Number	Percentage of total SSI	Number	Percentage of total SSI
1982	127,900	3.3	91,900	5.9	36,000	1.6
1985	210,800	5.1	146,500	9.7	64,300	2.4
1990	435,600	9	282,400	19.4	153,200	4.6
1991	519,660	10.2	329,690	22.5	189,970	5.2
1992	601,430	10.8	372,930	25.4	228,500	5.6
1993	683,150	11.4	416,420	28.2	266,730	5.9
1994	738,140	11.7	440,000	30	298,140	6.2
1995	785,410	12.1	459,220	31.8	326,190	6.3
1996	724,990	11	417,360	29.5	307,630	5.9
1997	650,830	10	367,200	27	283,630	5.5
1998	669,630	10.2	364,980	27.4	304,650	5.8
1999	684,930	10.4	368,330	28.2	316,600	6
2000	692,590	10.5	364,470	28.3	328,120	6.2
2001	695,650	10.4	364,550	28.9	331,100	6.1
2002	703,515	10.4	364,827	29.1	338,688	6.1
2003	696,772	10.1	356,298	28.9	340,474	6

SOURCE: "Table 7. E6. Number of Noncitizens Receiving Federally Administered Payments as a Percentage of SSI Recipients, by Eligibility Category, December 1982–2003, Selected Years," in *Annual Statistical Supplement, 2004*, Social Security Online, http://www.socialsecurity.gov/policy/docs/statcomps/supplement/2004/7e.html#table7.e6 (accessed March 10, 2005)

were lawfully admitted for permanent residence under the Immigration and Nationality Act (INA) and had a total of forty credits of work in the United States (work credits from the spouse or parent might also count).

Some other noncitizens could be eligible for SSI payments, including:

- Active duty members of the U.S. armed forces
- American Indians born outside the United States
- Certain noncitizens admitted as Amerasian immigrants
- Cuban or Haitian entrants

Tax System Favors Federal Government over States

In their testimony before the House Subcommittee on Immigration and Claims at the hearing "The U.S. Population and Immigration" in August 2001, Michael E. Fix and Jeffrey S. Passel noted that in measuring taxes paid by immigrants against the costs of providing assistance, the federal government was the winner ("U.S. Immigration at the Beginning of the 21st Century," Washington, DC: The Urban Institute, August 2, 2001). More taxes were paid to the federal government, but the states assumed the highest costs associated with immigrants—the costs of educating children. Increasingly, the border states in particular complained of rising costs associated with illegal immigration.

REMITTANCES—THE FLOW OF MONEY OUT OF THE UNITED STATES TO LATIN AMERICA

In an opinion article titled "Mexicans in the U.S. Send Billions Home—And It All Comes Back," for the *Rocky Mountain News* (February 19, 2005), Benjamin

P. Gochman and Rutilio Martinez, of Consulting Group of the Americas LLC, stated that "[i]n 2004 Mexicans working in the U.S. sent back $16.4 billion to their families in Mexico. This number is expected to top $19.2 billion by the end of 2005. Money transfers (called remittances) to families in Mexico from relatives in the U.S. have surpassed foreign direct investment as the second most important source of revenues for Mexico after oil (Bank of Mexico, 2004)."

Gochman and Martinez reported that interest on Mexico's $136 billion debt with U.S. banks, plus profits returned to the United States by American corporations in Mexico, averaged over $14 billion per year during the years 1995–2003. Until 2003 the return of this money was enough to offset the remittances sent to Mexico. In 2004 the amount of remittances surpassed the amount returned to the United States from Mexico. The authors suggested, however, that the remittances would, in part, increase spending by Mexican citizens in U.S. border towns. They argued that with increased border exports of goods to Mexico, the American economy would not be adversely affected. Border exports included consumer goods, used cars, firearms, capital goods such as agricultural machinery, and a small number of luxury cars. While the U.S. Department of Commerce did not register these as exports, the U.S.–Mexico Chamber of Commerce estimated border exports at $20 billion in 1998. Remittances sent to Mexico had become the main source of income for many Mexican families. Gochman and Martinez argued that these families were part of the middle and upper class who made regular shopping expeditions to U.S.-border or near-border towns. They opposed a proposal to tax remittances as this would not only "adversely affect Mexico's poor and working class families" but would reduce the growth rate of American exports to Mexico.

Marcela Cortes, writing for EFE News Service ("Illegal Mexican Immigrants Send the Most Money Home," http://www.efenews.com, December 17, 2004), cited a study by Banco de Mexico that indicated that 83% of the remittances sent to Mexico came from illegal immigrants, most of whom were working in the United States. The study found that Mexican migrants sent home $13.8 billion between January and October 2004, an increase of more than 23% from the same period of 2003. Ms. Cortes quoted Carlos Villanueva, chairman of the Association of Mexicans Abroad, who said, "Remittances are estimated to total $17 billion this year, but such figures come up short because they do not take into account nontraditional ways of sending money, such as services or in kind. It is a fact that remittances are the top driving force of the Mexican economy."

The Value of Remittances to Families Back Home

The May 2004 report *Sending Money Home: Remittance to Latin America and the Caribbean*, produced by Inter-American Development Bank (http://www.iadb.org), provided an interesting analysis of remittances. The report noted that "one aspect of globalization ... has attracted relatively little attention: the flow of workers to fill jobs in more developed countries, and the subsequent financial flows back to their families in countries of origin ... delivering desperately needed resources ... to more than one hundred million families worldwide." According to the report this phenomenon is nowhere more apparent than in Latin America and the Caribbean.

While migrants have traveled to other Latin American countries, Europe, and most recently to Japan, for the past two decades the overwhelming migration has been to the United States. According to the Inter-American Development Bank report, "in 2003 remittance floes exceeded all combined Foreign Direct Investment and Official Development Assistance to the Region (Latin America and the Caribbean) ... and accounted for at least 10% of gross domestic product in Haiti, Nicaragua, El Salvador, Jamaica, the Dominican Republic, and Guyana." Remittances to Mexico exceeded total tourism revenues, and equaled more than two-thirds of the value of petroleum exports and about 180% of total agricultural exports.

The report also cited a survey by the Pew Hispanic Center (*Remittance Senders and Receivers: Tracking the Transnational Channels*, Washington, DC, 2003) in which half of Latino migrants in the United States who had been away from home five years or less reported that they sent remittances home. After migrants were in the

FIGURE 6.4

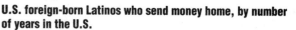
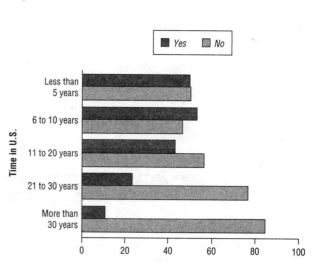

U.S. foreign-born Latinos who send money home, by number of years in the U.S.

SOURCE: "U.S. Foreign-Born Latinos: Who Sends Money Home," in *Sending Money Home: Remittance to Latin America and the Caribbean*, Inter-American Development Bank, Multilateral Investment Fund, May 2004, http://www.iadb.org/mif/V2/files/StudyPE2004eng.pdf (accessed March 15, 2005)

FIGURE 6.5

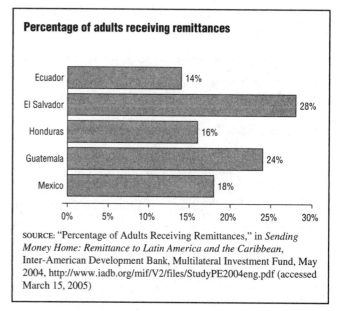

Percentage of adults receiving remittances

SOURCE: "Percentage of Adults Receiving Remittances," in *Sending Money Home: Remittance to Latin America and the Caribbean*, Inter-American Development Bank, Multilateral Investment Fund, May 2004, http://www.iadb.org/mif/V2/files/StudyPE2004eng.pdf (accessed March 15, 2005)

United States ten years, the likelihood of sending remittances began to decline gradually. However, about 10% of those who had been in the United States for more than thirty years still sent remittances. (See Figure 6.4.)

Some 28% of adults in El Salvador and 24% of adults in Guatemala received remittances from family members who left the country to find work. In Mexico remittances arrived for 18% of adults. (See Figure 6.5.) Most workers sent remittances at least once a month. In

FIGURE 6.6

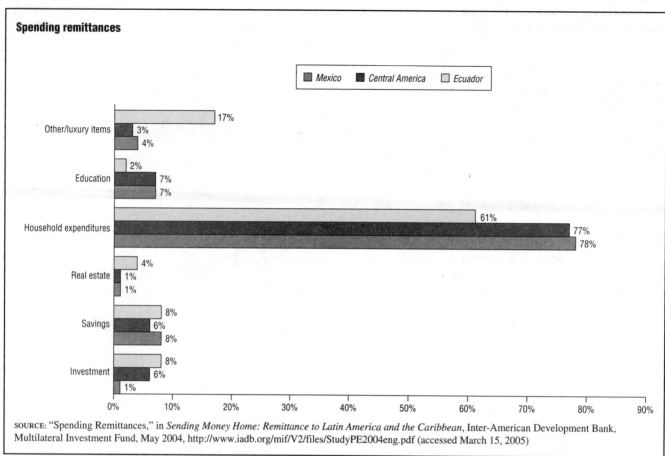

Spending remittances

SOURCE: "Spending Remittances," in *Sending Money Home: Remittance to Latin America and the Caribbean*, Inter-American Development Bank, Multilateral Investment Fund, May 2004, http://www.iadb.org/mif/V2/files/StudyPE2004eng.pdf (accessed March 15, 2005)

Mexico 78% of remittance funds were spent on household needs (housing, food, and utilities), 7% on education, and 8% to savings. Most Mexican recipients of remittances spent just 4% of funds received on luxury items. (See Figure 6.6.)

In its *Survey of Mexican Migrants, Part Two: Attitudes about Voting in Mexican Elections and Ties to Mexico*, released March 14, 2005, the Pew Hispanic Center in Washington, D.C., reported that 78% of Mexican migrants sent remittances. The survey also explored the close ties that Mexican migrants maintained with family back home. Fifty-four percent of migrants surveyed said they spoke by telephone to their families in Mexico at least once a week. Of those who had been in the United States ten years or more, close to half (46%) said they were still in weekly contact with family in Mexico. Among the primarily younger and more educated migrants surveyed, 17% said they maintained regular contact with their families by computer.

GOVERNMENT SPENDING ON IMMIGRATION
The Department of Homeland Security Budget

A recent contributor to immigration costs has been the stepped-up border security measures since the terrorist attacks of September 11, 2001. On October 18, 2004,

President George W. Bush signed the fiscal year (FY) 2005 Homeland Security Appropriations Act. The $40.2 billion budget as proposed by the president for the Department of Homeland Security (DHS) represented a 10% increase in funding over the previous year.

Included in the FY 2005 budget were increases targeted for specific initiatives. New funding amounting to $419.2 million was designated to enhance border and port security activities, including the detection of individuals attempting to illegally enter the United States. Another substantial increase was $179 million for improvements in immigration enforcement both domestically and overseas, including $123 million for the detention and removal of illegal aliens. The remaining $56 million in additional funding would be used to detect and locate individuals in the United States in violation of immigration laws or engaged in immigration-related fraud. Another $160 million in total resources was devoted to continuing progress toward a six-month processing time for all immigration applications and reducing the backlog of applications. A total of $340 million was allocated to the continued expansion of the US-VISIT program. Direct immigration-related functions received 30% of the total DHS budget; Customs and Border Patrol, 15%; Immigration and Customs Enforcement, 10%; Citizenship and Immigration, 4%; and US-VISIT, 1%. (See Table 6.9.)

TABLE 6.9

Department of Homeland Security FY 2005 budget

[Dollars in millions]

Organization	FY 2003	FY 2004[b]	FY 2005	(+/−) Change FY 2004 to FY 2005
Security, enforcement & investigations	21,566	22,606	24,691	2,085
BTS Under Secretary	0	8	10	2
US VISIT	380	328	340	12
Bureau of Customs & Border Protection	5,887	5,942	6,199	257
Bureau of Immigration & Customs Enforcement	3,262	3,654	4,011	357
Transportation Security Administration	4,648	4,405	5,297	892
United States Coast Guard	6,196	6,935	7,471	536
United States Secret Service	1,193	1,334	1,363	29
Preparedness & recovery	5,175	5,493	7,372	1,879
EP&R Federal Emergency Management Agency (less Biodefense)[a]	5,175	4,608	4,844	236
Biodefense	0	885	2,528	1,643
Research, Development, Training, Assessments & Services	2,330	3,591	3,810	219
Bureau of Citizenship & Immigration Services	1,422	1,653	1,711	58
Federal Law Enforcement Training Center	170	191	196	5
Information Analysis & Infrastructure Protection Directorate	185	834	864	30
Science & Technology Directorate	553	913	1,039	126
Departmental management and operations	2,111	4,851	4,294	−557
Departmental Management	2,040	4,771	4,212	−559
Departmental operations	22	211	405	194
Technology investments	47	184	226	42
Counter-Terrorism Fund	10	10	20	10
Office for Domestic Preparedness	1,961	4,366	3,561	−805
Inspector General	71	80	82	2
Total	**31,182**	**36,541**	**40,167**	**3,626**

[a]FY 2003 includes supplemental funding for EP&R: FEMA ($1,426 M); all other supplemental funding has been excluded.
[b]FY 2004 total excludes war supplemental funding.

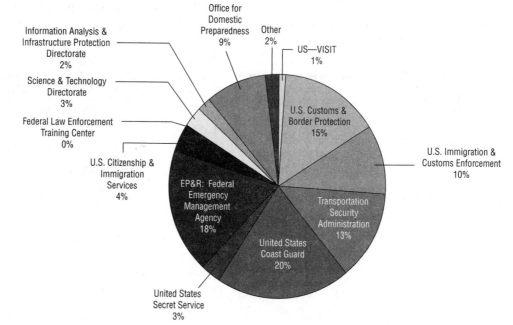

*Other includes: BTS Under Secretary, Office of the Inspector General, Departmental Operations, Department-wide Technology Investments and Counterterrorism Fund.

SOURCE: "Total Budget Authority by Organization as of January 31, 2004 (Dollars in Millions)," and "FY 2005 Total Budget Authority by Organization," in *Homeland Security Budget in Brief: Fiscal Year 2005*, U.S. Department of Homeland Security, 2005, http://www.dhs.gov/interweb/assetlibrary/FY_2005_BIB_4.pdf (accessed April 6, 2005)

U.S. Aid for Refugees

U.S. refugee policy has been based on the premise that the care of refugees and other conflict victims as well as the pursuit of permanent solutions for refugee crises are shared international responsibilities. The more refugees assist in their home regions, the fewer that might ultimately require resettlement outside those regions. Following this philosophy, the U.S. Department

TABLE 6.10

Migration and Refugee Assistance (MRA) program summary, FY 2001–03

[Dollars in thousands]

	FY 2001 actual	FY 2002 estimate[c]	FY 2003 request[c]	Increase or decrease(−)
Overseas assistance	$ 531,270	$ 537,000	$ 524,000	$ (13,000)
Africa	190,900	195,600	195,600	0
East Asia[b]	21,223	15,800	15,500	(300)
Europe[b]	104,153	88,000	77,000	(11,000)
Near East/North Africa	106,959	103,400	103,400	0
South Asia[b]	35,840	45,500	45,500	0
Western hemisphere	13,626	15,000	14,700	(300)
Multiregional activities[b]	58,569	57,700	56,600	(1,100)
Migration[a]		16,000	15,700	(300)
Refugee admission[b]	92,854	92,000	105,000	13,000
Refugees to Israel	59,868	60,000	60,000	0
Administrative expenses	15,010	16,556	16,565	9
Appropriation total[b]	**$699,002**	**$705,556**	**$705,565**	**9**

[a]In FY 2000 and FY 2001, funds for migration activities were included within the individual overseas assistance regions. In FY 2002, they will be separated out into a new overseas assistance category.

[b]Of the $622.6 million appropriated in FY 2000, $21.0 million was not made available until September 30, 2000. These funds have been allotted in FY 2001 as follows: $1 million for overseas. Assistance in East Asia, $3.6 million for overseas assistance in Europe, $250,000 for overseas assistance in South Asia, $1.5 million for multiregional activities, and $14.7 million for refugee admissions. This $21 million is included in the FY 2002 column of the chart above.

[c]The FY 2002 and FY 2003 levels above do not reflect current program estimates for overseas assistance and refugee admissions. The current level for both years for overseas assistance is $499 million and for refugee admissions is $130 million.

SOURCE: "MRA Program Summary (Dollars in Thousands)," in *Migration and Refugee Assistance: Emergency Refugee and Migration Assistance, Fiscal Year 2003*, U.S. Department of State, Bureau of Population, Refugees, and Migration, Congressional Presentation Document and Bureau Performance Plan, http://www.state.gov/documents/organization/14382.pdf (accessed March 3, 2005)

of State annually contributes to overseas assistance funds administered by international organizations and nongovernmental organizations that carry out relief services.

In its report *Migration and Refugee Assistance: Emergency Refugee and Migration Assistance, Fiscal Year 2003* (http://www.state.gov/g/prm/rls/rpt/2002/14280.htm), the Bureau of Population, Refugees and Migration (PRM) projected a decrease of $13 million in Migration and Refugee Assistance (MRA) in FY 2003 over FY 2002. The report noted that after September 11, 2001, refugee admissions were suspended (until December 10, 2001) and case adjudications were disrupted while security procedures were tightened. A slow recovery in the number of admissions was anticipated during subsequent years. The report also noted that new security procedures had significantly increased the per capita cost of the refugee program. The cost of refugee admissions in 2001 was $92.8 million and rose to $105 million in the FY 2003 budget request. (See Table 6.10.)

Funding for overseas assistance was a major part (71%) of the MRA budget. This compares to the 15%

FIGURE 6.7

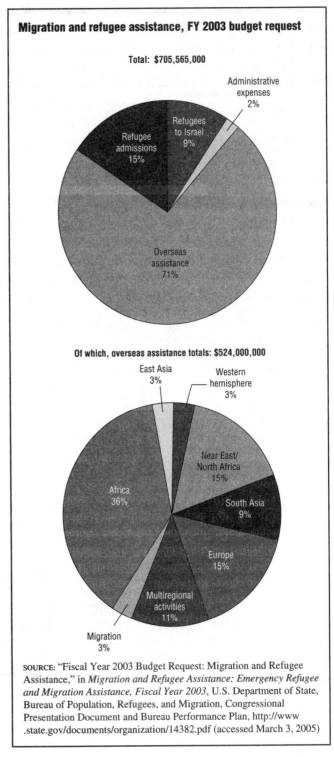

Migration and refugee assistance, FY 2003 budget request

Total: $705,565,000

- Administrative expenses 2%
- Refugees to Israel 9%
- Refugee admissions 15%
- Overseas assistance 71%

Of which, overseas assistance totals: $524,000,000

- East Asia 3%
- Western hemisphere 3%
- Near East/North Africa 15%
- South Asia 9%
- Europe 15%
- Multiregional activities 11%
- Migration 3%
- Africa 36%

SOURCE: "Fiscal Year 2003 Budget Request: Migration and Refugee Assistance," in *Migration and Refugee Assistance: Emergency Refugee and Migration Assistance, Fiscal Year 2003*, U.S. Department of State, Bureau of Population, Refugees, and Migration, Congressional Presentation Document and Bureau Performance Plan, http://www.state.gov/documents/organization/14382.pdf (accessed March 3, 2005)

allocated to refugee admissions into the United States. (See Figure 6.7.) The PRM report noted that overseas assistance funds were allocated to five primary organizations: the United Nations High Commissioner for Refugees (UNHCR), the International Committee of the Red Cross (ICRC), the United Nations Relief and Works Agency for Palestinian Refugees in the Near East, the International Organization for Migration (IOM), and the World Food Program (WFP).

2005 Budget Allocations for Overseas Refugee Relief

According to *Funding Actions Finalized with Organizations* (Washington, DC: U.S. Department of State, Bureau of Population, Refugees, and Migration, February 9, 2005), PRM committed a total of $13.9 million to four specific refugee-related programs in FY 2005:

- $562,500—International Catholic Migration Commission, for the initial funding for oversees processing in Turkey, 10/1/04–9/30/05

- $578,000—Shelter for Life, to support permanent water supply system development in Iraq, 1/1/05–12/31/05

- $9,452,053—United Israel Appeal, to facilitate resettlement and integration of humanitarian migrants to Israel, 10/1/04–9/30/05

- $2,720,000—World Food Program, to support provision of returnee food rations in Burundi, 11/1/04–10/31/05

In a January 31, 2005, press release ("U.S. Contributes $125 Million to the UN High Commissioner for Refugees," http://www.state.gov/r/pa/prs/ps/2005/41400.htm), the U.S. Department of State announced an initial contribution of $125 million to the UNHCR for 2005 Annual Programs. The funds were allocated as follows:

- Africa—$50.0 million

- Near East—$2.9 million

- Europe—$14.1 million

- South Asia—$20.3 million

- East Asia—$5.2 million

- Western Hemisphere—$4.6 million

- Global Operations and Reserves—$27.9 million

Refugee Resettlement Expenses

As reported in the State Department's International Information Programs *Washington File*, Arthur "Gene" Dewey, Assistant Secretary of State for Refugees, told a group of international journalists in November 2004 that "[t]he United States did its share, more than its share, really" (Charlene Porter, "United States Leads World in Refugee Resettlement," November 26, 2004). He went on to say that the United States accepted more refugees than the ten other countries involved in resettlement, offering a new start to 54% of the world's refugees resettled in fiscal year 2004. (The other nations with refugee resettlement programs were Australia, Canada, Denmark, Finland, Ireland, the Netherlands, New Zealand, Norway, Sweden, and the United Kingdom.)

Dewey noted that resettlement of refugees had become far more complicated in recent times. "Now we receive refugees from about forty-six different locations, much smaller clusters around the world," Dewey said. "And there are about sixty different nationalities." In addition, the threat of terrorism since 2001 has made U.S. officials more cautious in the evaluation of candidates for resettlement in the United States.

These combined factors increased the cost of resettlement significantly, according to Dewey. The State Department's Bureau of Population, Refugees, and Migration reported that U.S. costs of resettlement for fiscal year 2004 were $3,500 per refugee admitted, compared to $2,200 in 2001. The almost 60% increase created what Dewey called a "funding impediment," which he predicted could curtail the resettlement effort in fiscal year 2005.

COST OF ILLEGAL IMMIGRATION TO SOUTHWEST BORDER COUNTIES

According to the *2003 Yearbook of Immigration Statistics* (Washington, DC: U.S. Department of Homeland Security, Office of Immigration Statistics, September 2004), of the 931,557 deportable aliens located by Border Patrol agents in 2003, approximately 95% were Mexicans attempting to enter the United States over the southwest border. A significant portion of the Department of Homeland Security budget for Border Patrol activities was focused on the southwest border, particularly to implement electronic monitoring and airplane coverage of great open distances between towns or ports of entry.

The Front Line—Twenty-Four U.S. Counties on the Border

In a study conducted for the United States/Mexico Border Counties Coalition (USMBCC), researchers from the University of Texas at El Paso, New Mexico State University, and San Diego State University found that the twenty-four border counties along the U.S.–Mexico border spent about $108.2 million providing law enforcement, criminal justice, and emergency health-care services to illegal aliens apprehended in fiscal year 1999 (*Illegal Immigrants in U.S./Mexico Border Counties*, Washington, DC: U.S./Mexico Border Counties Coalition, February 2001).

Another study conducted by MGT of America for the USMBCC, *Medical Emergency: Costs of Uncompensated Care in Southwest Border Counties* (September 2002), analyzed the cost of providing emergency medical care to illegal immigrants who crossed the border for health care (including mothers ready to deliver babies) or who were injured in attempted border crossings. The Emergency Medical Treatment and Active Labor Act of 1986 (42 U.S.C. 1395 dd) requires hospitals and emergency personnel to screen, treat, and stabilize anyone who seeks emergency medical care regardless of income or immigration status.

This 2002 USMBCC report cited an American Hospital Association survey, which found that the hospitals in the twenty-four border counties incurred $832 million in uncompensated care in 2000. The report attributed about $190 million of uncompensated emergency care to undocumented immigrants. The USMBCC study also determined that if the twenty-four border counties were combined into one state, by comparison to the other forty-nine states it would have the lowest per capita income, the highest unemployment rate, the highest percentage of children living in poverty, and the highest percentage of residents without health insurance.

In July 2004 the Associated Press reported in two separate stories ("Texas to Get $47.5 Million in Funds for Uninsured," July 22, 2004, and "Arizona to Get Reimbursed for Illegal Immigrants' Hospital Care," July 23, 2004) that hospitals and other health-care facilities in Arizona and Texas would receive compensation for the care they provided to the uninsured, including illegal immigrants. Arizona facilities were to receive $42 million and Texas providers $47.5 million annually over four years as part of a $1 billion, four-year federal program administered by the Centers for Medicare and Medicaid Services. The program was designed to help hospitals and other health-care providers across the United States recoup their estimated $1.45 billion losses for medical care to uninsured patients, many of whom are illegal immigrants. Of the $250 million to be disbursed for each of the four years to hospitals across the country, Arizona and Texas facilities would receive more than one-third (36%).

U.S. towns along the southwestern border also face the burden of identifying and burying the bodies of illegal immigrants who died while attempting to enter the United States. Between October 2003 and September 2004, 314 people died crossing the U.S.–Mexico border ("Cost of Illegal Immigration Seen in Graveyards," Associated Press, September 24, 2004). The average burial cost for an unclaimed body was reported to be $900 while the cost of investigating the death and identifying the body could be as high as $2,500. Imperial County, California, expected to pay $30,000 in 2004 for autopsies of bodies found along the border.

Border issues divide communities and politicians. In a story for the *Philadelphia Inquirer* ("'Neighborhood Watch' at the Nation's Borders," February 2, 2004), Dave Montgomery related: "Thousands of furious Arizonans complain that undocumented workers consume millions of dollars in public services and wrest jobs from U.S. citizens." Citizen "watchdog groups" threatened to patrol the borders in an effort to stem the flood of illegal immigrants crossing public as well as private property, while human rights activists described the self-appointed groups as "paramilitary vigilantes 'driven by hate.'"

During the month of April 2005 an estimated 900 volunteers, working in eight-hour shifts, conducted stationary patrols of a twenty-three-mile stretch of border in Cochise County, Arizona. Although some volunteers came armed, their mission was simply to alert Border Patrol agents of border crossers. Organizers called the "Minute Man Project" a success. They reported that calls to Border Patrol agents resulted in arrests of 335 illegal immigrants and brought national attention to the problem of border control ("Minuteman Project Draws to Close in Arizona," Associated Press, April 30, 2005).

A 2004 study by the Federation of American Immigration Reform (FAIR) estimated that illegal immigration cost the state of Arizona $1.3 billion per year (*The Costs of Illegal Immigration to Arizonans*, Washington, DC, June 2004). The study considered the cost of education, health care, and incarceration for the illegal alien population. It also credited the estimated $257 million per year in taxes paid by illegal immigrants. FAIR published a similar study focusing on California (*The Costs of Illegal Immigration to Californians*, Washington, DC, November 2004). They concluded that the illegal alien population in California cost the state's taxpayers $10.5 billion. Taking into account the estimated $1.6 billion in taxes paid illegal immigrants, the total cost was approximately $9 billion. Another recent FAIR report analyzed the costs of illegal immigration on the state of Texas (*The Costs of Illegal Immigration to Texans*, Washington, DC, April 2005). The report estimated that the illegal population in Texas cost the state $4.7 billion, or $725 per Texas household headed by a native-born resident. The study asserted that $1 billion of that overall cost was offset by the taxes of these illegal immigrants.

CHAPTER 7
THE IMPACT OF IMMIGRATION ON TWENTY-FIRST CENTURY AMERICA

The same things are said today of Puerto Ricans and Mexicans that were once said of the Irish, Italians, Germans and Jews: "They'll never adjust; they can't learn the language; they won't be absorbed."

—John F. Kennedy, *A Nation of Immigrants*

CHANGING AMERICA

In a series of articles published in late 2003, S. Lynne Walker chronicled the reopening of a large meat-packing company in Beardstown, Illinois, a town of 7,000 people ("Beardstown: Reflection of a Changing America," *State Journal-Register*, November 9–November 12, 2003). The revived industry brought not only jobs for local residents but an influx of immigrants, mostly from Mexico. Suddenly the local school was faced with students who did not speak English and a Catholic church had requests for a Spanish-speaking priest. Local people resented the newcomers who were "different" and some locals moved away. Mexican families missed familiar goods and services. Over time the makeup of the mostly white Midwestern community became 30% Hispanic. Eventually the disparate populations learned to coexist, and in some cases even appreciate their diversity. For better or worse, the town was forever changed.

IMMIGRATION'S IMPACT—A STUDY OF NEW YORK CITY

New York was already a bustling seaport of 33,000 people by 1789 when George Washington was sworn in as president of the new republic on the balcony of the city's Federal Hall. Although the Dutch first settled the site in 1624, they were soon joined by the British and an influx of people from many other nations. New York quickly became a favored port of arrival. The Statue of Liberty was installed in New York Harbor in 1886, with those famous words of Emma Lazarus carved on her base: "Give me your tired, your poor, your huddled masses yearning to breathe free."

Newcomers struggled to survive in the city on hard work and low wages but settled in neighborhoods populated by friends and relatives from back home, or at least people who spoke the same language. The city became a conglomeration of races, tongues, and customs—and somehow managed to tolerate, even appreciate, them all. In the late 1930s European intellectuals, musicians, and artists sought refuge there and the city emerged from World War II as a world cultural center. The burgeoning population spread over five boroughs—Brooklyn, the Bronx, Manhattan, Queens, and Staten Island—and each grew into the equivalent of a major city.

The City Studied Its Modern Immigrants

In 1992 the New York City Department of City Planning prepared a detailed analysis of the city's immigration patterns during the 1980s. The information was designed to help policymakers and service providers gain perspective on the city they served. The information proved so valuable that the Planning Department continued to study the city's immigration patterns and publish periodic reports. Based on the 2000 census, the fourth such study, *The Newest New Yorkers, 2000: Immigrant New York in the New Millennium*, was released in October 2004.

The report noted that after 1950 most U.S. cities in the Northeast and Midwest experienced population declines. The thriving postwar economy made houses affordable; subsequently, many families moved to new homes in the suburbs. New shopping and business centers followed, resulting in economic changes and job losses for established urban areas. While New York experienced similar suburban flight, a steady influx of immigrants replenished the city's population. In 2000, New York City's total population reached a peak of more than eight million. Among those were 2.9 million foreign-born residents, the greatest

FIGURE 7.1

FIGURE 7.2

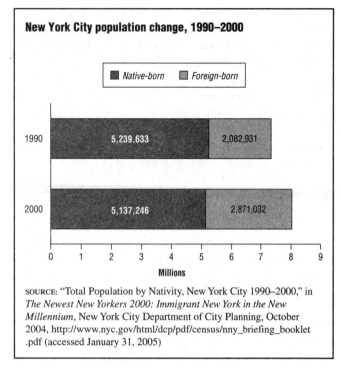

New York City population change, 1990–2000

SOURCE: "Total Population by Nativity, New York City 1990–2000," in *The Newest New Yorkers 2000: Immigrant New York in the New Millennium*, New York City Department of City Planning, October 2004, http://www.nyc.gov/html/dcp/pdf/census/nny_briefing_booklet .pdf (accessed January 31, 2005)

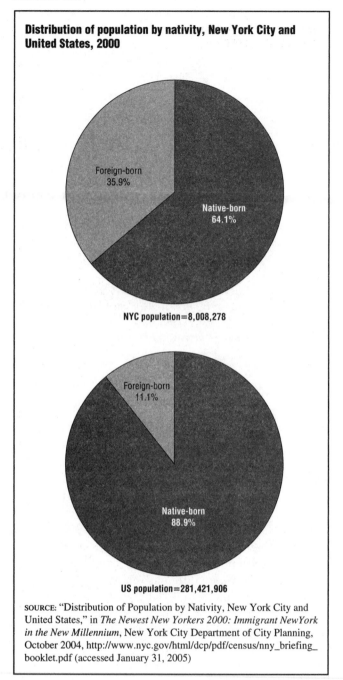

Distribution of population by nativity, New York City and United States, 2000

NYC population=8,008,278

US population=281,421,906

SOURCE: "Distribution of Population by Nativity, New York City and United States," in *The Newest New Yorkers 2000: Immigrant NewYork in the New Millennium*, New York City Department of City Planning, October 2004, http://www.nyc.gov/html/dcp/pdf/census/nny_briefing_ booklet.pdf (accessed January 31, 2005)

number of immigrants in the city's history. Figure 7.1 illustrates the decline of the city's native-born population and the growth of the foreign-born population from 1990 to 2000.

Immigration Gave the City Stability

The introduction to *The Newest New Yorkers* summed up the impact of immigrants and illegal aliens on the city:

> New York City's demography is not static, but a dynamic process defined by the ebb and flow of people. As some people leave the city for points in the region and beyond, the city's population continues to be replenished by the flow of new immigrants. These demographic processes result in a unique level of diversity: 43% of the city's 2.9 million foreign-born residents arrived in the U.S. in the previous ten years; 46% of the population speaks a language other than English at home; in just thirty years, what was primarily a European population has now become a place with no dominant race/ethnic or nationality group. Indeed, New York epitomizes the world city.
>
> The importance of immigration in stabilizing New York City's population is only exceeded by the huge impact it has had on the city's racial and ethnic composition. With the passage of the 1965 amendments to the Immigration and Nationality Act, the countries from which immigrants originated shifted from southern and eastern Europe to Latin America, Asia, and the Caribbean. As a result, New York City experienced a dramatic shift in its racial composition, from a population that was mostly European to one where no group comprises a majority.

New York City and the United States Compared

Immigrants accounted for 11% of the total U.S. population in 2000. By contrast, foreign-born residents comprised 36% of New York City's 2000 population. (See Figure 7.2.) The share of foreign-born residents in New York City rose by 8% over 1990 census figures, while the country as a whole experienced a 3% rise. New York City's foreign-born residents reached a peak of 41% of the city's population in 1910.

In addition, the regions of origin of New York City's foreign-born population differed from those of immigrants to the country as a whole. While almost half (46.6%) of

FIGURE 7.3

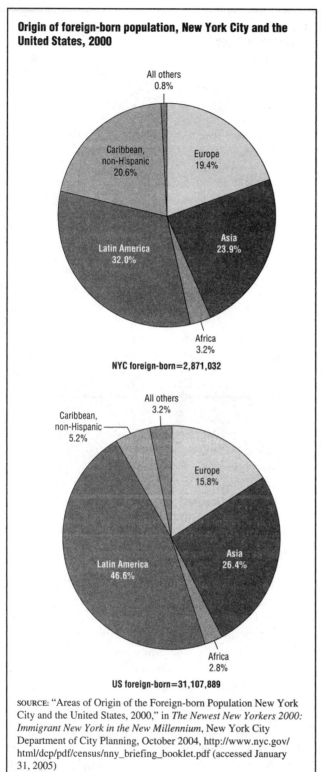

Origin of foreign-born population, New York City and the United States, 2000

All others
0.8%

Caribbean,
non-Hispanic
20.6%

Europe
19.4%

Asia
23.9%

Latin America
32.0%

Africa
3.2%

NYC foreign-born=2,871,032

All others
3.2%

Caribbean,
non-Hispanic
5.2%

Europe
15.8%

Asia
26.4%

Latin America
46.6%

Africa
2.8%

US foreign-born=31,107,889

SOURCE: "Areas of Origin of the Foreign-born Population New York City and the United States, 2000," in *The Newest New Yorkers 2000: Immigrant New York in the New Millennium*, New York City Department of City Planning, October 2004, http://www.nyc.gov/html/dcp/pdf/census/nny_briefing_booklet.pdf (accessed January 31, 2005)

from "all other" countries compared to 3.2% of the overall U.S. foreign-born population. (See Figure 7.3.) (Note: "non-Hispanic Caribbean" countries includes Anguilla, Antigua-Barbuda, Aruba, Bahamas, Barbados, Belize, British Virgin Islands, Cayman Islands, Dominica, French Guiana, Grenada, Guadeloupe, Guyana, Haiti, Jamaica, Martinique, Montserrat, Netherlands Antilles, St. Kitts and Nevis, St. Lucia, St. Vincent and the Grenadines, Surinam, Trinidad and Tobago, Turks and Caicos Islands. "All other" countries includes Australia, Bermuda, Canada, Fiji, French Polynesia, Kiribati, Marshall Islands, Nauru, New Caledonia, New Zealand, Northern Mariana Islands, Papua New Guinea, Tonga, Vanuatu, and Western Samoa.)

The mix of foreign-born residents in New York City was quite different from that of the overall United States. Almost one-third (29.5%) of all U.S. foreign-born residents recorded by the 2000 census were from Mexico. Yet, in New York City, Mexicans accounted for just 4.3% of foreign-born residents. Vietnam, Cuba, Canada, El Salvador, and Germany were among the top ten countries of origin for immigrants to the United States, but those countries were not even in the top twenty sources of immigrants for New York City. More than half of all immigrants from the Dominican Republic lived in New York City in 2000 and they made up 12.8% of the city's foreign-born population. Yet, the Dominican Republic was not among the top ten countries of origin for the overall U.S. immigrant population. Table 7.1 and Figure 7.4 offer a comparison of the top countries of birth for all U.S. immigrants and for those living in New York City.

In 1970 white non-Hispanics represented almost two-thirds of the city's population; by 2000, no single group comprised a majority according to the Planning Department study. White non-Hispanics dropped to 24% of the population while Hispanics became the largest group at 34%. The graph in Figure 7.5 illustrates the balancing of racial and ethnic groups over three decades of population change.

Changes in Immigration Laws Altered Sources of Immigrants

According to *The Newest New Yorkers*, the 1990 Immigration Act changed the countries of origin for immigrants arriving in New York City. The number of naturalized citizens grew from 855,000 in 1990 to 1.3 million in 2000. These new citizens made increasing use of the "immediate relatives" visas to bring in spouses, minor children, and parents. The most dramatic change came in the increased share of refugees, rising from 5.1% in the 1980s to 13.5% in the 1990s. (See Figure 7.6.) The majority of refugee arrivals came from former Soviet republics. The increased use of "diversity" visas brought more immigrants from Poland, Ireland, Bangladesh, Ghana, Nigeria, and Albania. (See Table 7.2.)

U.S. immigrants came from Latin America, only one-third of New York's foreign-born residents were from that region. By contrast about one-fifth (20.6%) of the immigrants in New York City came from non-Hispanic Caribbean countries compared to just 5.2% of all U.S. immigrants. New York City was home to less than 1% of immigrants

TABLE 7.1

Foreign-born population by country of birth, New York City, 1990 and 2000

| | 2000 | | 1990 | | Growth, 1990–2000 | |
	Rank	Number	Rank	Number	Number	Percent
Total, Foreign-born	—	2,871,032	—	2,082,931	788,101	37.8
Dominican Republic	1	369,186	1	225,017	144,169	64.1
China	2	261,551	2	160,399	101,152	63.1
Jamaica	3	178,922	3	116,128	62,794	54.1
Guyana	4	130,647	6	76,150	54,497	71.6
Mexico	5	122,550	17	32,689	89,861	274.9
Ecuador	6	114,944	10	60,451	54,493	90.1
Haiti	7	95,580	7	71,892	23,688	32.9
Trinidad & Tobago	8	88,794	12	56,478	32,316	57.2
Colombia	9	84,404	8	65,731	18,673	28.4
Russia	10	81,408	*	*	*	*
Italy	11	72,481	4	98,868	(26,387)	−26.7
Korea	12	70,990	11	56,949	14,041	24.7
Ukraine	13	69,727	*	*	*	*
India	14	68,263	14	40,419	27,844	68.9
Poland	15	65,999	9	61,265	4,734	7.7
Philippines	16	49,644	16	36,463	13,181	36.1
Bangladesh	17	42,865	42	8,695	34,170	393.0
Pakistan	18	39,165	29	14,911	24,254	162.7
Honduras	19	32,358	27	17,890	14,468	80.9
Greece	20	29,805	18	31,894	(2,089)	−6.5

*The USSR was ranked 5th in 1990 with 80,815 residents. If it were a single entity in 2000, it would have ranked 4th with approximately 164,000 persons.

SOURCE: "Foreign-Born Population by Country of Birth, New York City, 1990 and 2000," in *The Newest New Yorkers 2000: Immigrant New York in the New Millennium*, New York City Department of City Planning, October 2004, http://www.nyc.gov/html/dcp/pdf/census/nny_briefing_booklet.pdf (accessed January 31, 2005)

FIGURE 7.4

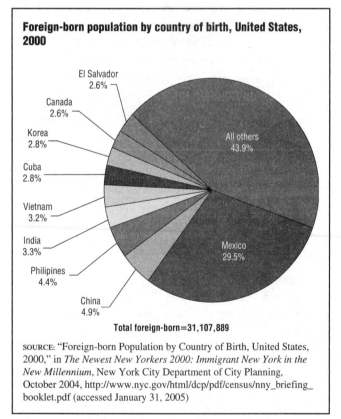

Foreign-born population by country of birth, United States, 2000

El Salvador 2.6%
Canada 2.6%
Korea 2.8%
Cuba 2.8%
Vietnam 3.2%
India 3.3%
Philipines 4.4%
China 4.9%
All others 43.9%
Mexico 29.5%

Total foreign-born = 31,107,889

SOURCE: "Foreign-born Population by Country of Birth, United States, 2000," in *The Newest New Yorkers 2000: Immigrant New York in the New Millennium*, New York City Department of City Planning, October 2004, http://www.nyc.gov/html/dcp/pdf/census/nny_briefing_booklet.pdf (accessed January 31, 2005)

Demographic profiles of New York City's foreign-born residents provide a variety of cultural and family information. The New York City sex ratio (the number of males per one hundred females) was 90 in the year 2000. However, for immigrants from Pakistan the sex ratio was 161. Men from that culture often immigrated alone, established themselves in the United States, and then sent for wives and children. In non-Hispanic Caribbean cultures, women tended to immigrate first and the men followed. Thus the sex ratio for Trinidad and Tobago was just 70. Households with immigrants from Bangladesh, China, Pakistan, and Greece typically were comprised of married couples. The highest rate of married couple households was 78.8% among immigrants from Bangladesh. Female-headed households were more likely among immigrants from the Dominican Republic (38.8%), Jamaica (33.1%), and Honduras (32.3%). (See Table 7.3.)

Impact of Education, Language, and Job Skills on Immigrant Assimilation

The New York City study demonstrates the challenges of simply surviving in America. New immigrants depended on the education and skills they brought with them and the support system of already established immigrants who spoke their language. Many immigrant families shared housing with extended family and needed multiple workers to support the household. Even with pooled resources, many families struggled in the city. Foreign-born males had a higher rate of participation in the labor force (66.9%) than native-born

FIGURE 7.5

FIGURE 7.6

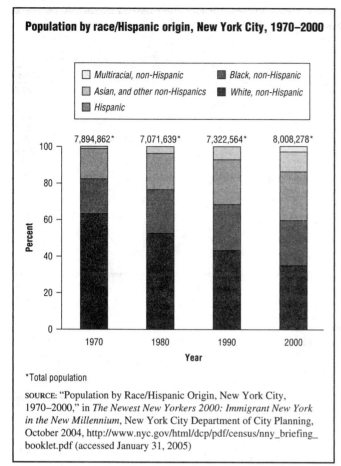

Population by race/Hispanic origin, New York City, 1970–2000

*Total population

SOURCE: "Population by Race/Hispanic Origin, New York City, 1970–2000," in *The Newest New Yorkers 2000: Immigrant New York in the New Millennium*, New York City Department of City Planning, October 2004, http://www.nyc.gov/html/dcp/pdf/census/nny_briefing_booklet.pdf (accessed January 31, 2005)

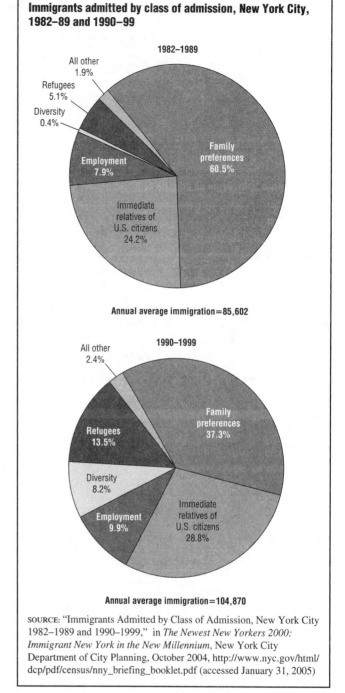

Immigrants admitted by class of admission, New York City, 1982–89 and 1990–99

SOURCE: "Immigrants Admitted by Class of Admission, New York City 1982–1989 and 1990–1999," in *The Newest New Yorkers 2000: Immigrant New York in the New Millennium*, New York City Department of City Planning, October 2004, http://www.nyc.gov/html/dcp/pdf/census/nny_briefing_booklet.pdf (accessed January 31, 2005)

males (62.6%). However, the mean annual earnings of all foreign-born male workers ($39,060) were less than 65% of those of native-born male workers ($60,754). (See Table 7.4.)

Immigrants from the Philippines arrived in New York City with high educational levels (93.4% were high school graduates). Although one-fourth of these immigrants were not proficient in English, as a group they attained the highest median household income of any immigrant group ($70,500), suggesting that many had college educations. They also had an average of 1.6 workers per household and high labor force participation rates for both men (73.7%) and women (67.4%). Only 5.3% of immigrants from the Philippines lived in poverty. (See Table 7.4.)

In comparison, just one-third of Mexican immigrants had completed high school and 76.2% were not proficient in English. They had the highest average number of workers per household at 1.8 and the highest poverty rate at 32%. (See Table 7.4.)

ENGLISH PROFICIENCY IS DOWN. In "Proficiency in English Decreases Over a Decade" (*New York Times*, January 19, 2005), Nina Bernstein reported that growing numbers of adults in New York City had difficulty speaking English. She cited city statistics that between 1990 and 2000 the population of those with deficient English language skills had increased 30% to 1.5 million people. Almost half lived in households where no one spoke English with proficiency. In one-fourth of these households the only member proficient in English was a child.

The problem of providing English language classes to meet the needs of new residents was compounded,

TABLE 7.2

Top users of employment and diversity visas by country of birth, New York City, 1990–99

	Annual average employment visas				Annual average diversity visas		
	Total	Employment	Employment as a % of total		Total	Diversity	Diversity as a % of total
Total	**104,870**	**10,391**	**9.9**	**Total**	**104,870**	**8,557**	**8.2**
China	11,127	2,915	26.2	Poland	2,985	1,407	46.9
Philippines	2,657	1,115	42.0	Ireland	1,391	1,236	88.9
India	2,851	475	16.6	Bangladesh	2,899	1,231	42.5
Trinidad & Tobago	2,859	464	16.2	Ghana	919	441	48.0
Korea	1,531	426	27.8	Ukraine	5,494	348	6.3
Jamaica	6,112	373	6.1	Pakistan	2,107	292	13.9
Guyana	5,144	325	6.3	Nigeria	794	290	36.5
Poland	2,985	292	9.8	Russia	3,034	288	9.5
Ecuador	2,963	277	9.3	Albania	423	250	59.2
Israel	717	260	36.2	Egypt	757	215	28.4

SOURCE: "Top Users of Employment and Diversity Visas by Country of Birth, New York City, 1990–1999," in *The Newest New Yorkers 2000: Immigrant New York in the New Millennium*, New York City Department of City Planning, October 2004, http://www.nyc.gov/html/dcp/pdf/census/nny_briefing_booklet.pdf (accessed January 31, 2005)

TABLE 7.3

Selected demographic characteristics by country of birth, New York City, 2000

	Population			Households				
	Total	% ages 18 to 64	Sex ratio*	Total	% married couple	% female head, no spouse	% owner-occupied	% overcrowded
Total, NYC	**8,008,278**	**64.2**	**90**	**3,020,980**	**37.9**	**18.8**	**30.3**	**14.6**
Native-born	5,137,246	55.9	89	1,816,243	31.0	18.9	31.6	7.5
Foreign-born	2,871,032	79.0	91	1,204,737	48.2	18.7	28.3	25.4
Dominican Republic	369,186	81.7	80	142,042	38.9	38.6	8.5	38.0
China	261,551	79.2	94	95,086	65.6	9.0	42.2	34.2
Jamaica	178,922	81.0	71	80,990	33.8	33.1	36.9	16.5
Guyana	130,647	83.3	87	48,054	55.5	21.9	48.5	22.6
Mexico	122,550	85.1	154	32,201	55.8	13.7	5.7	66.1
Ecuador	114,944	84.7	115	37,276	55.2	19.2	17.6	41.7
Haiti	95,580	80.3	76	40,694	43.2	30.7	30.2	26.4
Trinidad & Tobago	88,794	81.7	70	40,036	38.5	31.6	32.3	18.1
Colombia	84,404	82.7	75	31,705	42.3	24.3	20.8	34.9
Russia	81,408	70.8	83	37,624	52.0	10.8	20.9	18.0
Italy	72,481	60.3	92	42,938	58.7	8.8	64.5	2.6
Korea	70,990	84.1	83	25,979	58.4	9.2	20.0	35.5
Ukraine	69,727	63.4	84	32,388	58.6	10.0	19.8	20.0
India	68,263	84.8	123	26,889	68.4	4.9	32.7	31.5
Poland	65,999	64.4	87	33,226	48.5	9.0	31.4	10.8
Philippines	49,644	83.5	70	18,840	52.4	15.9	41.1	26.3
Bangladesh	42,865	79.9	137	11,585	78.8	3.3	18.4	60.8
Pakistan	39,165	76.3	161	12,294	64.6	2.6	17.6	53.2
Honduras	32,358	85.5	85	11,800	41.3	32.3	9.8	37.7
Greece	29,805	73.2	115	15,067	64.1	7.7	54.9	7.6

*Males per 100 females

SOURCE: "Selected Demographic Characteristics by Country of Birth, New York City, 2000," in *The Newest New Yorkers 2000: Immigrant New York in the New Millennium*, New York City Department of City Planning, October 2004, http://www.nyc.gov/html/dcp/pdf/census/nny_briefing_booklet.pdf (accessed January 31, 2005)

according to Ms. Bernstein, by the fact that the city's foreign-born population spoke 175 to 200 different languages. An added difficulty in teaching new residents to read and write English was the low educational level of many immigrants, who often were not able to read and write their own language. Adding to the long-term problem, the foreign-born groups with the highest rates of difficulty with English also had the highest birth rate.

A meeting of public and private agencies involved in teaching English to newcomers identified further challenges. They concluded that many existing literacy programs were not located in or near areas where the people with the greatest need lived. Furthermore, some funding sources for literacy programs required participants to provide a Social Security number when registering. As a result, many illegal residents feared participation could lead to deportation.

TABLE 7.4

Selected socioeconomic characteristics by country of birth, New York City, 2000

	% not English proficient	% high school graduate	Average workers per hhld	Median household income	% in poverty	Males, ages 16+		Females, ages 16+	
						Labor force particip. rate	Mean earnings (full time)	Labor force particip. rate	Mean earnings (full time)
Total, NYC	23.7	72.3	1.1	$37,700	21.1	64.5	$50,771	52.0	$40,369
Native-born	8.6	78.4	1.0	$39,900	21.5	62.6	$60,754	53.1	$45,960
Foreign-born	48.2	64.7	1.2	$35,000	20.4	66.9	$39,060	50.6	$32,293
Dominican Republic	70.0	43.8	1.1	$25,300	30.9	60.6	$25,746	46.4	$21,342
China	74.6	54.6	1.5	$33,320	21.7	66.0	$31,799	52.8	$28,278
Jamaica	1.7	68.7	1.3	$38,500	14.6	70.0	$35,967	64.7	$32,323
Guyana	3.1	65.4	1.5	$41,960	13.4	72.9	$32,895	60.7	$29,178
Mexico	76.2	34.7	1.8	$32,000	32.0	72.2	$21,284	39.7	$16,737
Ecuador	71.2	52.8	1.5	$36,000	21.9	69.0	$24,254	46.9	$20,937
Haiti	49.9	68.8	1.3	$36,000	19.1	64.7	$31,576	56.3	$29,785
Trinidad & Tobago	1.5	73.0	1.3	$36,300	16.5	71.1	$35,054	63.6	$32,756
Colombia	69.1	64.5	1.3	$35,000	20.2	66.6	$29,904	54.0	$25,290
Russia	58.0	85.4	1.0	$28,000	22.2	60.0	$45,090	46.8	$36,209
Italy	50.8	46.7	1.0	$39,500	10.4	51.6	$56,466	31.2	$41,744
Korea	69.8	83.4	1.3	$35,200	17.7	68.9	$44,054	53.5	$35,505
Ukraine	70.6	84.8	0.9	$23,100	20.8	55.9	$43,121	42.5	$36,373
India	36.7	79.9	1.5	$50,000	14.4	76.2	$47,887	47.2	$44,482
Poland	56.9	69.3	0.9	$33,100	14.1	60.1	$37,690	42.8	$29,993
Philippines	24.9	93.4	1.6	$70,500	5.3	73.7	$42,958	67.4	$51,051
Bangladesh	58.6	74.5	1.5	$33,300	31.0	73.8	$27,960	29.4	$22,051
Pakistan	51.8	67.6	1.4	$36,500	26.1	72.1	$34,572	22.2	$36,171
Honduras	64.5	42.3	1.1	$27,000	27.7	67.0	$26,998	44.2	$21,030
Greece	56.5	50.9	1.2	$43,930	13.4	61.8	$51,023	36.8	$35,667

SOURCE: "Selected Socioeconomic Characteristics by Country of Birth, New York City, 2000," in *The Newest New Yorkers 2000: Immigrant New York in the New Millennium*, New York City Department of City Planning, October 2004, http://www.nyc.gov/html/dcp/pdf/census/nny_briefing_booklet.pdf (accessed January 31, 2005).

The Foreign-Born in the Workforce

Given that the foreign-born accounted for 43% of all workers, according to *The Newest New Yorkers*, immigrants were a vital part of the city's labor force in 2000. They represented 64% of manufacturing workers and 58% of construction workers. More than one-third of foreign-born workers in manufacturing were employed in textile and apparel-producing industries. Immigrants represented more than half (54%) of all workers in accommodation, food, and other services. While the largest number (100,400) worked in restaurants, 23,800 were employed in private households and 21,100 worked in hotels or other traveler accommodation businesses. The city's hospitals, home health-care businesses, nursing facilities, schools, colleges, and universities employed 311,300 foreign-born workers. (See Figure 7.7.)

A number of entrepreneurial foreign-born residents established their own businesses. Many imported and sold goods from their home countries to other immigrants and tourists. Ethnic restaurants have long been an attraction of the city's neighborhoods and each new wave of immigrants added different scents and flavors that attracted city dwellers and visitors alike. Maggie Leung, as profiled by Joseph Berger for the *New York Times* ("Spotting a Niche, and Knowing How to Fill It; She Gave Customers What They Wanted: Work Uniforms," February 26, 2005), was an example of an immigrant woman who found a need and filled it. While working in her uncle's Brooklyn store, the Hong Kong immigrant heard customers ask if he sold waiter's jackets, or waitress's blouses. Ms. Leung enlisted the help of her sisters and began making uniforms. As Berger put it, if you "want to know what jobs people hold, just gaze in the window of Maggie Leung's uniform store ... She sells burgundy vests for waiters, smocks with orange piping for beauticians, pink aprons for manicurists, [and] heavy cotton coats for meat cutters."

Immigrant women comprised one of the fastest growing groups of business owners in the United States, according to Susan C. Pearce ("Today's Immigrant Entrepreneur," *Immigration Policy in Focus*, Vol. 4, no. 1, January 2005). Immigrant women were more likely than nonimmigrant women to own their own business. Pearce cited the 2000 census, which revealed that 8.3% of all employed immigrant women were business owners, compared to 6.2% of employed native-born women. Since 1990 immigrant women business owners had increased nearly 190%. According to Pearce, "Immigrant entrepreneurs represent a potential source of continued new business growth that brings a broad range of international skills to the work force."

Many foreign-born residents worked hard to realize the American dream of home ownership. Not surprisingly, those who had lived in the city longer and established

FIGURE 7.7

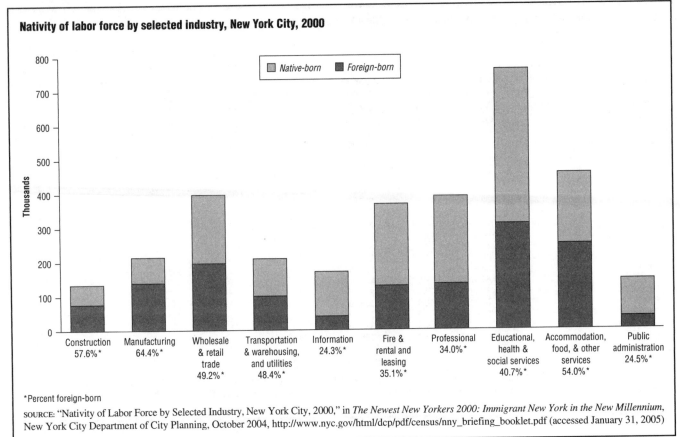

Nativity of labor force by selected industry, New York City, 2000

*Percent foreign-born

SOURCE: "Nativity of Labor Force by Selected Industry, New York City, 2000," in *The Newest New Yorkers 2000: Immigrant New York in the New Millennium*, New York City Department of City Planning, October 2004, http://www.nyc.gov/html/dcp/pdf/census/nny_briefing_booklet.pdf (accessed January 31, 2005)

TABLE 7.5

Housing type by nativity of household head, New York City, 2002

| | Household heads | | | | Percent distribution | | | |
| | | Foreign-born | | | | | Foreign-born | | |
	Total	Total	Entered before 1990	Entered 1990 or later	Total	Total	Entered before 1990	Entered 1990 or later
Total New York City	3,005,323	1,291,309	861,033	430,276	100.0	43.0	28.7	14.3
Owner-occupied	981,815	392,847	335,963	56,884	100.0	40.0	34.2	5.8
Conventional	632,921	284,365	253,924	30,441	100.0	44.9	40.1	4.8
Co-op/condo	348,894	108,482	82,039	26,443	100.0	31.1	23.5	7.6
Renter-occupied	2,023,508	898,462	525,070	373,392	100.0	44.4	25.9	18.5
Market rate	638,368	309,515	161,570	147,945	100.0	48.5	25.3	23.2
Controlled/stabilized	1,047,719	491,594	291,412	200,182	100.0	46.9	27.8	19.1
Government assisted	151,523	57,361	39,849	17,512	100.0	37.9	26.3	11.6
Public housing	185,898	39,992	32,239	7,753	100.0	21.5	17.3	4.2

SOURCE: "Housing Type by Nativity of Household Head, New York City, 2002," in *The Newest New Yorkers 2000: Immigrant New York in the New Millennium*, New York City Department of City Planning, October 2004, http://www.nyc.gov/htm/dep/pdf/census/nny_briefing_booklet.pdf (accessed January 31, 2005)

themselves in jobs were more able to buy homes. Of all owner-occupied dwellings in the city, 34.2% were owned by foreign-born residents who arrived before 1990, compared to just 5.8% owned by those who arrived during or after 1990. While the foreign-born population accounted for 43% of all households, they represented just 21.5% of

public housing residents and 37.9% of those receiving government-housing assistance. (See Table 7.5.)

Impact of Immigration on the City's Population

The New York City Planning Department study defined population change as the net result of births, deaths, and

TABLE 7.6

Total births rank ordered by mother's birthplace, New York City, 2000

	Number	Percent
Total births	**120,989**	**100.0**
Foreign-born mothers	62,489	51.6
Dominican Republic	8,942	7.4
Mexico	6,408	5.3
China	5,676	4.7
Jamaica	4,050	3.3
Guyana	2,723	2.3
Ecuador	2,595	2.1
Haiti	2,052	1.7
Trinidad & Tobago	1,941	1.6
India	1,587	1.3
Bangladesh	1,414	1.2
Pakistan	1,396	1.2
Colombia	1,371	1.1
Russia	1,042	0.9
Korea	1,014	0.8
Israel	995	0.8

SOURCE: "Total Births Rank Ordered by Mother's Birthplace, New York City, 2000," in *The Newest New Yorkers 2000: Immigrant New York in the New Millennium*, New York City Department of City Planning, October 2004, http://www.nyc.gov/html/dcp/pdf/census/nny_briefing_booklet.pdf (accessed January 31, 2005)

FIGURE 7.8

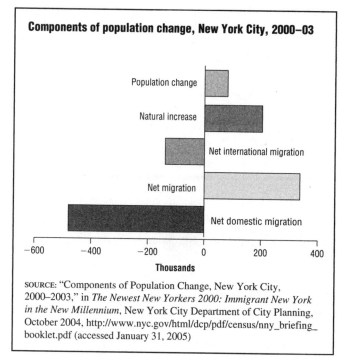

Components of population change, New York City, 2000–03

SOURCE: "Components of Population Change, New York City, 2000–2003," in *The Newest New Yorkers 2000: Immigrant New York in the New Millennium*, New York City Department of City Planning, October 2004, http://www.nyc.gov/html/dcp/pdf/census/nny_briefing_booklet.pdf (accessed January 31, 2005)

migration (persons entering and leaving the city) in a given period of time. Between 2000 and 2003 the population of New York City grew by about 1%, or roughly 77,000 people. Births exceeded deaths by more than 200,000. More than half of all births were to foreign-born women. Together, women originating in the Dominican Republic and Mexico accounted for 13% of all births in the city. (See Table 7.6.) During the same period, 475,000 residents left the city to live elsewhere. This loss was substantially offset by 339,000 people who moved into the city from within the United States and from other countries. (See Figure 7.8.)

The authors of *The Newest New Yorkers* concluded that "the post-1965 flow of immigrants to New York mitigated catastrophic population losses in the 1970s, stabilized the city's population in the 1980s, helped the city reach a new population peak in 2000, and continues to play a crucial role in the city's population growth."

BLACK IMMIGRANTS FROM AFRICA DIFFER FROM AMERICAN BLACK POPULATION

According to the *New York Times* (Sam Roberts, "More Africans Enter U.S. Than in Days of Slavery," February 21, 2005), more people of African descent arrived in the United States voluntarily from 1990 to 2000 than the total who came as slaves prior to 1807 when the country outlawed the slave trade. In 1800 about 20% of the 5 million people in the United States were black compared to 13% of the nearly 300 million people in the country as of 2000. While the American-born black population increased 18% from 1990 to 2000 (28,034,275 to 33,048,095), the African-born population more than doubled from 229,488 to 612,548. By 2000 about 50,000 black legal immigrants were arriving each year. According to the *New York Times* article, New York state attracted the greatest number of immigrants from African nations. Nigeria and Ghana were among the top twenty sources of immigrants to the state. In the United States, Nigeria was the leading source of African immigrants, followed by Ghana, Ethiopia, Liberia, Somalia, and Kenya.

By 2000, one-in-three black persons living in New York City had been born in foreign countries. They began to come as refugees and students; more recently, they have come through family reunification and diversity visas. *The Newest New Yorkers* found that recent immigrants often segregated from other blacks. Large community clusters of Nigerians, Canarsie, and Ghanaians were identified within the city. "As with European ethnics at the turn of the century, ethnicity has been a powerful force in shaping black residential settlement in New York," explained Joseph J. Salvo, director of the Population Division of the Department of City Planning, as quoted in the *New York Times* article.

The *New York Times* reported that immigrants from Africa have been "redefining what it means to be African-American." Immigrants from Africa lack the perspective of American history that drove affirmative action and diversity programs aimed at "redress[ing] the legacy of history." Many speak English, have been raised in large cities with capitalist economies, live in families headed by married couples, and are generally more highly educated than American-born blacks. They also tend to have higher paying jobs.

Although New York City had a significant African immigrant population, as of 2000 Washington, D.C., had the largest black African-born population. In Minneapolis/St. Paul, the black African-born population grew 628% between 1990 and 2000, moving the twin cities into the top five list of metropolitan areas with the largest black populations: Washington, D.C.; New York City; Atlanta; Minneapolis/St. Paul; and Los Angeles.

FOREIGN STUDENTS AT U.S. COLLEGES AND UNIVERSITIES

In a statement before the Senate Foreign Relations Committee at an October 6, 2004, hearing entitled "Addressing the New Reality of Current Visa Policy on International Students and Researchers," Allan E. Goodman, President and CEO of the Institute of International Education, spelled out the cultural and economic benefits to the United States of welcoming foreign students to college campuses:

> The United States is the destination of choice for most foreign students seeking to study abroad. The education available at our 4,000 accredited colleges and universities is recognized and envied around the world. ... There are more seats in higher education in California, for example, than in all of China. Only nine countries in the entire world have more institutions of higher education than the states of California and New York. ... Educational exchange programs ... are the best investment that America can make in reducing misunderstanding of our culture, our people and our policies. An educational experience in America pays dividends to our nation's public diplomacy over many years ...

> There are other benefits to having foreign students on our campuses. ... They come into the classroom with a very different worldview from American students. Raised in a different culture with a different history, they enrich the classroom discussion and share their global perspectives with American classmates, many of whom may never have the opportunity to study or travel abroad. ... Less than 200,000 American students study abroad for credit each year, a tiny fraction of approximately 15 million enrolled in U.S. colleges and universities. For the vast majority who will never study abroad, academic dialog with foreign students on U.S. campuses may well be their only training opportunity before entering careers which will almost certainly be global, whether in business, government, academia, or the not-for-profit sector.

According to the *Open Doors 2004* survey conducted by the Institute of International Education (IIE), 572,509 international students were enrolled in U.S. colleges and universities during the 2003–04 academic year compared to 586,323 the previous year. (See Table 7.7.) The IIE determined that this 2.4% decrease represented the first absolute decline in foreign enrollments since the 1971–72 academic year.

TABLE 7.7

Total international student enrollment, selected years 1954–2003

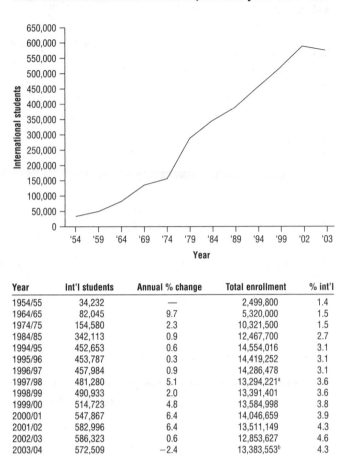

Year	Int'l students	Annual % change	Total enrollment	% int'l
1954/55	34,232	—	2,499,800	1.4
1964/65	82,045	9.7	5,320,000	1.5
1974/75	154,580	2.3	10,321,500	1.5
1984/85	342,113	0.9	12,467,700	2.7
1994/95	452,653	0.6	14,554,016	3.1
1995/96	453,787	0.3	14,419,252	3.1
1996/97	457,984	0.9	14,286,478	3.1
1997/98	481,280	5.1	13,294,221[a]	3.6
1998/99	490,933	2.0	13,391,401	3.6
1999/00	514,723	4.8	13,584,998	3.8
2000/01	547,867	6.4	14,046,659	3.9
2001/02	582,996	6.4	13,511,149	4.3
2002/03	586,323	0.6	12,853,627	4.6
2003/04	572,509	−2.4	13,383,553[b]	4.3

[a]In 1997, The College Board changed its data collection process.
[b]The College Board Annual Survey of Colleges data on U.S. higher education enrollment.

SOURCE: "Total International Student Enrollment," in *Open Doors 2004 Fast Facts*, Institute of International Education, 2004, http://opendoors.iienetwork.org/file_depot/0-10000000/0-10000/3390/folder/37224/OpenDoors2004 FastFacts.pdf (accessed March 11, 2005)

India accounted for 13.9% of all foreign students enrolled in American colleges and universities in the 2003–04 academic year. Despite the overall decline in international students, the number of students from India increased 6.9% from 74,603 in 2002–03 to 79,736 in 2003–04, the greatest percentage gain of any country. Indonesia and Thailand recorded the greatest decreases in share of international students at 14.9% and 10.5%, respectively. (See Table 7.8.)

Not Enough American Students Apply for Teaching and Research Assistantships

Goodman noted in his statement before the Senate Foreign Relations Committee that foreign students had become an important source of graduate-level teaching and research assistants in U.S. universities, particularly in science and engineering fields, because not enough American students applied to fill the available positions.

TABLE 7.8

Leading place of origin of international students, 2002/03 and 2003/04

Rank	Place of origin	2002/03	2003/04	2003/04 % change	2003/04 % of total
	World total	586,323	572,509	−2.4	
1	India	74,603	79,736	6.9	13.9
2	China	64,757	61,765	−4.6	10.8
3	Korea, Republic of	51,519	52,484	1.9	9.2
4	Japan	45,960	40,835	−11.2	7.1
5	Canada	26,513	27,017	1.9	4.7
6	Taiwan	28,017	26,178	−6.6	4.6
7	Mexico	12,801	13,329	4.1	2.3
8	Turkey	11,601	11,398	−1.7	2.0
9	Thailand	9,982	8,937	−10.5	1.6
10	Indonesia	10,432	8,880	−14.9	1.6
11	Germany	9,302	8,745	−6.0	1.5
12	United Kingdom	8,326	8,439	1.4	1.5
13	Brazil	8,388	7,799	−7.0	1.4
14	Colombia	7,771	7,533	−3.1	1.3
15	Kenya	7,862	7,381	−6.1	1.3
16	Hong Kong	8,076	7,353	−9.0	1.3
17	Pakistan	8,123	7,325	−9.8	1.3
18	France	7,223	6,818	−5.6	1.2
19	Malaysia	6,595	6,483	−1.7	1.1
20	Nigeria	5,816	6,140	5.6	1.1

SOURCE: "Leading Place of Origin of International Students, 2002/03 and 2003/04," in *Open Doors 2004 Fast Facts*, Institute of International Education, 2004, http://opendoors.iienetwork.org/file_depot/0-10000000/0-10000/3390/folder/37224/OpenDoors2004FastFacts.pdf (accessed March 11, 2005)

TABLE 7.9

Fields of study of international students, 2002/03 and 2003/04

Field of study	2002/03 Int'l students	2003/04 Int'l students	2003/04 % of total	% change
Business & management	114,777	108,788	19.0	−5.2
Engineering	96,545	95,221	16.6	−1.4
Math & computer science	71,926	67,693	11.8	−5.9
Other*	58,473	60,273	10.5	3.1
Social sciences	45,978	54,153	9.5	17.8
Physical & life sciences	43,549	44,607	7.8	2.4
Fine & applied arts	31,018	31,882	5.6	2.8
Undeclared	36,395	29,313	5.1	−19.5
Health professions	28,120	25,749	4.5	−8.4
Humanities	19,153	16,622	2.9	−13.2
Education	16,004	15,909	2.8	−0.6
Intensive English language	17,620	15,006	2.6	−14.8
Agriculture	6,763	7,293	1.3	7.8
Total	**586,323**	**572,509**	**100.0**	**−2.4**

*"Other" mainly includes liberal/general studies, communications and journalism, multi/interdisciplinary studies and law.

SOURCE: "Fields of Study of International Students, 2002/03 and 2003/04," in *Open Doors 2004 Fast Facts*, Institute of International Education, 2004, http://opendoors.iienetwork.org/file_depot/0-10000000/0-10000/3390/folder/37224/OpenDoors2004FastFacts.pdf (accessed March 11, 2005)

Business and management programs were the top field of study for 19% of undergraduate- and graduate-level international students in the 2003–04 academic year. Another 16.6% were enrolled in engineering and 11.8% in math and computer science programs. These three leading fields of study all showed decreased enrollments in 2003–04 compared to 2002–03. By contrast, international student enrollment in social sciences grew 17.8% in the same period. (See Table 7.9.)

Foreign Students Contribute to U.S. Economy

"Educational exchange [is] one of the leading American service export industries, according to the U.S. Department of Commerce," Goodman told the Senate Foreign Relations Committee. He also noted, "International students make important financial contributions to their host institution and to the local communities in which they live during their stay. Each year students from abroad bring some $12 billion into the U.S. economy."

The University of Southern California had the largest international student population with 6,647 foreign students representing 21% of the school's 31,606 total enrollment in 2003–04. (See Table 7.10.) California was also the state with the greatest number of international students: 77,186 in the 2003–04 academic year. Of the states with the most international students, only Ohio, Indiana, Minnesota, and North Carolina reported growth in their foreign student populations in the 2003–04

TABLE 7.10

U.S. institutions with the largest number of international students, 2002/03 and 2003/04

Rank	Institution	State	Int'l students	Total enrollment
1	University of Southern California	CA	6,647	31,606
2	Columbia University	NY	5,362	23,609
3	Purdue University, main campus	IN	5,094	38,847
4	New York University	NY	5,070	38,188
5	University of Texas at Austin	TX	4,827	51,426
6	University of Illinois at Urbana—Champaign	IL	4,769	38,747
7	University of Michigan—Ann Arbor	MI	4,583	39,031
8	Boston University	MA	4,518	29,049
9	University of California—Los Angeles	CA	4,320	38,598
10	The Ohio State University, main campus	OH	4,263	50,731
11	Texas A&M University	TX	3,815	44,813
12	University of Maryland College Park	MD	3,726	35,329
13	Indiana University at Bloomington	IN	3,715	38,589
14	Penn State University	PA	3,693	41,445
15	SUNY at Buffalo	NY	3,664	27,275
16	University of Pennsylvania	PA	3,557	22,769
17	University of Wisconsin—Madison	WI	3,435	41,507
18	Harvard University	MA	3,403	19,690
19	Florida International University	FL	3,397	33,401
20	University of Houston	TX	3,368	34,699

SOURCE: "U.S. Institutions with the Largest Number of International Students, 2002/03 and 2003/04," in *Open Doors 2004 Fast Facts*, Institute of International Education, 2004, http://opendoors.iienetwork.org/file_depot/0-10000000/0-10000/3390/folder/37224/OpenDoors2004FastFacts.pdf (accessed March 11, 2005)

academic year compared to the previous year, and the increase in both Ohio and Indiana was less than 1%. (See Table 7.11.)

According to Goodman, about two-thirds of foreign students were supported by personal funds. He reported

TABLE 7.11

TABLE 7.12

States with the most international students, 2002/03 and 2003/04

Rank	State	2002/03	2003/04	% change
1	California	80,487	77,186	−4.1
2	New York	63,773	63,313	−0.7
3	Texas	45,672	45,150	−1.1
4	Massachusetts	30,039	28,634	−4.7
5	Florida	27,270	25,861	−5.2
6	Illinois	27,116	25,609	−5.6
7	Pennsylvania	24,470	23,428	−4.3
8	Michigan	22,873	22,277	−2.6
9	Ohio	18,668	18,770	0.5
10	Indiana	13,529	13,586	0.4
11	New Jersey	13,644	13,163	−3.5
12	Maryland	12,749	12,633	−0.9
13	Virginia	12,875	12,531	−2.7
14	Georgia	12,267	12,010	−2.1
15	Washington	11,430	10,756	−5.9
16	Missouri	10,181	9,973	−2.0
17	Arizona	10,325	9,907	−4.0
18	Minnesota	8,985	9,142	1.7
19	North Carolina	8,599	8,826	2.6
20	Oklahoma	9,026	8,764	−2.9

SOURCE: "States with the Most International Students, 2002/03 and 2003/04," in *Open Doors 2004 Fast Facts*, Institute of International Education, 2004, http://opendoors.iienetwork.org/file_depot/0-10000000/ 0-10000/3390/folder/37224/OpenDoors2004FastFacts.pdf (accessed March 11, 2005)

Primary source of funding of international students, 2003/04

Primary source of funds	2003/04 int'l students	2003/04 % of total
Personal & family	385,543	67.3
U.S. college or university	134,015	23.4
Home government/university	13,699	2.4
U.S. private sponsor	2,921	0.5
Foreign private sponsor	12,326	2.2
Current employment	11,888	2.1
U.S. government	10,111	1.8
International organization	1,964	0.3
Other sources	42	0.0
Total	**572,509**	**100.0**

SOURCE: "Primary Source of Funding of International Students, 2003/04," in *Open Doors 2004 Fast Facts*, Institute of International Education, 2004, http://opendoors.iienetwork.org/file_depot/0-10000000/0-10000/3390/ folder/37224/OpenDoors2004FastFacts.pdf (accessed March 11, 2005)

TABLE 7.13

Net contribution to U.S. economy by foreign students, 2002/03

Total number of foreign students:	**586,322**
Contribution from tuition and fees to U.S. economy:	$7,143,000,000
Contribution from living expenses:	$10,138,000,000
Total contribution by foreign students:	**$17,281,000,000**
Less U.S. support of 28.4%	−$4,908,000,000
Plus dependents' living expenses:	+$479,000,000

SOURCE: "Part 1. Net Contribution to U.S. Economy by Foreign Students, 2002/03," in *Open Doors 2004*, Institute of International Education, 2004, http://opendoors.iienetwork.org/file_depot/0-10000000/0-10000/3390/ folder/28491/Economic+Impact+Data+USA.pdf (accessed March 11, 2005)

that "for many states, the tuition, fees and living expenses paid by international students exceed the revenues generated by professional football and basketball combined."

In the IIE *Open Doors 2004* survey, 67.3% of international students reported that they and/or their families provided primary funding for their 2003–04 educational expenses in the United States. The U.S. colleges and universities were the other major source of funds for 23.4% of foreign students through scholarships, grants, loans, and assistantships. (See Table 7.12.)

For the academic year 2002–03 the IIE reported that the 586,322 foreign students enrolled in U.S. colleges and universities contributed $12.9 billion to the U.S. economy. Financial aid provided by the academic institutions was subtracted from the total tuition and living expenses paid by the students. (See Table 7.13.) Just 12.4% of international students were married and most of these students (85%) brought their families with them to the United States. An estimated 72,617 spouses and 43,570 children accompanied these enrolled foreign students. Living expenses paid by students for these family members were estimated at $479 million annually. (See Table 7.14.)

The IIE survey estimated that California, with the greatest number of international students, realized $1.7 billion in tuition and other fees as well as living expenses paid by students and their dependents for academic year 2002–03. New York was close behind at $1.5 billion. Wyoming, with the fewest international

students among the forty-eight contiguous states and Washington, D.C., garnered $9.3 million from international students in the same period.

In his address to the Senate Foreign Relations Committee, Goodman acknowledged U.S. security concerns about possible student visa abuse, but made a plea for expediting student visa processing so that foreign students did not arrive late for the start of school semesters. He also stated that foreign students faced lengthy delays because they had to reapply for visa approval each time they returned home, even for short visits during holiday breaks. Goodman recommended student visa approval be awarded for the entire period of study in the United States.

CALIFORNIA'S ROLE IN IMMIGRATION

The influx of illegal aliens into the state of California in the 1980s has inspired controversy, particularly regarding California's role in the problem. Many commentators have rejected the assertion that California is the helpless victim of illegal aliens and the federal government. They argue that some policies promoted in the 1980s actively

TABLE 7.14

Contribution to U.S. economy by foreign students' dependents, 2002/03

Spouses' contribution		Children's contribution	
Percent of married students:	12.4%	Number of couples in the U.S.:	72,617
Percent of spouses in the U.S.:	85.0%	Number of children per couple:	0.6
Number of spouses in the U.S.:	72,617	Number of children in the U.S.:	43,570
Additional expenses for a spouse: (% of student living expenses)	25.0%	Additional expenses for a child: (% of student living expenses)	20.0%
Spouses' contribution:	$306,000,000	Children's contribution:	$173,000,000
(No. of spouses × 85% × 25% × student living expenses)		(No. of couples × .6 × 20% × student living expenses)	
Net contribution to U.S. economy by foreign students' dependents:			**$479,000,000**

SOURCE: "Part 2. Contribution to U.S. Economy by Foreign Students' Dependents, 2002/03," in *Open Doors 2004*, Institute of International Education, 2004, http://opendoors.iienetwork.org/file_depot/0-10000000/0-10000/3390/folder/28491/Economic+Impact+Data+USA.pdf (accessed March 11, 2005)

encouraged illegal immigration. For example, in 1984 and 1985 city councils in Los Angeles, San Francisco, and many other California cities passed resolutions making their cities sanctuaries for illegal aliens from Central American countries regarded as having repressive governments supported by the United States.

Furthermore, many California homeowners and businesses hired illegal aliens to maintain their homes, care for their children, or work in stores, factories, and on farms. Illegal aliens went to California because other refugees from similar areas of the world had established vibrant communities there. Finally, refugees, like many Americans, were attracted to California's pleasant climate. The Immigration and Naturalization Service (INS) warned that the word would spread and illegal aliens would flock to California. In *Estimates of the Unauthorized Immigrant Population Residing in the United States: 1990 to 2000* (Washington, DC: Office of Policy and Planning, U.S. Immigration and Naturalization Service, January 2003) the INS calculated that in 2000 about 2.2 million illegal aliens, or 32% of the total number of illegal residents in the United States, lived in California.

Governor Pete Wilson's Role

Former governor Pete Wilson has also been charged with complicity in California's illegal alien problem. When the Immigration Reform and Control Act of 1986 (IRCA) was being debated in the U.S. Senate, Wilson (a senator at the time) supported a special amnesty for illegal aliens who could prove that they worked as farm laborers for at least ninety days between May 1985 and May 1986. The Special Agricultural Worker (SAW) program became part of IRCA. When the INS demanded proof that the applicants for legalization under SAW had indeed fulfilled their employment requirement, Wilson opposed it.

Some experts believe that many undocumented aliens legalized under the SAW program were admitted under fraudulent circumstances. Although the program was supposed to grant amnesty to about 350,000 workers, nearly 1.3 million illegal immigrants gained permanent resident status through the program; most settled in California (Eric Schlosser, "In the Strawberry Fields," *Reefer Madness: Sex, Drugs, and Cheap Labor in the American Black Market*, Boston: Houghton Mifflin, 2003). After the workers were legalized, hundreds of thousands of family members entered the United States illegally. Most were women and children—those most likely to use medical and educational services.

Welfare Dependence after Welfare Reform

In *How Are Immigrants Faring after Welfare Reform? Preliminary Evidence from Los Angeles and New York City* (Randy Capps, et al., Washington, DC: Urban Institute, March 2002), the authors found that by 1999–2000 low-income immigrant families had lower public assistance program participation rates than low-income native families. In Los Angeles, 13% of low-income immigrant families received food stamps, compared with 34% of low-income native families. The study suggested that the percentages might have been higher but for immigrants' fears of being branded "public charges"—that is, dependent on the state—which could lead to the denial of an immigrant's application for legal permanent resident status.

Public Education and California's Immigrant Children

In California, education has been the public service most affected by both legal and illegal immigration. According to data from the California Department of Education, enrollments in California's primary and secondary schools rose significantly from 1950 to 2002. This was primarily a result of the steady influx of school-age immigrants and the growing numbers of American-born children of immigrants. The California Department of Finance projected that Hispanic K–12 enrollment would grow from 45.4% of the total in 2002–03 to 52.4% in 2011–12 (Stephen J. Carroll, et al., *California's K–12 Public Schools: How Are They Doing?*, Santa Monica, CA: The RAND Corporation, 2005). In *The Well-Being of California's Children* (San Francisco, CA: Public Policy Institute of California, 2003), Frank F. Furstenberg reported that in 1999, nearly half of all children in California under the age of six had a foreign-born parent.

These children were mostly Hispanic, came from the poorest families in California, and had parents with low levels of educational attainment. Such children tended to have limited English proficiency and to experience greater problems in school.

ENGLISH LANGUAGE PROFICIENCY IMPORTANT TO EDUCATIONAL SUCCESS

In a study of immigration's impact on the nation's schools, Michael E. Fix and Jeffrey S. Passel noted that as of 2000 one out of every five K–12 students was the child of immigrants and of these about 25% were themselves foreign-born (*U.S. Immigration: Trends and Implications for Schools*, Washington, DC: The Urban Institute, January 2003). Fix and Passel estimated that 5% of U.S. students had limited English proficiency (LEP). The authors also noted a recent dispersal trend—immigrants were moving in greater numbers into states that previously had not attracted significant numbers of immigrants. This created new challenges for schools that previously had not had to meet the needs of LEP students. In addition to the cost and availability of qualified bilingual teachers, schools faced the potential loss of certain federal funding according to the No Child Left Behind Act of 2002 should students—including LEP students—fail to make adequate academic progress on standardized tests.

Do Immigrants Improve English Skills with Succeeding Generations?

Some commentators have expressed concerns that today's immigrants, particularly those who speak Spanish, may not be as willing to learn and use English as have past generations. The Lewis Mumford Center for Comparative Urban and Regional Research studied this issue and found that "English is almost universally accepted by the children and grandchildren of the immigrants who have come to the U.S. in great numbers since the 1960s" (Richard Alba, *Language Assimilation Today: Bilingualism Persists More Than in the Past, but English Still Dominates*, Albany, NY: University of Albany, December 2004).

The study found that most second-generation children spoke another language at home, but almost all were proficient in English. Among second-generation Hispanics, 85% spoke some Spanish at home compared to 61% of second-generation Asians. Except among Spanish-speaking groups, the study found that by the third generation (the grandchildren of immigrants) English was the primary language. Among third-generation Asians, 92% spoke only English compared to 72% of Hispanics. For Mexican-American children, maintaining bilingual skills was most common in communities near the U.S.–Mexico border. Away from the border, third-generation Mexican-American children were unlikely to be bilingual.

HOW WELL DO IMMIGRANT CHILDREN COMPETE WITH NATIVE CHILDREN?

A survey conducted in 2003 by the Pew Hispanic Center and the Kaiser Family Foundation explored attitudes of Hispanic adults, or Latinos, toward schools and education. The study, *National Survey of Latinos: Education* (Washington, DC, January 2004), paid particular attention to differences between recent immigrants and those who had been in the United States for a generation or more. When asked to evaluate public schools on an "A, B, C, D, or Failing" scale, 33% of foreign-born Latino parents gave their community schools an "A" compared to 16% of native-born Latino parents, 13% of African-American parents, and 19% of white parents. Foreign-born Latino parents were similarly more positive about the nationwide public school system. (See Figure 7.9.) If the school failed to meet performance standards, 69% of foreign-born Latino parents would require students to remain in the school compared to 50% of native Latino parents and 35% of white parents. Foreign-born Latino parents were generally more optimistic about U.S. schools. Authors of the survey noted that these findings suggested foreign-born parents might lack an understanding of major educational reforms such as the No Child Left Behind Act, vouchers, and charter schools.

When it came to understanding their child's curriculum, just 43% of foreign-born Latino parents said they knew a lot compared to 66% of native Latino parents and a similar share of African-American and white parents. (See Figure 7.10.) While 99% of all Latino parents thought it was important for schools to teach English to the children of immigrants, 93% of foreign-born Latino parents thought schools should also help students maintain their native tongue. Native Latino parents were somewhat less interested (81%) in having schools provide such instruction.

National Standardized Test Scores

Educational achievement in core subjects like reading, math, and science was considered by educators as a predictor of children's likelihood of completing high school, attending college, and attaining high-paying careers. According to the Pew Hispanic Center fact sheet "Hispanic School Achievement: Catching Up Requires Running Faster than White Youth" (Washington, DC, January 2004), in 2000 the average score on a standardized math test for kindergartners was 45.5 for white children, 40.0 for all Hispanic children, and 38.4 for African-American children. Children whose parents were born in Mexico, the Dominican Republic, and Puerto Rico on average scored significantly lower than their white peers. However, children whose parents were born in Cuba (46.1 score) outperformed their white peers. (See Table 7.15.) The number of generations a Hispanic child

FIGURE 7.9

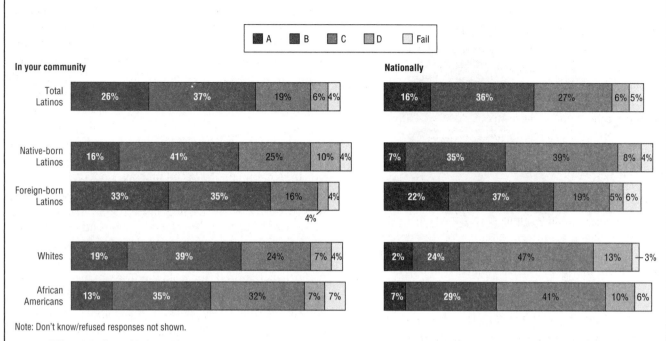

Ratings of schools, by demographic characteristics, 2003

STUDENTS ARE OFTEN GIVEN THE GRADES A, B, C, D OR FAIL. SUPPOSE THE PUBLIC SCHOOLS WERE GRADED IN THE SAME WAY. WHAT GRADE WOULD YOU GIVE SCHOOLS...

Note: Don't know/refused responses not shown.

SOURCE: "Chart 1. Ratings of Schools," in *National Survey of Latinos: Education*, Pew Hispanic Center/Kaiser Family Foundation, January 2004, http://pewhispanic.org/files/factsheets/7.pdf (accessed March 19, 2005) © 2004, Pew Hispanic Center, a Pew Research Center project.

FIGURE 7.10

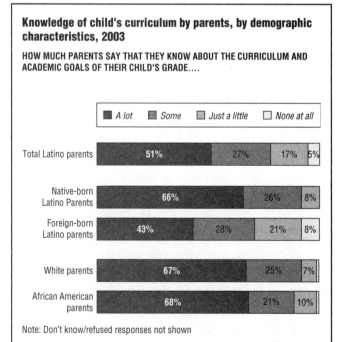

Knowledge of child's curriculum by parents, by demographic characteristics, 2003

HOW MUCH PARENTS SAY THAT THEY KNOW ABOUT THE CURRICULUM AND ACADEMIC GOALS OF THEIR CHILD'S GRADE....

Note: Don't know/refused responses not shown

SOURCE: "Chart 7. Knowledge of Child's Curriculum," in *National Survey of Latinos: Education,* Pew Hispanic Center/Kaiser Family Foundation, January 2004, http://pewhispanic.org/files/factsheets/7.pdf (accessed March 19, 2005) © 2004, Pew Hispanic Center, a Pew Research Center project.

TABLE 7.15

Average math test scores of 1st- and 2nd-generation kindergartners, by parental country of birth

Parental birth place	
Mexico	38.6
Dominican Republic	35.7
Puerto Rico	37.3
Cuba	46.1
El Salvador	39.7
Other Central America	39.4
South America	42.4

SOURCE: "Average Math Test Score of 1st and 2nd Generation Kindergartners," in *Fact Sheet—Hispanic School Achievement: Catching Up Requires Running Faster than White Youth*, Pew Hispanic Center, January 2004, http://pewhispanic.org/files/factsheets/7.2.pdf (accessed April 6, 2005) © 2004, Pew Hispanic Center, a Pew Research Center project.

was removed from the country of origin appeared to make no difference in educational achievement. Eighth-grade math scores and middle-school grade point averages were very similar regardless of whether the child was native-born or foreign-born.

In 2000 the dropout rate for Hispanic students age sixteen to nineteen was 21.1% ("High School Dropout Rates for Latino Youth," *ERIC Clearinghouse on Urban*

FIGURE 7.11

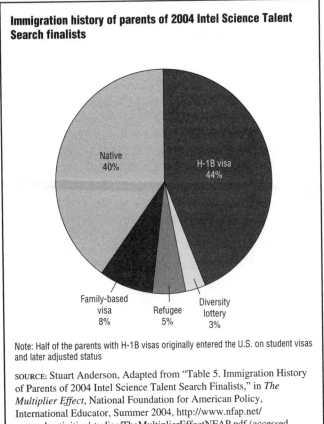

Immigration history of parents of 2004 Intel Science Talent Search finalists

Native 40%

H-1B visa 44%

Family-based visa 8%

Refugee 5%

Diversity lottery 3%

Note: Half of the parents with H-1B visas originally entered the U.S. on student visas and later adjusted status

SOURCE: Stuart Anderson, Adapted from "Table 5. Immigration History of Parents of 2004 Intel Science Talent Search Finalists," in *The Multiplier Effect*, National Foundation for American Policy, International Educator, Summer 2004, http://www.nfap.net/researchactivities/studies/TheMultiplierEffectNFAP.pdf (accessed March 18, 2005)

Education Digest, No. 193, December 2003). While this figure reflected a decrease in the 1990 dropout rate (21.8%) of Latino youth, it was about three times the rate of 6.9% for white, non-Hispanic students in 2000.

Children of Immigrants Succeed in Math and Science Competitions

A study by the National Foundation for American Policy (NFAP) found that "an astounding 60% of the top science students in the United States and 65% of the top math students are the children of immigrants. In addition, foreign-born high school students make up 50% of the 2004 U.S. Math Olympiad's top scorers, 38% of the U.S. Physics Team, and 25% of the Intel Science Talent Search finalists," which is considered the most prestigious award for young scientists and mathematicians in the United States (Stuart Anderson, *The Multiplier Effect*, Arlington, VA: National Foundation for American Policy, 2004). NFAP described itself as a nonprofit, nonpartisan organization engaged in public policy research on trade, immigration, and other national issues.

While the study focused on prestigious competitions that attracted outstanding science and math students, children of immigrants made an impressive showing. Eighteen of the forty finalists in the 2004 Intel Science Talent Search

had parents who entered the United States on professional status H-1B visas. Clearly these students had at least one highly educated parent. However, the parents of three finalists entered the country as family-sponsored immigrants, the parents of two competitors came as refugees, and one parent won a diversity lottery visa. (See Figure 7.11.) Stuart Anderson, author of the NFAP study, commented, "If those who most oppose immigration had succeeded over the past two decades, two-thirds of the most outstanding future scientists and mathematicians in the United States would not be in the country."

CALIFORNIA'S EFFORTS TO LEGISLATE AGAINST ILLEGAL ALIENS

In November 1994 increasing concern about the effects of a large number of illegal aliens culminated in California voters approving Proposition 187 by a margin of 59% to 41%. The ballot initiative prohibited illegal aliens and their children from receiving any welfare services, education, or emergency health care. It further required local law-enforcement authorities, educators, medical professionals, and social-service workers to report suspected illegal aliens to state and federal authorities. It also considered the manufacture, distribution, and sale of fraudulent documents a state felony punishable by up to five years in prison.

The day after California voters approved Proposition 187, civil rights groups filed a lawsuit in federal district court to block implementation of the ballot initiative. One week later U.S. District Court Judge Matthew Byrne issued a temporary restraining order.

In November 1995 U.S. District Court Judge Mariana Pfaelzer ruled unconstitutional Proposition 187's provision involving elementary and secondary education for undocumented children. The judge cited the U.S. Supreme Court decision in a Texas case, *Plyler v. Doe* (457 U.S. 202, 1982), which held that the equal protection clause of the Fourteenth Amendment prohibited states from denying education to illegal immigrants. Civil rights and education groups had argued that states had no legal rights to regulate immigration, which was a federal responsibility.

In March 1998 Judge Pfaelzer permanently barred Proposition 187's restrictions on benefits for aliens and declared much of the legislation unconstitutional. Pfaelzer allowed the criminal provision to consider as a felony the manufacture, distribution, and use of false documents.

Former governor Pete Wilson appealed Pfaelzer's decision. In April 1999 Wilson's successor, Governor Gray Davis, announced that the state of California would ask a federal appeals court to mediate the legal disputes over Proposition 187. Although Davis opposed the ballot initiative, he claimed he had no authority to disregard the voters' wishes or to rule on Proposition 187's constitutionality. Some individuals on both sides of the issue charged that the new governor had taken the easy way out. In July 1999 Governor Davis and the civil rights groups agreed to end the litigation, in effect nullifying the public votes banning public education and social services to illegal aliens. Only the criminal provision pertaining to false documents was to be implemented.

Arizona Succeeds Where California Failed

In November 2004, 56% of Arizona voters approved a ballot initiative called Proposition 200 that would require proof of citizenship when registering to vote and applying for public benefits. It also required state, county, and municipal employees to report suspected undocumented immigrants to immigration authorities. The Mexican American Legal Defense and Educational Fund filed suit to block implementation of Proposition 200 and some opponents called the measure "racist." On December 22, 2004, U.S. District Judge David Bury lifted a temporary order barring implementation of Proposition 200 and it became law in Arizona.

Meanwhile the courts were left to determine the definition of "public benefits." The state's attorney general issued an opinion that limited the definition of "public benefits" to welfare. The Federation for American Immigration Reform (FAIR) and a state support group filed suit to broaden the definition to include benefits such as public housing, post-secondary education, grants, loans, and food assistance.

The apparent success of Arizona's Proposition 200 sparked interest in similar laws in other states. The *Arizona Republic* reported that an initiative called "Protect Arkansas NOW" had been introduced in that state's legislature (Yvonne Wingett, "Prop. 200 Spurs Efforts Nationwide," January 21, 2005). Tyche Hendricks of the *San Francisco Chronicle* reported on February 28, 2005, that copycats were being pushed by groups in Colorado, Georgia, Mississippi, Louisiana, Washington, and Oregon ("Issue of Illegals Roiling Arizona: New Law Denies Public Services to Such Immigrants").

PUBLIC OPINION—CHANGING VIEWS ON IMMIGRATION

The results of the 2000 census added to the continuing debate on the effects of immigration on population growth and wages. The terrorist attacks of September 11, 2001, fed the debate over immigration levels. According to the U.S. Census Bureau report *Population Change and Distribution: 1990–2000* (Washington, DC, April 2001), the U.S. population grew by more than 13%, from 248.7 million in 1990 to 281.4 million in 2000. The additional 32.7 million people represented the largest increase in the country's history. The foreign-born population grew 57% during the

decade—from 19.8 million to 31.1 million, accounting for an estimated 11.1% of the total population in 2000 (*The Foreign-Born Population: 2000*, Washington, DC: U.S. Census Bureau, December 2003).

A Gallup poll entitled "Americans Have Mixed Opinions about Immigration" (Jeffrey M. Jones, Washington, DC: The Gallup Organization, June 19, 2001), found that 42% of the American public supported keeping immigration at the current level, while 41% wanted to lower the number of admissions. One month after the September 11, 2001, terrorist attacks, a joint CNN/Gallup/*USA Today* poll found that the percentage of Americans in favor of decreased immigration levels rose to 58% ("Opinions on Immigration," October 21, 2001). By June 2003 attitudes toward immigration were somewhat less negative, with 47% in favor of reduced immigration and 37% in favor of maintaining the current level ("Nearly Half of Americans Say Immigration Levels Should Be Decreased," The Gallup Organization, July 10, 2003). As of January 2005, however, attitudes had again shifted. Fifty-two percent of respondents surveyed in a Gallup poll favored reduced levels of immigration in America ("Most Americans Say Immigration Should Be Decreased," January 5, 2005).

Some Americans felt threatened by immigrants who they believed were unable or unwilling to assimilate into American culture. Others felt that just as previous waves of immigrants had added richness and a distinctive quality to American life, future influxes of foreign-born people would contribute more than just their numbers to American society. In the aforementioned June 2001 poll, the Gallup Organization asked Americans about the impact of immigration on society. Nearly half of respondents thought immigration made taxes and crime worse while more than half believed that food, music, and the arts were improved by immigrants.

In *Elite vs. Public Opinion: An Examination of Divergent Views on Immigration* (Washington, DC: Center for Immigration Studies, December 2002), Roy Beck and Steven A. Camarota examined the results of a national poll conducted from May through July 2002 by the Chicago Council on Foreign Relations. The authors contended that the poll results showed a wide gap between the opinions of the American public toward immigration and the opinions of American policymakers. This poll found that 60% of the public considered current immigration levels to be a "critical threat to the vital interests of the United States," while only 14% of the nation's leadership believed this to be true. More than half (55%) of the public believed current immigration levels should be reduced, compared with only 18% of "opinion leaders." The public ranked illegal immigration as the biggest foreign policy problem facing the nation, while the nation's leadership ranked it 26th in importance. According to the authors, "[t]he very large difference between elite and public opinion explains the current political stalemate on immigration. For example, supporters of an amnesty for illegal immigrants have broad elite support ranging from religious to business and union leaders. Normally elite support of this kind would lead to policy changes, but on this issue public opposition is so strong that it creates a political stalemate."

The Debate over Amnesty and Guest Worker Programs

David Simcox reported in *Measuring the Fallout: The Cost of the IRCA Amnesty after 10 Years* (Washington, DC: Center for Immigration Studies, 1997) that ten years after IRCA legalization, the illegal aliens who had received amnesties had cost the government a total of $102.1 billion in terms of twenty public assistance programs. During the same period, the amnestied illegal aliens paid taxes of only $78 billion. In addition, Simcox estimated indirect costs related to the legalized population at $54.6 billion—$9.9 billion for aid to displaced native workers, $36.1 billion in aid to American-born children of legalized women, and $8.6 billion in public education costs for the undocumented children of legalized aliens.

After his election in 2000, President George W. Bush proposed a guest worker program that would provide illegal immigrants in the United States with an opportunity to register for available jobs and move gradually toward permanent resident status. According to the president, the term "amnesty" did not apply to the program he had in mind.

In August 2001, shortly before Mexico's President Vicente Fox became the first official state visitor to the Bush White House, ABCNews.com conducted a random sample survey in which 43% of adults said they would support a plan "in which illegal immigrants from Mexico would be allowed to live and work legally in the United States" ("Border Lines Poll Shows Public Opinion Split On Residency for Mexican Illegals," August 29, 2001). Almost half (49%) of respondents said they would oppose such a plan. Despite the president's arguments, many people saw his proposal as amnesty disguised by another label.

Guest workers took a backseat to greater security issues following the terrorist attacks of September 2001. However, the idea did not disappear. In another ABCNews.com poll taken between January 7 and 11, 2004 ("Most Oppose Bush Immigration Plan," January 12, 2004), 52% of Americans opposed any program "in which illegal immigrants from Mexico should be allowed to live and work legally in the United States." Yet, in his January 20, 2004, State of the Union address, President Bush proposed a new temporary worker program:

> Tonight I also ask you to reform our immigration laws, so they reflect our values and benefit our economy.

FIGURE 7.12

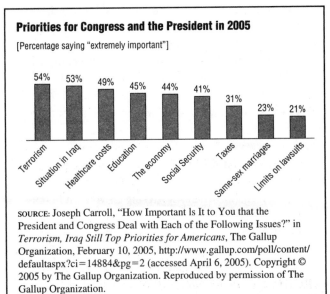

Priorities for Congress and the President in 2005

[Percentage saying "extremely important"]

SOURCE: Joseph Carroll, "How Important Is It to You that the President and Congress Deal with Each of the Following Issues?" in *Terrorism, Iraq Still Top Priorities for Americans*, The Gallup Organization, February 10, 2005, http://www.gallup.com/poll/content/defaultaspx?ci=14884&pg=2 (accessed April 6, 2005). Copyright © 2005 by The Gallup Organization. Reproduced by permission of The Gallup Organization.

I propose a new temporary worker program to match willing foreign workers with willing employers, when no Americans can be found to fill the job. ... I oppose amnesty, because it would encourage further illegal immigration, and unfairly reward those who break our laws. My temporary worker program will preserve the citizenship path for those who respect the law, while bringing millions of hardworking men and women out from the shadows of American life.

GUEST WORKER PROGRAM LACKED PUBLIC SUPPORT. While immigration was high on the president's priority list, it was less important overall to the majority of Americans. In a December 2004 poll by the Gallup organization ("Terrorism, Iraq Still Top Priorities for Americans"), immigration was not among the issues Americans considered to be "extremely important." (See Figure 7.12.) Less than 3 in 10 Americans listed immigration as a priority issue for Congress and the president in 2005.

A Washington Post/ABC News poll reported in January 2005 that 56% of those surveyed disapproved of President Bush's handling of immigration issues ("Presidential Peril? Bush's Popularity Is Narrowly Based; Democrats Match Him in Public Trust," *Washington Post*, January 19, 2005). Many people viewed his proposal to allow undocumented workers already in the United States to become legally recognized temporary workers as an amnesty program.

In his February 2, 2005, State of the Union speech, President Bush reiterated his intention to propose a guest worker program. He said, "it is time for an immigration policy that permits temporary guest workers to fill jobs Americans will not take, that rejects amnesty, that tells us who is entering and leaving our country, and that closes the border to drug dealers and terrorists."

CHAPTER 8

IMMIGRATION AND ILLEGAL ALIENS ARE MORE
A BLESSING THAN A BURDEN

**ARCHIVES OF RUDOLPH W. GIULIANI,
KENNEDY SCHOOL OF GOVERNMENT,
CAMBRIDGE, MASSACHUSETTS, THURSDAY,
OCTOBER 10, 1996**

... I'm pleased to be with you this evening to talk about the anti-immigrant movement in America.... And why I believe this movement endangers the single most important reason for American greatness, namely, the renewal, reformation and reawakening that's provided by the continuous flow of immigrants who are seeking to create better lives for themselves and their families ... and who succeed in doing so.

... I believe the anti-immigration movement in America is one of our most serious public problems. And Washington is only making the problem worse. The anti-immigration movement can be seen in legislation passed by Congress and the President. It can be seen in the negative attitudes being expressed by many of the politicians in America today.... And it can be seen in a growing sense of unease in the American workforce that somehow there aren't enough jobs to go around.

But the immigration issue is not being discussed in places where it really should be most visible. For example, immigration was not mentioned in last Sunday's Presidential debate. And that's unfortunate.... America needs an open and frank discussion about immigration. This critical issue should be decided in public debate, not behind closed doors in Washington.

I am speaking out because I believe that a threat to immigration can be a threat to the future of our country. Just as they did in years past, immigrants today revitalize and reinvigorate the culture and economy of our cities and states. But history also shows that America goes through periods—like the one we're in today—where people become fearful of immigration.

In 1923, an anti-immigration song was published in New York called "Close the Gates!" The lyrics went like this:

Close the gates of our nation,

Lock them firm and strong!

Before this mob from Europe,

Shall drag our colors down.

Unfortunately, this kind of fear mongering often works. One year later, in 1924, Congress passed new immigration quotas, severely restricting the flow of new arrivals, especially from Italy, Greece, and eastern Europe. Immigration from China and Japan was effectively banned altogether. Commenting on the 1924 quota law, the *New York Times* said, "America the melting pot comes to an end."

Today, about 100 million Americans are descended from the immigrants who passed through Ellis Island between 1892 and 1954. And millions more are descended from the immigrants who disembarked in Boston, beginning with the Puritans in 1630. Between 1880 and 1930, over 500,000 Italians entered America through Boston. Between 1830 and 1930, over 700,000 Irish arrived in Boston.

A member of my staff, Clark Whelton, has special reason to be grateful to Boston's historic role as a haven for new Americans. In 1848, his great-grandparents escaped the potato famine in Ireland and found new homes in Boston. Although they worked hard, they never had much money. But their only son, Daniel A. Whelton, became Mayor of Boston in 1905.

That's the magic of immigration.... That's the magic of America. That same magic has worked for many of us.

My grandfather, Rodolfo Giuliani, arrived in New York City without much money in his pocket, but with a dream in his heart. And his dream of freedom and success became my dream. His dream of opportunity and achievement was shared by millions of immigrants from every part of the world. Their dreams transformed New York City, and Boston, and Los Angeles. Their dreams became the American dream.

Each one of us owes so much to immigration. That's why anti-immigration movements eventually die out. In the past we have always returned to the recognition that new Americans are good for our country. We realize that any effort to eliminate immigration or unfairly burden immigrants could destroy the very process that is the key to American success.

America became the most successful nation in history because of our constant process of re-evaluation, reform and revitalization, a process that is driven by immigrants who come here to create better lives for themselves and their children. We are constantly being reinvented, not just by the free flow of ideas but by the free flow of people. This process has really defined the United States. It makes us what we are.

Abraham Lincoln said that Americans are not bound together by a common race, religion, or ethnicity, but by their agreement on a set of principles centered on a strong belief in equality, democracy and opportunity. But sometimes our belief in those principles weakens. Today America is once again going through a period where it doubts that we need new people. In periods like this, fear prevails over optimism. Self-doubt prevails over confidence. Americans begin to think that our country is too crowded. When they see new people, they see problems.

I don't share that pessimism. When I see new people, I see new opportunities. I would like to take you to Kennedy Airport—which in many ways is the Ellis Island of today—and show you people coming to America from many different parts of the world.

In some ways they may look different and speak differently than the millions who came through Ellis Island. But the look in their eyes is the same. You can see in their eyes the same determination. You can see that they are looking for a chance to build new lives in a country that provides freedom and opportunity. And they are exactly what America needs today.

They help our country tremendously. They help us with the work they do; they challenge us with new ideas, and with new perspectives. They remind us how lucky we are, and that America is something special. Basically, new immigrants to America are no different than the old immigrants to America. And the anti-immigration movement now sweeping America is no different than earlier anti-immigration movements.

We need only look back at the "Know-Nothing" movement that swept America in the mid-nineteenth century. The "Know-Nothings" encouraged Americans to fear foreigners and stop immigration. No part of our country was immune from this hysteria. Even Massachusetts—birthplace of the American revolution—was gripped by a fear of foreigners.

In 1855, a young Irish immigrant named Mary Williams and her infant daughter Bridget were charged with the crime of poverty, and forcibly returned to Ireland. Even though she was not a pauper, and had never been a public charge, her passage back to Ireland—which cost $12—was paid by the Commonwealth of Massachusetts. With her on the boat—also against their will—went thirty-five other immigrants. A reporter for the *Boston Daily Advertiser* called Mary Williams "a victim of know-nothing intolerance."

But it was also in 1855 that one of America's greatest leaders had the courage to stand up and oppose the "Know-Nothings." He was Abraham Lincoln. Lincoln lamented the state of a nation that began with the phrase "all men are created equal."

"When the know-nothings get control," Lincoln wrote, "it will read: all men are created equal, except Negroes, and foreigners, and Catholics. If the Know-Nothings come to power," continued Lincoln, "I should prefer emigrating to some country where they make no pretense of loving liberty—to Russia, for instance, where despotism can be taken pure and without the base alloy of hypocrisy."

Abraham Lincoln was not solely a romantic about the value of immigration, and neither am I. The fact is, immigration makes economic sense. Immigrants work hard. In New York City, foreign-born males are 10% more likely to be employed than native-born males. Foreign-born women are employed at the same rate as native-born women.

In New York City, immigrants own businesses in higher percentages than other Americans. And immigrants in New York City are 10% less likely than native-born Americans to be on public assistance. The fact is, immigrants are achievers. Nationwide, immigrants account for 50% of all professors of engineering. Immigrants account for 21% of all U.S. physicians. Immigrants are net contributors to our economy. They are creators of wealth. They pay their own way.

STATEMENT OF SENATOR EDWARD M. KENNEDY BEFORE THE 105TH CONGRESS, APRIL 15, 1997

As tax day is here, it is worth considering the contributions of legal immigrants to Uncle Sam.

A new study by the Library of Congress highlights the extraordinary level of Federal taxes paid by legal immigrants. Recent immigrants—including both those who have not yet naturalized and those who have become citizens—paid an estimated $55 billion in Federal income taxes in 1995. Without immigration, the Government would have had $55 billion less to pay for key services or deficit reduction.

We have long known of the major contributions of immigrants in developing innovative technologies, creating jobs for American workers, vitalizing our inner cities, serving in our Armed Forces, and in many other ways. But this report also shows that immigrants pay their way in Federal taxes.

The $55 billion that recent immigrants contributed is almost three times what the Federal Government will spend this year on law enforcement to deal with crime. It is twice what the Federal Government will invest in education. It is nine times the budget of the Environmental Protection Agency.

Often in recent years, Congress has been too quick to engage in immigrant-bashing, or too slow to recognize the immense contributions of immigrants to the Nation's heritage and history. Studies like this help to redress the balance, by demonstrating the continuing important role of immigration in our modern society.

STATEMENT OF SENATOR PATRICK LEAHY, RANKING MEMBER, SENATE JUDICIARY COMMITTEE IMMIGRATION SUBCOMMITTEE HEARING ON "IMMIGRANT CONTRIBUTIONS TO THE U.S. ARMED FORCES," MAY 26, 1999

… It has become fashionable for Congress over the last several years to use immigrants as scapegoats and blame them for society's problems. So I am pleased when we focus attention on the many ways in which immigrants have contributed to our country and serve our nation.

According to the Cato Institute, immigrants account for more than 20% of all recipients of the Congressional Medal of Honor—the country's highest award for battlefield valor. That is more than 700 immigrants who served this country in time of war and displayed heroism "beyond the call of duty." Many lost their lives or were seriously injured.

Today's witnesses provide further evidence—if evidence is needed—that immigrants share a commitment to defending this nation and are willing, if necessary, to give what Abraham Lincoln called "the last full measure of devotion" in support of America's interests.

As we pay tribute today to our immigrant veterans, we should ask ourselves why we are often so quick to turn our backs on them. Under the immigration "reform" legislation enacted in 1996, Congress passed and the President endorsed a broad expansion of the definition of what makes a legal resident deportable. In the rush to be tough on illegal immigration, the bill also vastly limited relief from deportation and imposed mandatory detention for thousands of permanent residents in deportation proceedings. These harsh new measures have now snared immigrants who spilled their blood for our country. As the INS prepares to deport these American veterans, we have not even been kind enough to thank them for their service with a hearing to listen to their story and consider whether, just possibly, their military service or other life circumstances outweigh the government's interest in deporting them.

Here is the cold and ugly side of our "tough" immigration policies. Here are the human consequences of legislating by thirty-second political ad. Unfortunately the checks and balances of our government have failed these veterans because Congress and this Administration were determined not to be outdone by each other. "Tough" in this case meant blinding the INS to the personal consequences of these people. It meant substituting discretion with a cold rubber stamp that can only say "no."

Just last month, a fifty-two-year-old Vietnam veteran named Gabriel Delgadillo was deported for a crime he committed in 1988. The crime, burglary, was reclassified as a mandatory deportation offense under the 1996 law. Delgadillo left behind a wife and seven children, all U.S. citizens.

Ralph Hesselbach enlisted in the U.S. Army in the summer of 1967, when he was seventeen years old, and fought in active combat in Vietnam. As a scout dog handler with the 33rd Scout Dog Platoon of the 4th Infantry Division, Specialist Hesselbach served as a permanent point man and led scouting missions to uncover mines, trip wires and intercept ambushes. In late 1968, he was severely injured and permanently disabled in an explosion at base camp. He was honorably discharged to medical retirement and was awarded the National Defense Service Medal, the Combat Infantry Badge, the Vietnam Service Medal, the Vietnam Campaign Medal and the Good Conduct Medal. Hesselbach challenged the retroactive application of the 1996 law, but was ordered deported by an immigration judge. His service and sacrifice got him no consideration whatever.

Rafael Ramirez is a thirty-five-year-old New Yorker who emigrated from the Dominican Republic at the age of seven and who, nine years after his honorable discharge from the Army as a sergeant, faced deportation. His offense: in 1990, just months after leaving the Army, he pled guilty to possessing marijuana.

I brought Sergeant Ramirez's case to the attention of INS Commissioner Meissner, and I was pleased that some semblance of justice was eventually achieved. But in too many cases, the INS maintains that the 1996 law stripped it of any discretion to consider whether military service or other life circumstances may outweigh the government's interest in deportation. We need to ensure that every veteran's case is carefully reviewed by an immigration judge empowered to do justice.

Our national policy on deportation of veterans is particularly disgraceful at a time when we are sending tens of thousands of U.S. servicemen and women, including untold numbers of non-naturalized immigrants, into harm's way in the Balkans. Why on earth has Congress asked the INS to devote its limited resources to hunting down immigrants who previously answered this country's call to duty, some of whom were permanently disabled in the course of their service?

A few weeks ago, I introduced the Fairness to Immigrant Veterans Act of 1999, S.871. This bill would restore for veterans the opportunity to go before an immigration judge to present the equities of their case and to have a federal court review any deportation decision. It would also restore for veterans the opportunity to be released from detention and at home with their families while their case is under consideration.

The injustice addressed by this legislation is just one egregious example of how recent immigration "reform" has resulted in the break-up of American families and the deportation of people who have made significant contributions to our country. This Congress needs to address the broader injustices that the prior one-upmanship caused. In the meantime, as Memorial Day approaches, the Senate should take an important step in the right direction by passing the Fairness to Immigrant Veterans Act.

"IMMIGRANTS AND THE U.S. ECONOMY," TESTIMONY OF STEPHEN MOORE, SENIOR FELLOW IN ECONOMICS, CATO INSTITUTE, BEFORE THE SENATE JUDICIARY COMMITTEE SUBCOMMITTEE ON IMMIGRATION, APRIL 4, 2001

... [A] consensus seems to have emerged in the Congress that immigrants are—as they have been throughout most of our history—beneficial to our economy and assets to our society in other ways as well. This favorable attitude regarding immigration on Capitol Hill is evidenced by the pro-immigrant legislation that has passed the House and Senate in recent years and the wise rejection of many anti-immigration measures.

This pro-immigration environment that has emerged on Capitol Hill reflects the growing consensus within the economics profession that immigrants are on balance economic assets, not liabilities. To be sure, economists still argue about the size of the benefit of immigration to the U.S. economy, but almost all of the best research indicates that the direction of the impact is on balance positive. There is also lively debate about whether some groups of Americans—the lowest skilled Americans, blacks, earlier arriving immigrants, for example—are adversely impacted by immigration. But even here, I am pleased to report that more and more of the research findings seems to suggest that the extent to which low income Americans are hurt by the presence of immigrants has been exaggerated.

Let us start with the big picture. The past twenty years has been a period of fairly high levels of immigration, particularly in absolute numbers.... Over the past twenty years, the United States has legally admitted roughly fifteen million immigrants and refugees. We now admit almost four new immigrants per year for every 1,000 Americans, which is higher than in the past fifty years, but about half the historical average.... Still, the percentage of Americans that are foreign born has risen from about 6% in the 1970s to almost 10% today....

At earlier times in our nation's history, as many as 15% of Americans were foreign born. So although our current levels of immigration are by no means unprecedented, it is true, nonetheless, that for the past twenty-five years, the U.S. has been quite generous in immigrant admissions and that we are now in the midst of a new great wave of immigration to these shores not experienced since the great wave of Europeans who arrived through Ellis Island at the turn of the last century.

If immigrants were economically harmful, we would certainly expect to see visible signs of the damage to the economy by now. In fact, twenty years ago, many advocates of a lower level of immigration, or even in some extreme cases, a moratorium on immigration, argued that continued high levels of immigration would lead to such economic problems as:

1. increased unemployment for native-born workers
2. higher poverty rates of native-born Americans
3. lower incomes for American workers
4. increased economic problems for minority workers
5. a huge surge in welfare dependency, and
6. lower overall rates of economic growth.

But it didn't happen. None of these claims have been evidenced in the U.S economy.

Now it is undeniable that when immigrants come to the United States, the labor force competition may very well cause some American-born workers to lose their jobs (in the short term) through displacement; they may cause some wage rates to fall or not rise as fast as they might have otherwise, and some immigrants do take advantage of the welfare system. The relevant policy question is whether we have observed these impacts on an economy-wide level. And here there is little debate. High levels of immigration have corresponded with improvement in each of these areas, not with the problems getting worse. For example:

Unemployment—In the period 1978–82 the U.S. unemployment rate was between 6 and 8%. Today, the U.S. unemployment rate is between 4 and 5%. The U.S. economy has shown a remarkable ability to absorb new workers into the economy—both natives and immigrants—without causing job losses. Between 1980 and 2000 the U.S. became a job creation machine, with some thirty-five million more Americans employed today than twenty years ago. The U.S. has created more new jobs in the past twenty years than all of Japan and Europe combined since 1980. In fact, despite the fact that the U.S. takes in nearly as many immigrants in a year as does all of Japan and Europe combined, it is the U.S.—the nation of immigrants—that now has the lowest unemployment rate in the industrialized world.

Poverty—The poverty rate for Americans has fallen over the past twenty years for all races. The latest poverty rate statistics indicate that poverty is lower than at anytime since the mid 1970s.... A recent study by the Center for Immigration Studies reports that since 1980 the rate of poverty among immigrants has risen. Of course, if the overall level of poverty has fallen during this period, it means that the reduction in poverty for native-born Americans has been all the more impressive. In sum, there is no evidence that immigrants increase poverty among natives, in fact the evidence suggests the opposite effect.

Incomes—Median family income in the U.S. has risen over the period 1981–1998 from $39,000 to $45,800 or by roughly 16%, according to recent Census Bureau data. With inflation properly measured, median family income has risen since 1981 by closer to 25%. Again, wage suppression does not appear to have occurred in this period of high immigration.

Economic Advancement of Minorities—There is still in America far too wide an income gap between the races. But over the past twenty years of high levels of immigration, the income gap has actually shrunk, not widened.... For example, since the early 1980s, the growth of incomes for black families has exceeded the growth for white families. The black unemployment rate has fallen much faster than the white unemployment rate, as has the black poverty rate.

The income gap between blacks and whites and between men and women has narrowed to its lowest level in recorded history. From 1981 to 1998, the black incomes relative to whites shrunk from 60% to 69%—the highest ever recorded. For women, the gap narrowed from 89% to 94%. In sum, we have had record immigration and we have had record economic improvements for blacks.

What can we conclude about the impact of immigration on the U.S. economy since 1980? Over the past twenty years the U.S. economy has experienced a $10 to $15 trillion increase in net wealth, according to the Federal Reserve Board data, the GDP has grown by nearly 80% (after inflation), and the inflation rate has fallen to nearly zero. The National Bureau of Economic Research recently described the past eighteen years as the longest and strongest period of sustained prosperity in the U.S. in this century. If immigrants are somehow a "cost" to the U.S. economy, that cost has been virtually invisible. The experience of the past two decades puts a huge burden on the shoulders of those who contend that immigrants are economically burdensome.

But I believe a stronger case can be made. Immigrants have contributed directly to America's unprecedented economic expansion of the past two decades. Moreover, I believe the demographic evidence suggests that it will be in America's self-interest to continue admitting immigrants over at least the next twenty years.

In 1998 I completed a study jointly published by the Cato Institute on the economic and fiscal impact of immigrants to the United States. The study was entitled "A Fiscal Portrait of the Newest Americans."... [A]llow me to now relate to you the major conclusions based on our own research findings and corroborated by several dozen prestigious economic studies published in major economic journals.

1) Immigrants and their children increase economic growth. In the most comprehensive study ever conducted on immigration, the National Research Council of the National Academy of Sciences found that immigrants inflate the incomes of U.S.-born workers by at least $10 billion each year. This estimate is highly conservative because it does not include the impact of immigrant-owned businesses or the impact of high-skilled immigrants on overall productivity. Still, the NRC estimates that the typical immigrant and his or her children pay an estimated $80,000 more in taxes than they will receive in local, state and federal benefits over their lifetimes.

2) Immigrants pay their own way when it comes to services used and taxes paid. Immigrants use many government services—particularly at the state and local levels—but they ... also pay a lot in taxes. Conservatively estimated, in 1998 immigrant households paid an estimated $133 billion in direct taxes to federal, state and local governments. Adding the tax receipts paid by immigrant businesses brings the total annual tax contributions of immigrants to about $162 billion for 1998. In any given year, immigrants may use more in services than they pay in taxes, but over their lifetimes, immigrants are a fiscal bargain to native taxpayers. As their earnings rise over time, immigrant taxes exceed the benefits received....

3) Not all immigrants make the same tax payments or impose the same costs. The best predictors of immigrant

success and thus their tax payments are their skill levels, education attainment, and ability to speak English. In general, low-skilled, low-educated immigrants and non-English speaking immigrants use more government services and pay less in taxes than those with high skills.

4) Immigrants have a rapid rate of economic assimilation after they arrive in the U.S. As noted above, one of the most important economic characteristics of immigrants is that their earnings rise over time in the U.S. Hence, during their first years after arrival in the U.S. earnings are low and immigrants typically are net drains on the public coffers. But over time—usually after ten–fifteen years in the U.S—they turn into net contributors. This economic assimilation pattern varies by ethnicity and country of origin, but is still evident today as it was thirteen years ago when researchers first began to study the rate of economic success by immigrants over time....

5) The age profile of immigrants is a huge demographic bonus to native-born Americans. Most immigrants arrive in the United States in the prime of their working years. For example, more than 70% of immigrants who come to the U.S. are above the age of eighteen upon arrival. This means that there are roughly 17.5 million immigrants in the U.S. today whose educational and rearing costs were borne by the citizens of the sending country, not American taxpayers.... The total discounted present value windfall to the United States of obtaining this human capital at no expense to American taxpayers is roughly $1.43 trillion. Immigration can be thought of as an enormous $1.4 trillion transfer of wealth from the rest of the world to the United States.

6) Immigrants are huge net contributors to the Social Security and Medicare programs. Only 3% of immigrants enter the U.S. over the age of sixty-five, whereas 12% of Americans are over sixty-five —and that percentage will grow to 15% within twenty years. Based on the calculations of the actuaries at the Social Security Administration, this study estimates the total value to the Social Security system from current levels of immigration. I find that the total net benefit (taxes paid over benefits received) to the Social Security system in 1998 dollars from continuing current levels of immigration is nearly $500 billion from 1998–2022 and nearly $2.0 trillion through 2072. Continuing immigration is an essential component to solving the long term financing problem of the Social Security system.

7) Immigrant entrepreneurs are a major source of new jobs and vitality in the American economy. Most immigrant businesses—like most businesses started by American-born entrepreneurs—are not highly successful or large employers. But many of America's largest and most profitable businesses today were started by immigrants. Immigrants who entered the U.S. as refugees, economic immigrants, or family-sponsored immigrants are now at the helm of some of the nation's leading and rapidly growing technology businesses: Hungarian-born Andrew S. Grove, recently retired as Chairman and CEO of Intel; Algerian-born Eric Benhamou, heads 3Com Corp; Iranian-born brothers Farzad and Farid Dibachi founded and head Diba, Inc.; and Uganda-born Ajay Shah, is the chief executive of Smart Modules Technologies.... Ten highly successful immigrant firms ... alone generated $28 billion in revenues and employed 75,000 American workers in 1997. The tax revenue paid in 1997 by the companies directly and their employees was at least $3 billion.

Immigration and the Demographic Crisis in Developed Nations—One of the greatest unheralded economic challenges facing the industrialized nations is the demographic bubble due to unprecedented low birth rates. Economists are just starting to confront the huge economic challenge that the population implosion represents to the developed nations of the world. The birth rates in nations like Japan, Germany, France, Spain, and Italy are well below replacement level fertility. The U.S. is just slightly below replacement level fertility, but we have a demographic safety valve: immigration.

Consider, for example, the level of unfounded liabilities in pension programs around the world. As bad as our Social Security liability problem is, it is dwarfed by the huge levels of red ink in the European nations. Immigration will allow the U.S. to smooth out the bumps in our demographic wave in productive ways that most of our competitor nations will not or cannot allow. Our immigrant heritage allows us to bring in productive immigrant workers, who will help pay the cost of the retirement benefits of everyone sitting in this hearing room.

Policy Conclusions—The U.S. legal immigration system works remarkably well, given that it has been crafted in a piecemeal way over many years. Most immigrants who come to the U.S. today are economic contributors on net. The system of family and employer sponsored immigration is effective in getting high quality immigrants to come to the U.S. and absorbing them rapidly into the labor force and the culture. Immigrant workers have brought a flexibility and a work ethic to the U.S. labor market that is sorely absent in many of our major competitor nations.

It is noteworthy that it was not so many years ago that anti-immigration groups would point glowingly to Japan as an example of a nation that prospers without immigration. Japan is now entering its second decade of depression. Part of the problem in Japan has been economic policy mistakes. But some of its economic maladies are a result of low birth rates.... Also, the aging of the workforce in Japan is a horrendous demographic crisis in that nation. The absence of immigrants in Japan has already come to haunt this once formidable economic powerhouse.

It would be economically advantageous to the U.S. to admit more—perhaps twice as many—highly skilled immigrants each year. This is not to say that low skilled immigrants are undesirable. But the economic benefits to natives of immigrants with high skill and education levels is higher than of immigrants with low skill and education levels. It is also true that younger working age immigrants are more beneficial than older immigrants.

It is worth emphasizing that many of the immigrants who have made the largest contributions in our society in recent times came to the U.S. without the characteristics that often presage success. The initial starting place of an immigrant is not always predictive of future success on these shores. Andrew Grove, co-founder of Intel, came to America as a refugee and from a family that had no money, no skills, and no special prospects for greatness. No economist would have likely predicted the greatness he achieved. Social scientists have begun to try to build profiles of immigrant success—by examining skill levels, education, ethnicity, and so on. Such studies are not always very predictive of economic success in the U.S.

It is in America's economic self-interest—and in the interests of immigrants themselves—that we keep the golden gates open to newcomers from every region of the world. The net gains to U.S. workers and retirees are in the trillions of dollars. Given the coming retirement of some seventy-five million baby boomers, we need the young and energetic immigrants now more than ever before.

"U.S. IMMIGRATION AT THE BEGINNING OF THE TWENTY-FIRST CENTURY," TESTIMONY PREPARED FOR THE SUBCOMMITTEE ON IMMIGRATION AND CLAIMS HEARING ON "THE U.S. POPULATION AND IMMIGRATION," COMMITTEE ON THE JUDICIARY, U.S. HOUSE OF REPRESENTATIVES, AUGUST 2, 2001, BY JEFFREY S. PASSEL AND MICHAEL FIX, IMMIGRATION STUDIES PROGRAM, URBAN INSTITUTE, WASHINGTON, D.C.

... In the past decade, a number of studies have been attempted to address the question of fiscal impacts [of immigration]. Several conclusions have emerged upon which there appears to be fairly widespread agreement. First, immigrants (and immigrant households) pay a considerable amount in taxes to all levels of government. However, because immigrant incomes are generally lower than native incomes when considered on a cross-sectional basis, the taxes from immigrants on a per capita or per household basis are lower than for natives. Similarly, the net balance of taxes and social spending directed toward families is more positive for native families than for immigrant families. This result derives principally from three factors: the previously-mentioned income differences; the biggest cost associated with immigrant families in general is the cost of educating children; and immigrant families have more children than native families.

The National Academy of Sciences (1997) attempted the most extensive study of this issue to date. In their study, the Academy attempted to model costs and taxes on a longitudinal basis and take into account the future generations derived from immigrants. Their main conclusion was that, on average, an additional immigrant generated a positive net contribution to the country. This varied considerably according to a number of factors. In general, the younger the immigrant, the greater the net contribution because younger immigrants have longer working times in the U.S. when they pay taxes. The more highly educated the immigrant the greater the net contribution. Again, this result is related to income. More highly educated immigrants tend to have higher incomes and pay higher taxes.

The balance of taxes versus costs tends to favor the federal government. More taxes are directed to the federal government than to state and local governments. On the other hand, the highest "costs" associated with immigrants tend to be for educating children and most of these costs are incurred by state and local governments. This particular result points out some of the major problems with these analyses. Most of the costs of educating immigrant children are spent on natives (the U.S.-born children). Yet, the research shows clearly the payoffs to education. Moreover, since this is the most critical factor for the integration of immigrants and their offspring, it is the most critical for the long-term health of the U.S. economy....

CHAPTER 9

IMMIGRATION AND ILLEGAL ALIENS ARE MORE A BURDEN THAN A BLESSING

FLOOR SPEECH OF CONGRESSMAN BILL YOUNG BEFORE THE U.S. HOUSE OF REPRESENTATIVES IN SUPPORT OF IMMIGRATION IN THE NATIONAL INTEREST ACT OF 1995 (H.R. 2202), MARCH 21, 1996

Mr. Chairman, the problem of illegal immigration has reached historic proportions. Past attempts by Congress to reform immigration laws have provided nothing more than greater incentives and promised benefits for illegal aliens. The result is the present system which actually encourages immigrants to come to America illegally.

Today, I am proud to support an historic change in our Nation's immigration policy. Today, we are going to pass a reform bill with real teeth in it. A bill that cracks down on illegal immigrants already here, and one that secures our borders against future immigrants who would seek to enter illegally. Past legislation this House has considered, which I strongly opposed, did nothing to alleviate the problems of illegal immigration. At long last, I look forward to supporting a bill which acknowledges these problems and takes action to address them.

While past legislation sent the message you could come to the U.S. illegally and expect to receive welfare benefits, food stamps and free health care, this legislation finally puts an end to this outrage. As a Member from the State of Florida, I have seen first-hand the financial burden these ill-gotten attempts at reform have placed on States forced to bear the brunt of this failed immigration policy. Past Congresses refused to stop the excessive flow of illegal immigrants and to eliminate the enormous costs associated with this broken system. Today, we own-up to our responsibilities with a hard-nosed approach that substantially increases border control, provides the Immigration and Naturalization Service with the tools necessary to find and deport illegal aliens, and pays for the Federal Government's financial obligations to the States.

Mr. Chairman, my State of Florida has long been overburdened by the flood of illegal immigration. Since the Mariel boatlift in 1980, we have been the destination of a disproportionate number of immigrants, making us the third-largest recipient of immigrants among our fifty States. Although immigration policy is the sole jurisdiction of the United States Government, history has proven that states like Florida are typically left with the cost and responsibility of providing expensive social services to illegal aliens.

With the enactment of H.R. 2202, we have an opportunity to minimize the enormous expenses that we force upon our States by denying most public benefits to illegal aliens, removing public charges, and holding sponsors personally responsible for the financial well-being of an immigrant they bring into our country. Most importantly, this bill requires the Federal Government to reimburse States and localities for any expenses incurred from providing federally mandated services to illegal immigrants. Based upon various formulas, it is estimated that the State of Florida has spent an average of $651 million per year from 1989–1993, or a total of $3.25 billion for services provided to illegal immigrants. If the costs to local governments are included, the total burden rises to $15 billion for that same five-year period.

Unlike past immigration reform bills, H.R. 2202 will actually discourage the illegal entry of immigrants by increasing our border control agents by 5,000 personnel, improving physical barriers along our borders, including a triple-layer fence, authorizing advanced border equipment to be used by the Immigration and Naturalization Service, and instituting an effective removal process to discharge illegal immigrants with no documentation. This bill provides the Department of Justice with twenty-five new U.S. Attorneys General and authorizes 350 new INS inspectors to investigate and prosecute aliens and alien smugglers.

This bill also strongly supports the American worker by cracking down on the use of fraudulent documents that illegal immigrants use to get American jobs and by enforcing strict penalties for employers who knowingly violate these laws. The Department of Labor has authorized 150 new investigators to enforce the bill's labor provisions barring the employment of illegal aliens.

Mr. Chairman, the American people demand that Congress take action to secure our borders against illegal immigrants. With the explosion in the amount of drugs and criminals coming across our borders, and with the flood of illegal immigrants, many of whom settle in Florida, it is eminently important that we do all we can to protect our national borders.

While past Congresses refused to address this national crisis, today we deliver, with a much needed and long overdue first step in this renewed effort. Today we will approve legislation with unprecedented prevention and enforcement mechanisms. The message to illegal aliens is no longer one of indifference. The new message is simple—try to enter the United States illegally and we will stop you, should you get in, we will find and deport you, and should you remain in hiding, don't expect much in the way of support.

OPENING STATEMENT, CHAIRMAN LAMAR SMITH, MARCH 11, 1999, HEARING ON THE IMPACT OF IMMIGRATION ON RECENT IMMIGRANTS AND BLACK AND HISPANIC CITIZENS, SUBCOMMITTEE ON IMMIGRATION AND CLAIMS

...How often do we hear that some businesses refuse to hire young black or Hispanic men for entry-level jobs, but then clamor to hire those from other countries? How often do we hear comments about the growing gap between the well-to-do and the working poor that don't mention that almost half of the relative decline in wages of high school dropouts is caused by immigration?

Think of a single mother barely surviving in a minimum wage job who sees her annual wages depressed by a thousand dollars because she must compete with more and more unskilled immigrants. She very well might be a recent immigrant seeking a better life for herself and her children. Or she might be able to trace her roots in this country back generations and is simply seeking the American Dream denied her ancestors.

Think what she could do for herself and her children with that lost money—buy a used car so she doesn't have to take a bus to work, put a down payment on a modest home, fix the furnace before winter comes. Worse, think what will happen if she actually loses her job because of the never-ending competition from new arrivals. It is certainly not the immigrants themselves who are to blame and who understandably want to come to America, it is

our immigration policy. But who knows how many people have been hurt by the unintended consequences of our outdated immigration policy?

A series of recent studies have all documented the effects of immigration policy on low-skilled American workers and recent immigrants:

The National Research Council of the National Academy of Sciences concludes that immigration was responsible for "about 44% of the total decline in relative wage[s] of high school dropouts...between 1980 and 1994."

The RAND Corporation reports that, in California, "the widening gap between the number of jobs available for non-college-educated workers and the increasing number of new non-college-educated immigrants signals growing competition for jobs and, hence, a further decline in relative earnings at the low end of the labor market."

The U.S. Commission on Immigration Reform, chaired by Barbara Jordan, a predecessor of the ranking member, finds that "immigration of unskilled immigrants comes at a cost to unskilled U.S. workers...."

The Hudson Institute states that "U.S. immigration policy serves primarily to increase the number of U.S. residents who lack even a high-school degree. America must stop recruiting workers for jobs that do not exist or exist only at the lowest wages."

The Brookings Institution publishes a paper concluding that "immigration has had a marked adverse impact on the economic status of the least skilled U.S. workers...."

The Center for Immigration Studies calculates that "immigration may reduce the wages of the average native in a low-skilled occupation by...$1,915 a year."

These studies just reinforce what common sense tells us. Add three facts together:

First: Immigrants will account for half of the increase in the workforce in the 1990s.

Second: The skill level of immigrants relative to Americans has been declining for years—35% of immigrant workers who have arrived since 1990 do not have a high school education, compared to 9% of native-born workers. Some 300,000 legal immigrants without high school educations arrive each year—and will total three million this decade.

Third: Close to 90% of all future jobs will require post-high school education.

Our policy must create opportunity for all. Current immigration policy would have many Americans and recent immigrants competing with hundreds of thousands of newcomers without high school degrees for a fixed number of low-skilled jobs. This is a recipe for disaster for millions of blue-collar workers and their families.

No one should complain about the plight of the working poor or the persistence of minority unemployment or the levels of income inequality without acknowledging the unintended consequences of our present immigration policy.

Of course, immigration is neither all good nor all bad. Immigrants benefit America in many ways. But we should design our immigration policy so that it enhances rather than diminishes opportunities for American workers. We should protect the jobs of the working poor. We can make a better life for all Americans, wherever they were born.

The destruction of the jobs and wages of blue-collar workers cries out for a bipartisan solution. The people's representatives should look out for the people.

"IMMIGRATION POLICY AND THE PLIGHT OF UNSKILLED WORKERS," STATEMENT OF VERNON M. BRIGGS, JR., CORNELL UNIVERSITY, BEFORE THE SUBCOMMITTEE ON IMMIGRATION U.S. HOUSE COMMITTEE OF THE JUDICIARY, WASHINGTON, D.C., MARCH 11, 1999

…Immigration policy has been captured by special interests who peddle the notion that immigration is an unmitigated benefit to the nation and that it is costless. Nothing could be further from the truth. The immigration myth is based on the premise that attention need only be paid to the benefits while the costs can be totally ignored. Only with respect to the formulation of immigration policy is such nonsense tolerated as conventional wisdom.

If the scale of immigration was small—as it was from the 1930s through to the mid-1960s—the nation could live with the myth that immigration yields only benefits. But it is not. In 1965, the foreign-born accounted for only 4.4% of the population—the lowest percentage since such data started being collected prior to the Civil War. The percentage had been falling for over fifty years. By 1997, however, the percentage had risen to 9.7% (plus some unknown additional increment of statistical undercount due to the estimated six million illegal immigrants currently in the country). Until there are legislative changes, the percentage will continue to rise. Thus, about one of every ten Americans in 1997 was foreign-born. In absolute terms, the foreign-born population grew from 8.6 million persons in 1965 to 25.8 million persons in 1997. In the process, immigration has again become a key feature of American life. Indeed, the U.S. Bureau of the Census has projected that immigration will be the most important factor influencing the growth of the American population over the next fifty years. Given its

momentum, the welfare of the nation can ill-afford to live with the "unrealistic" immigration myth—no matter how "persistent" and "persuasive" are the voices of its proponents.

The Point of Focus—Although the subject of immigration involves multiple considerations, they all have one common juncture point: the labor market. It is a truism that immigrants must work or they must be supported by those who do. So no matter how many other issues are thrown into the immigration caldron, the critical issue is what are the labor market consequences of what immigration policy produces or tolerates. For it must always be remembered that immigration is entirely a discretionary act. The mass immigration that the United States is currently experiencing is entirely a policy-driven phenomenon. No one has a right to immigrate or to seek refuge in the United States—legally or illegally. The "costs" of immigration need to be taken into account as much as do the "benefits" when it comes to designing the appropriate policy. The concerns of the "losers" are as relevant as those of the "winners." Such is especially the case when those most adversely impacted are the least advantaged persons in the population and labor market.

Labor Market Effects—Due to differences in the age and gender distribution of the foreign-born population from the native-born population, immigrants comprise a larger portion of the labor force than they do of the population as a whole. In 1997, foreign-born workers comprised 11.5% of the U.S. labor force (or almost one of every eight U.S. workers). In absolute numbers, 15.5 million workers were foreign-born. These are big numbers and, when concentrated in specific segments of the labor market, they have significant influences.

As in the past, post-1965 mass immigration is geographically concentrated. In 1997, five states (California, New York, Florida, Texas, and Illinois) accounted for 65% of the entire foreign-born population and 66% of the entire foreign-born labor force. The foreign-born are also overwhelmingly concentrated in only a handful of urban areas—especially in their central cities. These particular labor markets, however, are among the nation's largest in size: Los Angeles, New York, San Francisco, Miami, and Chicago. Collectively, these five cities accounted for 51% of all foreign-born workers. Although somewhat less numerous, immigrants also comprise significant percentages of the labor force of a number of other cities and increasingly in some rural towns.

The most significant labor market characteristic of the foreign-born labor work force, however, is the fact that it is disproportionately characterized by workers with low human capital endowments. The 1990 Census revealed that 25% of foreign-born adults who were twenty-five years and older had less than a ninth-grade education (compared with only 10% of native-born adults). Moreover, 42% of the foreign-born adult population did not have the equivalent of a high school diploma (compared to 23% of the native-born adult population). Thus, it is the low-skilled, low wage sector of the nation's major urban labor markets that are the most impacted by immigrant job-seekers. Not only do low-skilled immigrants compete with each other for whatever opportunities exist at the bottom of the nation's job hierarchy, but they also compete with the low-skilled native-born workers. Indeed, when the National Research Council (NRC) calculated in 1997 that immigration provides a net "benefit" to the U.S. economy of from $1 to $10 billion a year, the "benefit" was based largely on the result of the wage suppression of the wages of low-skilled workers whose wages are lower than they would have otherwise been. This, of course, is only a "benefit" that an economist can appreciate. It is certainly no "benefit" to low-skilled workers who are already at the bottom of the nation's income distribution. It is an artificially imposed hardship imposed by government policy on native-born low-skilled workers. The only actual wage "benefit" in this process is received by the immigrant workers themselves who typically earn considerably more at the bottom of the U.S. wage scale than they would have earned in his/her homeland. Low-skilled native-born workers lose; low-skilled foreign-workers benefit. Whose interests are U.S. policymakers supposed to protect?

STATEMENT OF TERRY ANDERSON BEFORE THE HOUSE SUBCOMMITTEE ON IMMIGRATION AND CLAIMS, JUNE 10, 1999

I am a black American who has lived on the same street in South Central Los Angeles for forty-five years. When I first moved there it was mostly white. And though there were a few (very few) people who did not like us because of our race we were generally treated with respect and dignity. We went to the same schools as the white kids and no special arrangements were made for us. The white folks would give us jobs and we all spoke the same language. We were ALL AMERICANS. We had a common culture, the American culture. Over the years the community changed gradually from white to black but basically (aside from race) remained the same.

About ten to fifteen years ago things began to change, drastically. We started to see an influx of people from south of the border. Mexico, Central America, South America and others. As these people got here our community began to change, for the worse.

When you here in Washington hear about illegal immigration you will only hear about "the poor immigrant who comes here for a better life" or the poor, poor immigrant child who "must" have an education. You hear about how "hard working" they are and about their great work ethic. You hear the lie about how [they] don't use public services and how they ONLY take the jobs that NOBODY else wants. You hear from all of the liberal organizations who advocate for the illegal aliens. You also hear from the racist organizations like MALDEF, LULAC, MEChA, and La Raza. They will tell you all the reasons why the illegal alien is good for America.

What [they] don't tell you about is the seventeen-year-old kid on my street that can't get a McDonald's job because he can't speak Spanish. They don't tell you about the eight-year-old boy on my street who like thousands of other black kids is thrown into a bilingual classroom and listens to translations all day long. His six-hour school day is turned into three hours. When his mother asks for an English only classroom she is told "there are none." They won't tell you about the $100,000 house in my neighborhood that sold for $137,000 because the real estate company put five families of "newly arrived Hispanics" who spoke no English on the deed. Now when a black family wants to buy a house, they too have to find four other families to share the ridiculous cost. They won't tell you how skilled black workers in Los Angeles can no longer apply their trade. Body and fender, roofers, framers, drywallers, gardeners, and now even truck drivers. They won't dare tell you about all of the race riots in our schools where the blacks are told to take their black asses back to Africa. Even the news media has refused to tell of this while we know that they are aware of it. There is NEVER a mention of all of the billboards in Spanish and how Chevron is now advertising in Spanish on English language TV.

. . . We, black Americans are being displaced in Los Angeles. We are being systematically and economically replaced. And the next time somebody tells you that the illegals only take jobs that blacks won't do, just remember that WE were doing those jobs before the illegal got here AND in places of the country where there is not yet a problem with illegals, you can STILL get your grass cut, your dinner served, your dishes bussed and your hotel room cleaned. Funny how in those places Americans are doing those jobs. We would still be doing them in Los Angeles if it was not for the fact that the illegal will work for $3.00 an hour. Breaking the law by working for less than minimum wage means nothing to somebody who broke the law to get here. And to those who would ask "How do you know they are illegal" I would say, there is NO WAY that this many people could come here this fast in these vast numbers under our current immigration system.

STATEMENT OF TOBIN ARMSTRONG BEFORE THE HOUSE SUBCOMMITTEE ON IMMIGRATION AND CLAIMS, JUNE 10, 1999

My name is Tobin Armstrong. My residence is at Armstrong, Texas, in the center of Kenedy County. There are 460 people in Kenedy County—three people per square mile. It is sixty miles north of Mexico on the Gulf of Mexico and has no cultivated land. It is all native pastureland and has a thick cover of thorn trees and live oak trees. I have lived in Kenedy County all my life, have served as a county official since 1948, and am presently County Commissioner for my precinct. I am the managing partner of the Armstrong Ranch, which is a family partnership involving 49,300 acres and 2,500 cattle units.

Since about 1993 my home county has experienced an escalation in traffic of illegal aliens resulting in increasing:

1. destruction of property

2. burglary

3. auto and equipment theft

4. death by starvation, exposure, disease, auto and train accidents and murder

5. illegal alien smuggling

6. narcotics trafficking

7. forage contamination

8. massive littering of our pastures

9. and most distressing of all, the introduction of diseases uncommon in the U.S.

Health authorities say there is no way to prevent illegal immigrants' bringing in these disease[s]. In October 1998 two women, a mother and daughter from El Salvador, were discovered in our pasture by the Border Patrol. Both had malaria and were at death's door. They were treated in the Spohn Memorial Hospital for ten days and released at a cost to the hospital of over $39,000. The mosquito that carries malaria is found as far north as Corpus Christi, Texas, 150 miles north of the Mexican border.

Mary Lee Grant, well regarded reporter for the *Corpus Christi Caller-Times*, and her co-worker contracted T.B. while doing investigative reporting on the conditions in the *colonias* in Nueces County. She conservatively estimates that, based on numerous interviews conducted, 70% of the people in the *colonias* are illegal aliens, which leads us to strongly suspect that the sharp increase in T.B. in South Texas is due to the influx of these illegal transients.

Other diseases being brought into the U.S. by illegal immigrants include encephalitis, cholera, rheumatic fever, salmonella, intestinal parasites, smallpox, measles, HIV and VDs.

The threat of the introduction of foot and mouth and other devastating livestock diseases is staggering. The toll on the illegals themselves is appalling.

We have found five bodies in the county since January 1 and have been averaging twenty per year for the past four or five years. Who knows how many bodies will never be found in these remote pastures?

Last year six illegals were run over and killed while sleeping on the rails adjacent to our pasture.

In March, twelve illegal aliens were severely injured, one of them permanently paralyzed, when the Suburban they were being smuggled in turned over and crashed through our ranch fence. Local hospitals and taxpayers must pay these bills.

In April 1999, 123 illegals were found locked in a semi-trailer truck at the Sarita Immigration Checkpoint six miles north of my home. The driver of the truck was carrying $25,000 in cash.

Thirty illegals were found in a truck the week before. This has become a common occurrence along our frontiers.

About 2,000 illegals per month are apprehended in the Sarita Checkpoint. 1,555,776 were apprehended in the district in fiscal year ending October 31, 1998.

It is common opinion that this is but a fraction of the numbers that are getting through.

Smuggling organizations are increasingly large, well financed and well connected with sharp scouts, decoys, guides and hi-tech communications. Smuggling has become big business.

Some bus drivers are able to pick up illegals, pocket the fares, and issue no tickets.

Make no mistake about it: the word is out that if you can get to the U.S. interior you are home free. That is why illegals will continue to come in increasing numbers. The situation is getting worse, not better. Interdiction hasn't significantly deterred illegal entry—it just redirects it.

"THE IMPACT OF IMMIGRATION ON U.S. POPULATION GROWTH," TESTIMONY PREPARED FOR THE HOUSE JUDICIARY COMMITTEE SUBCOMMITTEE ON IMMIGRATION AND CLAIMS, JULY 19, 2001, BY STEVEN A. CAMAROTA, DIRECTOR OF RESEARCH, CENTER FOR IMMIGRATION STUDIES

While there should be no real debate about the overall impact of immigration on population growth, there is, and should be, a debate over whether this kind of increase in population is desirable for the country. Below I examine some of the consequences that would seem to be unavoidable if the population continues to grow dramatically. There are clearly benefits from population growth; many advocates of high immigration, for example, point to the increase in equity for owners of real estate and greater opportunities and choices it should create for businesses and consumers. Nonetheless, there are clearly real costs as well:

Sprawl and Congestion—If we accept the admittedly low [population] projections discussed above, which indicate immigration will add seventy-six million people to the population over the next fifty years, it means that we will have to build something like thirty million more housing units than would otherwise have been necessary, assuming average household size. This must have some implications for worsening the problems of sprawl, congestion, and loss of open spaces, even if one makes optimistic assumptions about successful urban planning and "smart growth." A nation simply cannot add nearly eighty million people to the population and not have to develop a great deal of undeveloped land.

Can we quantify the role that population growth plays in causing land to become built up, which is a basic definition of sprawl? It turns out that we can. At its simplest level, there are only three possible reasons for an increase in developed land. Either each person is taking up more land, there are more people, or some combination of the two. It's the same with any natural resource. For example, if one wants to know why the United States consumes more oil annually now than it did say twenty years ago, it is either because there are more Americans, or because each of us is using more oil, or some combination of the two. In the case of sprawl, the natural resource being consumed is land.

If one compares the increase in developed land in the nation's 100 largest urbanized areas between 1970 and 1990, it turns out that the causes of sprawl are split right down the middle between population growth and increases in per person land consumption. Of course, this is not true in every city, but overall, population growth contributed to sprawl in equal proportions. While we cannot say with absolute certainty that population growth will continue to cause more and more land to be developed, both past experience and common sense strongly suggest that population growth of this kind has important implications for the preservation of farm land, open space, and the overall quality of life in many areas of the country.

Size of the School-Age Population—In the last few years, a good deal of attention has been focused on the dramatic increases in enrollment experienced by many school districts across the country. The Department of Education recently reported that the number of children in public schools has grown by nearly eight million in the last two decades. All observers agree that this growth has strained the resources of many school districts. Increased funding for education at the state, local, and federal levels has barely been able to keep pace with new construction and prevent class size from growing. While it has been suggested that this increase is the result of the children of baby boomers reaching school age (the so called "baby boom echo"), it is clear from the Current Population Survey that immigration policy explains the growth in the number of children in public schools.

We know that immigration accounts for the dramatic increase in school enrollment because the CPS not only asks all respondents their age and if they are immigrants, it also asks when they came to live in the United States. In addition, the CPS asks all persons if their parents were immigrants. With this data, it is a very simple matter to estimate the impact of recent immigration on public schools. In 2000, there were about eight million school-age children (ages five to seventeen) of immigrants who had arrived since 1970. The children of immigrants account for such a large percentage of the school-age population because a higher proportion of immigrant women are in their childbearing years and because immigrants tend to have more children than natives. Thus immigration accounts for virtually all of the increase in the school-age population in the United States over the last few decades. More importantly, without a change in immigration policy, the number of children in our already overtaxed schools will continue to grow. The absorption capacity of American public education is clearly an important issue that needs to be taken into account when formulating a sensible immigration policy. Failure to consider this capacity may have very real consequences for public education in the United States.

TESTIMONY OF BILL (WILLIAM G.) ELDER, CHAIRPERSON OF A NETWORK OF SIERRA CLUB MEMBERS THAT HAS BEEN COMMONLY REFERRED TO AS SIERRANS FOR U.S. POPULATION STABILIZATION, TO THE 107TH CONGRESS OF THE U.S. HOUSE OF REPRESENTATIVES, COMMITTEE ON THE JUDICIARY, SUBCOMMITTEE ON IMMIGRATION AND CLAIMS OVERSIGHT HEARING: THE UNITED STATES POPULATION AND IMMIGRATION, AUGUST 2, 2001

While some economic interests welcome the short-term profits of population booms, we do not. Looking ahead, we see long-term environmental and economic disaster for our country. We've already lost 95% of the old growth forests and 50% of the wetlands of this nation. We have grown well beyond the energy supply within our borders. Water supplies are declining.

Whether the issue is sprawl, endangered species, wetlands, clean air and water, forest or wilderness preservation—the environmental (and quality of life) impact of adding thirty-three million people per decade is extremely harmful. It is the equivalent of shoehorning another state the size of California—including all its homes, office buildings, shopping centers, schools and churches, freeways, power, water and food consumption, and waste products—to an already crowded and stressed U.S. environment. And not just doing it once, but then over and over, decade after decade after decade.

The role of immigration in this population boom is crucial. At least 60% of our population growth in the '90s (twenty million) was from immigration and children born to immigrants. Some put the figure higher, at 70%. With no change in immigration legislation, this growth will continue unabated and constitute the sole cause of population growth in the U.S. as the momentum and "echoes" of the baby boom fades away. The Census Bureau projects that unless current trends are changed, U.S. population will double within the lifetime of today's children.

The American people did their part to solve the environmental problems presented by the baby boom. We voluntarily adopted replacement level reproduction averaging two births per woman (although this is still high compared to 1.4 in other developed nations). We have also made some "gains"—albeit very limited—in reducing consumption per capita in areas such as electric power and use of lower polluting technologies.

But Congress, intentionally or not, has completely undone this sacrifice of the American people and our progress towards a stable and sustainable population by creating an "immigration boom." Immigration that averaged about two million per decade over the history of our nation has been expanded four fold by various acts of Congress beginning in 1965. (Since about two million people now leave the U.S. per decade, immigration of this traditional level would represent replacement level immigration.)

This new population boom must be addressed, not only for the sake of the quality of environment and life we pass to future generations of Americans, but also to be responsible to the citizens of the rest of the world who should not have to bear the burden of ever increasing resource consumption of our country.

We urge Congress to enact a comprehensive population policy for the United States that includes an end to U.S. population growth at the earliest possible time through reduction in natural increase (births minus deaths) and net immigration (immigration minus emigration).

APPENDIX I
FEDERAL PROTECTIONS AGAINST NATIONAL ORIGIN DISCRIMINATION—U.S. DEPARTMENT OF JUSTICE: POTENTIAL DISCRIMINATION AGAINST IMMIGRANTS BASED ON NATIONAL ORIGIN

This brochure, which was issued in October 2000 and is reprinted virtually in its entirety below, is available on the USDOJ Web site at http://www.usdoj.gov/crt/legalinfo/nordwg_brochure.html. The brochure is available in Arabic, Cambodian, Chinese, English, Farsi, French, Haitian Creole, Hindi, Hmong, Korean, Laotian, Punjabi, Russian, Spanish, Tagalog, Urdu, and Vietnamese:

INTRODUCTION

Federal laws prohibit discrimination based on a person's national origin, race, color, religion, disability, sex, and familial status. Laws prohibiting national origin discrimination make it illegal to discriminate because of a person's birthplace, ancestry, culture or language. This means people cannot be denied equal opportunity because they or their family are from another country, because they have a name or accent associated with a national origin group, because they participate in certain customs associated with a national origin group, or because they are married to or associate with people of a certain national origin.

The Department of Justice's Civil Rights Division is concerned that national origin discrimination may go unreported in the United States because victims of discrimination do not know their legal rights, or may be afraid to complain to the government. To address this problem, the Civil Rights Division has established a National Origin Working Group to help citizens and immigrants better understand and exercise their legal rights. . . .

CRIMINAL VIOLATIONS OF CIVIL RIGHTS

- *A young man of South Asian descent is assaulted as he leaves a concert at a nightclub. The assailant, a member of a skinhead group, yells racial epithets as he beats the victim unconscious in the club's parking lot with fists and a pipe.*

- *At Ku Klux Klan meetings, a Klansman tells other members that Mexicans and Puerto Ricans should go back where they came from. They burn a cross in the front yard of a young Hispanic couple in order to frighten them and force them to leave the neighborhood. Before burning the cross, the defendant displays a gun and gives one of his friends another gun in case the victims try to stop them.*

- *An American company recruits workers in a small Mexican town, promising them good work at high pay. The company smuggles the Mexicans to the United States in an empty tanker truck. When they finally arrive in the U.S., the workers are threatened, told that if they attempt to leave their factory they will be killed.*

The Criminal Section of the Civil Rights Division prosecutes people who are accused of using force or violence to interfere with a person's federally protected rights because of that person's national origin. These rights include areas such as housing, employment, education, or use of public facilities. You can reach the Criminal Section at (202) 514-3204.

DISABILITY RIGHTS

- *An HMO that enrolls Medicaid patients tells a Mexican American woman with cerebral palsy to come back another day for an appointment while it provides immediate assistance to others.*

This example may be a violation of federal laws that prohibit discrimination because of disability as well as laws that prohibit discrimination because of national origin. If you believe you have been discriminated against because you have a disability you may contact the Disability Rights Section at (800) 514-0301 (voice) or 800-514-0383 (TTY).

EDUCATION

- *A child has difficulty speaking English, but her school does not provide her with the necessary assistance to help her learn English and other subjects.*

- *A majority Haitian school does not offer honors classes. Other schools in the district that do not have many Haitian students offer both honors and advanced placement courses.*

These examples may be violations of federal law, which prohibits discrimination in education because of a person's national origin. The Division's Educational Opportunities Section enforces these laws in elementary and secondary schools as well as public colleges and universities. The Education Section's work addresses discrimination in all aspects of education, including assignment of students to schools and classes, transportation of students, hiring and placement of faculty and administrators, distribution of school resources, and provision of educational programs that assist limited English speaking students in learning English.

To file a complaint or for more information, contact the Education Section at (202) 514-4092.

EMPLOYMENT

- *A transit worker's supervisor makes frequent racial epithets against the worker because his family is from Iran. Last week, the boss put up a fake sign on the bulletin board telling everyone not to trust the worker because he is a terrorist.*

- *A woman who immigrated from Russia applies for a job as an accountant. The employer turns her down because she speaks with an accent even though she is able to perform the job requirements.*

- *A food processing company requires applicants who appear or sound foreign to show work authorization documents before allowing them to complete an employment application while native born Caucasian applicants are not required to show any documents before completing employment applications. Moreover, the documents of the ethnic employees are more closely scrutinized and more often rejected than the same types of documents shown by native born Caucasian employees.*

These examples may be violations of the law that prohibits discrimination against an employee or job applicant because of his or her national origin. This means an employer cannot discipline, harass, fire, refuse to hire or promote a person because of his or her national origin.

If you believe an employer, labor organization or employment agency has discriminated against you because of your national origin, contact:

Equal Employment Opportunity Commission

(800) 669-4000

(Employers with 15 or more employees)

Office of Special Counsel

(800) 255-7688

(Employers with 4 to 14 employees)

Employment Litigation Section

(202) 514-3831

(State or local government employer with a pattern or practice of illegal discrimination)

In addition, an employer may violate federal law by requiring specific work authorization documents, such as a green card, or rejecting such documents only from applicants of certain national origins. For more information or to file a charge, contact the Division's Office of Special Counsel at the above toll-free number.

HOUSING

- *A Native Hawaiian family is looking for an apartment. They are told by the rental agent that no apartments are available, even though apartments are available and are shown to white applicants.*

- *A realtor shows a Latino family houses only in Latino neighborhoods and refuses to show the family houses in white neighborhoods.*

These examples may be violations of the federal Fair Housing Act. That law prohibits discrimination because of national origin, race, color, sex, religion, disability, or familial status (presence of children under 18) in housing. Individual complaints of discrimination may be reported to the Department of Housing and Urban Development (HUD) at (800) 669-9777. If you believe there is a pattern or practice of discrimination, contact the Division's Housing and Civil Enforcement Section at (202) 514-4713.

LENDING

- *A Latina woman is charged a higher interest rate and fees than white male customers who have similar financial histories and apply for the same type of loan.*

This example may be a violation of federal laws that prohibit discrimination in lending because of national origin, race, color, sex, religion, disability and marital status or because any of a person's income comes from public assistance. If you believe you have been denied a loan because of your national origin or other protected reason, you may ask the lender for an explanation in writing of why your application was denied.

If the loan is for a home mortgage, home improvement, or other housing-related reasons, you may file a complaint with the Department of Housing and Urban Development at (800) 669-9777. If the loan is for purposes other than housing (such as a car loan), you may file a complaint either with the Division's Housing and Civil Enforcement Section or with the lender's regulatory agency. If your experience was part of a pattern or practice of discrimination you may also call the Housing and Civil Enforcement Section at (202) 514-4713, to obtain more information about your rights or to file a complaint.

PUBLIC ACCOMMODATIONS

- *In a restaurant, a group of Asian Americans waits for over an hour to be served, while white and Latino customers receive prompt service.*

- *Haitian American visitors to a hotel are told they must pay in cash rather than by credit card, are charged higher rates than other customers, and are not provided with the same amenities, such as towels and soap.*

These examples may be violations of federal laws that prohibit discrimination because of national origin, race, color, or religion in places of public accommodation. Public accommodations include hotels, restaurants, and places of entertainment. If you believe you have been denied access to or equal enjoyment of a public accommodation where there is a pattern or practice of discrimination, contact the Housing and Civil Enforcement Section at (202) 514-4713.

POLICE MISCONDUCT

- *Police officers constantly pull over cars driven by Latinos, for certain traffic violations, but rarely pull over white drivers for the same violations.*

- *A police officer questioning a man of Vietnamese origin on the street gets angry when the man is unable to answer his questions because he does not speak English. The Officer arrests the man for disorderly conduct.*

These examples may be violations of the Equal Protection Clause of the United States Constitution. They may also be violations of the Omnibus Crime Control and Safe Streets Act of 1968. That law prohibits discrimination because of national origin, race, color, religion, or sex by a police department that gets federal funds through the U.S. Department of Justice. They may also violate Title VI of the Civil Rights Act of 1964, which prohibits discrimination by law enforcement agencies that receive any federal financial assistance, including asset forfeiture property.

Complaints of individual discrimination can be filed with the Coordination and Review Section at 1-888-848-5306.

Complaints of individual discrimination may also be filed with the Office of Justice Programs at Office for Civil Rights, (202) 307-0690.

The Special Litigation Section investigates and litigates complaints that a police department has a pattern or practice of discriminating on the basis of national origin. To file a complaint, contact the Special Litigation Section at (202) 514-6255.

CIVIL RIGHTS OF INSTITUTIONALIZED PERSONS

- *A jail will not translate disciplinary hearings for detainees who do not speak English.*

- *A state's psychiatric hospital has no means of providing treatment for people who do not speak English.*

These examples may be violations of the Equal Protection Clause of the United States Constitution. The Special Litigation Section enforces the constitutional rights of people held in state or local government institutions, such as prisons, jails, juvenile correctional facilities, mental health facilities, developmental disability or mental retardation facilities, and nursing homes. If you are a resident of any such facility and you believe there is a pattern or practice of discrimination based on your national origin, contact the Special Litigation Section at (202) 514-6255.

FEDERALLY ASSISTED PROGRAMS

- *A local social services agency does not provide information or job training in Korean even though one quarter of local residents speak only Korean.*

- *A hospital near the Texas/Mexico border dresses its security officers in clothes that look like INS uniforms to scare Latinos away from the emergency room. Latino patients are told to bring their own translators before they can see a doctor.*

These examples may be violations of federal laws that prohibit discrimination because of national origin, race or color by recipients of federal funds. If you believe you have been discriminated against by a state or local government agency or an organization that receives funds from the federal government, you may file a complaint with the Division's Coordination and Review Section at (888) 848-5306. The Coordination and Review Section will refer the complaint to the federal funding agency that is primarily responsible for enforcing nondiscrimination prohibitions applicable to its recipients.

VOTING

- *Despite requests from voters in a large Spanish-speaking community, election officials refuse to provide election materials, including registration forms and sample ballots, in Spanish or to allow Spanish speakers to bring translators into the voting booth.*

- *A polling official requires a dark-skinned voter, who speaks with a foreign accent and has an unfamiliar last name, to provide proof of American citizenship, but does not require proof of citizenship from white voters.*

The election officials' conduct may violate the federal laws prohibiting voting discrimination. The Voting Rights Acts do not specifically prohibit national origin discrimination. However, provisions of the Acts make it illegal to limit or deny the right to vote of any citizen not only because of race or color, but also because of membership in a language minority group. In addition, the Acts also require in certain jurisdictions that election materials and assistance be provided in languages other than English.

Additionally, Section 208 of the Voting Rights Act, allows voters, who need help because of blindness, disability or because they cannot read or write, to bring someone (other than an employer or union representative) to help. This means that a voter who needs help reading the ballot in English can bring a friend or family member to translate. In some places, election officials must provide information, such as voter registration and the ballot, in certain language(s) other than English. This can include interpreters to help voters vote.

If you believe that you have been discriminated against in voting or denied assistance in casting your ballot, you may contact the Division's Voting Section at (800) 253-3931.

APPENDIX II
MAPS OF THE WORLD

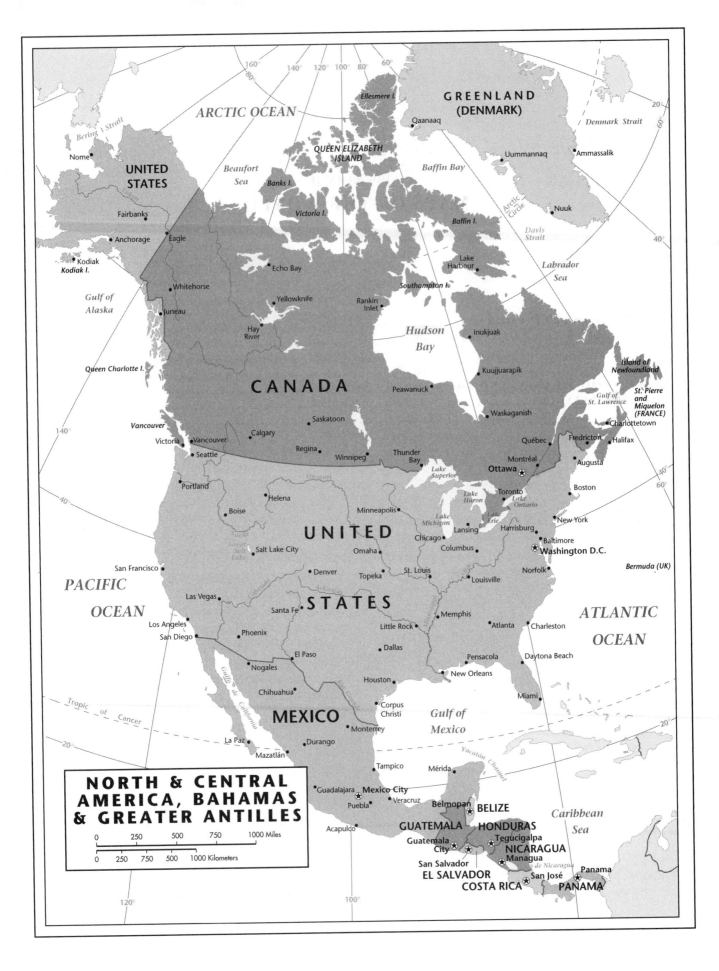

EUROPE

0   200   400 Miles

0   200   400 Kilometers

RUSSIA

0   250   500 Miles

0   250   500 Kilometers

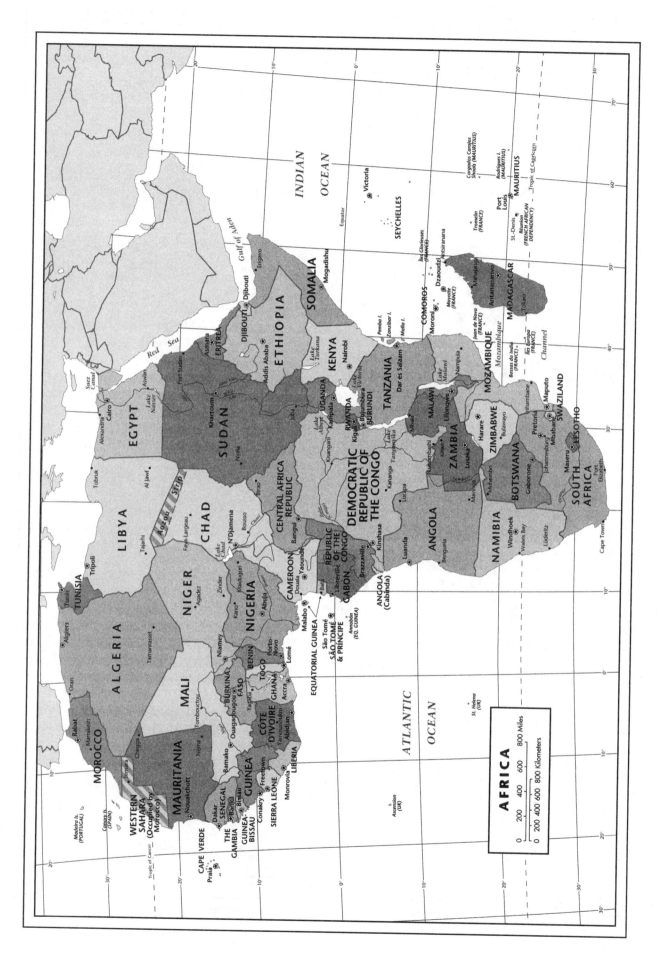

AFRICA

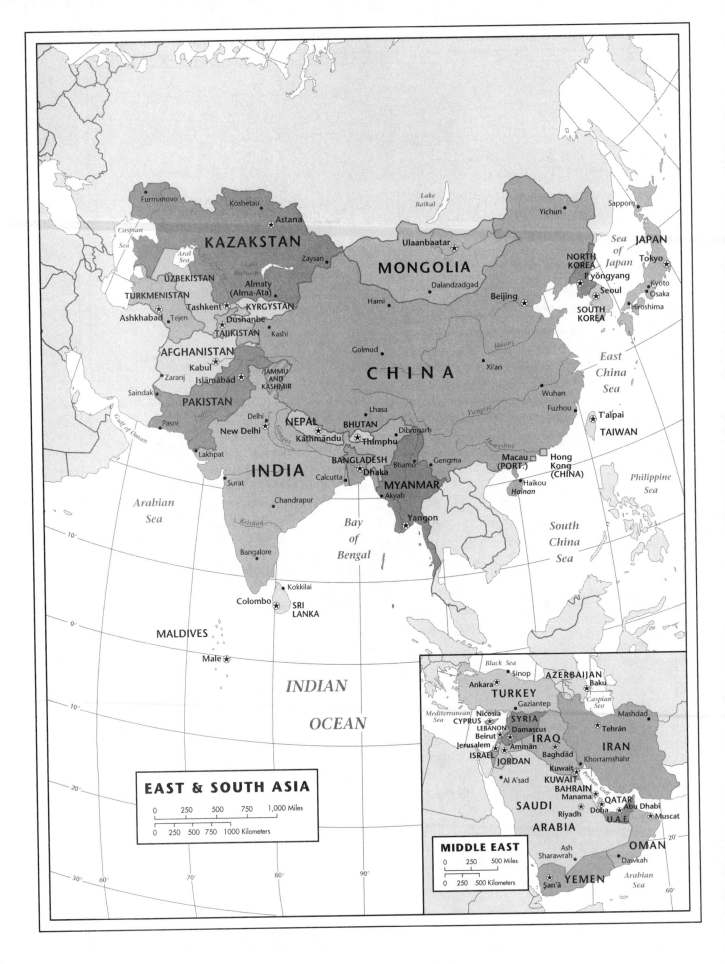

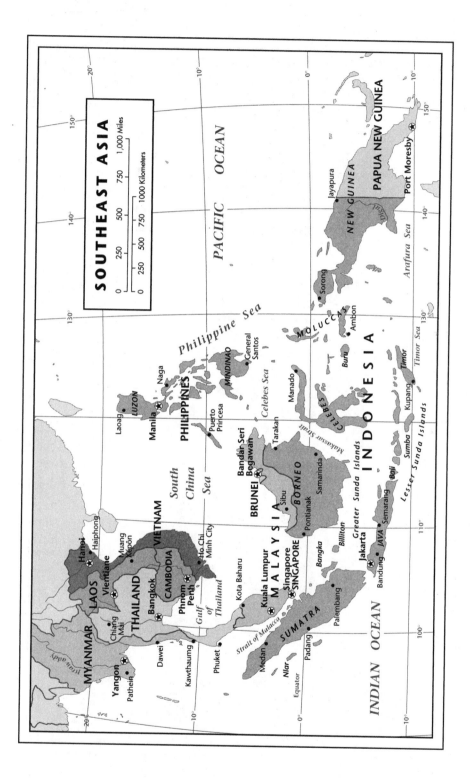

SOUTHEAST ASIA

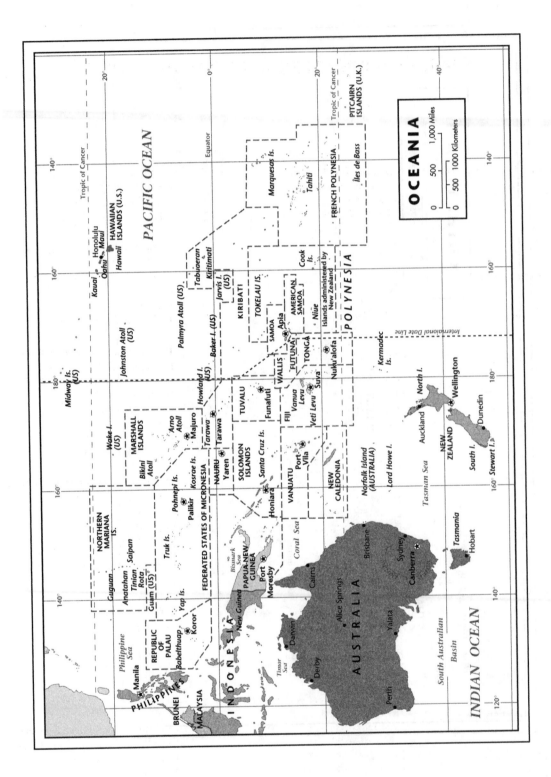

IMPORTANT NAMES AND ADDRESSES

American Civil Liberties Union (ACLU)
125 Broad St., 18th Fl.
New York, NY 10004-2400
(212) 549-2500
E-mail: aclu@aclu.org
URL: http://www.aclu.org

American Immigration Lawyers Association (AILA)
918 F St. NW
Washington, DC 20004-1400
(202) 216-2400
FAX: (202) 783-7853
E-mail: membership@aila.org
URL: http://www.aila.org

American Refugee Committee
430 Oak Grove St., Ste. 204
Minneapolis, MN 55403
(612) 872-7060
FAX: (612) 607-6499
E-mail: archq@archq.org
URL: http://www.archq.org/

Amnesty International USA
5 Penn Plaza, 14th Fl.
New York, NY 10001
(212) 807-8400
FAX: (212) 627-1451
E-mail: aimember@aiusa.org
URL: http://www.amnestyusa.org

The Cato Institute
1000 Massachusetts Ave. NW
Washington, DC 20001-5403
(202) 842-0200
FAX: (202) 842-3490
URL: http://www.cato.org

Center for Immigration Studies
1522 K St. NW, Ste. 820
Washington, DC 20005-1202
(202) 466-8185
FAX: (202) 466-8076
E-mail: center@cis.org
URL: http://www.cis.org

Church World Service
28606 Phillips St.
P.O. Box 968
Elkhart, IN 46515
(574) 264-3102
1-800 297-1516
FAX: (574) 262-0966
E-mail: info@churchworldservice.org
URL: http://www.churchworldservice.org

Episcopal Migration Ministries
Episcopal Church Center
815 Second Ave.
New York, NY 10017
(212) 716-6000
1-800 334-7626
E-mail: emm@episcopalchurch.org
URL: http://www.episcopalchurch.org/emm.htm

Ethiopian Community Development Council
901 South Highland St.
Arlington, VA 22204
(703) 685-0510
FAX: (703) 685-0529
E-mail: info@ecdcinternational.org
URL: http://www.ecdcinternational.org

The Federation for American Immigration Reform (FAIR)
1666 Connecticut Ave. NW, Ste. 400
Washington, DC 20009
(202) 328-7004
FAX: (202) 387-3447
E-mail: comments@fairus.org
URL: http://www.fairus.org

Hebrew Immigrant Aid Society
333 Seventh Ave., 17th Fl.
New York, NY 10001-5004
(212) 967-4100
FAX: (212) 967-4483
E-mail: info@hias.org
URL: http://www.hias.org

Human Rights Watch
350 Fifth Ave., 34th Fl.
New York, NY 10118-3299

(212) 290-4700
FAX: (212) 736-1300
E-mail: hrwnyc@hrw.org
URL: http://www.hrw.org

Institute of International Education
809 United Nations Plaza
New York, NY 10017
(212) 883-8200
FAX: (212) 984-5452
URL: http://www.iie.org

International Committee of the Red Cross
(For U.S.A. and Canada)
2100 Pennsylvania Ave. NW, Ste. 545
Washington, DC 20037
(202) 293-9430
FAX: (202) 293-9431
E-mail: washington.was@icrc.org
URL: http://www.icrc.org

International Immigrants Foundation
1435 Broadway, 2nd Fl.
New York, NY 10018
(212) 302-2222
FAX: (212) 221-7206
E-mail: IIF@10.org
URL: http://www.10.org

Lutheran Immigration and Refugee Service
700 Light St.
Baltimore, MD 21230
(410) 230-2700
FAX: (410) 230-2890
E-mail: lirs@lirs.org
URL: http://www.lirs.org/

Migration and Refugee Services
United States Conference of Catholic Bishops
3211 Fourth St. NE
Washington, DC 20017-1194
(202) 541-3352
FAX: (202) 722-8755
E-mail: mrs@usccb.org
URL: http://www.usccb.org/mrs

Migration Policy Institute
1400 16th St. NW, Ste. 300
Washington, DC 20036
(202) 266-1940
FAX: (202) 266-1900
E-mail: info@migrationpolicy.org
URL: http://www.migrationpolicy.org/

National Council of La Raza
1126 16th St. NW, Ste. 1000
Washington, DC 20036
(202) 785-1670
FAX: (202) 776-1792
E-mail: info@nclr.org
URL: http://www.nclr.org

National Foundation for American Policy
2111 Wilson Blvd., Ste. 700
Arlington, VA 22201
(703) 351-5042
E-mail: info@nfap.net
URL: http://www.nfap.net

National Immigration Forum
50 F St. NW, Ste. 300
Washington, DC 20001
(202) 347-0040
FAX: (202) 347-0058
URL: http://www.immigrationforum.org

New York Immigration Coalition
275 Seventh Ave., 9th Fl.
New York, NY 10001
(212) 627-2227
FAX: (212) 627-9314
URL: http://www.thenyic.org

Pew Hispanic Center
1615 L St. NW, Ste. 700
Washington, DC 20036
(202) 419-3600
FAX: (202) 419-3608
E-mail: info@pewhispanic.org
URL: http://www.pewhispanic.org

Refugee Council USA
3211 Fourth St. NE
Washington, DC 20017
(202) 541-5402
FAX: (202) 722-8737
E-mail: council@refugeecouncilusa.org
URL: http://www.refugeecouncilusa.org

United Nations High Commissioner for Refugees
United States
1775 K St. NW, Ste. 300
Washington, DC 20006
(202) 296-5191
FAX: (202) 296-5660
E-mail: usawa@unhcr.ch
URL: http://www.unhcr.ch

Urban Institute
2100 M St. NW
Washington, DC 20037
(202) 833-7200
E-mail: paffairs@ui.urban.org
URL: http://www.urban.org

U.S. Census Bureau
4700 Silver Hill Rd.
Washington, DC 20233-0001
(301) 763-2422
E-mail: director@census.gov
URL: http://www.census.gov

U.S. Department of Health and Human Services
Office of Refugee Resettlement
370 L'Enfant Promenade SW, 6th Fl./East
Washington, DC 20447
(202) 401-9246
FAX: (202) 401-5487
URL: http://www.acf.hhs.gov/programs/orr/

U.S. Department of Homeland Security
U.S. Citizenship and Immigration Services
2675 Prosperity Ave.

Fairfax, VA 22031
1-800 375-5283
URL: http://www.uscis.gov/

U.S. Department of Labor
Bureau of International Labor Affairs
200 Constitution Ave. NW, Rm. C-4325
Washington, DC 20210
(202) 693-4770
FAX: (202) 693-4780
E-mail: contact-ilab@dol.gov
URL: http://www.dol.gov/ilab/
welcome.html

U.S. Department of State
Bureau of Population, Refugees, and Migration
2201 C St. NW
Washington, DC 20520
(202) 647-8472
URL: http://www.state.gov/g/prm

U.S. House of Representatives Committee on the Judiciary
Subcommittee on Immigration, Border Security, and Claims
2138 Rayburn House Office Bldg.
Washington, DC 20515
(202) 225-3951
E-mail: Judiciary@mail.house.gov
URL: http://www.house.gov/judiciary/
immigration.htm

U.S. Senate Committee on the Judiciary
Subcommittee on Immigration, Border Security, and Citizenship
224 Dirksen Senate Office Bldg.
Washington, DC 20510
(202) 224-7840
FAX: (202) 224-9102
URL: http://judiciary.senate.gov/
subcommittees/immigration109.cfm

RESOURCES

The United States government provides most of the statistical information concerning immigration and naturalization. Much of the information comes from various branches of the Department of Homeland Security (DHS). The primary sources are the *2003 Statistical Yearbook of Immigration Statistics* (Office of Immigration Statistics, Department of Homeland Security, 2003) and *Yearbook of Immigration Statistics* (2003, ongoing), an online publication of DHS's U.S. Citizenship and Immigration Services (USCIS), which assumed the responsibilities of the U.S. Immigration and Naturalization Service (INS) on March 1, 2003. The USCIS is responsible for processing visas and petitions for naturalization, asylum, and refugee status. These publications are the most complete statistical compilations available on immigrants, illegal aliens, and refugees who come to the United States. The INS also published *Estimates of the Unauthorized Immigrant Population Residing in the United States: 1990 and 2000* (2003) and *Legalization Effects: Lawful Permanent Residence and Naturalization through 2001* (2002). The DHS Office of Immigration Statistics tracked workers admitted on temporary visas in *Characteristics of Specialty Occupation Workers (H-1B): Fiscal Year 2003*. DHS published the *Department of Homeland Security Budget in Brief: Fiscal Year 2005*.

Because immigration affects so many areas, several other government agencies are also involved. The Office of Refugee Resettlement of the U.S. Department of Health and Human Services (HHS) monitors the nation's efforts to resettle incoming refugees. *Office of Refugee Resettlement (ORR) Annual Report to Congress—2003* reviews the refugee situation and analyzes the impact and financial cost of refugee admissions. HHS also published *Temporary Assistance for Needy Families (TANF) Program: Fifth Annual Report to Congress* (2003). The HHS Centers for Disease Control and Prevention (CDC) monitors communicable diseases worldwide and provides reports of trends within the United States, including "Trends in TB Cases in the U.S. 2003" (CDC 2005).

The Bureau of Consular Affairs of the U.S. Department of State detailed results of the diversity lottery in *Diversity Visa Lottery 2005 (DV-2005) Results*, tracked past refugee arrivals and anticipated future refugee levels in *Proposed Refugee Admissions for Fiscal Year 2005—Report to Congress*, reported U.S. and international data in *Trafficking in Persons Report* (2004), and tracked nonimmigrant visas issued in *Report of the Visa Office* (December 2004). The Bureau of Population, Refugees, and Migration, an agency of the State Department, administers U.S. refugee assistance and admissions programs. Its data on refugee admissions ceilings and admissions were used in developing this book along with *Emergency Refugee and Migration Fiscal Year 2003* and *Summary of Refugee Admissions for Fiscal Year 2004*.

The U.S. Department of Justice published *Follow-Up Report on INS Efforts to Improve the Control of Nonimmigrant Overstays* (2002) and *The Immigration and Naturalization Service's Removal of Aliens Issued Final Orders* (2003). The Department of Justice (DOJ) issued a June 2004 report, *Assessment of U.S. Government Activities to Combat Trafficking in Persons*. The DOJ detailed discrimination issues that might affect immigrants in *Federal Protections against National Origin Discrimination*.

The U.S. Department of Labor tracked wages and H-2A visa employers in *United States Department of Labor H-2A Crop Activity Summary, Fiscal Year 2003*. The U.S. Department of Agriculture Food and Nutrition Service compiled data on "State-Funded Programs for Legal Immigrants." The Social Security Administration, an agency of the HHS, provides data on noncitizens receiving Supplemental Security Income in *Annual Statistical Supplement 2004*.

The U.S. Commission on Civil Rights, an independent agency that evaluates federal laws and makes recommendations to the President and Congress, published

"Summary of Migrant Civil Rights Issues along the Southwest Border" (2003). The Congressional Budget Office prepared *A Description of the Immigrant Population* (November 2004).

The U.S. Census Bureau collects and distributes the nation's statistics. Demographic data from the bureau include *Profile of the Foreign-Born Population in the United States: 2000* (2001), *The Foreign-Born Population in the United States: 2003* (August 2004), *Current Population Reports* (2004), and projections of the resident population for the nation, published by the Population Projections Program on the Internet (http://www.census.gov/population/www/projections/natsum-T5.html).

The U.S. General Accountability Office (GAO), the investigative arm of Congress, has studied many aspects of immigration. Some of the reports used in this publication include *Overstay Tracking: A Key Component of Homeland Security and Layered Defense* (March 2, 2004), *Major Management Challenges and Program Risks: Department of Justice* (2003), *Illegal Aliens: Opportunities Exist to Improve the Expedited Removal Process* (2000), *Border Security: New Policies and Procedures Are Needed to Fill Gaps in the Visa Revocation Process* (2003), *Homeland Security: Justice Department's Project to Interview Aliens after September 11, 2001* (2003), and *Homeland Security: Challenges to Implementing the Immigration Interior Enforcement Strategy* (2003).

The Congressional Research Service (CRS), an arm of The Library of Congress (Washington, D.C.), is a think tank that works exclusively for members and committees of Congress. CRS publications used in the preparation of the book include *Mexico-U.S. Relations: Issues for the 107th Congress* (K. Larry Storrs, 2001), *Immigration of Agricultural Guest Workers: Policy, Trends, and Legislative Issues* (Ruth Ellen Wasem and Geoffrey K. Collver, 2001), *Cash and Noncash Benefits for Persons with Limited Income: Eligibility Rules, Recipient and Expenditure Data, FY 1998–FY 2000* (Vee Burke, 2002), *Refugee Admissions and Resettlement Policy* (Andorra Bruno, 2002), *Welfare Reform: An Issue Overview* (Vee Burke, 2003), and *Unauthorized Aliens in the United States: Estimates since 1986* (September 15, 2004).

The Office of the United Nations High Commissioner on Refugees (UNHCR) provided international data on asylum seekers in *Asylum Levels and Trends in Industrialized Countries, 2004.*

Organizations that support and oppose immigration have published extensive information on various immigration issues. Reports used in this book include *A Fiscal Portrait of the Newest Americans* (Stephen Moore, National Immigration Forum and the Cato Institute,

Washington, D.C., 1998), *Undocumented Immigrants: Facts and Figures* (Jeffrey S. Passel et al., Urban Institute, January 12, 2004), *Immigrant Families and Workers: Facts and Perspectives* (Randolph Capps et al., Urban Institute, 2003), *Health Insurance of Children in Mixed-Status Immigrant Families* (Randolph Capps et al., Urban Institute, November 2003), *Snapshots of America's Families III, No. 12* (Randy Capps et al., Urban Institute, October 2003), *Trends in Naturalization* (Michael E. Fix et al., Urban Institute, September 2003), and *The Health and Well-Being of Young Children of Immigrants* (Randolph Capps et al., Urban Institute, February 8, 2005). The Center for Immigration Studies (CIS) produced *Measuring the Fallout: The Cost of the IRCA Amnesty after 10 Years* (David Simcox, CIS, 1997), "The Coming Conflict over Asylum: Does America Need a New Asylum Policy?" (Don Barnett, CIS, *Backgrounder*, March 2002), "Another 50 Years of Mass Mexican Immigration: Mexican Government Report Projects Continued Flow Regardless of Economics or Birth Rates" (David Simcox, CIS, *Backgrounder*, March 2002), *The Costs of Immigration* (Federation for American Immigration Reform, Washington, D.C., 2000), "Immigration from Mexico: Assessing the Impact on the United States" (Steven A. Camarota, CIS, *Backgrounder*, July 2001), "Back Where We Started: An Examination of Trends in Immigrant Welfare Use since Welfare Reform" (Steven A. Camarota, CIS, *Backgrounder*, March 2003), "The Deportation Abyss: 'It Ain't Over 'Til the Alien Wins'" (Michelle Malkin, CIS, *Backgrounder*, September 2002), *The Economy Slowed, but Immigration Didn't: The Foreign-Born Population, 2000–2004* (Stephen A. Camarota, CIS, November 2004), and *A Jobless Recovery? Immigrant Gains and Native Losses* (Stephen A. Camarota, CIS, October 2004). Amnesty International published *Why Am I Here? Children in Immigration Detention* (New York, NY, 2003). The Pew Hispanic Center studied the Mexican Immigrant population in *Survey of Mexican Migrants: Attitudes about Immigration and Major Demographic Characteristics* (Roberto Suro, March 2005), studied Hispanic attitudes toward education in *National Survey of Latinos: Education*, and evaluated academic achievement of Hispanic students in *Hispanic School Achievement: Catching Up Requires Running Faster than White Youth* (January 2004). Public Agenda conducted surveys of immigrants for *Now That I'm Here: What America's Immigrants Have to Say About Life in the U.S. Today* (January 14, 2003). The Gale Group thanks all these organizations for permission to reproduce their data and graphics. As always, The Gale Group thanks the Gallup Organization for permission to use its opinion polls.

The Newest New Yorkers 2000: Immigrant New York in the New Millennium (New York City Department of

City Planning, October 2004), is the latest in a quadrennial series of in-depth studies of changing demographic trends, costs, and contributions of the immigrant population of the city. In *The Multiplier Effect* the National Foundation for American Policy studied immigrant children who were finalists in national math and science competitions. The Institute of International Education provided information about international students studying in the United States in *Open Doors 2004 Fast Facts* (2004). The Inter-American Bank, Multilateral Investment Fund completed an in-depth analysis of remittances sent to countries of origin by immigrants working in the United States in *Sending Money Home: Remittance to Latin America and the Caribbean* (May 2004). The Gale Group thanks these researchers for permission to reproduce their data and graphics.

INDEX

Beck, Roy, 123–124
Benefits
    for refugee transition, 70–71
    taxes paid by immigrants and, 129–130
    See also Welfare
Benhamou, Eric, 130
Berger, Joseph, 113
Bernstein, Nina, 111–112
BIA (Board of Immigration Appeals), 68
Biometric passports, 53, 55
Birth certificates, 27
Birth rates, 130
Birthright citizenship, 25
Births
    in New York City, 115
    New York City, total births
        rank ordered by mother's
        birthplace, 115*t*
Board of Immigration Appeals (BIA), 68
Bonner, Robert, 80
"Border Agency Reports First-Year
    Successes" (U.S. Customs and Border
    Protection), 80
Border exports, 100
"Border Lines Poll Shows Public Opinion
    Split On Residency for Mexican
    Illegals" (ABCNews.com), 124
Border Patrol. *See* U.S. Border Patrol
Border security
    cost of illegal immigration, 106
    government spending on
        immigration, 102
    Homeland Security Act and, 26
    U.S. Border Patrol, 79–80
Borjas, George J., 93
Boston Daily Advertiser (newspaper), 126
Bracero Program, 86
Brazil, 51
Brever, Charles R., 86
Briggs, Vernon M., Jr., 135–136
Brookings Institution, 134
Bryne, Matthew, 122
Bureau of Citizenship and Immigration
    Services
    immigration forms filed, 24
    temporary protected status, 22
Bureau of Immigration, 8
Bureau of Immigration and
    Naturalization, 8
Bureau of Population, Refugees, and
    Migration
    Migration and Refugee Assistance,
        FY 2003 budget request, 104*f*
    Migration and Refugee Assistance
        (MRA) program summary, 104*t*
    refugee admissions, 61
    refugee aid, 104, 105
    refugees from Near East,
        South Asia, 65
Burmese refugees, 64
Bury, David, 123

Bush, George W.
    Border Patrol and, 80
    budget for ORR, 70
    Department of Homeland Security
        budget, 102
    detainees and, 28
    East Asian refugee information, 64
    guest worker program proposal of, 124
    Homeland Security Act of 2002 signed
        by, 26
    immigration proposal of, 27
    Intelligence Reform and Terrorism
        Prevention Act of 2004, 27
    priorities for Congress and President
        in 2005, 124*f*
    *Proposed Refugee Admissions for FY
        2005—Report to Congress*, 65, 66
    refugee admission limits, 61
    trafficking in persons and, 69
"Bush Vows Push on Immigration"
    (Curl), 27
Business people, nonimmigrant visas
    for, 46
Businesses
    immigrant contributions to economy,
        129, 130
    of New York City immigrants, 113

C

California
    cost of illegal immigration, 106
    foreign-born populations in, 33–34
    foreign students in, 117, 118
    gangs in, 83
    illegal aliens in, efforts to legislate
        against, 122–123
    immigrant/native employment in, 95
    refugee resettlement in, 63
    role in immigration, 118–120
California Department of Education, 119
California Department of Finance, 119
*California's K12 Public Schools: How Are
    They Doing?* (Carroll et al.), 119
Camarota, Steven A.
    illegal aliens, number of, 74
    immigrant/native employment, 95
    immigrant welfare report, 23
    immigrants, natives, characteristics of,
        34–35
    immigration and economy, 33
    "The Impact of Immigration on U.S.
        Population Growth," 137–138
    public opinion on immigration, 123–124
Canada
    nonimmigrant overstays from, 75–76
    North American Free Trade
        Agreement, 86
Capps, Randy, 73, 119
Caribbean
    immigrants from, 33, 109
    immigrants from, quota laws and, 10

immigrants from, sex ratio, 110
refugee admission limits, 61
refugees from, 66
remittances, value to families in, 101
Carroll, Stephen J., 119
Cash assistance, 70
Cato Institute
    fiscal impact of immigrants, 98
    Immigrants and the U.S. Economy, 99
    immigrants, contributions of, 127
    testimony of Stephen Moore,
        128–131
CBP (U.S. Customs and Border
    Protection)
    apprehension of illegal aliens, 80–83
    enforcement of immigration laws,
        79–80
CDC (Centers for Disease Control),
    52–53
Center for Immigration Studies (CIS)
    *The Coming Conflict over Asylum: Does
        America Need a New Asylum
        Policy?*, 68
    fiscal impact of immigrants, 99
    illegal aliens, number of, 74
    illegal immigrants study, 93–94
    immigrant/native employment, 95
    immigrant welfare report, 23
    immigrants, natives, characteristics of,
        34–35
    immigration and economy, 33
    impact of illegal immigrants on
        unskilled labor, 134
    poverty rate, 129
    public opinion on immigration,
        123–124
*Center for National Security Studies, et al., v.
    U.S. Department of Justice*, 28
Centers for Disease Control (CDC),
    52–53
Central America
    human trafficking from, 84–85
    immigrants from, 33
    immigrants from, educational
        attainment of, 94
    immigrants from, incomes of, 37
    map of, 146
Central Asia, refugee admission limits, 61
"Change in Law Hurting the Needy"
    (Hernandez), 91
Change of address, 26
*Characteristics of Specialty Occupation
    Workers (H-1B): Fiscal Year 2003*
    (Office of Immigration Statistics), 51
Chicago Council on Foreign Relations,
    123–124
Chicago Police Department, 30
"Chicago Police Videos Offer Insights
    into Various Faiths" (Kinzer), 30
Child Citizenship Act of 2000, 25
Child predators, 83